ISSN 1532-1185

MINORITIES
RACE AND ETHNICITY IN AMERICA

Melissa J. Doak

INFORMATION PLUS® REFERENCE SERIES
Formerly Published by Information Plus, Wylie, Texas

GALE
CENGAGE Learning™

Detroit • New York • San Francisco • New Haven, Conn • Waterville, Maine • London

GALE
CENGAGE Learning

Minorities: Race and Ethnicity in America

Melissa J. Doak

Paula Kepos, Series Editor

Project Editors: Kathleen J. Edgar, Elizabeth Manar

Rights Acquisition and Management: Jennifer Altschul, Mollika Basu, Jermaine Bobbitt

Composition: Evi Abou-El-Seoud, Mary Beth Trimper

Manufacturing: Cynde Bishop

Product Management: Carol Nagel

For product information and technology assistance, contact us at
Gale Customer Support, 1-800-877-4253.
For permission to use material from this text or product,
submit all requests online at **www.cengage.com/permissions.**
Further permissions questions can be e-mailed to
permissionrequest@cengage.com

Cover photograph: Image copyright digitalskillet, 2008. Used under license from Shutterstock.com.

Gale
27500 Drake Rd.
Farmington Hills, MI 48331-3535

ISBN-13: 978-0-7876-5103-9 (set)
ISBN-13: 978-1-4144-0765-4

ISBN-10: 0-7876-5103-6 (set)
ISBN-10: 1-4144-0765-3

ISSN 1532-1185

This title is also available as an e-book.
ISBN-13: 978-1-4144-3819-1 (set)
ISBN-10: 1-4144-3819-2 (set)
Contact your Gale sales representative for ordering information.

Printed in the United States of America
1 2 3 4 5 6 7 12 11 10 09 08

TABLE OF CONTENTS

PREFACE

Minorities: Race and Ethnicity in America is part of the *Information Plus Reference Series.* The purpose of each volume of the series is to present the latest facts on a topic of pressing concern in modern American life. These topics include today's most controversial and studied social issues: abortion, capital punishment, care for the elderly, crime, health care, the environment, immigration, minorities, social welfare, women, youth, and many more. Even though this series is written especially for high school and undergraduate students, it is an excellent resource for anyone in need of factual information on current affairs.

By presenting the facts, it is the intention of Gale, a part of Cengage Learning, to provide its readers with everything they need to reach an informed opinion on current issues. To that end, there is a particular emphasis in this series on the presentation of scientific studies, surveys, and statistics. These data are generally presented in the form of tables, charts, and other graphics placed within the text of each book. Every graphic is directly referred to and carefully explained in the text. The source of each graphic is presented within the graphic itself. The data used in these graphics are drawn from the most reputable and reliable sources, in particular from the various branches of the U.S. government and from major independent polling organizations. Every effort has been made to secure the most recent information available. Readers should bear in mind that many major studies take years to conduct, and that additional years often pass before the data from these studies are made available to the public. Therefore, in many cases the most recent information available in 2008 is dated from 2005 or 2006. Older statistics are sometimes presented as well, if they are of particular interest and no more-recent information exists.

Even though statistics are a major focus of the *Information Plus Reference Series,* they are by no means its only content. Each book also presents the widely held positions and important ideas that shape how the book's subject is discussed in the United States. These positions are explained in detail and, where possible, in the words of their proponents. Some of the other material to be found in these books includes historical background; descriptions of major events related to the subject; relevant laws and court cases; and examples of how these issues play out in American life. Some books also feature primary documents, or have pro and con debate sections giving the words and opinions of prominent Americans on both sides of a controversial topic. All material is presented in an even-handed and unbiased manner; readers will never be encouraged to accept one view of an issue over another.

HOW TO USE THIS BOOK

Race and ethnicity have acted as some of the most divisive factors in U.S. history. Many people, from all racial and ethnic backgrounds, have struggled, sometimes at great peril to themselves, to provide equality for all people in the United States. Nevertheless, it is an undeniable fact that African-Americans, Hispanics, Native Americans, Asian-Americans, and other minority groups have a different experience living in the United States than do whites. This book reports on and examines the differences between minority groups and white Americans across the economic, political, and social spectrums.

Minorities: Race and Ethnicity in America consists of eight chapters and three appendixes. Each chapter is devoted to a particular aspect of minorities. For a summary of the information covered in each chapter, please see the synopses provided in the Table of Contents at the front of the book. Chapters generally begin with an overview of the basic facts and background information on the chapter's topic, then proceed to examine subtopics of particular interest. For example, Chapter 4: Minorities in the Labor Force begins with a historical perspective of the role that African-Americans, Asian-Americans, and Hispanics played in the U.S. labor force. From there, it examines the labor force participation and unemployment of minorities, the types of discrimination that minorities experience on the job, and workforce projections through 2016. Next, the chapter notes some of the different types of jobs that minorities hold in various industries and in the federal government. It then discusses the state of minority-owned businesses—including minority women-owned businesses—and how they are increasing in number. This discussion covers minority set-aside programs and the court cases that are shaping the impact of these programs. The chapter concludes with detailing the pros and cons of Native American casinos. Readers can find their way through a chapter by looking for the section and subsection headings, which are clearly set off from the text. Or, they can refer to the book's extensive index if they already know what they are looking for.

Statistical Information

The tables and figures featured throughout *Minorities: Race and Ethnicity in America* will be of particular use to readers in learning about this issue. These tables and figures represent an extensive collection of the most recent and important statistics on minorities, as well as related issues—for example, graphics in the book cover the number of different minority peoples living in the United States overall and in specific regions; their average earnings as compared to whites; the rates at which they are the victims of various crimes; and the health problems that disproportionately afflict certain minority groups. Gale, a part of Cengage Learning, believes that making this information available to readers is the most important way to fulfill the goal of this book: to help readers understand the issues and controversies surrounding minorities and reach their own conclusions about them.

Each table or figure has a unique identifier appearing above it, for ease of identification and reference. Titles for the tables and figures explain their purpose. At the end of each table or figure, the original source of the data is provided.

To help readers understand these often complicated statistics, all tables and figures are explained in the text. References in the text direct readers to the relevant statistics. Furthermore, the contents of all tables and figures are fully indexed. Please see the opening section of the index at the back of this volume for a description of how to find tables and figures within it.

Appendixes

Besides the main body text and images, *Minorities: Race and Ethnicity in America* has three appendixes. The first is the Important Names and Addresses directory. Here readers will find contact information for a number of government and private organizations that can provide further information on aspects of minorities. The second appendix is the Resources section, which can also assist readers in conducting their own research. In this section, the author and editors of *Minorities: Race and Ethnicity in America* describe some of the sources that were most useful during the compilation of this book. The final appendix is the index.

ADVISORY BOARD CONTRIBUTIONS

The staff of Information Plus would like to extend its heartfelt appreciation to the Information Plus Advisory Board. This dedicated group of media professionals provides feedback on the series on an ongoing basis. Their comments allow the editorial staff who work on the project to continually make the series better and more user-friendly. Our top priorities are to produce the highest-quality and most useful books possible, and the Advisory Board's contributions to this process are invaluable.

The members of the Information Plus Advisory Board are:

* Kathleen R. Bonn, Librarian, Newbury Park High School, Newbury Park, California

* Madelyn Garner, Librarian, San Jacinto College–North Campus, Houston, Texas

* Anne Oxenrider, Media Specialist, Dundee High School, Dundee, Michigan

* Charles R. Rodgers, Director of Libraries, Pasco-Hernando Community College, Dade City, Florida

* James N. Zitzelsberger, Library Media Department Chairman, Oshkosh West High School, Oshkosh, Wisconsin

COMMENTS AND SUGGESTIONS

The editors of the *Information Plus Reference Series* welcome your feedback on *Minorities: Race and Ethnicity in America*. Please direct all correspondence to:

Editors
Information Plus Reference Series
27500 Drake Rd.
Farmington Hills, MI 48331-3535

CHAPTER 1
WHO ARE MINORITIES?

MINORITIES ARE A GROWING PERCENTAGE OF THE NATION

The U.S. Census Bureau reports that in 2006 the U.S. population totaled 299.4 million people. (See Table 1.1.) Of that number, 198.7 million (66.4%) people identified themselves as non-Hispanic white alone. The other 33.6% were members of one or more minority racial or ethnic groups. Even though women are a majority of the nation's population (151.9 million women versus 147.5 million men), women are often considered a "minority" in social issues, because they have been historically discriminated against in American society. In this publication, however, women are treated only in relation to racial or ethnic minority groups.

The Census Bureau predicts that by 2020, 61.3% of Americans will be white non-Hispanics and 38.7% will belong to a minority group. (See Table 1.2.) Projections indicate that the proportion of white, non-Hispanic-Americans will shrink to only a bare majority (50.1%) by 2050. In that year, the Census Bureau projects that 49.9% of Americans will belong to a minority racial or ethnic group. The nation is increasingly diverse due to the growth in immigration and interracial marriages.

CHANGING RACIAL AND ETHNIC ORIGIN CLASSIFICATIONS

For the 1980 and 1990 censuses the Census Bureau divided the U.S. population into the four racial categories identified by the Office of Management and Budget—White, Black, American Indian/Alaska Native, and Asian/Pacific Islander—and added the category "Some Other Race." The U.S. government uses these race and ethnic origin data to make decisions, among other things, about funding and making laws. For example, federal programs use the race information to monitor and ensure that the civil rights of African-Americans and other minority groups are not violated, and states use the data to ensure compliance with political redistricting requirements.

As ethnic identity becomes more complex because of immigration and interracial marriages and births, a growing number of people object to categories based on race. It is no longer unusual to find Americans whose backgrounds include two or more races.

Katherine Wallman explains in "Data on Race and Ethnicity: Revising the Federal Standard" (*The American Statistician*, vol. 52, 1998) that these standards came under attack because many Americans believed they did not accurately reflect the diversity of the nation's population. Between 1993 and 1995 the Census Bureau conducted hearings and invited public comment on the proposal under consideration to add new choices to the categories that had been used in the 1990 census. Among the Census Bureau's findings were that Arab-Americans were unhappy with their official designation as "white, non-European." This group included people from the Middle East, Turkey, and North Africa. In addition, many indigenous Hawaiians wanted to be recategorized from Pacific Islander to Native American, reflecting historical accuracy and giving them access to greater minority benefits.

Some Hispanics wanted the Census Bureau to identify them as a race and not as an ethnic origin, and to replace the word *Hispanic* with *Latino*. They asserted that *Hispanic* recalled the colonization of Latin America by Spain and Portugal and argued that the term was as offensive as the term *Negro* is for African-Americans. However, when Hispanics were surveyed, the results showed they preferred to be identified by their families' country of origin, such as Puerto Rican, Colombian, Cuban, or sometimes just American.

A number of African-Americans wanted the Census Bureau to retire the term *Black*. Nevertheless, there was some difference of opinion. For example, people from the Caribbean preferred to be labeled by their families' country of origin, such as Jamaican-American or Haitian-American. Africans who were not American also found the term inaccurate. Even

TABLE 1.1

Population by sex, race, and Hispanic origin, 2006

Sex, race, and Hispanic or Latino origin	Population July 1, 2006
Both sexes	**299,398,484**
One race	294,679,815
White	239,746,254
Black	38,342,549
AIAN	2,902,851
Asian	13,159,343
NHPI	528,818
Two or more races	4,718,669
*Race alone or in combination:**	
White	243,825,488
Black	40,240,898
AIAN	4,497,895
Asian	14,907,198
NHPI	1,007,644
Not Hispanic or Latino	**255,077,446**
One race	250,987,070
White	198,744,494
Black	36,689,680
AIAN	2,258,877
Asian	12,881,639
NHPI	412,380
Two or more races	4,090,376
*Race alone or in combination:**	
White	202,266,112
Black	38,294,161
AIAN	3,629,247
Asian	14,446,354
NHPI	824,477
Hispanic or Latino	**44,321,038**
One race	43,692,745
White	41,001,760
Black	1,652,869
AIAN	643,974
Asian	277,704
NHPI	116,438
Two or more races	628,293
*Race alone or in combination:**	
White	41,559,376
Black	1,946,737
AIAN	868,648
Asian	460,844
NHPI	183,167
Male	**147,512,152**
One race	145,185,578
White	118,797,402
Black	18,284,591
AIAN	1,454,460
Asian	6,379,879
NHPI	269,246
Two or more races	2,326,574
*Race alone or in combination:**	
White	120,815,338
Black	19,210,221
AIAN	2,226,161
Asian	7,253,426
NHPI	506,827

TABLE 1.1

Population by sex, race, and Hispanic origin, 2006 [CONTINUED]

Sex, race, and Hispanic or Latino origin	Population July 1, 2006
Not Hispanic or Latino	**124,587,102**
One race	122,573,046
White	97,536,842
Black	17,471,866
AIAN	1,114,358
Asian	6,242,036
NHPI	207,944
Two or more races	2,014,056
*Race alone or in combination:**	
White	99,276,455
Black	18,251,963
AIAN	1,774,537
Asian	7,025,262
NHPI	412,498
Hispanic or Latino	**22,925,050**
One race	22,612,532
White	21,260,560
Black	812,725
AIAN	340,102
Asian	137,843
NHPI	61,302
Two or more races	312,518
*Race alone or in combination:**	
White	21,538,883
Black	958,258
AIAN	451,624
Asian	228,164
NHPI	94,329
Female	**151,886,332**
One race	149,494,237
White	120,948,852
Black	20,057,958
AIAN	1,448,391
Asian	6,779,464
NHPI	259,572
Two or more races	2,392,095
*Race alone or in combination:**	
White	123,010,150
Black	21,030,677
AIAN	2,271,734
Asian	7,653,772
NHPI	500,817
Not Hispanic or Latino	**130,490,344**
One race	128,414,024
White	101,207,652
Black	19,217,814
AIAN	1,144,519
Asian	6,639,603
NHPI	204,436
Two or more races	2,076,320
*Race alone or in combination:**	
White	102,989,657
Black	20,042,198
AIAN	1,854,710
Asian	7,421,092
NHPI	411,979

though the term *African-American* has become more prominent in spoken English in recent years, lack of agreement and the length of the term have been significant factors in preventing its adoption by the government.

The 2000 Census

Conforming to revised standards issued by the Office of Management and Budget, the 2000 census recategorized the races into White, Black/African-American/Negro, American Indian/Alaska Native, Native Hawaiian/Other Pacific Islander, and Asian. The Census Bureau also added a sixth category: Some Other Race. In addition, the Census Bureau included two ethnic categories: Hispanic/Latino and Not Hispanic/Not Latino. To provide an accurate count of multiracial Americans, the 2000 census allowed Americans to select more than one race. Write-in spaces allowed Native

TABLE 1.1

Population by sex, race, and Hispanic origin, 2006 [CONTINUED]

Sex, race, and Hispanic or Latino origin	Population July 1, 2006
Hispanic or Latino	**21,395,988**
One race	21,080,213
White	19,741,200
Black	840,144
AIAN	303,872
Asian	139,861
NHPI	55,136
Two or more races	315,775
*Race alone or in combination:**	
White	20,020,493
Black	988,479
AIAN	417,024
Asian	232,680
NHPI	88,838

*'In combination' means in combination with one or more other races. The sum of the five race groups adds to more than the total population because individuals may report more than one race.

Note: The April 1, 2000 population estimates base reflects changes to the Census 2000 population from the count question resolution program and geographic program revisions. Black=Black or African American; AIAN=American Indian and Alaska Native; NHPI=Native Hawaiian and other Pacific Islander.

SOURCE: Adapted from "Table 3. Annual Estimates of the Population by Sex, Race, and Hispanic or Latino Origin for the United States: April 1, 2000 to July 1, 2006," in *National Population Estimates—Characteristics*, U.S. Census Bureau, Population Division, May 17, 2007, http://www.census.gov/popest/national/asrh/NC-EST2006-srh.html (accessed November 2, 2007)

Americans to record their tribal affiliation, and individuals of Hispanic origin could write in a national affiliation other than the major groups of Mexican, Cuban, and Puerto Rican.

In "Impact of Census' Race Data Debated" (*USA Today*, March 12, 2001), Martin Kasindorf and Haya El Nasser explain that many Americans thought that the official recognition of multiracial Americans would profoundly change how Americans thought about race in the long term. Some believed that racial lines would blur until racial differences no longer became so important in American life. Others took a more pessimistic view, arguing that because African-Americans marry outside their racial categories less than other minorities, the difference between an "expanded majority" of whites and the African-American minority group would harden further.

A more in-depth discussion of the major race and ethnic groups follows.

HISPANICS

Hispanic is a broad term used to describe a varied ethnic group of individuals who trace their cultural heritage to Spain or to Spanish-speaking countries in Latin America. The term can also refer to people whose Spanish ancestors were residents of the southwestern region of the United States that was formerly under Spanish or Mexican control.

The Census Bureau indicates that in 2006, 44.3 million Hispanics lived in the United States. (See Table 1.1.) As 14.8% of the population, they were the largest minority group in the nation. Frank Hobbs and Nicole Stoops of the Census Bureau indicate in *Demographic Trends in the 20th Century* (November 2002, http://www.census.gov/prod/2002pubs/censr-4.pdf) that in 1980 Hispanics represented 14.6 million people (6.4% of the total U.S. population). In 1990 Hispanics totaled about 22.4 million people (9% of the total U.S. population). The 2000 census counted 35.6 million Hispanics living in the United States. (See Table 1.2.) The Hispanic population in the country increased by 141.7% between 1980 and 2000. The Census Bureau predicts that by 2050 there will be 102.6 million Hispanics living in the United States.

Immigration and high birth rates are two major reasons for the large growth of the Hispanic population. In *Estimates of the Unauthorized Immigrant Population Residing in the United States: January 2005* (August 2006, http://www.dhs.gov/xlibrary/assets/statistics/publications/ILL_PE_2005.pdf), Michael Hoefer, Nancy Rytina, and Christopher Campbell of the U.S. Department of Homeland Security estimate that as of January 2005 approximately 10.5 million illegal aliens lived in the United States, up from 8.5 million in January 2000. More than half of these illegal immigrants (6 million) came from Mexico, while El Salvador and Guatemala were the next leading source countries.

The Census Bureau's American Community Survey samples the U.S. population yearly and collects detailed information on characteristics of the population to provide more current data on the makeup of the U.S. population than the census, which is conducted every ten years. In *The American Community—Hispanics: 2004* (February 2007, http://www.census.gov/prod/2007pubs/acs-03.pdf), the Census Bureau finds that in 2004, 28% of the Hispanic community, particularly those who immigrated to the United States in recent years, had yet to become citizens. About 61% of all Hispanics had been born in the United States, and another 11% had become naturalized citizens. This varied by country of origin, however. Almost all Puerto Ricans had been born in the United States, because Puerto Rico is a U.S. territory. As of 2004 more Mexicans than any other foreign group had been born in the United States: 60.6% of Mexicans, 38.7% of Dominicans, and 36.7% of Cubans had been born in the United States. (See Figure 1.1.) Cubans had the highest proportion of those who had become naturalized citizens: 38.1% of Cubans, 28.3% of Colombians, 28.1% of Peruvians, and 28% of Dominicans had become naturalized citizens. Guatemalans had the highest percent of residents who were not citizens (55.7%), followed by Hondurans (50.5%) and Salvadorans (49.6%).

TABLE 1.2

Projected population of the United States, by race and Hispanic origin, selected years 2000–50

[In thousands except as indicated. As of July 1. Resident population.]

Population or percent and race or Hispanic origin	2000	2010	2020	2030	2040	2050
Population						
Total	282,125	308,936	335,805	363,584	391,946	419,854
White alone	228,548	244,995	260,629	275,731	289,690	302,626
Black alone	35,818	40,454	45,365	50,442	55,876	61,361
Asian alone	10,684	14,241	17,988	22,580	27,992	33,430
All other races*	7,075	9,246	11,822	14,831	18,388	22,437
Hispanic (of any race)	35,622	47,756	59,756	73,055	87,585	102,560
White alone, not Hispanic	195,729	201,112	205,936	209,176	210,331	210,283
Percent of total population						
Total	100.0	100.0	100.0	100.0	100.0	100.0
White alone	81.0	79.3	77.6	75.8	73.9	72.1
Black alone	12.7	13.1	13.5	13.9	14.3	14.6
Asian alone	3.8	4.6	5.4	6.2	7.1	8.0
All other races*	2.5	3.0	3.5	4.1	4.7	5.3
Hispanic (of any race)	12.6	15.5	17.8	20.1	22.3	24.4
White alone, not Hispanic	69.4	65.1	61.3	57.5	53.7	50.1

*Includes American Indian and Alaska Native alone, Native Hawaiian and other Pacific Islander alone, and two or more races.

SOURCE: "Table 1a. Projected Population of the United States, by Race and Hispanic Origin: 2000 to 2050," in *U.S. Interim Projections by Age, Sex, Race, and Hispanic Origin*, U.S. Census Bureau, March 18, 2004, http://www.census.gov/ipc/www/usinterimproj/natprojtab01a.pdf (accessed November 2, 2007)

Hispanic Origins

Hispanic-Americans trace their origins to a number of countries. The Census Bureau reports that in 2006, 65.5% of the Hispanics in the United States were of Mexican heritage. (See Figure 1.2.) Approximately 8.6% were of Puerto Rican heritage, 3.7% were Cuban, and 8% were from other countries. Another 8.2% were of Central American and 6% were of South American origin. The differences in origin can often mean significant variations in where Hispanics live in the United States and in their educational attainment, income, and living conditions.

Geographic Distribution

Different areas of the United States have more Hispanics living in them. The West has the highest proportion of Hispanics (26.6%). (See Figure 1.3.) By contrast, the South is 14.5% Hispanic, the Northeast is 11.3% Hispanic, and the Midwest is only 5.3% Hispanic. In *American Community—Hispanics*, the Census Bureau reports that New Mexico had the highest Hispanic population; 43.4% of its residents in 2004 were Hispanic, followed by 34.9% of the residents of both Texas and California, 28.1% of the residents of Arizona, and 22.9% of the residents of Nevada. Even though New Mexico had the highest proportion of Hispanic residents, 30.3% of all Hispanic people living in the United States lived in California in 2004. Roberto R. Ramirez and G. Patricia de la Cruz of the Census Bureau note in *The Hispanic Population in the United States: March 2002* (June 2003, http://www.census.gov/prod/2003pubs/p20-545.pdf) that

the likelihood of Hispanics living in a particular region depends primarily on their country of origin. They find that in 2002 Mexican-Americans were the most likely to live in the West (54.6% of them did so) and the South (34.3%), Puerto Ricans were the most likely to live in the Northeast (58%), and Cubans were the most likely to live in the South (75.1%).

Mexican-Americans

Many Hispanic-Americans are descendants of the Spanish and Mexican people who lived in the West and Southwest when these regions were controlled by Spain (starting in the 1500s) and later by Mexico (after Mexico gained its independence from Spain in 1821). Their forebears were absorbed into the United States when Texas revolted, broke away from Mexico, became a republic, and then finally joined the United States during the 1840s. The Mexican-American War (1846–1848) added California, Arizona, New Mexico, Utah, Colorado, and territories north of the Rio Grande boundary to the United States with the signing of the Treaty of Guadalupe Hidalgo in 1848. As a result, Hispanics living in these areas became Americans.

The Mexican-origin population, which more than doubled in the last two decades of the twentieth century, continues to grow in the twenty-first century. According to the Census Bureau, in *American Community—Hispanics*, 25.9 million people, or about 9.1% of the U.S. population, were of Mexican origin in 2004. Mexican-Americans represented 65.5% of the Hispanic population in the United States in 2006. (See Figure 1.2.) Ramirez and de la Cruz

FIGURE 1.1

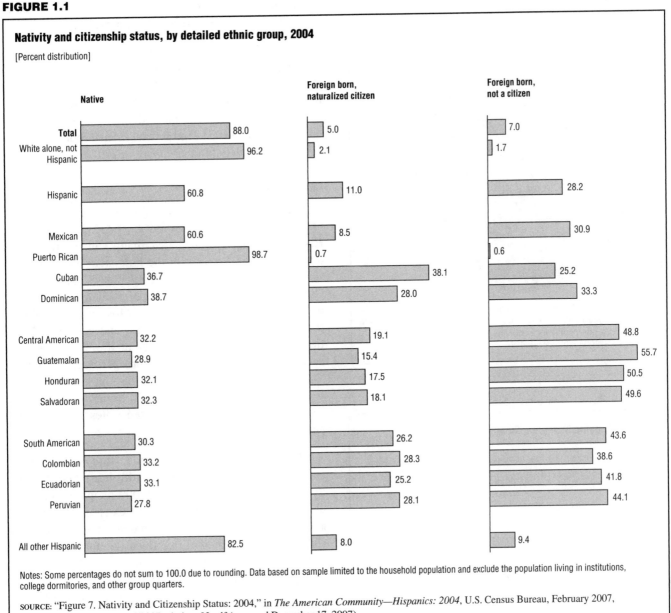

Nativity and citizenship status, by detailed ethnic group, 2004

[Percent distribution]

	Native	Foreign born, naturalized citizen	Foreign born, not a citizen
Total	88.0	5.0	7.0
White alone, not Hispanic	96.2	2.1	1.7
Hispanic	60.8	11.0	28.2
Mexican	60.6	8.5	30.9
Puerto Rican	98.7	0.7	0.6
Cuban	36.7	38.1	25.2
Dominican	38.7	28.0	33.3
Central American	32.2	19.1	48.8
Guatemalan	28.9	15.4	55.7
Honduran	32.1	17.5	50.5
Salvadoran	32.3	18.1	49.6
South American	30.3	26.2	43.6
Colombian	33.2	28.3	38.6
Ecuadorian	33.1	25.2	41.8
Peruvian	27.8	28.1	44.1
All other Hispanic	82.5	8.0	9.4

Notes: Some percentages do not sum to 100.0 due to rounding. Data based on sample limited to the household population and exclude the population living in institutions, college dormitories, and other group quarters.

SOURCE: "Figure 7. Nativity and Citizenship Status: 2004," in *The American Community—Hispanics: 2004*, U.S. Census Bureau, February 2007, http://www.census.gov/prod/2007pubs/acs-03.pdf (accessed December 17, 2007)

find that Mexican-Americans remained concentrated for the most part in the West (54.6%) and in the South (34.3%).

Puerto Ricans

The situation of Puerto Ricans is unique in American society. The Caribbean island of Puerto Rico, formerly a Spanish colony, became a U.S. commonwealth after it was ceded to the United States by the Treaty of Paris in 1898, which ended the Spanish-American War (1898). In 1917 the Revised Organic Act (the Jones Act) granted the island a bill of rights and its own legislature. It also conferred U.S. citizenship to all Puerto Ricans.

Ruth Glasser states in "Tobacco Valley: Puerto Rican Farm Workers in Connecticut" (*Hog River Journal*, vol.

1, 2002) that following World War II (1939–1945) an industrialization program was launched in Puerto Rico. Even though the program benefited many, it sharply reduced the number of agricultural jobs on the island, driving many rural residents to the cities. Combined with a high birth rate, this led to unemployment, overcrowding, and poverty. These conditions forced many Puerto Ricans to move to the mainland United States, particularly New York City. Since 1993, when President Bill Clinton (1946–) eliminated tax exemptions for manufacturing firms in Puerto Rico, industries have moved away from the island in search of cheaper labor, further compounding the economic problems of Puerto Rico. According to Virginia E. Sánchez Korrol, in *From Colonia to Community: The History of Puerto Ricans in New York City* (1994), in 1940 fewer than seventy thousand Puerto

FIGURE 1.2

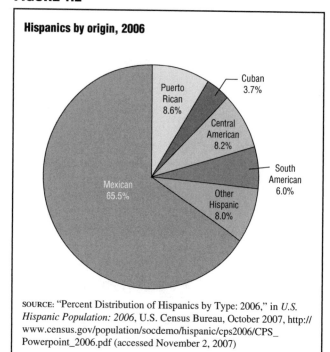

Hispanics by origin, 2006

SOURCE: "Percent Distribution of Hispanics by Type: 2006," in *U.S. Hispanic Population: 2006*, U.S. Census Bureau, October 2007, http://www.census.gov/population/socdemo/hispanic/cps2006/CPS_Powerpoint_2006.pdf (accessed November 2, 2007)

FIGURE 1.3

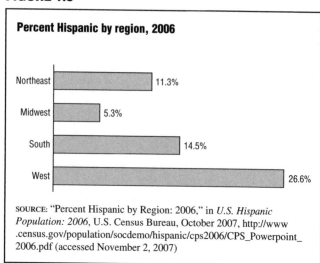

Percent Hispanic by region, 2006

SOURCE: "Percent Hispanic by Region: 2006," in *U.S. Hispanic Population: 2006*, U.S. Census Bureau, October 2007, http://www.census.gov/population/socdemo/hispanic/cps2006/CPS_Powerpoint_2006.pdf (accessed November 2, 2007)

Ricans lived in the contiguous United States. The Census Bureau notes in *American Community—Hispanics* that by 2004, 3.9 million Puerto Ricans called the United States home. Partly because of the relative ease with which Puerto Ricans can travel in the United States, many move freely back and forth between the United States and Puerto Rico.

Joseph Berger explains in "A Puerto Rican Rebirth in El Barrio; After Exodus, Gentrification Changes Face of East Harlem" (*New York Times*, December 10, 2002) that most of the first Puerto Ricans who arrived in the United States settled in New York City in the Manhattan neighborhood of East Harlem, which came to be known as El Barrio (the Neighborhood). Eventually, Puerto

Rican immigrants moved in greater numbers to other boroughs of the city and into New Jersey.

In 2006 Puerto Ricans represented 8.6% of the Hispanic population living in the United States. (See Figure 1.2.) Ramirez and de la Cruz state that Puerto Ricans were more likely to live in the Northeast (58%) than in other areas. Puerto Ricans were even more likely than other Hispanic groups to reside inside central cities in metropolitan areas—57.4% of them lived in these areas in 2002.

Cuban-Americans

In *Cubans in the United States* (August 25, 2006, http://pewhispanic.org/files/factsheets/23.pdf), the Pew Hispanic Center explains that many Cubans fled Cuba during the early 1960s after the Fulgencio Batista (1901–1973) regime was overthrown by Fidel Castro (1926–). Cuban immigrants tended to settle in Miami, Florida, and in the surrounding Dade County. Most of these political refugees were older, middle class, and educated. Many fled to maintain a capitalist way of life, and many succeeded in achieving economic prosperity in the United States. A second phase of Cuban immigration took place from about 1965 to 1974, legally bringing middle- and working-class Cubans to the United States through Cuban and U.S. government programs.

In *Mariel Boatlift* (April 2005, http://www.globalsecurity.org/military/ops/mariel-boatlift.htm), GlobalSecurity.org reports that in 1980, 125,000 people seeking refuge from Castro's government fled Cuba in what became known as the Mariel Boatlift, named after the town in Cuba from which they sailed. Because most of these new immigrants were from less wealthy and less educated backgrounds than their predecessors, and some were actually criminals or people who were mentally ill, many had difficulty fitting into the existing Cuban communities in the United States. Also, unlike the Cubans who came before them, they had spent twenty years living under a dictatorship that was vastly different from the democratic government they encountered in the United States. This difference led to further difficulties in adjustment to their new homes.

Mireya Navarro reports in "Last of Refugees from Cuba in '94 Flight Now Enter U.S." (*New York Times*, February 1, 1996) that in 1994 more than twenty-nine thousand Cubans tried to enter the United States after fleeing a severe economic crisis in their own country. Most attempted the trip by boats and rafts but were intercepted by the U.S. Coast Guard and taken back to Cuba, where they were detained at Guantánamo Bay, the U.S. naval base. By January 1996 most detainees had been allowed to enter the United States, and the detention camps were closed. The Pew Hispanic Center notes that under current U.S. policy, Cubans who are able to reach the United States are allowed to stay, whereas those intercepted at sea are returned to Cuba.

Even though language differences cause initial difficulties for Cuban immigrants, the Pew Hispanic Center explains that most adapt well and that Cubans are the most economically successful of the Hispanic ethnic groups. Unlike Americans of Mexican and Puerto Rican backgrounds, who began migrating throughout the country during the 1990s, the Cuban population has generally remained concentrated in Florida, even though large numbers also live in New Jersey, New York, and California.

AFRICAN-AMERICANS

In 1619 the first Africans arrived in colonial North America. Subsequently, their numbers increased rapidly to fill the growing demand for slave labor in the new land. The first slaves were brought into this country by way of the West Indies, but as demand increased, they were soon brought directly to the English colonies on the mainland in North America. Most were delivered to the South and worked on plantations, where they supplied cheap labor.

The vast majority of African-Americans in the United States were kept as slaves until the Civil War (1861–1865). According to the 1860 census (http://www2.census.gov/ prod2/decennial/documents/1860a-02.pdf), the states that comprised the Confederacy in the South at the outbreak of hostilities had a slave population of 3.5 million, compared to a white population of nearly 5.5 million. By contrast, the Union states and territories in the North had a white population of 21.5 million, with slaves numbering 432,650.

In 1863 President Abraham Lincoln (1809–1865) issued the Emancipation Proclamation, which technically freed slaves in the Confederate states, although those states did not recognize the legality of the proclamation. In 1865 the Thirteenth Amendment to the U.S. Constitution abolished slavery throughout the United States. In 1868 the Fourteenth Amendment afforded former slaves and other African-Americans equal protection under the law, and in 1870 the Fifteenth Amendment granted them the right to vote. The present population of African-Americans in the United States includes not only those descended from former slaves but also those who have since emigrated from Africa, the West Indies, and Central and South America.

According to the Census Bureau, in 2006, 36.7 million people who identified their race as non-Hispanic, black alone lived in the United States; 38.3 million people identified their race as black alone or in combination. (See Table 1.1.) Generally, even mixed-race individuals in the United States identify as African-American due to the rigid politics of race in the nation. In 2006 African-Americans made up 12.8% of the population, up from 12.3% in 2000, as reported by the Census Bureau, in *Profiles of General Demographic Characteristics 2000* (May 2001, http://www.census.gov/prod/cen2000/dp1/ 2kh00.pdf).

Geographic Distribution

Few African-Americans voluntarily migrated from the southern farms and plantations that had been their homes in the first decades after the abolition of slavery. As a result, at the beginning of the twentieth century a large majority of African-Americans still lived in the South. However, when World War I (1914–1918) interrupted the flow of migrant labor from Europe, large numbers of African-Americans migrated from the rural South to northern industrial cities to take advantage of new work opportunities there. Compared to the oppressive system of segregation in the South, economic and social conditions were better in the North for many African-Americans, thereby encouraging a continuous flow of migrants. According to the article "North by South: The African-American Great Migration" (2005, http://northbysouth.kenyon.edu/), between 1900 and 1960, 4.8 million African-Americans fled the South and settled in northern cities such as Chicago, Detroit, Cleveland, Pittsburgh, and New York. The African-American migrations following World War I and World War II are among the largest voluntary internal migrations in U.S. history.

Most African-Americans moved to the Northeast and Midwest, although after 1940 significant numbers also moved West. The traditional migration from the South to the North dwindled dramatically in the 1970s. In fact, after 1975, largely due to the favorable economic conditions developing in the booming Sunbelt cities, African-Americans started migrating in droves to the South. In 2004 five out of the six states whose populations were more than 25% African-American were in the deep South: Mississippi (37.2%), Louisiana (32.5%), Georgia (28.7%), South Carolina (28.9%), and Alabama (26%). (See Figure 1.4.) States in the Midwest and Northwest had low proportions of African-Americans.

White Flight

African-Americans are significantly more likely than non-Hispanic whites to live in metropolitan areas, inside of central cities. According to Jesse McKinnon of the Census Bureau, in *The Black Population in the United States: March 2002* (April 2003, http://www.census.gov/ prod/2003pubs/p20-541.pdf), more than one out of two (51.5%) African-Americans lived in these areas in 2002, compared to only 21.1% of non-Hispanic whites. In contrast, a higher proportion of whites lived inside metropolitan areas, but outside of central cities, than did African-Americans (56.8% and 36%, respectively), as well as in nonmetropolitan areas (22.1% and 12.5%, respectively).

FIGURE 1.4

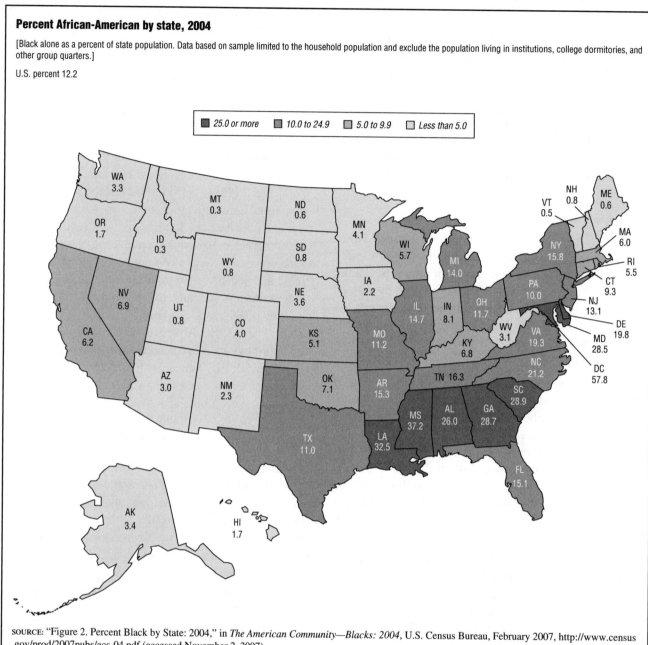

Percent African-American by state, 2004

[Black alone as a percent of state population. Data based on sample limited to the household population and exclude the population living in institutions, college dormitories, and other group quarters.]

U.S. percent 12.2

Legend: ■ 25.0 or more ■ 10.0 to 24.9 ■ 5.0 to 9.9 □ Less than 5.0

WA 3.3
OR 1.7
MT 0.3
ND 0.6
MN 4.1
WI 5.7
MI 14.0
NY 15.8
VT 0.5
NH 0.8
ME 0.6
MA 6.0
RI 5.5
CT 9.3
NJ 13.1
DE 19.8
ID 0.3
WY 0.8
SD 0.8
IA 2.2
IL 14.7
IN 8.1
OH 11.7
PA 10.0
NV 6.9
UT 0.8
NE 3.6
MD 28.5
DC 57.8
CA 6.2
CO 4.0
KS 5.1
MO 11.2
KY 6.8
WV 3.1
VA 19.3
NC 21.2
AZ 3.0
NM 2.3
OK 7.1
AR 15.3
TN 16.3
SC 28.9
MS 37.2
AL 26.0
GA 28.7
LA 32.5
TX 11.0
FL 15.1
AK 3.4
HI 1.7

SOURCE: "Figure 2. Percent Black by State: 2004," in *The American Community—Blacks: 2004*, U.S. Census Bureau, February 2007, http://www.census .gov/prod/2007pubs/acs-04.pdf (accessed November 2, 2007)

Cities with particularly high proportions of African-Americans in 2003 included New York–White Plains–Wayne (24.7%), Philadelphia (22.3%), Washington, D.C.–Arlington–Alexandria (30.1%), Atlanta–Sandy Springs–Marietta (29.2%), and Baltimore-Towson (27.3%). (See Table 1.3.) However, the suburban areas around these metropolitan areas have lower proportions of African-Americans. For example, only 9.8% of the population of Nassau and Suffolk counties, the suburbs of New York City, was African-American, compared to 24.7% of New York City itself. Even though Chicago was 19.7% African-American, its suburbs in Lake and Kenosha counties were only 6.9% African-American.

Eric Bickford explains in "White Flight: The Effect of Minority Presence on Post–World War II Suburbanization" (September 1999, http://eh.net/Clio/Publications/ flight.shtml) that a primary reason for the high proportion of African-Americans in central cities has been "white flight." Beginning in the 1950s, as African-Americans moved to northeastern and midwestern cities, whites who were economically able to do so moved to suburban areas. Before the Civil Rights Act of 1964, which prohibited discrimination in housing, African-Americans were not given the same opportunities to move away from cities, whether or not they were economically able to do so. As wealthier whites abandoned city neighborhoods,

TABLE 1.3

Population of twenty largest metropolitan statistical areas with metropolitan divisions, by race/ethnicity, 2003

Rank	Metropolitan statistical area/metropolitan division	Population characteristics, 2003 (percent)					
		White alone	Black or African American alone	Asian alone	American Indian, Alaska Native alone	Native Hawaiian and other Pacific Islander alone	Hispanic or Latino (any race)
1	New York-Northern New Jersey-Long Island, NY-NJ-PA	69.2	20.2	8.6	0.5	0.1	20.9
	Edison, NJ	82.2	7.8	8.7	0.2	0	10
	Nassau-Suffolk, NY	84.3	9.8	4.5	0.3	0.1	12.1
	Newark-Union, NJ-PA	71.6	22.7	4.4	0.3	0.1	14.4
	New York-White Plains-Wayne, NY-NJ	62.5	24.7	10.3	0.6	0.1	26.4
2	Los Angeles-Long Beach-Santa Ana, CA	75.6	8.1	13.2	1	0.3	43
	Los Angeles-Long Beach-Glendale, CA	74.3	9.9	12.7	1.1	0.3	46.3
	Santa Ana-Anaheim-Irvine, CA	80	1.8	14.9	0.9	0.3	32.1
3	Chicago-Naperville-Joliet, IL-IN-WI	75.1	18.5	4.9	0.3	0.1	17.9
	Chicago-Naperville-Joliet, IL	73.5	19.7	5.3	0.4	0.1	18.9
	Gary, IN	79.2	18.5	0.9	0.3	0.1	10.3
	Lake County-Kenosha County, IL-WI	87	6.9	4.3	0.4	0.1	15
4	Philadelphia-Camden-Wilmington, PA-NJ-DE-MD	74.2	20.6	3.8	0.2	0	5.4
	Camden, NJ	78.6	16.5	3.2	0.2	0.1	6.8
	Philadelphia, PA	72.1	22.3	4.3	0.2	0	4.9
	Wilmington, DE-MD-NJ	78	17.9	2.6	0.3	0	5.1
5	Dallas-Fort Worth-Arlington, TX	79.7	14	4.3	0.6	0.1	24.3
	Dallas-Plano-Irving, TX	78.1	15.2	4.8	0.6	0.1	26.1
	Fort Worth-Arlington, TX	82.8	11.6	3.5	0.6	0.1	20.8
6	Miami-Fort Lauderdale-Miami Beach, FL	75.7	20.9	1.9	0.3	0.1	36.8
	Fort Lauderdale-Pompano Beach-Deerfield Beach, FL	71.3	24.3	2.7	0.3	0.1	20.2
	Miami-Miami Beach-Kendall, FL	76.2	20.9	1.4	0.3	0.1	60.5
	West Palm Beach-Boca Raton-Boynton Beach, FL	80.8	15.9	1.8	0.4	0.1	14.9
7	Houston-Sugar Land-Baytown, TX	76.1	16.8	5.4	0.5	0.1	31.1
8	Washington-Arlington-Alexandria, DC-VA-MD-WV	63.5	26.4	7.7	0.4	0.1	10.1
	Bethesda-Gaithersburg-Frederick, MD	73.6	13.3	10.8	0.3	0.1	10.6
	Washington-Arlington-Alexandria, DC-VA-MD-WV	60.6	30.1	6.9	0.4	0.1	10
9	Atlanta-Sandy Springs-Marietta, GA	65.6	29.2	3.7	0.3	0.1	7.7
10	Detroit-Warren-Livonia, MI	72.4	23	2.9	0.3	0	3.1
	Detroit-Livonia-Dearborn, MI	53.6	42.4	2.1	0.4	0	4.2
	Warren-Farmington Hills-Troy, MI	87.8	7	3.5	0.3	0	2.3
11	Boston-Cambridge-Quincy, MA-NH	85.6	7.5	5.4	0.3	0.1	7
	Boston-Quincy, MA	79.9	12.9	5.6	0.3	0.1	7.7
	Cambridge-Newton, Framingham, MA	87.1	4	7.6	0.2	0	4.8
	Essex County, MA	90.3	4.7	2.8	0.3	0.1	13.2
	Rockingham County-Strafford County, NH	96.8	0.7	1.4	0.2	0.1	1.2
12	San Francisco-Oakland-Fremont, CA	65.2	9.5	20.9	0.6	0.7	18.9
	Oakland-Fremont-Hayward, CA	64.2	12.5	18.6	0.7	0.6	20.2
	San Francisco-San Mateo-Redwood City, CA	66.7	5.2	24.3	0.5	0.8	17.1
13	Riverside-San Bernardino-Ontario, CA	83.1	8.2	4.6	1.4	0.4	40.9
14	Phoenix-Mesa-Scottsdale, AZ	89.4	4	2.4	2.5	0.2	28.1
15	Seattle-Tacoma-Bellevue, WA	79.8	5.5	9.5	1.2	0.6	6.2
	Seattle-Bellevue-Everett, WA	79.7	4.9	10.7	1.1	0.5	6.1
	Tacoma, WA	80.3	7.3	5.4	1.5	0.9	6.3
16	Minneapolis-St. Paul-Bloomington, MN-WI	86.9	5.9	4.7	0.7	0.1	3.8
17	San Diego-Carlsbad-San Marcos, CA	80.3	5.9	9.4	1	0.5	28.7
18	St. Louis, MO-IL	78.8	18.1	1.7	0.2	0	1.7
19	Baltimore-Towson, MD	68	27.3	3.1	0.3	0.1	2.1
20	Tampa-St. Petersburg-Clearwater, FL	84.8	11.2	2.2	0.4	0.1	12

SOURCE: Adapted from "Table 1. Annual Estimates of the Population of Metropolitan and Micropolitan Statistical Areas: April 1, 2000 to July 1, 2006," in *Metropolitan and Micropolitan Statistical Area Estimates*, U.S. Census Bureau, April 2007, http://www.census.gov/population/www/estimates/CBSA-est2006-annual.html and "Table B-3. Metropolitan Areas—Population by Age, Race, and Sex," in *State and Metropolitan Area Data Book: 2006*, U.S. Census Bureau, July 2006, http://www.census.gov/prod/2006pubs/smadb/smadb-06tableb.pdf (accessed December 12, 2007)

taking their tax dollars with them, city neighborhoods rapidly deteriorated, leaving poor and nonwhite residents to deal with increasing crime and neighborhood deterioration.

ASIAN-AMERICANS

The term *Asian-American* is a catch-all term that did not gain currency until the late 1960s and early 1970s. It was not until 1980 that the Census Bureau created the "Asian and Pacific Islander" category, a departure from the previous practice of counting several Asian groups separately. Even though seemingly a geographic description, "Asian and Pacific Islander" contains racial overtones, given that natives of Australia and New Zealand are not included, nor are whites born in the Asian region of the former Soviet Union. In 2006, 13.2 million Asian-Americans lived in the United States, making up 4.4% of the country's population. (See Table 1.1.) Native Hawaiians and Pacific Islanders had a population of 528,818, making up 0.2% of the total U.S. population.

Chinese Immigration in the 1800s

In "Chinese Immigration" (September 1, 2003, http://memory.loc.gov/learn/features/immig/chinese.html), the Library of Congress explains that the first major immigration of people from Asia to the United States involved the Chinese. From the time of the California gold rush of 1849 until the early 1880s, it is estimated that as many as 250,000 Chinese immigrated to the United States, with the vast majority coming from the Pearl River delta of Guangdong Province. Many hoped to strike it rich in California, the "Golden Mountain," and then return home. A few fulfilled that dream, but most stayed in the United States, two-thirds in California, where they faced intense discrimination. They became the object of political posturing that portrayed "cheap Chinese labor" as a threat to U.S. workers.

After the Civil War, at the same time most African-Americans were able to gain citizenship with the adoption of the Fourteenth Amendment in 1868, an exception was carved out for Asian immigrants. They were designated "aliens ineligible to citizenship." The Chinese Exclusion Act of 1882 then stopped the entry of Chinese into the country altogether, except for a few merchants and students. As a result, China became the source of the United States' first illegal aliens. Claire Lui states in "How Illegal Immigration Was Born" (May 7, 2007, http://www.americanheritage.com/) that besides jumping ship or illegally crossing borders, many Chinese immigrants took advantage of the 1906 earthquake in San Francisco, which destroyed the city's vital statistics records, to gain legal status by forging U.S. birth certificates. By law, any male of Chinese heritage born in the United States had the right to return to China for any children he fathered (although he could not bring back the alien mother). As a result, many of these

fraudulent U.S. citizens escorted to the United States a host of "paper sons." Despite this traffic and other means of illegal entry, the Chinese-American population declined from the 1880s to the 1920s. Laws regulating Chinese immigration to the United States did not change until World War II, when China became an ally. President Franklin D. Roosevelt (1882–1945) persuaded Congress to repeal the Chinese Exclusion Act in 1943.

People of other nationalities that comprise the Asian-American category also began immigrating to the United States before World War II. The Japanese first came to the United States in significant numbers during the 1890s, although many laborers had previously settled in Hawaii. Like the Chinese, the Japanese mostly lived in the western United States. There was some call for a "Japanese Exclusion Act," but because Japan was an emerging Pacific power, such legislation was never passed. Overall, Japanese immigrants fared better than their Chinese counterparts and soon outpaced them in population. However, the Library of Congress notes in "Japanese Immigration" (February 2, 2004, http://memory.loc.gov/learn/features/immig/japanese.html) that when Japan and the United States went to war in 1941, over one hundred thousand Americans of Japanese descent, including many who were native-born U.S. citizens, were removed from their homes and confined in detention camps. By 1945 approximately 125,000 people of Japanese descent had been sent to these camps. It is noteworthy that even though the United States was also at war with Germany and Italy, citizens of German and Italian descent or birth were not subject to incarceration due to their heritage.

Before World War II Filipinos, Asian-Indians, and Koreans represented a negligible share of the Asian-American population. In *Historical Census Statistics on Population Totals by Race, 1790 to 1990, and by Hispanic Origin, 1970 to 1990, for the United States, Regions, Division, and States* (September 2002, http://www.census.gov/population/documentation/twps0056/twps0056.pdf), Campbell Gibson and Kay Jung of the Census Bureau state that in 1940 there were 254,918 Asian-Americans living in the United States; 126,947 were Japanese, 77,504 were Chinese, and 45,563 were Filipino. Asian-Indians totaled some 2,405, and Koreans numbered even fewer. As was the case with Puerto Ricans, Filipinos began to immigrate to the United States in the years following the Spanish-American War, when their country was annexed and eventually granted commonwealth status. Designated "American nationals," Filipinos held a unique position: They were not eligible for citizenship, but they also could not be prevented from entering the United States. Many Filipinos immigrated during the 1920s looking for work, but the Great Depression of the 1930s stemmed this flow.

Asian-Indians had come to the United States in small numbers, generally settling in New York City and other eastern ports, but it was not until the early years of the twentieth century that they began immigrating to the West Coast, generally entering through western Canada. Koreans came to the United States from Hawaii, where several thousand had immigrated between 1903 and 1905. Both Asian-Indians and Koreans lost their eligibility to enter the United States following the Immigration Act of 1917, accounting for their small populations before World War II. Once the Chinese Exclusion Act was repealed, however, the door was also open for Filipinos and Asian-Indians to gain entry to the United States as well as to earn citizenship during the postwar years. The Korean War (1950–1953) led to a long-term U.S. military presence in Korea, resulting in a number of Korean-born wives of military personnel relocating to the United States. In addition, many Korean-born children were adopted and brought to the United States. A larger influx of Korean families immigrated during the mid-1960s.

Sharp Rise in Immigration

Asian immigration during the 1980s can be divided into two "streams." The first stream came from Asian countries that already had large populations in the United States (such as the People's Republic of China, Korea, and the Philippines). These immigrants, many of whom were highly educated, came primarily for family reunification and through employment provisions of the immigration laws. The second stream consisted primarily of immigrants and refugees from the war-torn countries of Southeast Asia (Vietnam, Laos, and Cambodia). They were admitted under U.S. policies that supported political refugees after the Vietnam War (1954–1975), as well as those escaping unstable economic and political conditions in neighboring countries. In "Southeast Asian Communities" (2008, http://www.searac.org/commun.html), the Southeast Asia Resource Action Center notes that between 1975 and 1998 an estimated 1.3 million refugees arrived in the United States from Southeast Asia.

According to the 2006 American Community Survey (http://www.census2010.gov/acs/www/), China was the top Asian country of origin for Asian immigrants—3.1 million U.S. residents traced their roots to China. Almost 2.5 million U.S. residents traced their roots to India, and over 2.3 million traced their roots to the Philippines. Over 1.3 million people living in the United States had ancestral origins in Korea, and almost 1.5 million had origins in Vietnam. Among Native Hawaiians and Pacific Islanders, Native Hawaiians had the highest population, at 148,598.

Geographic Distribution

In 2004 Asians and Pacific Islanders were much more likely than non-Hispanic whites to live in the West (47.9% and 19.4%, respectively). (See Figure 1.5.) Twenty percent

FIGURE 1.5

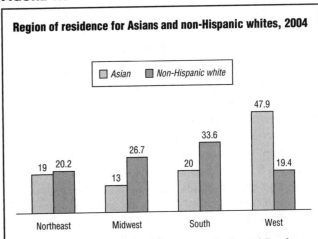

Region of residence for Asians and non-Hispanic whites, 2004

SOURCE: Adapted from "Table 20. Population by Region and Sex, for Asian Alone and White Alone, Not Hispanic: March 2004," in *The Asian Alone Population in the United States: March 2004*, U.S. Census Bureau, 2004, http://www.census.gov/population/socdemo/race/api/ppl-184/tab20.pdf (accessed November 10, 2007)

of Asian-Americans lived in the South, 19% lived in the Northeast, and only 13% lived in the Midwest.

In *The Asian and Pacific Islander Population in the United States: March 2002* (May 2003, http://www.census.gov/prod/2003pubs/p20-540.pdf), Terrance Reeves and Claudette Bennett of the Census Bureau report that in 2002, 95% of Asians and Pacific Islanders lived in metropolitan areas, whereas only 78% of non-Hispanic whites lived in metropolitan areas. Jessica S. Barnes and Claudette E. Bennett of the Census Bureau state in *The Asian Population: 2000* (February 2002, http://www.census.gov/prod/2002pubs/c2kbr01-16.pdf) that in 2000 New York, Los Angeles, and San Jose, California, were the three cities with the largest populations of Asian-Americans. Likewise, Elizabeth M. Grieco of the Census Bureau notes in *The Native Hawaiian and Other Pacific Islander Population: 2000* (December 2001, http://www.census.gov/prod/2001pubs/c2kbr01-14.pdf) that Honolulu, Los Angeles, and San Diego, California, were the three cities with the largest Native Hawaiian and Pacific Islander populations in 2000.

NATIVE AMERICANS

Most historians agree that the people known as Native Americans and Alaskan Natives arrived in North America from northeast Asia at least thirty thousand years ago during the last of the Ice Age glaciations (coverings of large areas of Earth with ice). At that time the two continents were connected by a land bridge over what is currently the Bering Strait. However, according to Charles W. Petit in "Rediscovering America: The New World May Be 20,000 Years Older Than Experts

Thought" (*U.S. News and World Report*, October 12, 1998), some archaeologists dispute this theory by citing evidence that indicates that migrants may have actually arrived many thousands of years earlier, perhaps by boat.

Migrants who settled on the northern coast of Alaska and the Yukon River valley, which were free of ice barriers, became known as Eskimos and Aleuts. Those who ventured farther south followed the eastern slope of the Rocky Mountains and continued along the mountainous spine of North America into Central and South America. There, they moved east throughout the central plains and eastern highlands of both continents and were later erroneously named Indians by exploring Spaniards. The misnomer is attributed to Christopher Columbus (1451–1506), who, on landing in the Bahamas in 1492, thought he had reached the islands off the eastern region of Asia, called the Indies. He therefore greeted the inhabitants as "Indians." In the twenty-first century many descendants of the original settlers prefer to be called Native Americans.

Most Native American groups have historically had a close relationship with the earth. Some have been farmers, whereas others have specialized in hunting and fishing. The arrival of the Europeans eventually changed the way of life of Native American tribes. Devastating wars, disease, the annihilation of the buffalo, and the loss of land fit for cultivation to Europeans led to the elimination of much of their population.

In 2006, 2.9 million Native Americans and Alaskan Natives lived in the United States, making up approximately 1% of the population. (See Table 1.1.) An additional 1.6 million people claimed they were Native American or Alaskan Native in combination with one or more other races.

Geographic Distribution

Stella U. Ogunwole of the Census Bureau reports in *The American Indian and Alaska Native Population: 2000*, February 2002, http://www.census.gov/prod/2002pubs/c2kbr01-15.pdf) that in 2000, the most recent year for which data are available, 48% of Native Americans and Alaskan Natives lived in the West. Another 29.3% lived in the South, 16.1% lived in the Midwest, and 6.6% lived in the Northeast. Individuals who were Native American or Alaskan Native in combination with one or more other races were slightly less likely to live in the West and slightly more likely to live in the Northeast, Midwest, or South.

Many Native Americans live on or near reservations and are members of groupings called "tribes." Ogunwole notes that in 2000 the largest tribal groupings were the Cherokee, with 729,533 members, followed by the Navajo, with 298,197 members, and the Latin Native Americans, with 180,940 members. Many Alaskan Natives are

also members of such groups. The largest tribal groupings of Alaskan Natives in 2000 were the Eskimos, with 54,761 members, followed by the Tlingit-Haida, with 22,365 members, the Alaska Athabascan, with 18,838 members, and the Aleut, with 16,978 members.

RELATIONS BETWEEN WHITES AND MINORITY GROUPS

In *Whites, Blacks, Hispanics Assess Race Relations in the U.S.* (August 6, 2007, http://www.gallup.com/poll/28312/Whites-Blacks-Hispanics-Assess-Race-Relations-US.aspx), Joseph Carroll of the Gallup Organization reports on a 2007 poll about relations between racial and ethnic groups. Overall, 83% of Americans maintained that relations between whites and Asian-Americans were "very/somewhat good," 71% thought that relations between whites and African-Americans were "somewhat/very good," and 68% thought relations between whites and Hispanics were "somewhat/very good." Non-Hispanic whites were significantly more than African-Americans to perceive relations between whites and African-Americans as good (75% and 55%, respectively). (See Figure 1.6.) Carroll notes that African-Americans' perceptions of relations between blacks and whites was the worst it had been since 2001.

According to Carroll, a smaller proportion of Americans characterized the relations between non-Hispanic whites and Hispanics as good; 66% described the relations in this way. Similar proportions of non-Hispanic whites (68%) and Hispanics (70%) viewed relations between the groups positively, whereas only 53% of African-Americans viewed relations between the groups positively. (See Figure 1.7.)

FIGURE 1.6

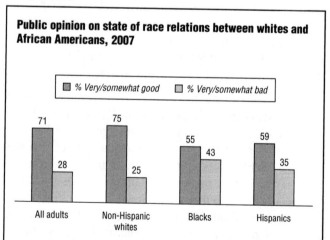

Public opinion on state of race relations between whites and African Americans, 2007

■ % *Very/somewhat good*   □ % *Very/somewhat bad*

All adults: 71, 28
Non-Hispanic whites: 75, 25
Blacks: 55, 43
Hispanics: 59, 35

SOURCE: Joseph Carroll, "Relations between Whites and Blacks," in *Whites, Blacks, Hispanics Assess Race Relations in the U.S.*, The Gallup Organization, August 6, 2007, http://www.gallup.com/poll/28312/Whites-Blacks-Hispanics-Assess-Race-Relations-US.aspx?version=print (accessed January 16, 2008). Copyright © 2008 by The Gallup Organization. Reproduced by Permission of The Gallup Organization.

FIGURE 1.7

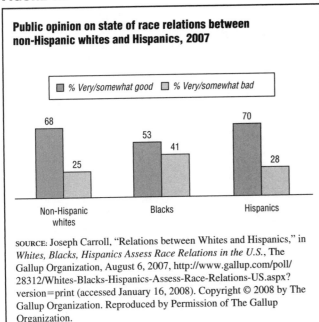

Public opinion on state of race relations between non-Hispanic whites and Hispanics, 2007

SOURCE: Joseph Carroll, "Relations between Whites and Hispanics," in *Whites, Blacks, Hispanics Assess Race Relations in the U.S.*, The Gallup Organization, August 6, 2007, http://www.gallup.com/poll/28312/Whites-Blacks-Hispanics-Assess-Race-Relations-US.aspx?version=print (accessed January 16, 2008). Copyright © 2008 by The Gallup Organization. Reproduced by Permission of The Gallup Organization.

Frank Newport of the Gallup Organization notes in *Update: Americans' Satisfaction with Aspects of Life in the U.S.* (January 27, 2005, http://www.gallup.com/poll/14611/Update-Americans-Satisfaction-Aspects-Life-US.aspx) that even though most Americans characterized relations between races and ethnic groups as "good" in 2005, only 9% of Americans were "very satisfied" with the state of race relations in the nation. Another 44% said that they were "somewhat satisfied," and 24% were "somewhat dissatisfied" with race relations in the United States.

In *Black Dissatisfaction Simmers beneath Good Race Relations* (August 22, 2003, http://www.gallup.com/poll/9100/Black-Dissatisfaction-Simmers-Beneath-Good-Race-Relations.aspx), Lydia Saad of the Gallup Organization reports that in 2003, 68% of white Americans believed that African-Americans in their own communities are treated as well as whites. This figure, however, masks a distinct divide, with only 40% of African-Americans reporting that African-Americans are treated as well as whites. African-American respondents indicated that they were generally dissatisfied with the way African-Americans are treated in society—39% felt "very dissatisfied," 20% felt "somewhat dissatisfied," and only 10% felt "very satisfied." Most African-Americans reported having experienced racial discrimination in public life or employment, with 26% reporting that they experienced it at least weekly. Four out of five (81%) believed that racial minorities did not have equal job opportunities as whites.

CHAPTER 2
FAMILY LIFE AND LIVING ARRANGEMENTS

Historically, the family has been regarded as the cornerstone of society in the United States. For many years, particularly when the United States was primarily an agricultural society, extended families (multiple generations living in the same household) were common. As the culture became more urban and mobile, nuclear families (two parents and their children) became the American norm.

However, the makeup of families and their role in society have been undergoing a massive change. Shifts in economics, employment, moral values, and social conditions have led to an increasing number of single men and women living alone, cohabitations without marriage, and single-parent families. A growing number of children, especially minority children, are being raised by only one parent or by neither parent, as in the case of children being raised by grandparents or foster parents. How these changes affect minorities in the United States can be best understood through a detailed look at minority families.

MARITAL STATUS

The U.S. Census Bureau (June 29, 2005, http://www.census.gov/population/socdemo/hh-fam/ms1.pdf) reports that in 2005, 127.1 million Americans (aged fifteen and older) were married, up from 95.3 million in 1970 and 112.6 million in 1990. This figure includes both people who did and people who did not live with their spouses. However, the proportion of people of marriage age who were married has decreased steadily since 1960, even though the absolute numbers of married people have increased. In 1960, 67.6% of the population aged fifteen and older was married, dropping to 64.2% in 1970, 60.9% in 1980, 58.7% in 1990, 56.2% in 2000, and to a low of 55.4% in 2004. The proportion of African-Americans who were married has been lower than the proportion of married adults in the general population since 1960 and has dropped faster as well. Of all African-

Americans aged fifteen and older, 60.3% in 1960, 55.4% in 1970, 46.5% in 1980, 42.4% in 1990, and 39.2% in 2000 were married. By 2006 only 32.3% of African-Americans aged fifteen and older were married. (See Table 2.1.) That same year, 58.6% of Asian-Americans, 56.4% of non-Hispanic whites, and 50.7% of Hispanics aged fifteen and older were married.

Never Married

Racial differences among never-married people are also significant. Among those over age fifteen, African-Americans are far more likely than non-Hispanic whites, Hispanics, or Asian-Americans to have never married. In 2006, 45.4% of African-Americans had never been married, compared to 25.4% of non-Hispanic whites, 31.5% of Asian-Americans, and 35.2% of Hispanics. (See Table 2.1.)

One reason that the proportion of never-married individuals aged fifteen years and older has increased over time is that the age at first marriage has steadily risen since 1970 for all races and ethnic groups. The median (average) age of first marriage for women rose from 20.8 in 1970 to 25.3 in 2005. (See Figure 2.1.) The median age of first marriage for men rose from 23.2 in 1970 to 27.1 in 2005. This rise in the age of first marriage accounts for some of the decreases in the proportion of adults who have ever married.

Interracial Marriage

Laws that prohibited interracial marriage were on the books in many states until 1967. In that year, the U.S. Supreme Court unanimously decided in *Loving v. Virginia* (388 U.S. 1) that prohibitions against interracial marriage were unconstitutional. However, interracial marriages were rare even into the 1970s. After 1980 interracial marriages became much more common. The Census Bureau reports that the number of interracial married couples more than tripled between 1980 and 2006. (See Table 2.2.) For example, in 1980 there were 167,000 African-American–white

TABLE 2.1

Marital status of people 15 years and over, by sex, race, and Hispanic origin, 2006

[Numbers in thousands, except for percentages]

All races	Total Number	Married spouse present Number	Married spouse absent Number	Widowed Number	Divorced Number	Separated Number	Never married Number	Total Percent	Married spouse present Percent	Married spouse absent Percent	Widowed Percent	Divorced Percent	Separated Percent	Never married Percent
All races														
Total 15+ Male	233,039	119,055	3,785	13,914	22,806	4,963	68,515	100.0	51.1	1.6	6.0	9.8	2.1	29.4
Total 15+ Female	113,073	59,528	2,096	2,624	9,679	2,059	37,086	100.0	52.6	1.9	2.3	8.6	1.8	32.8
15–64 years	99,679	51,023	1,300	2,679	11,275	2,693	30,708	100.0	51.2	1.3	2.7	11.3	2.7	30.8
White, non-Hispanic														
Total 15+ Male	161,116	89,081	1,735	10,584	16,500	2,358	40,859	100.0	55.3	1.1	6.6	10.2	1.5	25.4
Total 15+ Female	78,227	44,655	797	1,995	7,205	1,049	22,525	100.0	57.1	1.0	2.5	9.2	1.3	28.8
Total 15+	82,890	44,426	937	8,589	9,295	1,309	18,334	100.0	53.6	1.1	10.4	11.2	1.6	22.1
Black														
Total 15+ Male	28,554	8,670	544	1,790	3,198	1,388	12,964	100.0	30.4	1.9	6.3	11.2	4.9	45.4
Total 15+ Female	12,939	4,445	269	336	1,201	545	6,141	100.0	34.4	2.1	2.6	9.3	4.2	47.5
Total 15+	15,615	4,225	275	1,453	1,997	842	6,822	100.0	27.1	1.8	9.3	12.8	5.4	43.7
Asian														
Total 15+ Male	10,832	6,014	339	403	517	144	3,416	100.0	55.5	3.1	3.7	4.8	1.3	31.5
Total 15+ Female	5,172	2,790	196	59	202	46	1,879	100.0	53.9	3.8	1.1	3.9	0.9	36.3
Total 15+	5,660	3,224	142	344	315	98	1,537	100.0	57.0	2.5	6.1	5.6	1.7	27.2
Hispanic														
Total 15+ Male	30,613	14,356	1,174	1,007	2,246	1,065	10,765	100.0	46.9	3.8	3.3	7.3	3.5	35.2
Total 15+ Female	15,759	7,131	851	195	905	406	6,270	100.0	45.3	5.4	1.2	5.7	2.6	39.8
Total 15+	14,854	7,225	323	812	1,340	659	4,495	100.0	48.6	2.2	5.5	9.0	4.4	30.3

Notes: Hispanics may be of any race. Prior to 2001, this table included group quarters people.

SOURCE: Adapted from "Table A1. Marital Status of People 15 Years and over by Age, Sex, Personal Earnings, Race, and Hispanic Origin, 2006," in *America's Families and Living Arrangements: 2006*, U.S. Census Bureau, March 27, 2007, http://www.census.gov/population/www/socdemo/hh-fam/cps2006.html (accessed November 10, 2007)

interracial married couples; by 2006 there were 403,000 African-American–white interracial married couples. In 1980 there were 450,000 married couples with one white spouse and one spouse of a race other than white or African-American, such as Native American or Asian and Pacific Islander; in 2006 nearly 1.8 million married couples fit this description. Even though the proportion of interracial married couples is rising, the vast majority of married couples continue to be made up of two spouses of the same race. In 1980, 651,000 (1.3%) married couples were interracial; by 2006 there were 2.3 million (3.8%).

Why is the number of interracial and interethnic marriage rising? Michael J. Rosenfeld of Stanford University argues in "A Briefing Paper Prepared for the Council on Contemporary Families" (April 25, 2007, http://www.contemporaryfamilies.org/subtemplate.php?t=press Releases&ext=nontraditional) that the rise in immigra-

tion from Asian and Hispanic countries is partially responsible, because neither of these groups is as segregated from white society as African-Americans have historically been in the United States. He also cites a greater acceptance of diversity and improving race relations as reasons marriages between whites and African-Americans have increased.

In fact, considerable progress has been made in the public acceptance of interracial marriage. According to Joseph Carroll of the Gallup Organization, in *Most Americans Approve of Interracial Marriages* (August 16, 2007, http://www.gallup.com/poll/28417/Most-Americans-Approve-Interracial-Marriages.aspx), in 1958 only 4% of Americans were accepting of marriage between couples of different races, and as late as 1994, 48% of all Americans approved. By 2007, however, 77% of Americans said they approved of marriages between African-Americans and whites. Sup-

FIGURE 2.1

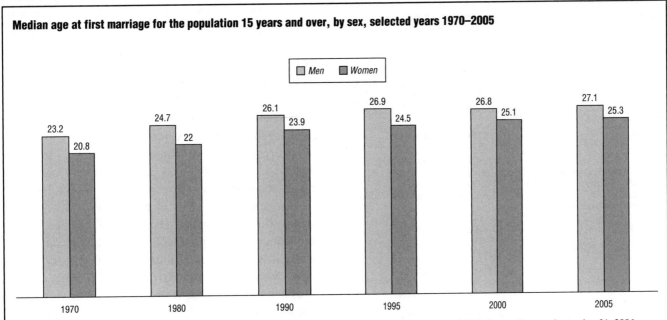

Median age at first marriage for the population 15 years and over, by sex, selected years 1970–2005

☐ Men ☐ Women

	1970	1980	1990	1995	2000	2005
Men	23.2	24.7	26.1	26.9	26.8	27.1
Women	20.8	22	23.9	24.5	25.1	25.3

SOURCE: Adapted from "Table MS-2. Estimated Median Age at First Marriage, by Sex: 1890 to the Present," U.S. Census Bureau, September 21, 2006, http://www.census.gov/population/socdemo/hh-fam/ms2.pdf (accessed December 6, 2007)

TABLE 2.2

Married couples by race and Hispanic origin of spouses, selected years, 1980–2006

[In thousands (49,714 represents 49,714,000). As of March. Persons 15 years old and over. Persons of Hispanic origin may be any race. Based on Current Population Survey.]

Race and origin of spouses	1980	1990	2000	2006
Married couples, total[a]	49,714	53,256	56,497	59,528
Interracial married couples, total	651	964	1,464	2,274
White/black[b]	167	211	363	403
Black husband/white wife	122	150	268	286
White husband/black wife	45	61	i95	117
White[b]/other race[c]	450	720	1,051	1,763
Black[b]/other race[c]	34	33	50	108
Hispanic origin				
Hispanic/Hispanic	1,906	3,085	4,739	6,065
Hispanic/other origin (not Hispanic)	891	1,193	1,743	2,226
All other couples (not of Hispanic origin)	46,917	48,979	50,015	51,236

[a]Includes other married couples not shown separately.
[b]Beginning with the 2003 Current Population Survey (CPS), respondents could choose more than one race. Beginning 2004, data shown represent persons who selected this race group only and exclude persons reporting more than one race. The CPS prior to 2003 only allowed respondents to report one race group.
[c]"Other race," is any race other than white or black, such as American Indian, Japanese, Chinese, etc. This total excludes combinations of other races by other races.

SOURCE: "Table 59. Married Couples by Race and Hispanic Origin of Spouses: 1980 to 2006," in *Statistical Abstract of the United States: 2008*, U.S. Census Bureau, December 2007, http://www.census.gov/compendia/statab/tables/08s0059.pdf (accessed January 6, 2008)

eighteen and forty-nine approved, whereas among adults over age fifty only 67% approved. These numbers indicate that the trend toward increasing acceptance of interracial marriage is likely to continue.

MIXED-RACE CHILDREN. The number of mixed-race births has kept pace with increases in interracial marriage and cohabitation. The change in the question of race for the 2000 census, which enabled people to identify themselves by multiple races, made it easier to track mixed-race Americans. According to the 2000 census, 3.9 million (1.4%) Americans identified themselves as belonging to two or more races. (See Table 2.3.) By 2005 this number had grown to nearly 4.6 million Americans, an increase of 17.5%.

In 2000, 465,051 Native Hawaiians and Pacific Islanders reported being of one race, whereas 910,907 Native Hawaiians or Pacific Islanders reported belonging to two or races. (See Table 2.3.) Therefore, 445,856 reported being of mixed race in 2000. By 2005 the Census Bureau estimated that 473,061 Native Hawaiians and Pacific Islanders were of mixed race. An estimated 1.6 million Native Americans and Alaskan Natives were multiracial in 2005, virtually unchanged since 2000. In 2000 there were 1.4 million Asian-Americans who reported that they were multiracial; by 2005 the Census Bureau reported there were 1.7 million multiracial Asian-Americans. The groups with the smallest proportion claiming a multiracial heritage in the 2000 census were African-Americans (1.4 million, which increased to 1.8 million in 2005) and non-Hispanic whites (3.4 million,

port for interracial marriages was higher among African-Americans (85%) than among whites (75%). Younger Americans were more accepting of interracial marriages than older Americans—85% of people between the ages of

TABLE 2.3

Resident population by race and Hispanic origin, 2000 and 2005

[Data shown are modified race counts]

Characteristic	Number 2000 (July)	Number 2005 (July)	Percent change, 2000 to 2005
Both sexes			
Total	282,193,477	296,410,404	5.3
One race	278,264,867	291,831,380	5.2
White	228,621,011	237,854,954	4.3
Black or African American	35,812,967	37,909,341	6.2
American Indian and Alaska Native	2,673,516	2,863,001	7.5
Asian	10,692,322	12,687,472	19.8
Native Hawaiian and other Pacific Islanders	465,051	516,612	11.7
Two or more races	3,928,610	4,579,024	17.5
Race alone or in combination:ᵇ			
White	231,978,939	241,806,816	4.5
Black or African American	37,231,510	39,724,136	7.1
American Indian and Alaska Native	4,236,490	4,453,660	5.4
Asian	12,122,242	14,376,658	19.7
Native Hawaiian and other Pacific Islanders	910,907	989,673	9.1
Not Hispanic or Latino	246,545,289	253,723,180	3.1
One race	243,113,423	249,749,485	2.9
White	195,769,254	198,366,437	1.4
Black or African American	34,413,010	36,324,593	5.9
American Indian and Alaska Native	2,103,966	2,232,922	6.5
Asian	10,458,303	12,420,514	19.9
Native Hawaiian and other Pacific Islanders	368,890	405,019	10.3
Two or more races	3,431,866	3,973,695	16.7
Race alone or in combination:ᵇ			
White	198,692,488	201,782,278	1.7
Black or African American	35,613,610	37,858,590	6.6
American Indian and Alaska Native	3,462,858	3,602,649	4.3
Asian	11,744,147	13,933,501	19.8
Native Hawaiian and other Pacific Islanders	754,872	812,287	8.0
Hispanic or Latino	35,648,188	42,687,224	20.9
One race	35,151,444	42,081,895	20.9
White	32,851,757	39,488,517	21.4
Black or African American	1,399,957	1,584,748	13.9
American Indian and Alaska Native	569,550	630,079	11.2
Asian	234,019	266,958	14.8
Native Hawaiian and other Pacific Islanders	96,161	111,593	16.9
Two or more races	496,744	605,329	23.2
Race alone or in combination:ᵇ			
White	33,286,451	40,024,538	21.4
Black or African American	1,617,900	1,865,546	16.2
American Indian and Alaska Native	773,632	851,011	10.6
Asian	378,095	443,157	18.2
Native Hawaiian and other Pacific Islanders	156,035	177,386	14.5

Notes:
ᵃThe April 1, 2000 population estimates base reflects changes to the Census 2000 population from the count question resolution program and geographic program revisions.
ᵇIn combination means in combination with one or more other races. The sum of the five race groups adds to more than the total population because individuals may report more than one race.

SOURCE: Adapted from "Table 13. Resident Population by Sex, Race, and Hispanic Origin Status: 2000 to 2005," in *Statistical Abstract of the United States: 2007*, U.S. Census Bureau, 2006, http://www.census.gov/compendia/statab/2007/population/estimates_and_projections_by_age_sex_raceethnicity.html (accessed February 1, 2008)

which increased to 4 million in 2005). The rigid politics of race in the United States probably leads to an underreporting of mixed-race backgrounds among these two groups.

Divorce

In 2006 the Census Bureau reported that 22.8 million adults (aged fifteen and older) were divorced. (See Table 2.1.) In other words, nearly one out of ten (9.8%) of all people aged fifteen years and older were divorced and had not remarried at the time of the survey—thus, the proportion of ever-divorced people is much higher. A similar proportion of African-Americans (11.2%) and non-Hispanic whites (10.2%) were divorced, whereas a much lower proportion of Hispanics (7.3%) and Asian-Americans (4.8%) were divorced. In *Marital Status and Living Arrangements: March 1994* (February 1996, http://www.census.gov/prod/1/pop/p20-484.pdf), Arlene F. Saluter of the Census Bureau reports that divorce for most groups rose sharply from 1970 to the 1990s, when 3.1% of whites, 3.9% of Hispanics, and 4.4% of African-Americans were divorced. The divorce rate leveled off in the 1990s, according to Jason Fields of the Census Bureau, in *America's Families and Living Arrangements: 2003* (November 2004, http://www.census.gov/prod/2004pubs/p20-553.pdf).

Because men are considerably more likely than women to remarry following a divorce, there are significantly higher proportions of currently divorced women than currently divorced men. In 2006, 1.2 million (9.3%) African-American men were currently divorced, compared to 1.9 million (12.8%) African-American women; and 7.2 million (9.2%) white, non-Hispanic men were divorced, compared to 9.3 million (11.2%) white, non-Hispanic women. (See Table 2.1.) Among those of Hispanic origin, 905,000 (5.7%) men and 1.3 million (9%) women were divorced. In the Asian and Pacific Islander community, 202,000 (3.9%) men and 315,000 (5.6%) women were divorced. Many more women of each race and ethnicity remained divorced than men.

Death of a Spouse

In 2006, 13.9 million (6%) people aged fifteen years and older in the United States were widowed. (See Table 2.1.) Across all racial and ethnic groups, more women than men were widowed because of the shorter average lifespan of men, the tendency of wives to be younger than their husbands, and the greater likelihood that men will remarry. This was particularly pronounced in the white and African-American communities. Nearly 8.6 million (10.4%) non-Hispanic white women were widowed, compared to only 1.9 million (2.5%) non-Hispanic white men. A similar proportion of African-American women (1.5 million, or 9.3%) were widowed, compared to 336,000 (2.6%) African-American men. Among Asian-

FIGURE 2.2

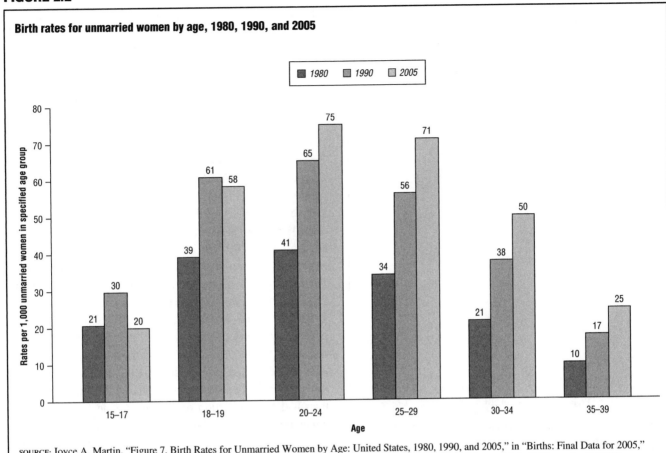

Birth rates for unmarried women by age, 1980, 1990, and 2005

■ *1980* ■ *1990* □ *2005*

(Rates per 1,000 unmarried women in specified age group)

Age	1980	1990	2005
15–17	21	30	20
18–19	39	61	58
20–24	41	65	75
25–29	34	56	71
30–34	21	38	50
35–39	10	17	25

SOURCE: Joyce A. Martin, "Figure 7. Birth Rates for Unmarried Women by Age: United States, 1980, 1990, and 2005," in "Births: Final Data for 2005," *National Vital Statistics Reports*, vol. 56, no. 6, December 5, 2007, http://www.cdc.gov/nchs/data/nvsr56/nvsr56_06.pdf (December 9, 2007)

Americans, 344,000 (6.1%) women were widowed, compared to only 59,000 (1.1%) men. Among Hispanics, 812,000 (5.5%) women were widowed, compared to 195,000 (1.2%) men.

TEENAGE PREGNANCY

Over the generations, a major change in American attitudes has removed much of the social stigma from unwed motherhood. Unmarried women of all ages are having children openly and with a regularity that was unheard of just a few generations ago. Many women do not feel the need to marry immediately when they become pregnant. Joyce A. Martin et al. indicate in "Births: Final Data for 2005" (*National Vital Statistics Reports*, vol. 56, no. 6, December 5, 2007) that in 2005, 36.9% of all births were to unmarried mothers. However, even though the proportion of all births to unmarried mothers has risen, between 1990 and 2005 the birth rate to unmarried teenagers decreased. (See Figure 2.2.) For example, among fifteen- to seventeen-year-olds, the birth rate decreased from thirty per one thousand women in 1990 to twenty births per one thousand women in 2005. Eighteen- to nineteen-year-olds also experienced a decrease, from sixty-one per one thousand births in 1990 to fifty-eight per one thousand births in 2005. However, the birth rate for teenagers rose markedly between 2005 and 2006, the first increase since 1991. The birth rate for teenagers fifteen to seventeen years old increased 3% to twenty-two births per one thousand females in 2006, and for teenagers aged eighteen to nineteen the rate increased 4% to seventy-three per one thousand births. (See Figure 2.3.)

Experts offer many possible explanations for the high rates of teenage motherhood. Among them are lack of access to birth control, lack of education, and little hope for the future, including absence of educational goals. What is certain is that the health of the babies born to teenagers, and especially to teenagers of a racial or ethnic minority group, is often at risk. According to Shih-Chen Chang et al., in "Characteristics and Risk Factors for Adverse Birth Outcomes in Pregnant Black Adolescents" (*Journal of Pediatrics*, vol. 143, no. 2, August 2003), African-American teenagers are twice as likely as white teenagers to deliver low-birthweight babies and 1.5 times more likely to have premature babies. Both low-birthweight and premature babies experience a number of serious health and developmental problems. In general, babies born to teenage mothers of all races suffer a higher risk of low birth weight, preterm delivery, and infant mortality when compared to babies born to older mothers.

FIGURE 2.3

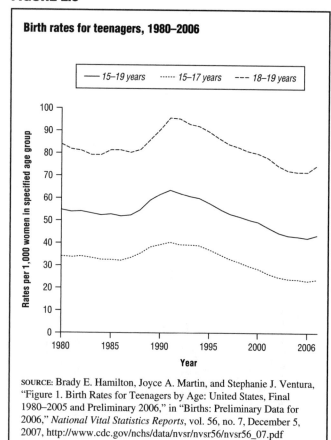

Birth rates for teenagers, 1980–2006

SOURCE: Brady E. Hamilton, Joyce A. Martin, and Stephanie J. Ventura, "Figure 1. Birth Rates for Teenagers by Age: United States, Final 1980–2005 and Preliminary 2006," in "Births: Preliminary Data for 2006," *National Vital Statistics Reports*, vol. 56, no. 7, December 5, 2007, http://www.cdc.gov/nchs/data/nvsr/nvsr56/nvsr56_07.pdf (accessed December 9, 2007)

The largest decline in teen birth rates between 1991 and 2005 was among African-American teens; the birth rate for this group fell from 118.2 to 60.9 births per 1,000 females. (See Figure 2.4.) African-American teens had the highest birth rate in 1991, but by 2005 they had the second-highest birth rate. Even though the teen Hispanic birthrate had fallen from 104.6 to 81.7 births per 1,000 women, these teens had the highest birthrate in 2005. In 2005 Native American teens had a birthrate of 52.7, non-Hispanic white teens had a birthrate of 25.9, and Asian-American teens had a birthrate of 17.

However, in 2006 the birthrate was up for all teenagers aged fifteen to nineteen years except Asian-American teens. The birthrate for African-American teens was up 5% to 63.7 births per 1,000 women. (See Table 2.4.) It was up 4% for Native American teens to 54.7, up 3% for non-Hispanic white teens to 26.6, and up 2% for Hispanic teens, to 83.

MINORITY FAMILY STRUCTURE
Married-Couple Families

The Census Bureau defines a family as two or more people living together who are related by birth, marriage, or adoption. A household, however, can be family or nonfamily and is simply all people who occupy a housing unit.

The proportion of married-couple families among all households declined from 1970 to 2003. According to Fields, 70.6% of all households in 1970 were married-couple families. By 2006 the Census Bureau (March 30, 2007, http://www.census.gov/compendia/statab/tables/08s0060.pdf) reports that the proportion of households that were married-couple families had dropped to 51%.

The proportion of married-couple families among all family households declined between 1970 and the mid-2000s for all races and ethnicities. In *Household and Family Characteristics: March 1994* (September 1995, http://www.census.gov/prod/1/pop/p20-483.pdf), Steve Rawlings and Arlene F. Saluter of the Census Bureau report numbers from 1970 and 1980, which here are compared with Fields's numbers from 2003. In 1970, 88.9% of white families were married-couple families, compared to 81.9% in 2003. Asian-Americans also maintained a proportion of married-couple families comparable to that among the white community. In 1980, 84.5% of Asian-American family households were headed by married couples; by 2003 this proportion had decreased to 80.4%. A high proportion of Hispanic families were headed by a married couple in 1970 (80.6%), but by 2003 this proportion had decreased more significantly (to 68.1%) than had the proportion of married-couple families among either non-Hispanic whites or Asian-Americans. However, the percentage of married-couple families was the lowest, and had decreased the most dramatically, among African-Americans between 1970 and 2003. In 1970, 68.3% of African-American families were married-couple families; by 2003 this proportion had dropped to 46.7%.

By 2006 only 51.5% of all people aged fifteen and older lived with a spouse. (See Table 2.1.) In comparison to this average, 55.3% of all adult non-Hispanic whites and 56.5% of all Asian-Americans lived with a spouse. In contrast, 46.9% of all Hispanic adults and only 30.4% of all African-American adults lived with a spouse.

Single-Parent Households

In 1970 there were 2.9 million families headed by a single mother, comprising 10% of all family households with children. (See Table 2.5.) By 2005 there were 8.3 million single-mother families, 23% of all families with children. Single-father families increased from 341,000 in 1970 to 2 million in 2005, increasing from 1% to 6% of families with children. Most single-parent households in the United States continue to be headed by women. The proportion of family households headed by women with no husband present has grown among all racial and ethnic groups.

In 2006 Asian-Americans and non-Hispanic whites had the lowest proportion of family households headed by single women. Among Asian-American family households,

FIGURE 2.4

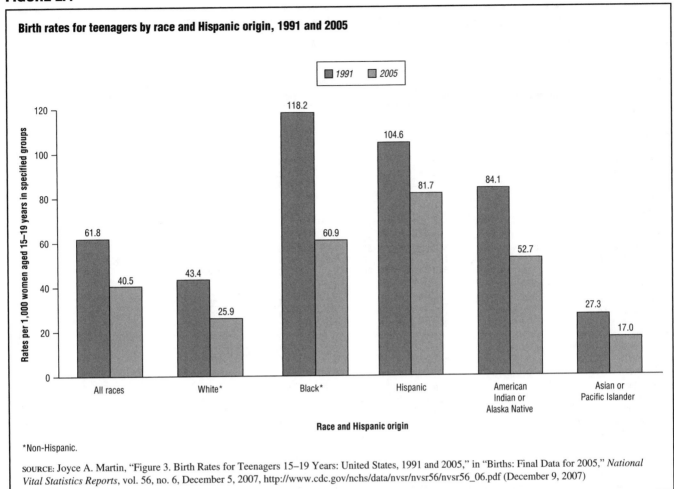

Birth rates for teenagers by race and Hispanic origin, 1991 and 2005

*Non-Hispanic.

SOURCE: Joyce A. Martin, "Figure 3. Birth Rates for Teenagers 15–19 Years: United States, 1991 and 2005," in "Births: Final Data for 2005," *National Vital Statistics Reports*, vol. 56, no. 6, December 5, 2007, http://www.cdc.gov/nchs/data/nvsr/nvsr56/nvsr56_06.pdf (December 9, 2007)

383,000 (11.9%) were headed by a female, and 9.1 million (14.4%) white, non-Hispanic family households were headed by a female. (See Table 2.6.) Hispanic women were nearly one and a half times as likely to head households as were non-Hispanic white women, and single African-American women were more than three times as likely as white women to head households. In 2006 there were 2.3 million (22.8%) Hispanic families headed by a female and 4.1 million (45.5%) African-American families headed by a female. Hispanic and African-American female-headed families were also more likely to contain children than female-headed families of other races and ethnic groups. Nearly two-thirds of Hispanic, female-headed families (65.3%) and African-American, female-headed families (64.1%) contained children under eighteen years old, compared to 57.8% of non-Hispanic white and 42.8% of Asian-American female-headed families.

Living Arrangements of Children

Changes in the marital circumstances of adults naturally affect the living arrangements of children. High divorce rates, an increased delay in first marriages, and more out-of-wedlock births have resulted in fewer children living with two parents. In 2006, 49.7 million (67.4%) children under age eighteen were living with two parents (not necessarily both birth parents), meaning that almost a third (32.6%) of children were living with either a single parent or no parents. (See Table 2.7.) Minority children have been particularly affected by these changes.

The Census Bureau notes in *America's Families and Living Arrangements: 2006* (March 30, 2007, http://www.census.gov/population/www/socdemo/hh-fam/cps2006.html) that divorced single women are on average older than never-married women and that they tend to have more education and higher incomes as well—leading their children to have an advantage over the children of never-married women. In 2006 African-American single mothers were the most likely to have never married (1.9 million, 63.1%) and the least likely to be divorced (595,000, 18.9%). Hispanic single mothers were more likely to have never married (908,000, 46.4%) than to be divorced (521,000, 26.6%). Non-Hispanic white single mothers were the most likely to be divorced (2.8 million, 42.2%) and only a third had never married (2.4 million, 35.8%). Asian-American single mothers were the least likely to have never married (sixty-three thousand, 28.9%) but also less likely than non-Hispanic white women to be divorced (seventy-six thousand, 34.7%), perhaps

TABLE 2.4

Birth rates for women aged 15–19 years, by age, race, and Hispanic origin, selected years, 1991–2006

[Data for 2006 are based on a continuous file of records received from the states. Rates per 1,000 women in the specified group]

Age and race and Hispanic origin of mother	Year				Percent change, 2005–2006	Percent change, 1991–2005
	2006	2005	2004	1991		
10–14 years						
All races and origins[a]	0.6	0.7	0.7	1.4	−14	−50
Non-Hispanic white[b]	0.2	0.2	0.2	0.5	0[†]	−60
Non-Hispanic black[b]	1.6	1.7	1.6	4.9	−6	−65
American Indian or Alaska Native total[b, c]	0.9	0.9	0.9	1.6	0[†]	−44
Asian or Pacific Islander total[b, c]	0.2	0.2	0.2	0.8	0[†]	−75
Hispanic[d]	1.3	1.3	1.3	2.4	0[†]	−46
15–19 years						
All races and origins[a]	41.9	40.5	41.1	61.8	3	−34
Non-Hispanic white[b]	26.6	25.9	26.7	43.4	3	−40
Non-Hispanic black[b]	63.7	60.9	63.1	118.2	5	−48
American Indian or Alaska Native total[b, c]	54.7	52.7	52.5	84.1	4	−37
Asian or Pacific Islander total[b, c]	16.7	17.0	17.3	27.3	−2	−38
Hispanic[d]	83.0	81.7	82.6	104.6	2	−22
15–17 years						
All races and origins[a]	22.0	21.4	22.1	38.6	3	−45
Non-Hispanic white[b]	11.8	11.5	12.0	23.6	3	−51
Non-Hispanic black[b]	36.1	34.9	37.1	86.1	3	−59
American Indian or Alaska Native total[b, c]	30.5	30.5	30.0	51.9	0[†]	−41
Asian or Pacific Islander total[b, c]	8.7	8.2	8.9	16.3	6	−50
Hispanic[d]	47.9	48.5	49.7	69.2	−1	−30
18–19 years						
All races and origins[a]	73.0	69.9	70.0	94.0	4	−26
Non-Hispanic white[b]	49.3	48.0	48.7	70.6	3	−32
Non-Hispanic black[b]	108.4	103.0	103.9	162.2	5	−36
American Indian or Alaska Native total[b, c]	92.8	87.6	87.0	134.2	6	−35
Asian or Pacific Islander total[b, c]	28.9	30.1	29.6	42.2	−4	−29
Hispanic[d]	139.7	134.6	133.5	155.5	4	−13

[†]Zero percent change.
[a]Includes Hispanic origin not stated.
[b]Race and Hispanic origin are reported seperately on birth certificates. Persons of Hispanic origin may be of any race. Race categories are consistent with the 1977 Office of Management and Budget (OMB) standards. Twenty-three states reported multiple-race data for 2006. The multiple-race data for these states were bridged to the single-race categories of the 1977 OMB standards for comparability with other states.
[c]Data for persons of Hispanic origin are included in the data for each race group according other person's reported race.
[d]Includes all persons of Hispanic origin of any race.

SOURCE: Brady E. Hamilton, Joyce A. Martin, and Stephanie J. Ventura, "Table 3. Birth Rates for Women Aged 15–19 Years, by Age, Race, and Hispanic Origin of Mother: United States, Final 1991, 2004, and 2005 and Preliminary 2006; and Percent Change in Rates, 1991–2005 and 2005–2006," in "Births: Preliminary Data for 2006," *National Vital Statistics Reports*, vol. 56, no. 7, December 5, 2007, http://www.cdc.gov/nchs/data/nvsr/nvsr56/nvsr56_07.pdf (accessed December 9, 2007)

because of the high proportion of Asian-American single mothers who were separated but not yet divorced (sixty thousand, 27.5%). As a group, then, the children of non-Hispanic white single mothers tend to have an economic advantage over the children of Hispanic or African-American single mothers, whereas the children of African-American single mothers, on average, tend to be the most economically disadvantaged of all minority groups.

AFRICAN-AMERICAN CHILDREN. In 2006, 4.3 million (35.4%) African-American children under the age of eighteen lived with two parents, whereas 6.2 million (50.6%) lived with their mothers only. (See Table 2.7.) A higher proportion of African-American children lived with neither parent (1.1 million, or 9.1%) than lived with their fathers only (608,000, or 4.9%). The Census Bureau (September 21, 2006, http://www.census.gov/population/socdemo/hh-fam/ch3.pdf) reports that in 1970 the propor-

tions of African-American children who lived with one parent (31.7%) or two parents (58.6%) were virtually the reverse of their living arrangements in 2006.

An increasing number of African-American children live with neither parent. A disproportionate number of them are in foster care. In *AFCARS Report* (September 2006, http://www.acf.hhs.gov/programs/cb/stats_research/afcars/tar/report13.pdf), the U.S. Department of Health and Human Services reports that on September 30, 2005, 32% of children in foster care were African-American. According to the Census Bureau, in "National Population Estimates—Characteristics" (May 17, 2007, http://www.census.gov/popest/national/asrh/), if the number of African-American children in foster care reflected their proportion in the general population, only 13.4% of children in foster care would be African-American.

TABLE 2.5

Number and percent of single and married parents, selected years, 1970–2005

[In thousands]

Family type	1970	1980	1985	1990	2000	2005
Total families	**51,456**	**59,550**	**62,706**	**66,090**	**72,025**	**77,010**
Married couple	44,728	49,112	50,350	52,317	55,311	58,109
Male householder*	1,228	1,733	2,228	2,884	4,028	4,893
Female householder*	5,500	8,705	10,129	10,890	12,687	14,009
Family households with children	**28,731**	**31,022**	**31,112**	**32,289**	**34,605**	**36,520**
Married couple	25,532	24,961	24,210	24,537	25,248	26,180
Male householder*	341	616	896	1,153	1,786	2,034
Female householder*	2,858	5,445	6,006	6,599	7,571	8,305
Percent distribution						
Family households with children	100	100	100	100	100	100
Married couple	89	81	78	76	73	72
Male householder*	1	2	3	4	5	6
Female householder*	10	18	19	20	22	23

*No spouse present.
Notes: Excludes members of Armed Forces except those living off post or with their families on post. Beginning 2001 population controls based on Census 2000 and an expanded sample of households.

SOURCE: Adapted from "Table 69. Family Households with Own Children under Age 18 by Type of Family and Age of Householder: 1970 to 2005," in *Statistical Abstract of the United States: 2007*, U.S. Census Bureau,2006,http://www.census.gov/compendia/statab/2007/tables/07s0069.xls (accessed February 1, 2008)

HISPANIC CHILDREN. In 2006 a higher proportion of Hispanic children (9.7 million, or 65.9%) than African-American children were living with two parents, but this proportion was still lower than the proportion of non-Hispanic white children who lived with two parents (32.5 million, or 76%). (See Table 2.7.) Almost 3.7 million (25%) Hispanic children lived with a single mother and 603,000 (4.1%) lived with a single father. This proportion was considerably higher than among non-Hispanic whites—6.8 million (15.9%) non-Hispanic white children lived with a single mother and 2.1 million (4.8%) lived with a single father—but well below the proportion of African-American children living with a single parent. Approximately 734,000 (5%) Hispanic children lived with neither parent. Some of these children likely lived with other relatives, such as a grandparents, or with foster parents.

ASIAN-AMERICAN CHILDREN. The Asian-American family is typically a close-knit unit, and members are traditionally respectful of the authority of the elder members of the family. As the younger generation becomes more assimilated into American culture, however, the unchallenged role of elders may not remain as strong. Even so, family tradition and honor are still held in high regard. In 2006, 2.9 million (82%) Asian-American children were living with both parents, a proportion higher than that of whites. (See Table 2.7.) About 380,000 (11%) Asian and Pacific Islander children lived with a single mother and 133,000 (3.8%) lived with a single father. Approximately 114,000 (3.3%) lived with neither parent.

HOUSING GRANDCHILDREN. Because of many factors, including the high cost of housing, substance abuse,

and the inability of some parents to care for their children, many children are living with their grandparents. It is especially common in the African-American community for children to live with their grandparents, with or without one or both of their parents present. In *America's Families and Living Arrangements: 2006*, the Census Bureau states that in 2006, 572,000 (5.1%) African-American children lived in a grandparent's home without either of their parents present. The proportion of children who lived in a grandparent's home is significantly higher when children who lived with one or both parents in the home of a grandparent are added to this total. More than one out of ten African-American children (1.2 million, or 10.5%) lived in the home of a grandparent, with or without a parent present, in 2006. In other words, more than one out of ten African-American children were living in the home of a grandparent in 2006, and nearly one out of twenty were being raised exclusively by a grandparent.

Only 266,000 (1.8%) Hispanic children lived in the home of a grandparent with neither parent present in 2006. This number jumps to 821,000 (5.6%) when children who lived with one or both parents in the home of a grandparent are added. Among Asian-Americans, twenty-eight thousand (1%) children under the age of eighteen lived in the home of a grandparent with neither parent present in 2006. This number climbs to ninety-five thousand (3.3%) when children who lived with one or both parents in the home of a grandparent are counted. Among non-Hispanic whites, only 548,000 (1.3%) children lived in the home of a grandparent with neither parent present in 2006; 1.4 million (3.3%) white children lived in the home of a grandparent with or without a parent present. African-American children, then,

TABLE 2.6

Families by number of own children under 18 years old, by race/ethnicity, 1990–2006

[As of March (66,090 represents 66,090,000). Based on Current Population Survey.]

Race, Hispanic origin, and year	Number of families (1,000)					Percent distribution				
	Total	No children	One child	Two children	Three or more children	Total	No children	One child	Two children	Three or more children
All families[a]										
1990	66,090	33,801	13,530	12,263	6,496	100	51	20	19	10
2000	72,025	37,420	14,311	13,215	7,080	100	52	20	18	10
2005	76,858	40,647	15,069	13,741	7,400	100	53	20	18	10
2006, total	77,402	40,936	15,528	13,664	7,275	100	53	20	18	9
Married couple	58,179	32,197	10,031	10,336	5,615	100	55	17	18	10
Male householder[b]	5,130	3,035	1,313	588	194	100	59	26	11	4
Female householder[b]	14,093	5,703	4,184	2,739	1,466	100	40	30	19	10
White families[c]										
1990	56,590	29,872	11,186	10,342	5,191	100	53	20	18	9
2000	60,251	32,144	11,496	10,918	5,693	100	53	19	18	9
2005	63,079	34,255	11,872	11,127	5,825	100	54	19	18	9
2006, total	63,401	34,465	12,150	10,988	5,799	100	54	19	17	9
Married couple	50,363	28,352	8,405	8,795	4,811	100	56	17	17	10
Male householder[b]	3,903	2,259	1,041	461	142	100	58	27	12	4
Female householder[b]	9,136	3,853	2,704	1,732	846	100	42	30	19	9
Black families[c]										
1990	7,470	3,093	1,894	1,433	1,049	100	41	25	19	14
2000	8,664	3,882	2,101	1,624	1,058	100	45	24	19	12
2005	8,902	4,077	2,059	1,641	1,125	100	46	23	18	13
2006, total	9,047	4,080	2,298	1,659	1,011	100	45	25	18	11
Married couple	4,126	2,105	879	693	449	100	51	21	17	11
Male householder[b]	805	497	187	89	32	100	62	23	11	4
Female householder[b]	4,117	1,478	1,232	876	530	100	36	30	21	13
Asian families[c]										
2005	3,142	1,535	730	646	230	100	49	23	21	7
2006, total	3,208	1,599	681	717	211	100	50	21	22	7
Married couple	2,590	1,201	535	660	194	100	46	21	25	7
Male householder[b]	235	179	32	17	7	100	76	14	7	3
Female householder[b]	383	219	114	39	11	100	57	30	10	3
Hispanic families[d]										
1990	4,840	1,790	1,095	1,036	919	100	37	23	21	19
2000	7,561	2,747	1,791	1,693	1,330	100	36	24	22	18
2005	9,521	3,528	2,130	2,163	1,699	100	37	22	23	18
2006, total	9,862	3,743	2,249	2,206	1,664	100	38	23	22	17
Married couple	6,642	2,307	1,415	1,643	1,276	100	35	21	25	19
Male householder[b]	969	654	186	90	38	100	67	19	9	4
Female householder[b]	2,252	782	648	472	350	100	35	29	21	16
Non-Hispanic white families[c, d]										
2005	54,257	30,965	9,924	9,151	4,217	100	57	18	17	8
2006, total	54,257	30,967	10,113	8,942	4,235	100	57	19	16	8
Married couple	44,116	26,182	7,086	7,257	3,591	100	59	16	16	8
Male householder[b]	3,003	1,644	877	377	106	100	55	29	13	4
Female householder[b]	7,138	3,141	2,150	1,308	539	100	44	30	18	8

[a]Includes other races, not shown separately.
[b]No spouse present.
[c]Beginning with the 2003 Current Population Survey (CPS), respondents could choose more than one race. Beginning 2005, data represent persons who selected this race group only and exclude persons reporting more than one race. The CPS prior to 2003 only allowed respondents to report one race group.
[d]Hispanic persons may be any race.

SOURCE: "Table 67. Families by Number of Own Children under 18 Years Old: 1990 to 2006," in *Statistical Abstract of the United States: 2008*, U.S. Census Bureau, December 2007, http://www.census.gov/compendia/statab/tables/08s0067.pdf (accessed January 14, 2008)

were the most likely to be living in the home of a grandparent, with or without a parent present, whereas Asian-American children were the least likely to be living with a grandparent. Children of all races and ethnicities were significantly more likely to be living with their mother in their grandparents' home rather than with the father in their grandparents' home.

HOMEOWNERSHIP

Owning one's home has traditionally been the American dream. However, for many Americans, especially minorities, purchasing a home can be difficult or impossible. The Census Bureau's Housing Vacancy Survey calculates homeownership rates by race and ethnicity of householder (the rate is computed by dividing the number

TABLE 2.7

Living arrangements of children, by age, race, and Hispanic origin, 2006

[Numbers in thousands]

	Total under 18 years[a]	Under 1 year	1–2 years	3–5 years	6–8 years	9–11 years	12–14 years	15–17 years	Total under 6 years	Total 6–11 years	Total 12–17 years
Total children, all races	73,664	4,053	8,214	12,132	11,670	11,996	12,568	13,031	24,399	23,666	25,599
Living with both parents	49,661	2,787	5,628	8,452	7,998	8,192	8,202	8,402	16,867	16,190	16,604
Living with mother only	17,161	902	1,898	2,732	2,671	2,801	3,087	3,069	5,532	5,472	6,157
Living with father only	3,458	229	387	466	536	532	609	699	1,083	1,068	1,307
Living with neither parent	3,383	135	300	482	465	471	669	861	917	935	1,530
Total non-Hispanic white children	42,744	2,261	4,523	6,775	6,691	6,999	7,432	8,062	13,559	13,691	15,494
Living with both parents	32,459	1,818	3,536	5,363	5,159	5,330	5,406	5,848	10,717	10,488	11,254
Living with mother only	6,831	293	682	989	1,010	1,130	1,353	1,375	1,964	2,140	2,728
Living with father only	2,067	105	185	248	323	333	397	476	538	656	873
Living with neither parent	1,386	45	121	175	200	207	276	362	340	407	639
Total black children	12,261	656	1,360	2,020	1,990	1,949	2,161	2,124	4,037	3,939	4,285
Living with both parents	4,338	209	484	694	708	699	789	754	1,387	1,407	1,543
Living with mother only	6,199	350	702	1,070	1,030	1,010	1,034	1,001	2,123	2,040	2,036
Living with father only	608	57	81	96	107	92	95	81	234	199	176
Living with neither parent	1,116	40	93	160	145	147	243	287	293	293	530
Total Asian children	3,476	193	428	592	549	621	540	554	1,213	1,170	1,093
Living with both parents	2,850	165	356	514	460	512	432	411	1,035	972	843
Living with mother only	380	20	46	42	62	65	61	84	108	127	145
Living with father only	133	5	16	17	11	32	21	31	38	43	52
Living with neither parent	114	2	10	20	16	12	26	28	32	28	54
Total Hispanic children[b]	14,697	942	1,867	2,674	2,357	2,352	2,335	2,170	5,484	4,709	4,505
Living with both parents	9,686	588	1,229	1,840	1,606	1,600	1,509	1,314	3,657	3,206	2,823
Living with mother only	3,674	246	463	620	565	585	614	581	1,329	1,150	1,195
Living with father only	603	67	97	95	89	73	90	93	259	162	183
Living with neither parent	734	42	79	118	97	94	121	182	239	191	304

[a]Excludes children in group quarters and those who are a family reference person or spouse.
[b]Hispanics may be of any race.

SOURCE: Adapted from "Table C2. Household Relationship and Living Arrangements of Children under 18 Years, by Age, Sex, Race, Hispanic Origin: 2006," in *America's Families and Living Arrangements: 2006*, U.S. Census Bureau, March 27, 2007, http://www.census.gov/population/www/socdemo/hh-fam/cps2006.html (accessed December 6, 2007)

of owner households by the total number of households). In 2006 the rate for non-Hispanic white householders who owned their home was 75.8%, for Asian and Pacific Islander householders it was 60.8%, for Native American or Alaskan Native householders it was 58.2%, for Hispanic householders it was 49.7%, and for African-American householders it was 47.9%. (See Table 2.8.)

Growth of Homeownership

Even though compared to non-Hispanic white homeownership the proportion of minority homeownership is low, these numbers actually reflect significant growth in the purchase of homes by minorities. Homeownership rates rose for all groups, but they rose faster among minority groups. From 1995 to 2006 the homeownership rate for non-Hispanic whites grew from 70.9% to 75.8%, for Hispanics it grew from 42.1% to 49.7%, and for African-Americans it grew from 42.7% to 47.9%. (See Table 2.8.) During this same period the homeownership rate for Asians and Pacific Islanders grew from 50.8% to 60.8% and for Native Americans or Alaskan Natives it grew from 55.8% to 58.2%.

A number of factors were responsible for the growth of minority homeownership in the 1990s. The administration of President Bill Clinton (1946–) provided more lending opportunities for minorities by revitalizing the Federal Housing Administration (FHA) and improving enforcement of the Community Reinvestment Act, which was passed by Congress in 1977 to encourage banks and other lending institutions to invest in the communities in which they operate. Furthermore, the U.S. Department of Housing and Urban Development (HUD) pressured the Federal National Mortgage Association (Fannie Mae) and the Federal Home Loan Mortgage Corporation (Freddie Mac) to initiate programs to help minority and low-income borrowers in securing mortgages. Fannie Mae is a private company that was created by Congress in 1938 to improve the housing industry during the Great Depression. Its smaller counterpart, Freddie Mac, is a shareholder-owned company created by Congress in 1970 to support homeownership. Both Fannie Mae and Freddie Mac buy mortgages, package them into bonds backed by the government, and sell them to investors, thereby freeing up money for additional mortgage lending. Besides these efforts, minority homeownership was

TABLE 2.8

Homeownership rates by race and ethnicity of householder, selected years, 1995–2006

	1995	2000
U.S. total	**64.7**	**67.4**
White, total	68.7	71.1
Non-Hispanic white	70.9	73.8
Black, total	42.7	47.2
All other races, total	47.2	53.5
American Indian or Alaskan Native	55.8	56.2
Asian or Native Hawaiian/Pacific Islander	50.8	52.8
Other	37.4	NA
Hispanic or Latino	42.1	46.3
Non-Hispanic	66.7	69.5

	2005	2006
U.S. total	**68.9**	**68.8**
White alone, total	72.7	72.6
Non-Hispanic white alone	75.8	75.8
Black alone, total	48.2	47.9
All other races alone, total*	59.2	59.9
American Indian or Alaskan Native alone	58.2	58.2
Asian or Native Hawaiian/Pacific Islander alone	60.1	60.8
Hispanic or Latino	49.5	49.7
Non-Hispanic	71.2	71.2

NA Not applicable.

*Asian, Native Hawaiian or other Pacific Islander, American Indian or Alaska Native (only one race reported) and two or more races.

SOURCE: Adapted from "Table 20. Homeownership Rates by Race and Ethnicity of Householder: 1994 to 2006," in *Housing Vacancies and Homeownership Annual Statistics: 2006*, U.S. Census Bureau, February 12, 2007, http://www.census.gov/hhes/www/housing/hvs/annual06/ann06t20 .html (accessed December 12, 2007)

also helped by a considerably strong economy and a robust stock market during the 1990s and by low mortgage rates during the early 2000s.

President George W. Bush (1946–) also made minority homeownership a priority of his administration. According to the White House, in *A Home of Your Own: Expanding Opportunities for All Americans* (June 2000, http://www.whitehouse.gov/infocus/homeownership/home ownership-policy-book-whole.pdf), in 2002 President Bush challenged the real estate industry to invest more to increase the number of minority homeowners by at least 5.5 million families by the end of the decade. His administration also announced several initiatives to help minority and low-income Americans buy homes. Acknowledging that many Americans can afford a monthly mortgage payment but lack the funds for a down payment, in 2003 President Bush signed the American Dream Down-payment Assistance Act, authorizing $200 million per year in down payment assistance to at least forty thousand low-income families. In "Fannie Mae's Commitment to Minority Homeownership" (July 2007, http://www.fanniemae .com/initiatives/minority/index.jhtml), Fannie Mae notes that in 2004 it pledged to help 1.8 million minority families buy their first home in the next decade. In 2007 it remained committed to minority homeownership.

Private-sector real estate lenders were likely to follow suit in targeting minorities for homeownership, in part as a simple acknowledgment of changing times. As the baby boomer generation (1946–1964) begins to leave the workforce, and because of the low birth rate of native-born Americans, minority groups (which are dominated by Hispanics) will make up a larger proportion of the population and as such are expected to play an increasing role in the economy. The 1990s saw a major influx of immigrants, who at first typically rented their homes but later became factors in the home-buying market. According to John Handley, in "Demographic Trends to Shape Future U.S. Housing Markets" (December 20, 2004, http://rismedia.com/wp/2004-12-20/demo graphic-trends-to-shape-future-us-housing-markets-2/), James Johnson of the University of North Carolina, Chapel Hill, estimates that ten million immigrants will reach their peak home-buying years between 2005 and 2015, making them a market to be courted by real estate lenders. Aside from the benefits enjoyed by the individual, an increase in the number of minority homeowners is likely to improve the quality of life in entire communities, improving areas such as safety and the quality of schools in neighborhoods in which minority homeowners have a stake.

CHAPTER 3
EDUCATION

In *The Condition of Education, 2005* (June 2005, http://nces.ed.gov/pubs2005/2005094.pdf), the National Center for Education Statistics (NCES) reports that two factors—rising immigration and the baby boom echo—boosted public school enrollment from the latter part of the 1980s and into the first half of the 2000s. Enrollment was projected to reach 49.6 million in 2007, and then set new enrollment records each year through 2016, according to the NCES, in *The Condition of Education, 2007* (June 2007, http://nces.ed.gov/pubs2007/2007064.pdf).

Along with this increase in enrollment came an increase in the proportion of public school students who were considered to be part of a minority group, due largely to the growth in the Hispanic public school population. The NCES notes that in 2005, 42.4% of public school students enrolled in kindergarten through twelfth grade belonged to a minority group. (See Table 3.1.) Hispanics (19.7%) and African-Americans (15.6%) accounted for the largest number of minority students in public schools. These figures represented a significant increase since 1972, when white students made up 77.8% and minority students only 22.2% of the public school population. However, minority enrollment in public schools differed from region to region. In 2005 the Midwest had the lowest proportion of minority students (26%) and the West had the highest (54%). (See Figure 3.1.) More than one out of three (37%) students in the West were Hispanic, whereas nearly one-quarter (24%) of students in the South were African-American.

RISK FACTORS IN EDUCATION

In the United States, education is often viewed as a way out of poverty to a better life. Many observers believe education is the key to narrowing the economic gap between the races. Even though many individual minority students strive for, and achieve, great educational success, on average minority students perform less well than white students in school and are generally more likely than their white counterparts to drop out of school. Asians and Pacific Islanders are the exception to this rule. Many Asian-American students accomplish stunning academic achievements. Educators point with pride to these high-achieving students, who have often overcome both language and cultural barriers. Why are some groups more at risk of failure, and other groups more likely to succeed in school?

The Early Childhood Longitudinal Study, Birth Cohort, a study by the NCES, attempts to begin answering this question by assessing preschoolers' readiness for school. The study collected information on a cohort (a group of individuals with several characteristics in common) of children born in 2001 and followed them through 2007, focusing on the children's early development and how parents prepared their children for school. Even though at nine months of age little variation in mental and motor skills was found by race or ethnic group, several demographic characteristics were related to the likelihood of families engaging in activities that help prepare children for school, including reading or telling them stories, singing to them, taking them on errands, playing peek-a-boo, and allowing them to play outside. The NCES indicates in *Condition of Education, 2005* that in 2001–02 Asian-American families were more likely than other minority groups to read to their children (26%), tell them stories (25%), and play peek-a-boo (73%), although they were less likely to facilitate outside playing (43%) and significantly less likely to take their children on errands (38%) than were other minority families.

In contrast, both African-American and Hispanic families were less likely to read to (23% and 21%, respectively) and tell their children stories (24% and 21%, respectively), and more likely to sing to them (73% and 70%, respectively) and play peek-a-boo (61% and 64%, respectively) than were non-Hispanic white

TABLE 3.1

Percentage distribution of the race/ethnicity of public school students enrolled in kindergarten through 12th grade, 1972–2005

		Minority enrollment							
Fall of year	White	Total	Black	Hispanic	Asian	Pacific Islander	American Indian/ Alaska Native	More than one race	Other
1972	77.8	22.2	14.8	6.0	—	—	—	—	1.4
1973	78.1	21.9	14.7	5.7	—	—	—	—	1.4
1974	76.8	23.2	15.4	6.3	—	—	—	—	1.5
1975	76.2	23.8	15.4	6.7	—	—	—	—	1.7
1976	76.2	23.8	15.5	6.5	—	—	—	—	1.7
1977	76.1	23.9	15.8	6.2	—	—	—	—	1.9
1978	75.5	24.5	16.0	6.5	—	—	—	—	2.1
1979	—	—	—	—	—	—	—	—	—
1980	—	—	—	—	—	—	—	—	—
1981	72.4	27.6	16.0	8.7	—	—	—	—	2.9
1982	71.9	28.1	16.0	8.9	—	—	—	—	3.2
1983	71.3	28.7	16.1	9.2	—	—	—	—	3.4
1984	71.7	28.3	16.1	8.5	—	—	—	—	3.6
1985	69.6	30.4	16.8	10.1	—	—	—	—	3.5
1986	69.1	30.9	16.6	10.8	—	—	—	—	3.6
1987	68.5	31.5	16.6	10.8	—	—	—	—	4.0
1988	68.3	31.7	16.5	11.0	—	—	—	—	4.2
1989	68.0	32.0	16.6	11.4	3.0*	*	0.9	—	0.1
1990	67.6	32.4	16.5	11.7	3.0*	*	0.9	—	0.3
1991	67.1	32.9	16.8	11.8	3.2*	*	0.8	—	0.2
1992	66.8	33.2	16.9	12.0	3.3*	*	0.8	—	0.2
1993	67.0	33.0	16.6	12.1	3.3*	*	0.8	—	0.2
1994	65.8	34.2	16.7	13.7	2.5*	*	0.8	—	0.5
1995	65.5	34.5	16.9	14.1	2.3*	*	0.6	—	0.6
1996	63.7	36.3	16.6	14.5	4.1*	*	1.2	—	—
1997	63.0	37.0	16.9	14.9	3.9*	*	1.2	—	—
1998	62.4	37.6	17.2	15.4	4.0*	*	1.1	—	—
1999	61.9	38.1	16.5	16.2	4.5*	*	1.0	—	—
2000	61.3	38.7	16.6	16.6	4.2*	*	1.3	—	—
2001	61.3	38.7	16.5	16.6	4.3*	*	1.3	—	—
2002	60.7	39.3	16.5	17.6	4.0*	*	1.2	—	—
2003	58.3	41.7	16.1	18.6	3.7	0.3	0.6	2.4	—
2004	57.4	42.6	16.0	19.3	3.9	0.2	0.8	2.4	—
2005	57.6	42.4	15.6	19.7	3.7	0.2	0.7	2.5	—

— Not available.

*From 1989 through 2002, Asian and Pacific Islander students were not reported separately; therefore, Pacific Islander students are included with Asian students during this period.

Note: Figures include all public school students enrolled in kindergarten through 12th grade. Race categories exclude persons of Hispanic ethnicity. Over time, the Current Population Survey (CPS) has had different response options for race/ethnicity. In 1994, the survey methodology for the CPS was changed and weights were adjusted. In 1996, the Census revised procedures for editing and allocating the race variable to offset an underestimation of Asians/Pacific Islanders. One should use caution when making comparisons between data for 1995 and 1996 and later of Asians/Pacific Islanders. Detail may not sum to totals because of rounding.

SOURCE: "Table 5-1. Percentage Distribution of the Race/Ethnicity of Public School Students Enrolled in Kindergarten through 12th Grade: Fall 1972–2005," in *The Condition of Education 2007*, U.S. Department of Education, National Center for Education Statistics, June 2007, http://nces.ed.gov/programs/coe/2007/pdf/05_2007.pdf (accessed December 13, 2007)

families in 2001–02. This may be partly because poor families are much less likely to read to their children or tell them stories than are nonpoor families, and African-American and Hispanic families are disproportionately poor. African-American families, non-Hispanic white families, and Hispanic families were about equally likely to take their children on errands and facilitate outside playing.

In its third wave, the Early Childhood Longitudinal Study, Birth Cohort collected more specific information about the readiness of preschoolers for school. Researchers assessed children between the ages of forty-eight and fifty-seven months. In *Preschool: First Findings from the Preschool Follow-up of the Early Childhood Longitudinal*

Study, Birth Cohort (October 2007, http://nces.ed.gov/pubs2008/2008025.pdf), the NCES indicates that this study found that children's language knowledge—or ability to understand words or retell a story—varied by race and ethnicity, with non-Hispanic white children scoring the highest (9.2), followed by African-American children (8), Asian-American children (7.9), Native American children (7.9), and Hispanic children (7.4). Overall literacy, such as letter recognition and understanding aspects of reading such as reading from left to right, also varied by race and ethnicity. Non-Hispanic whites scored high on the overall literacy score (14.2), although Asian-American children scored higher (17.5), followed by African-American children (12), Hispanic children (10.7), and Native American children (9.6). Asian-American pre-

FIGURE 3.1

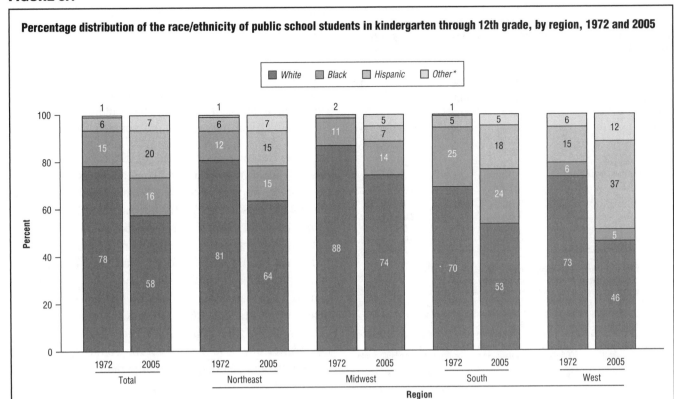

Percentage distribution of the race/ethnicity of public school students in kindergarten through 12th grade, by region, 1972 and 2005

#Rounds to zero.
*In 1972, "other" includes all students who did not identify themselves as white, black, or Hispanic. In 2005, "other" includes Asian students, Pacific Islander students, American Indian/Alaska Native students, and students of more than one race.
Note: Race categories exclude persons of Hispanic ethnicity. Figures include all public school students enrolled in kindergarten through 12th grade. Detail may not sum to totals because of rounding.

SOURCE: "Minority Enrollment: Percentage Distribution of the Race/Ethnicity of Public School Students in Kindergarten through 12th Grade, by Region: Fall 1972 and 2005," in *The Condition of Education 2007*, U.S. Department of Education, National Center for Education Statistics, June 2007, http://nces.ed.gov/programs/coe/2007/pdf/05_2007.pdf (accessed December 13, 2007)

schoolers scored the highest on mathematics knowledge and skills (26.3), followed by non-Hispanic white preschoolers (24.2), African-American preschoolers (20.6), Hispanic preschoolers (20.1), and Native American preschoolers (17.6). Therefore, overall, Native American, Hispanic, and African-American children were less prepared for school than were either non-Hispanic white or Asian-American children.

PREPRIMARY EDUCATION. One thing that can help preschoolers prepare for elementary school is attending center-based early childhood programs. Angelina KewalRamani et al. state in *Status and Trends in the Education of Racial and Ethnic Minorities* (September 2007, http://nces.ed.gov/pubs2007/2007039.pdf) that "research has suggested that intensive, high-quality preschool programs can have positive effects on the cognitive and academic development of low-income minority children, both in the short- and long-term." In 2005, 57.2% of all three- to five-year-olds who were not yet enrolled in kindergarten were enrolled in center-based preschools. (See Table 3.2.) However, nonpoor children were more likely than poor children to be

enrolled in these programs (59.9% and 47.2%, respectively). Among nonpoor preschoolers, Asian and Pacific Islander preschoolers were the most likely to be enrolled (73.4%), followed by African-American preschoolers (67.8%), white preschoolers (61%), Native American preschoolers (53.1%), and Hispanic students (47.8%). Among poor preschoolers, African-American children were the most likely to be enrolled (64.8%), followed by white students (44.6%) and Hispanic students (36%).

Educational Progress

The Early Childhood Longitudinal Study, Kindergarten Class of 1998–99, another research study conducted by the NCES, collected information on a cohort of children who began kindergarten in the fall of 1998 and followed them through the spring of 2004. The study specifically looked at children's achievement in mathematics and reading as they progressed through school. The study found that the number of family risk factors (poverty, non-English primary home language, mother's lack of a high school diploma/general education diploma, or a single-parent household) inversely related to gains in

TABLE 3.2

Percentage of 3- to 5-year-olds enrolled in center-based preprimary programs, by poverty status and race/ethnicity, 1995, 1999, 2001, and 2005

Poverty status and race/ethnicity	1995	1999	2001	2005
Total	55.1	59.7	56.4	57.2
Poor*	45.6	51.9	46.4	47.2
White	43.6	42.9	46.2	44.6
Black	55.3	72.7	57.7	64.8
Hispanic	32.0	41.7	35.4	36.0
Asian/Pacific Islander	‡	‡	‡	‡
American Indian/Alaska Native	‡	‡	‡	‡
Nonpoor*	58.5	62.2	59.6	59.9
White	59.6	62.7	61.1	61.0
Black	65.4	73.7	68.0	67.8
Hispanic	42.3	46.5	43.0	47.8
Asian/Pacific Islander	58.1	64.2	75.9	73.4
American Indian/Alaska Native	‡	‡	‡	53.1

‡Reporting standards not met. Sample size too small.
*Total includes race/ethnicity categories not separately shown.
Note: Estimates are based on children who have yet to enter kindergarten. Center-based programs include day care centers, Head Start program, preschool, prekindergarten, and other early childhood programs. "Poor" is defined to include those families below the poverty threshold; "nonpoor" is defined as 100 percent or more than the poverty threshold. As the 2005 poverty thresholds were not yet available at the time this table was prepared, an approximation was used for analyses using National Household Education Survey (NHES):2005 data. Race categories exclude persons of Hispanic origin.

SOURCE: Angelina KewalRamani et al., "Table 6. Percentage of 3- to 5-Year-Olds Enrolled in Center-Based Preprimary Programs, by Poverty Status and Race/Ethnicity: Selected Years, 1995–2005," in *Status and Trends in the Education of Racial and Ethnic Minorities*, U.S. Department of Education, National Center for Education Statistics, Institute of Education Sciences, September 2007, http://nces.ed.gov/pubs2007/2007039.pdf (accessed December 13, 2007)

mathematics and reading through third grade. Minority children tend to have higher numbers of risk factors than do non-Hispanic white children. However, even when controlling for family risk factors, African-American children had lower average achievement scores than other racial and ethnic groups when they began kindergarten, and the gap in these achievement scores widened from the start of kindergarten through the end of third grade. Researchers have not yet proposed an explanation for this difference, but it may be due to entrenched racism within American culture and the school system—if children of a particular group are expected to perform poorly, they may in fact do so.

According to the NCES, in *The Condition of Education, 2004* (June 2004, http://nces.ed.gov/pubs2004/2004077.pdf), the study found that by the end of third grade the mean (average) scale scores for reading achievement were highest for non-Hispanic whites (112) and Asians and Pacific Islanders (111), followed by Hispanics (105) and African-Americans (98). The same pattern held true in mathematics. The mean scale scores for mathematics achievement were highest for non-Hispanic whites (89) and Asians and Pacific Islanders (88), followed by Hispanics (82) and African-Americans (73). From the start of kindergarten through third grade, non-Hispanic whites, Asians and Pacific Islanders, and

Hispanics made similar gains in both reading and mathematics; however, African-Americans lagged behind in both areas.

READING PERFORMANCE. The ability to read is fundamental to most aspects of education. When students cannot read well, they usually cannot succeed in other subject areas and will eventually have additional problems in a society requiring increasingly sophisticated job skills.

The National Assessment of Educational Progress (NAEP) measures reading and mathematics proficiency on a scale from zero to five hundred and reports the percentage of students performing at three achievement levels: basic, proficient, and advanced. In 2005 the NAEP found that a higher percentage of non-Hispanic white and Asian and Pacific Islander fourth graders performed at or above proficient in reading (41% and 42%, respectively) than did African-American fourth graders (13%), Hispanic fourth graders (16%), or Native American fourth graders (18%). (See Figure 3.2.) This difference in reading proficiency also held true for eighth graders and twelfth graders, although by eighth grade a lower proportion of African-American, Hispanic, and Native American students were performing at below basic levels. (See Figure 3.3 and Figure 3.4.) Between eighth and twelfth grade more African-American, Hispanic, and Native American students achieved at least basic reading proficiency. Interestingly, between eighth and twelfth grades the proportion of non-Hispanic white students and Asian-American students below basic reading proficiency actually increased. The reason for this remains unclear.

MATHEMATICS PERFORMANCE. In a time when science and technology are considered vital to the nation's economy and position in the international community, education observers are concerned about the generally poor American performance in mathematics and science. Since 1971 the NAEP has tested students to determine their mathematical knowledge, skills, and aptitudes. The measurement assesses students in five content areas: number sense, properties, and operations; measurement; geometry and spatial sense; data analysis, statistics, and probability; and algebra and functions.

In 2005 Asians and Pacific Islanders outperformed all other racial and ethnic groups in mathematics for each grade reported. Over half (55%) of Asian-American fourth graders were at or above proficient, and nearly half (47%) of non-Hispanic white fourth graders achieved this level. (See Figure 3.5.) By contrast, only 21% of Native American fourth graders, 19% of Hispanic fourth graders, and 13% of African-American fourth graders achieved proficiency or above. Only one out of ten non-Hispanic white and Asian-American fourth graders failed to achieve basic proficiency, compared to 40% of African-American fourth

FIGURE 3.2

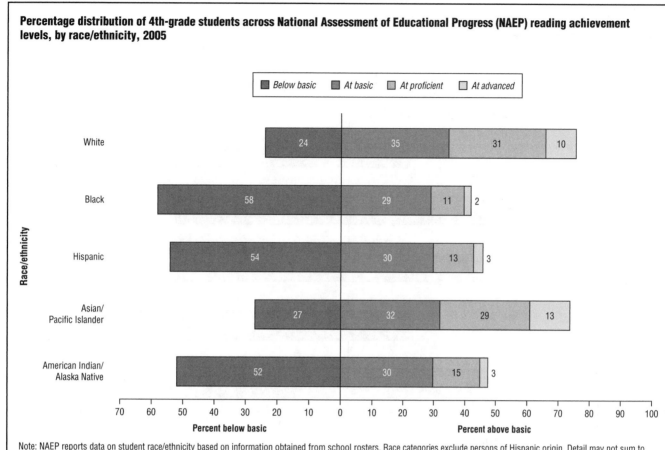

Percentage distribution of 4th-grade students across National Assessment of Educational Progress (NAEP) reading achievement levels, by race/ethnicity, 2005

Note: NAEP reports data on student race/ethnicity based on information obtained from school rosters. Race categories exclude persons of Hispanic origin. Detail may not sum to totals because of rounding.

SOURCE: Angelina KewalRamani et al., "Figure 10.1a. Percentage Distribution of 4th-Grade Students across NAEP Reading Achievement Levels, by Race/Ethnicity: 2005," in *Status and Trends in the Education of Racial and Ethnic Minorities*, U.S. Department of Education, National Center for Education Statistics, Institute of Education Sciences, September 2007, http://nces.ed.gov/pubs2007/2007039.pdf (accessed December 13, 2007)

graders and 32% of Hispanic and Native American fourth graders.

As students aged, the proportion of students in every race and ethnic group below basic proficiency increased, whereas the proportion of students at or above proficiency decreased. By eighth grade only 47% of Asian-American and 39% of non-Hispanic white students were at or above proficiency, whereas 19% of Asian-American students and 20% of non-Hispanic white students were below basic proficiency. (See Figure 3.6.) More than half (58%) of African-American eighth graders were below basic proficiency, as were nearly half of Hispanic (48%) and Native American (47%) eighth graders. By their senior year in high school, 70% of African-American students, 60% of Hispanic students, and 58% of Native American students were failing to demonstrate basic mathematics skills, and few were at or above proficiency. (See Figure 3.7.) The percentage of non-Hispanic white students and Asian-American students at or above proficiency in mathematics had dropped as well (29% and 36%, respectively).

Dropping Out

When students drop out or fail to complete high school, both the individual and society suffer. Dropping out of school often results in limited occupational and economic opportunities for these individuals. KewalRamani et al. note that individuals who drop out of school have higher unemployment rates and lower earnings than individuals who graduate high school. For society, high dropout rates may result in increased costs of government assistance programs for these individuals and their families, costly public training programs, and higher crime rates.

In 2005, 10.5% of all sixteen- to twenty-four-year-olds had dropped out of high school. (See Table 3.3.) Far more foreign-born young adults had dropped out than had native-born individuals (25.2% and 8.6%, respectively). A far lower percentage of Asian-American (3.5%) and white, non-Hispanic (7.2%) young adults had dropped out of high school than had African-American (11.6%), Native American (15.5%), or Hispanic young adults (22.8%). However, since 1989 the percentage of dropouts

FIGURE 3.3

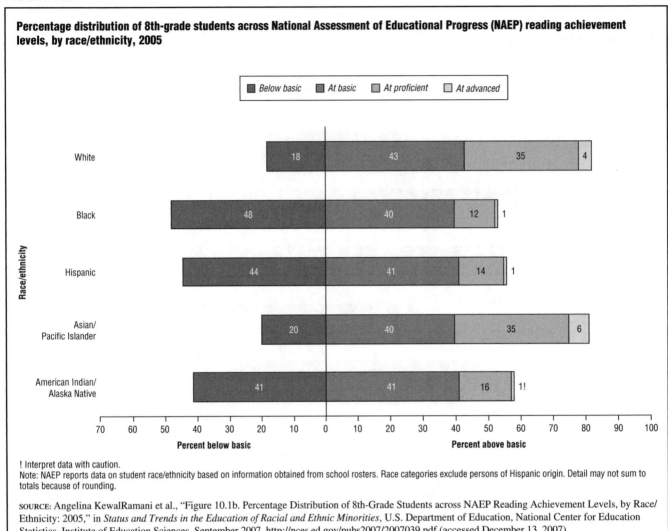

Percentage distribution of 8th-grade students across National Assessment of Educational Progress (NAEP) reading achievement levels, by race/ethnicity, 2005

! Interpret data with caution.
Note: NAEP reports data on student race/ethnicity based on information obtained from school rosters. Race categories exclude persons of Hispanic origin. Detail may not sum to totals because of rounding.

SOURCE: Angelina KewalRamani et al., "Figure 10.1b. Percentage Distribution of 8th-Grade Students across NAEP Reading Achievement Levels, by Race/Ethnicity: 2005," in *Status and Trends in the Education of Racial and Ethnic Minorities*, U.S. Department of Education, National Center for Education Statistics, Institute of Education Sciences, September 2007, http://nces.ed.gov/pubs2007/2007039.pdf (accessed December 13, 2007)

in this age group has decreased for all race and ethnic groups. (See Figure 3.8.)

Even though the proportion of young adults who had not completed school was highest among Hispanics, this proportion varied greatly by country of origin. Young adults who traced their roots to Mexico (25.5%) or Central America (32.6%) were the most likely to have dropped out of school, whereas those who traced their roots to South America (9.1%) were particularly unlikely to have drooped out. (See Table 3.3.) However, in all groups young adults who were foreign born were much more likely to have dropped out of school than were those who were native born.

One reason for the high dropout rate among foreign-born Hispanic young adults may be their undocumented immigration status. Some Hispanic youth who were brought to the United States as children see little benefit in graduating from high school as "illegal" residents. In 2007 advocacy groups urged Congress to pass the Development, Relief, and Education for Alien Minors Act. The act would have allowed students to remain in the United States for up to six years after high school graduation, as long as they either attended college or joined the military. The act would also have allowed these students to pay in-state tuition rates for college in the state in which they had resided for at least five years. At the end of this period, students who completed the two-year college or military requirement would be allowed to become permanent residents. However, in October 2007 the U.S. Senate failed to pass the act forward to a full debate, and the bill died.

MINORITY STUDENTS IN SCHOOL
Asian-American Students Often Excel

Jamie Lew, in "Burden of Acting Neither White nor Black: Asian American Identities and Achievement in Urban Schools" (*Urban Review*, vol. 38, no. 5, December 2006), and Stacey J. Lee, in "Additional Complexities: Social Class, Ethnicity, Generation, and Gender in Asian American Student Experiences" (*Race Ethnicity and Education*, vol. 9, no. 1, March 2006), indicate that

FIGURE 3.4

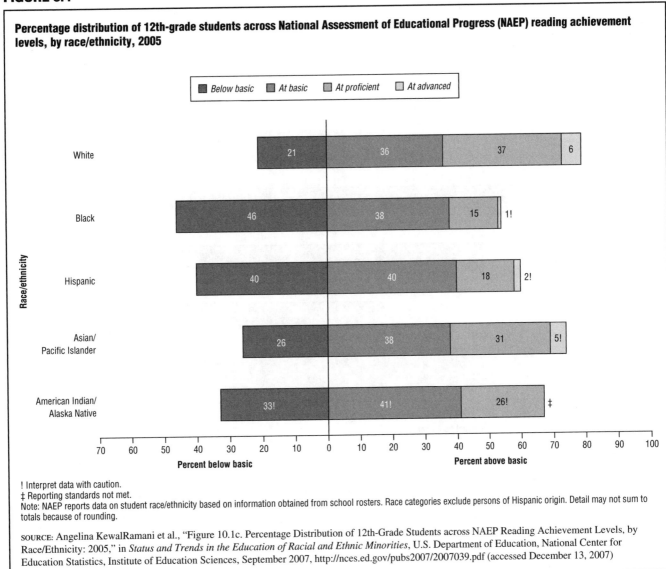

Percentage distribution of 12th-grade students across National Assessment of Educational Progress (NAEP) reading achievement levels, by race/ethnicity, 2005

■ *Below basic*   ■ *At basic*   ■ *At proficient*   □ *At advanced*

Race/ethnicity

White	21 / 36 / 37 / 6	
Black	46 / 38 / 15 / 1!	
Hispanic	40 / 40 / 18 / 2!	
Asian/Pacific Islander	26 / 38 / 31 / 5!	
American Indian/Alaska Native	33! / 41! / 26! / ‡	

70 60 50 40 30 20 10 0 10 20 30 40 50 60 70 80 90 100

Percent below basic   **Percent above basic**

! Interpret data with caution.
‡ Reporting standards not met.
Note: NAEP reports data on student race/ethnicity based on information obtained from school rosters. Race categories exclude persons of Hispanic origin. Detail may not sum to totals because of rounding.

SOURCE: Angelina KewalRamani et al., "Figure 10.1c. Percentage Distribution of 12th-Grade Students across NAEP Reading Achievement Levels, by Race/Ethnicity: 2005," in *Status and Trends in the Education of Racial and Ethnic Minorities*, U.S. Department of Education, National Center for Education Statistics, Institute of Education Sciences, September 2007, http://nces.ed.gov/pubs2007/2007039.pdf (accessed December 13, 2007)

Asian-American students often excel at school, sometimes performing better than their non-Hispanic white peers. Asian-American students generally have fewer family risk factors than do other minority children, including living below the poverty level, living in a household where the primary language is not English, having a mother whose highest education is less than a high school diploma or equivalent, and living in a single-parent household. When these risk factors are present, they affect the performance of Asian-American students as well as students from all racial and ethnic backgrounds.

However, some Asian-American children who do have risk factors are able to overcome them. In "Indochinese Refugee Families and Academic Achievement" (*Scientific American*, vol. 266, no. 2, February 1992), Nathan Caplan, Marcella H. Choy, and John K. Whitmore find that despite hardships and severe traumatic experiences in their native countries and despite attending schools

in low-income inner cities, most Indo-Chinese refugee students (which include children from Vietnam, Cambodia, Thailand, and Laos) performed well in school. The researchers also note that strong family traditions and values were important influences in these children's lives. The families were committed to a love of learning. They placed a high value on homework and did it as a family activity, with the older children helping the younger ones. Furthermore, parents read regularly to their children either in English or in their native language.

Progress for African-American Students

Even though the average academic performance of African-American students, in general, remains below that of non-Hispanic white students, high school graduation rates among African-Americans rose considerably in the second half of the twentieth century. Thomas D. Snyder, Sally A. Dillow, and Charlene M. Hoffman state in *Digest of Education Statistics, 2006* (July 2007, http://

FIGURE 3.5

Percentage distribution of 4th-grade students across National Assessment of Educational Progress (NAEP) mathematics achievement levels, by race/ethnicity, 2005

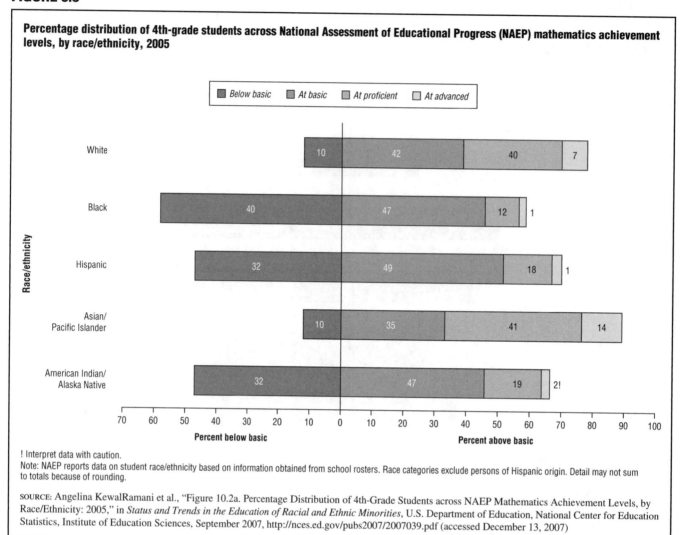

! Interpret data with caution.

Note: NAEP reports data on student race/ethnicity based on information obtained from school rosters. Race categories exclude persons of Hispanic origin. Detail may not sum to totals because of rounding.

SOURCE: Angelina KewalRamani et al., "Figure 10.2a. Percentage Distribution of 4th-Grade Students across NAEP Mathematics Achievement Levels, by Race/Ethnicity: 2005," in *Status and Trends in the Education of Racial and Ethnic Minorities*, U.S. Department of Education, National Center for Education Statistics, Institute of Education Sciences, September 2007, http://nces.ed.gov/pubs2007/2007039.pdf (accessed December 13, 2007)

nces.ed.gov/pubs2007/2007017.pdf) that 42.6% of African-American students and 38.5% of Hispanic students graduated from high school in 1975. The graduation rate has increased more dramatically for African-American students since 1975 than it has for Hispanic students. In 2006 African-Americans aged twenty-five and older were less likely than non-Hispanic whites to have earned a high school diploma, but they were more likely than Hispanics to have received a diploma. Four out of five (81.2%) African-Americans of this age had received a high school diploma.

Snyder, Dillow, and Hoffman note that the percent of African-American high school graduates who enrolled in college within the past twelve months fluctuated throughout the period from 1972 through 2005, from a low of 32.5% in 1973 to a high of 62.5% in 2004. In 2005 more than half (55.7%) of African-American students who had completed high school or earned a general education diploma in the past twelve months enrolled in college.

SCHOOL SEGREGATION. One reason African-American children have historically lagged behind non-Hispanic white children in educational achievement has been the separate

and inferior schools that they have been forced to attend. On May 17, 1954, in *Brown v. Board of Education of Topeka, Kansas* (347 US 483), the U.S. Supreme Court declared that separate schools for African-American children were inherently unequal and that schools had to desegregate. Over fifty years later, more and more school districts are questioning whether the federal courts need to continue supervising desegregation. However, despite regulations and busing, many inner-city schools are still not integrated, and academic achievement for African-American children is still lagging. Many non-Hispanic white students have moved (with their families' tax dollars) to the suburbs or transferred to private schools to avoid inner-city schools with high populations of minority students. For example, between 1993 and 2003 the percentage of central city public school students who were non-Hispanic white decreased from 44.3% to 35.2%, whereas the proportion of minority students increased from 55.7% to 64.8%. (See Table 3.4.) The percentage of African-American students in central city schools stayed relatively stable during that decade, whereas the percentage of Hispanic students rose dramatically.

FIGURE 3.6

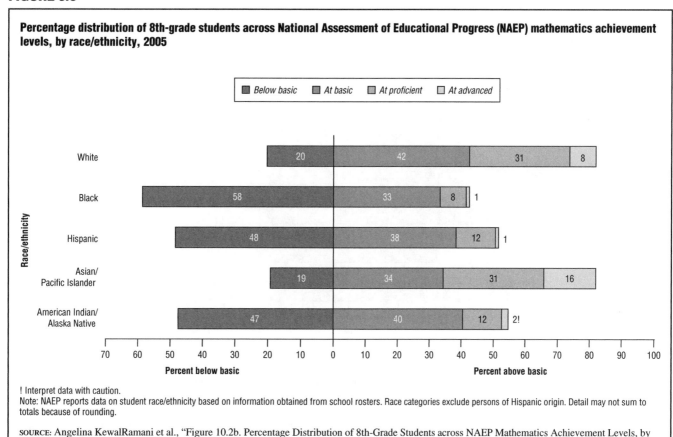

Percentage distribution of 8th-grade students across National Assessment of Educational Progress (NAEP) mathematics achievement levels, by race/ethnicity, 2005

! Interpret data with caution.
Note: NAEP reports data on student race/ethnicity based on information obtained from school rosters. Race categories exclude persons of Hispanic origin. Detail may not sum to totals because of rounding.

SOURCE: Angelina KewalRamani et al., "Figure 10.2b. Percentage Distribution of 8th-Grade Students across NAEP Mathematics Achievement Levels, by Race/Ethnicity: 2005," in *Status and Trends in the Education of Racial and Ethnic Minorities*, U.S. Department of Education, National Center for Education Statistics, Institute of Education Sciences, September 2007, http://nces.ed.gov/pubs2007/2007039.pdf (accessed December 13, 2007)

Half a century after *Brown*, the Supreme Court restricted the use of plans that use race as a factor in assigning students to schools in an effort to promote racial diversity in two cases decided on June 28, 2007: *Parents Involved in Community Schools v. Seattle School District* (No. 05-908) and *Meredith v. Jefferson County* (No. 05-915). The Court did not, however, declare that race could never be used to achieve diversity. Regardless, Robert Barnes reports in "Divided Court Limits Use of Race by School Districts" (*Washington Post*, June 29, 2007) that experts observe that many school districts will abandon policies designed to achieve racial diversity as a result of this ruling.

Resegregation began in the 1990s and most likely will accelerate as a result of the Supreme Court decision. In *Historic Reversals, Accelerating Resegregation, and the Need for New Integration Strategies* (August 1, 2007, http://www.civilrights.org/assets/pdfs/aug-2007-desegregation-report.pdf), Gary Orfield and Chungmei Lee of the Civil Rights Project state that "the trends . . . are those of increasing isolation and profound inequality." They note that the June 2007 Supreme Court decision was a dramatic reversal of the gains made during the civil rights era: "On average, segregated minority schools are inferior in terms of the quality of their teachers, the character of the cur-riculum, the level of competition, average test scores, and graduation rates."

In 2004, 65% of non-Hispanic white students attended public elementary or secondary schools where the percent of minority enrollment was less than 25%. (See Figure 3.9.) By contrast, only 25% of Native American students, 20% of Asian-American students, 9% of African-American students, and 8% of Hispanic students attended schools where minority enrollment was this low. Conversely, 58% of Hispanic students and 52% of African-American students attended schools where minorities made up 75% or more of the student population. A third (34%) of Asian-American students and 30% of Native American students attended schools with such high minority enrollment. However, only 3% of non-Hispanic white students attended schools where minorities made up 75% or more of the student population. These figures attest to the continued segregation of minority students in the U.S. public school system.

Hispanic Educational Attainment Holds Steady

Even though Hispanics made modest gains in education in the 1990s, low educational attainment has been a major hindrance to their economic advancement in the United States. In *Digest of Education Statistics, 2006*, the

FIGURE 3.7

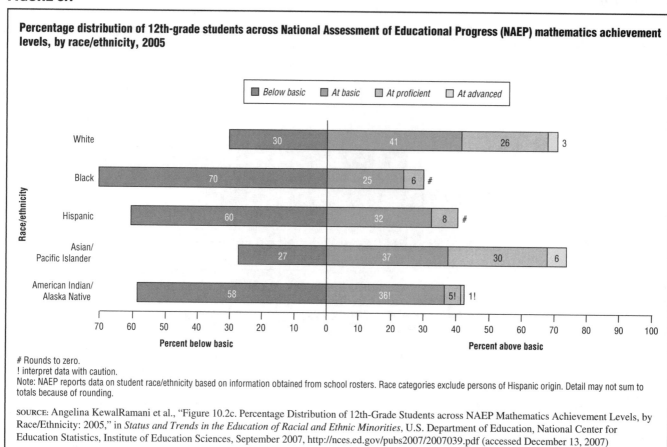

Percentage distribution of 12th-grade students across National Assessment of Educational Progress (NAEP) mathematics achievement levels, by race/ethnicity, 2005

Rounds to zero.
! interpret data with caution.
Note: NAEP reports data on student race/ethnicity based on information obtained from school rosters. Race categories exclude persons of Hispanic origin. Detail may not sum to totals because of rounding.

SOURCE: Angelina KewalRamani et al., "Figure 10.2c. Percentage Distribution of 12th-Grade Students across NAEP Mathematics Achievement Levels, by Race/Ethnicity: 2005," in *Status and Trends in the Education of Racial and Ethnic Minorities*, U.S. Department of Education, National Center for Education Statistics, Institute of Education Sciences, September 2007, http://nces.ed.gov/pubs2007/2007039.pdf (accessed December 13, 2007)

NCES finds that in 2006 Hispanics continued to trail behind other groups in high school graduation rates. Only 59.3% of Hispanics aged twenty-five and older had received high school diplomas, compared to 90.5% of non-Hispanic whites and 81.2% of African-Americans. Not surprisingly, in 2005 non-Hispanic whites, Asian-Americans, African-Americans, and Native Americans were more likely to have graduated from college than were Hispanics. (See Figure 3.10.)

Why do Hispanics trail other racial and ethnic groups in educational attainment? A language barrier may be one reason. In 2005 seven out of ten (70%) Hispanic students in kindergarten through twelfth grade spoke Spanish at home. (See Figure 3.11.) Almost one out of five (19%) Hispanic students spoke English with difficulty.

However, there are some signs that there has been slow but steady progress in the educational attainment of the Hispanic population in the United States. The NCES indicates in *Digest of Education Statistics, 2006* that the proportion of Hispanic adults with a high school diploma steadily rose from 1990 to 2006, from 50.8% in 1990 to 59.3% in 2006. Likewise, the proportion of Hispanics with a bachelor's degree also rose, from 9.2% in 1990 to 12.4% in 2006. The proportion of Hispanics aged twenty-five to twenty-nine with a high school diploma

was higher than the proportion of all Hispanics over age twenty-five with a diploma (63.2% and 59.3%, respectively), indicating that fewer young Hispanic adults than in previous generations are dropping out of school.

Native American Educational Attainment Remains Low

Native Americans have the lowest educational attainment of all minority groups, which is attributable in part to a high dropout rate. According to Catherine Freeman and Mary Ann Fox, in *Status and Trends in the Education of American Indians and Alaska Natives* (August 2005, http://nces.ed.gov/pubs2005/2005108.pdf), 45,828 students attended Bureau of Indian Affairs schools and tribal schools in 2003–04. In 2002, 624,298 Native American and Alaskan Native students attended public schools.

The Early Childhood Longitudinal Study, Birth Cohort, found that a high proportion of Native American children have certain risk factors that may affect their educational attainment. The study oversampled Native American children to better study their educational experiences. Fully a third (34%) of Native American children lived below the poverty line, compared to 23% of all children. (See Table 3.5.) A quarter (24%) of all Native American children lived with a single parent, compared to 20% of all children. In

TABLE 3.3

Percentage of 16- to 24-year-olds who were high school dropouts, by nativity and race/ethnicity with Hispanic and Asian subgroups, 2005

Race/ethnicity and subgroup	Number	Total	Native	Foreign-born
Total*	34,602,000	10.5	8.6	25.2
White	21,163,000	7.2	7.2	6.3
Black	4,786,000	11.6	11.8	8.5
Hispanic	6,190,000	22.8	13.2	38.1
Mexican	4,150,000	25.5	13.8	41.9
Puerto Rican	502,000	16.9	16.9	‡
Dominican	172,000	14.2	10.6!	17.7
Central American	469,000	32.6	9.9!	43.7
South American	267,000	9.1	4.8!	11.8
Other Hispanic or Latino	629,000	10.9	9.7	17.8
Asian	1,423,000	3.5	2.9	4.0
Asian Indian	236,000	3.1!	1.6!	4.0!
Chinese	297,000	2.2!	0.6!	3.8!
Filipino	266,000	3.2!	2.8!	3.6!
Japanese	55,000	2.1!	2.8!	#
Korean	167,000	2.0!	3.7!	1.0!
Vietnamese	166,000	2.0!	1.9!	5.6!
Other Asian	236,000	6.9	6.6!	7.2!
Native Hawaiian/Pacific Islander	53,000	9.8!	7.7!	18.2!
American Indian/Alaska Native	286,000	15.5	15.6	‡

#Rounds to zero.
!Interpret data with caution.
‡Reporting standards not met. Sample size too small.
*Total includes other race/ethnicity categories not separately shown.
Note: The data presented here represent status dropout rates, which is the percentage of civilian, non-institutionalized 16- to 24-year-olds who are not in high school and who have not earned a high school credential (either a diploma or equivalency credential such as a GED). The status dropout rate includes all dropouts regardless of when they last attended school, as well as individuals who may have never attended school in the United States, such as immigrants who did not complete a high school diploma in their home country. Another way of calculating dropout rates is the event dropout rate, which is the percentage of 15- to 24-year-olds who dropped out of grades 10 through 12 in the 12 months preceding the fall of each data collection year. Race categories exclude persons of Hispanic origin.

SOURCE: Angelina KewalRamani et al., "Table 17b. Percentage of 16- to 24-Year-Olds Who Were High School Status Dropouts, by Nativity and Race/Ethnicity with Hispanic and Asian Subgroups: 2005," in *Status and Trends in the Education of Racial and Ethnic Minorities*, U.S. Department of Education, National Center for Education Statistics, Institute of Education Sciences, September 2007, http://nces.ed.gov/pubs2007/2007039.pdf (accessed December 13, 2007)

addition, Native American parents had low educational attainment. A third (34%) of the mothers and 27% of the fathers had not completed high school, compared to 27% of all mothers and 17% of all fathers. Furthermore, only 9% of Native American mothers and 6% of Native American fathers had earned a bachelor's degree or higher, compared to 24% of all mothers and 24% of all fathers.

In 2005 Native American eighth graders had the highest rate of absences of any race or ethnic group in the preceding month—66% of Native American students had been absent, and 30% had been absent three or more times in the past month. (See Table 3.6.) A smaller proportion of Hispanic students (58%), non-Hispanic white students (56%), African-American students (56%), and Asian-American students (38%) had been absent in the past month, whereas only 25% of African-American students,

24% of Hispanic students, 20% of non-Hispanic white students, and 12% of Asian-American students had been absent three or more times in the past month. High rates of absenteeism were associated with lower rates of achieving at least a basic on the NAEP mathematics assessment. Only 41% of Native American students who had been absent three or more times achieved basic or above, compared to 56% of students who had been absent one or two times and 62% of students who had not been absent at all.

Freeman and Fox report that the Office of Indian Education Programs (OIEP), which was established in the late nineteenth century, works to improve educational opportunities and outcomes for the Native American population. In 2003–04 the OIEP oversaw 184 schools on 63 reservations in 23 states across the United States. On April 30, 2004, President George W. Bush (1946–) signed an executive order that established an Interagency Working Group on American Indian and Alaska Native Education with the goal of helping these students achieve the standards set by the No Child Left Behind Act.

REFORMING THE PUBLIC SCHOOL SYSTEM
No Child Left Behind

In January 2002 President Bush signed into law the No Child Left Behind (NCLB) Act, which was intended to improve the U.S. public school system and provide educational choice, especially for minority families. The law mandated that all public school students be proficient in reading and math by 2014, with progress measured by the administration of annual standardized tests. In addition, all subgroups—those with certain racial backgrounds, limited English proficiency, disabilities, or from low-income families—must meet the same performance standards as all students. Failure to make adequate yearly progress may result in escalating sanctions against the school, including the payment of transportation costs for students who wished to transfer to better-performing schools, extra tutoring for low-income students, replacement of the school staff, and potentially converting the school to a charter school or even turning to a private company to operate the school.

Even though the NCLB was passed with bipartisan support, critics quickly emerged, including those who charged that the mandate was underfinanced by the Bush administration. In "Federal Appeals Court Backs NEA Challenge to NCLB" (January 2008,http://www.nea.org/esea/nclblawsuit0108.html), Alain Jehlen notes that in January 2008 the National Education Association (NEA) and several state associations and school districts won a suit in the U.S. Court of Appeals arguing that the federal government could not force states and school districts to fund the provisions of the NCLB and that the federal government must pay for the act's implementation.

FIGURE 3.8

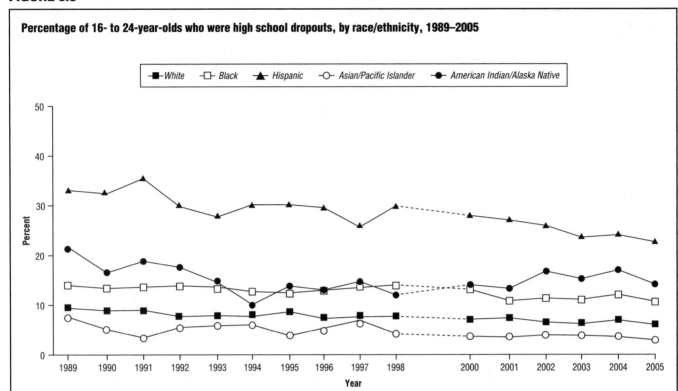

Percentage of 16- to 24-year-olds who were high school dropouts, by race/ethnicity, 1989–2005

Note: Some data for Asians/Pacific Islanders and American Indians/Alaska Natives should be interpreted with caution. The data presented here represent status dropout rates, which is the percentage of civilian, noninstitutionalized 16- to 24-years-olds who are not in high school and who have not earned a high school credential (either a diploma or equivalency credential such as a GED). The status dropout rate includes all dropouts regardless of when they last attended school, as well as individuals who may have never attended school in the United States, such as immigrants who did not complete a high school diploma in their home country. Another way of calculating dropout rates is the event dropout rate, which is the percentage of 15- to 24-year-olds who dropped out of grades 10 through 12 in the 12 months preceding the fall of each data collection year. Data for 1999 have been suppressed due to unstable estimates. Race categories exclude persons of Hispanic origin.

SOURCE: Angelina KewalRamani et al., "Figure 17. Percentage of 16- to 24-Year-Olds Who Were High School Status Dropouts, by Race/Ethnicity: 1989–2005," in *Status and Trends in the Education of Racial and Ethnic Minorities*, U.S. Department of Education, National Center for Education Statistics, Institute of Education Sciences, September 2007, http://nces.ed.gov/pubs2007/2007039.pdf (accessed December 13, 2007)

Sam Dillon, in "Schools Cut Back Subjects to Push Reading and Math" (*New York Times*, March 26, 2006), and Jennifer Booher-Jennings, in "Below the Bubble: 'Educational Triage' and the Texas Accountability System" (*American Educational Research Journal*, vol. 42, no. 2, 2005), report that many critics consider the law inflexible and so flawed that it actually undercuts the goals it seeks to achieve. Some question the reliance on high-stakes standardized tests, which force schools to spend a considerable amount of time preparing students to take the tests, an effort that produces no lasting educational benefit and requires a reallocation of resources. In many cases gifted students' programs have been cut back. Because low-income, minority gifted students lack the options of their white counterparts, they are left to languish in classes that fail to stimulate them.

Moreover, because of the strict testing requirements, many schools that were regarded as successful by almost all objective measures found themselves designated as failed schools. In some cases a school failed to meet its goal simply because two or three students in a subgroup failed to take a standardized test. In addition, the Center on

Education Policy explains in *From the Capital to the Classroom: Year 3 of the No Child Left Behind Act* (March 2005, http://www.cep-dc.org/pubs/nclby3/press/cep-nclby3_21 Mar2005.pdf) that the percentage of the nation's public schools that were identified as failed schools each year between 2001 and 2004 remained a stable 13%.

A further problem was that minority students who attended schools that were unquestionably substandard found that even if by law they had the right to transfer to another school, there were few places to go. In *Holding NCLB Accountable: Achieving Accountability, Equity, and School Reform* (2008), a multipart study that was conducted by the Civil Rights Project at Harvard University and edited by Gail L. Sunderman, the researchers find that no districts are able to approve all transfer requests. However well intentioned, the NCLB is proving difficult to implement, demonstrating once again that there are no easy answers to improving the U.S. educational system, especially for minority and low-income students.

Wendy Grigg, Patricia L. Donahue, and Gloria Dion indicate in *The Nation's Report Card: 12th-Grade Reading*

TABLE 3.4

Percentage distribution of public elementary and secondary school enrollment, by locale and race/ethnicity, 1993, 2000, and 2003

Year status and race/ethnicity	Total	Central city	Urban fringe	Town	Rural
1993					
White	66.0	44.3	68.8	78.4	83.5
Total minority	34.0	55.7	31.2	21.6	16.5
Black	16.6	28.7	13.6	10.4	8.7
Hispanic	12.7	21.4	11.8	8.3	4.4
Asian/Pacific Islander	3.6	5.0	5.4	1.3	1.1
American Indian/Alaska Native	1.1	0.7	0.5	1.5	2.3
2000					
White	61.0	37.0	64.8	73.5	81.5
Total minority	39.0	63.0	35.2	26.5	18.5
Black	17.0	29.6	12.9	13.8	8.6
Hispanic	16.6	26.8	16.4	9.5	6.1
Asian/Pacific Islander	4.2	5.7	5.2	1.0	1.6
American Indian/Alaska Native	1.2	0.8	0.7	2.2	2.2
2003					
White	58.7	35.2	63.5	70.5	79.1
Total minority	41.3	64.8	36.5	29.5	20.9
Black	17.2	27.7	13.3	13.6	9.9
Hispanic	18.5	29.8	17.5	11.5	7.4
Asian/Pacific Islander	4.4	6.6	4.9	1.7	1.3
American Indian/Alaska Native	1.2	0.8	0.7	2.7	2.3

Note: 1993 data exclude race/ethnicity information for Maine. 2000 and 2003 data exclude race/ethnicity information for Tennessee. Race categories exclude persons of Hispanic origin. Detail may not sum to totals because of rounding.

SOURCE: Angelina KewalRamani et al., "Table 7.1. Percentage Distribution of Public Elementary and Secondary School Enrollment, by Locale and Race/Ethnicity: 1993, 2000, and 2003," in *Status and Trends in the Education of Racial and Ethnic Minorities*, U.S. Department of Education, National Center for Education Statistics, Institute of Education Sciences, September 2007, http://nces.ed.gov/pubs2007/2007039.pdf (accessed December 13, 2007)

and Mathematics 2005 (February 2007, http://nces.ed.gov/ nationsreportcard/pdf/main2005/2007468.pdf) that the reading scores of twelfth graders declined between 1992 and 2002 and did not improve between the passage of the NCLB in 2002 and 2005. In addition, the NCLB had no effect on closing the gap between the performance of non-Hispanic white students and African-American or Hispanic students. Because changes were made in the twelfth-grade mathematics assessment in 2005, the test's results could not be compared to results of previous years. However, less than one-quarter of all twelfth graders tested at or above proficient in mathematics in 2005. Even though results of testing at the fourth-grade and eighth-grade levels were more encouraging, the twelfth-grade results still call into question the effectiveness of the NCLB.

School "Choice"

In *Condition of Education, 2004*, the NCES finds that the percentage of parents who enrolled their children in chosen public schools, rather than in their assigned public schools, increased from 11% in 1993 and to 15.4% in 2003. More than half (51%) the parents surveyed reported that they had the option to send their children to a chosen public school. Among those parents, 65% sent their children to their assigned public school, whereas 27% sent their children to a chosen public school. In 2003 African-American students were the most likely to attend a chosen public school (24%) and non-Hispanic whites were the least likely to attend one (12.9%), probably because whites were more likely to attend chosen private schools.

SCHOOL VOUCHERS. Despite the Supreme Court's rejection of segregated schools, many minority students have been relegated to failing neighborhood public schools with little diversity. One proposed solution to this problem is the school voucher, a concept pioneered by the Nobel Prize–winning economist Milton Friedman (1912–2006) in 1955. The Friedman Foundation for Educational Choice explains in "School Choice" (2007, http://www.friedman foundation.org/friedman/schoolchoice/) that the voucher program provides parents with a predetermined amount of money—in essence the tax dollars already collected by a community to be used for education—and allows parents to present that voucher to the public or private school of their choice. Proponents for vouchers believe that not only will minority children benefit but also that public schools, fearful of losing tax revenues, will gain an incentive to improve. Opponents of vouchers, such as the NEA in "Vouchers" (2008, http://www.nea.org/vouchers/index .html), maintain that choice will simply drain money from the public schools and worsen their condition, while not providing real choice for students from impoverished or low-income families.

Vouchers have been used on an experimental basis around the country—mostly in Cleveland, Ohio; Milwaukee, Wisconsin; and in Florida—and have produced mixed results. Even though some minority children have been able to use vouchers to escape inferior schools, many families still lack the money necessary to educate their children outside of the public system. The value of the vouchers, ranging from $1,250 to $3,700, is simply too small to cover the tuition for most traditional private schools, leading a number of parents to opt for Catholic schools, which can be less expensive. However, the funding of religious education may not hold up to constitutional scrutiny. In "Vouchers Are Constitutionally Suspect" (2001, http://www.adl.org/vouchers/vouchers _constit_suspect.asp), the Anti-Defamation League states that "voucher programs . . . would force citizens—Christians, Jews, Muslims and atheists—to pay for the religious indoctrination of school children at schools with narrow parochial agendas. In many areas, 80 percent of vouchers would be used in schools whose central mission is religious training."

Moreover, parents using vouchers incur additional costs, such as transportation and school lunches, that many have found they cannot afford. According to Andrew Stephen, in "America—Andrew Stephen on Magic Solutions for US Schools" (*New Statesman*, December 9, 2002), in Florida "a quarter of the kids who were signed up for

FIGURE 3.9

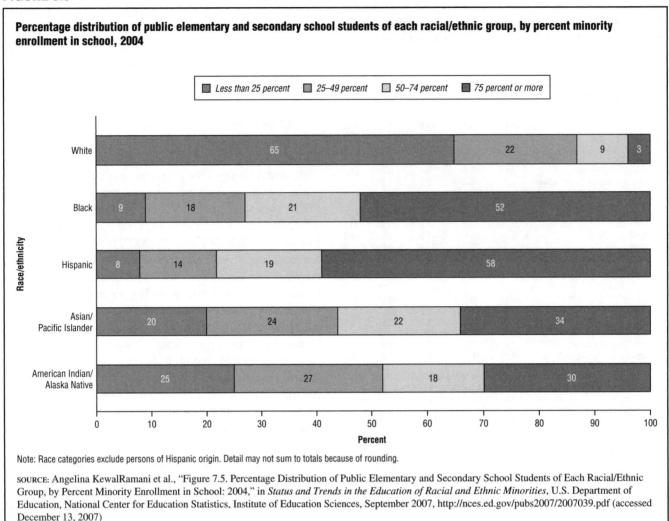

Percentage distribution of public elementary and secondary school students of each racial/ethnic group, by percent minority enrollment in school, 2004

Note: Race categories exclude persons of Hispanic origin. Detail may not sum to totals because of rounding.

SOURCE: Angelina KewalRamani et al., "Figure 7.5. Percentage Distribution of Public Elementary and Secondary School Students of Each Racial/Ethnic Group, by Percent Minority Enrollment in School: 2004," in *Status and Trends in the Education of Racial and Ethnic Minorities*, U.S. Department of Education, National Center for Education Statistics, Institute of Education Sciences, September 2007, http://nces.ed.gov/pubs2007/2007039.pdf (accessed December 13, 2007)

vouchers this school year have already found themselves back in the public system." In these cases, voucher programs end up not helping low-income children at all but segregating them further in neighborhood public schools while children from higher-income families who can afford the additional costs use the vouchers to attend private schools.

The voucher movement suffered a serious setback on January 5, 2006, when the Florida Supreme Court struck down that state's Opportunity Scholarship voucher system, saying that it violated the constitutional requirement of a uniform system of free public schools. With this argument, the court avoided the controversial issue of whether public school dollars could be used to fund parochial education. The NEA reports in "Florida High Court Rules against Vouchers" (January 6, 2006, http://www.nea.org/vouchers/flvouchers1-06.html) that even supporters of the voucher system in Florida admitted that the court's decision most likely threatened the two other voucher programs in use in the state. In "Utah Voters

Resoundingly Defeat School Voucher Ballot Issue" (December 7, 2007, http://www.nsba.org/), the National School Boards Association notes that a further setback occurred in Utah in November 2007, when voters rejected a statewide voucher program. In general, taxpayers do not support voucher programs. When put before voters, voucher programs have been defeated in all eleven referenda since 1990.

CHARTER SCHOOLS. Like vouchers, the idea of charter schools has also found proponents in the minority community. A charter school is publicly financed but operates independent of school districts, thereby combining the advantages of a private school with the free tuition of a public school. Parents, teachers, and other groups receive a charter from a state legislature to operate these schools, which in effect exist as independent school districts. They receive public funds and are accountable for both their financing and educational standards.

FIGURE 3.10

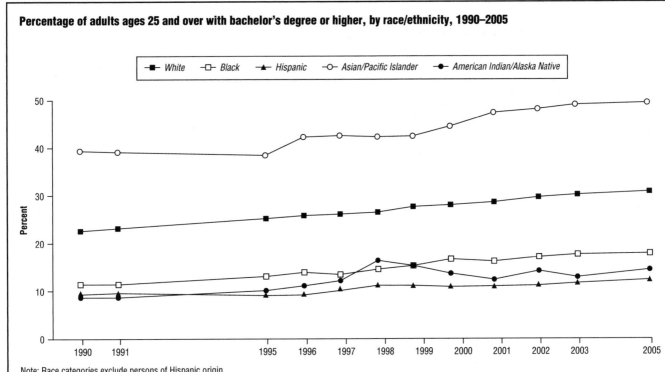

Percentage of adults ages 25 and over with bachelor's degree or higher, by race/ethnicity, 1990–2005

Note: Race categories exclude persons of Hispanic origin.

SOURCE: Angelina KewalRamani et al., "Figure 26.1. Percentage of Adults Ages 25 and over with Bachelor's Degree or Higher As Their Highest Level of Educational Attainment, by Race/Ethnicity: Selected Years, 1990–2005," in *Status and Trends in the Education of Racial and Ethnic Minorities*, U.S. Department of Education, National Center for Education Statistics, Institute of Education Sciences, September 2007, http://nces.ed.gov/pubs2007/2007039.pdf (accessed December 13, 2007)

According to Robin J. Lake and Paul T. Hill, in *Hopes, Fears, and Reality: A Balanced Look at American Charter Schools in 2005* (November 2005, http://www.ncsrp.org/downloads/HopesandFears2005_report.pdf), the charter school experiment started in Minnesota in 1992. By September 2004 almost one million students were enrolled in thirty-three hundred charter schools in forty states and Washington, D.C. As with vouchers, results have been uneven, with a number of notable successes offset by charter schools that failed to improve student achievement. Overall, however, the charter school movement has stood the test of time, and these schools have provided some parents with real options for their children's education.

However, one unintended consequence of charter schools is that they are more segregated than public schools. In "Charter Schools and Race: A Lost Opportunity for Integrated Education" (*Education Policy Analysis Archives*, vol. 11, no. 32, September 5, 2003), Erica Frankenberg and Chungmei Lee state that "seventy percent of all black charter school students attend intensely segregated minority schools compared with 34% of black public school students.... The pattern for Latino segregation is mixed; on the whole, Latino charter school students are less segregated than their black counterparts." The researchers report that 70% of African-American charter school stu-

dents were attending charter schools composed of 90% to 100% minority students.

HIGHER EDUCATION
Preparation for College

HIGH SCHOOL COURSE-TAKING. High school students are better prepared for college-level coursework if they take advanced courses while still in high school. Asian-American students are more likely than other students to take advanced math and science courses in high school. Non-Hispanic white students, while less likely to take these courses than Asian-American students, are significantly more likely than most minority students to take these courses. According to the College Board, in *College-Bound Seniors 2007* (2007, http://www.collegeboard.com/prod_downloads/about/news_info/cbsenior/yr2007/national-report.pdf), 54% of all college-bound seniors had taken physics, 53% had taken precalculus, and 30% had taken calculus in 2007. Among Asian-American students, 69% took physics, 69% took precalculus, and 50% took calculus. More than half of non-Hispanic white students took physics (55%) and precalculus (55%), and 31% took calculus. However, only 43% of African-American students took physics, 35% took precalculus, and 15% took calculus. Even though higher proportions of Hispanic and Native American

FIGURE 3.11

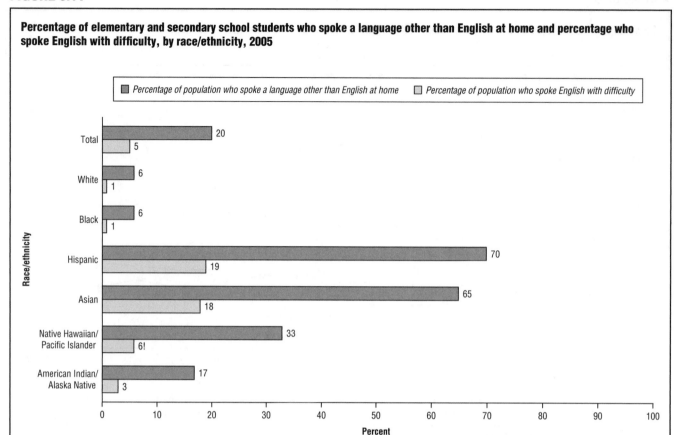

Percentage of elementary and secondary school students who spoke a language other than English at home and percentage who spoke English with difficulty, by race/ethnicity, 2005

■ *Percentage of population who spoke a language other than English at home*   □ *Percentage of population who spoke English with difficulty*

! Interpret data with caution.

Note: Respondents were asked if each child in the household spoke a language other than English at home. If they answered "yes," they were asked how well each child could speak English. Categories used for reporting were "very well," "well," "not well," and "not at all." All those who reported speaking English less than "very well" were considered to have difficulty speaking English. The percentages shown are of the total population for that particular race/ethnicity. Race categories exclude persons of Hispanic origin. Includes those students who are age 5 or older.

SOURCE: Angelina KewalRamani et al., "Figure 8.2. Percentage of Elementary and Secondary School Students Who Spoke a Language Other Than English at Home and Percentage Who Spoke English with Difficulty, by Race/Ethnicity: 2005," in *Status and Trends in the Education of Racial and Ethnic Minorities*, U.S. Department of Education, National Center for Education Statistics, Institute of Education Sciences, September 2007, http://nces.ed.gov/pubs2007/2007039.pdf (accessed December 13, 2007)

students took these upper-level courses than did African-American students, non-Hispanic white students were more likely to have taken them.

Asian-American students were more likely to achieve the highest academic levels in science, mathematics, and English in 2004. More than a third (38.8%) completed chemistry II, physics II, and/or advanced biology, compared to 20.3% of non-Hispanic white students, 10.8% of African-American students, 8.8% of Hispanic students, and 7.3% of Native American students. (See Table 3.7.) A third (33.4%) of Asian-American students completed a calculus course, compared to 16% of non-Hispanic white students, 6.8% of Hispanic students, 5.6% of Native American students, and 4.7% of African-American students. (See Table 3.8.) Almost half (43.1%) of Asian-American students completed at least some advanced academic level English courses, compared to a third (35.4%) of non-Hispanic white students and only 24.9% of Hispanic

students, 23.9% of African-American students, and 21.2% of Native American students. (Table 3.9.)

Even though a higher percentage of Asian-American students completed three years of a foreign language than did other students, Hispanic students were more likely to complete an advanced placement (AP) course, probably because many Hispanic students are bilingual. More than a quarter (27.2%) of Asian-American students completed three years of a foreign language course, but only 9.1% completed an AP course. (See Table 3.10.) By contrast, 15.1% of Hispanic students completed three years of a foreign language course, and only 10% completed an AP course. Less than 1% of African-American and Native American students completed an AP foreign language course.

AP courses are college-level courses offered to students in high school. The College Board developed thirty-seven courses in twenty subjects; college credit

TABLE 3.5

Percentage distribution of children born in 2001, by family characteristics when the children were about 9 months of age, 2001

Characteristic	Percent
American Indian and Alaska Native children (AIAN)	100
Poverty status[a]	
Below poverty threshold	34
At or above poverty threshold	66
Family type[b]	
Married, two biological parents	45
Married, two parents	#
Cohabiting, two biological parents	27
Cohabiting, two parents	2*
Single parent, lives alone	24
Other (guardian)	1
Child's mother's education[c]	
Less than high school	34
High school diploma/GED	21
Some college/vocational or technical	34
Bachelor's degree or higher	9
Child's father's education[d]	
Less than high school	27
High school diploma/GED	23
Some college/vocational or technical	21
Bachelor's degree or higher	6
All children	
Poverty status[a]	
Below poverty threshold	23
At or above poverty threshold	77
Family type[b]	
Married, two biological parents	64
Married, two parents	1
Cohabiting, two biological parents	14
Cohabiting, two parents	1
Single parent, lives alone	20
Other (guardian)	1
Child's mother's education[c]	
Less than high school	27
High school diploma/GED	22
Some college/vocational or technical	26
Bachelor's degree or higher	24
Child's father's education[d]	
Less than high school	17
High school diploma/GED	18
Some college/vocational or technical	21
Bachelor's degree or higher	24

Rounds to zero.
*Interpret data with caution.
[a]Poverty status is based on Census guidelines from 2001, where, for example, a family of 4 with an income of less than $18,104.00 was considered to be living in poverty.
[b]Married, two parents and cohabiting, two parents could be one biological parent and one nonbiological parent or two nonbiological parents (such as adoptive parents). Also, 95 percent of the time "single parent, lives alone" refers to the biological mother.
[c]Child's mother's education reflects the population of children living with their mother. Therefore, estimates may not sum to totals due to the omitted category no mother in household.
[d]Child's father's education reflects the population of children living with their father. Therefore, estimates may not sum to totals due to the omitted category no father in household.

SOURCE: Adapted from Kristin Denton Flanagan and Jen Park, "Table 2. Percentage Distribution of Children Born in 2001, by Family Characteristics When the Children Were About 9 Months of Age: 2001," in *American Indian and Alaska Native Children: Findings from the Base Year of the Early Childhood Longitudinal Study, Birth Cohort*, U.S. Department of Education, National Center for Education Statistics, August 2005, http://nces.ed.gov/pubs2005/2005116.pdf (accessed January 16, 2008)

TABLE 3.6

Percentage distribution of 8th-graders and percentage at or above *Basic* on the National Assessment of Educational Progress mathematics assessment, by race/ethnicity and number of days absent from school in the past month, 2005

Race/ethnicity	Total	No absences	1–2 absences	3 or more absences
		Percentage distribution		
Total*	100	45	34	21
White	100	44	36	20
Black	100	44	31	25
Hispanic	100	42	34	24
Asian/Pacific Islander	100	62	26	12
American Indian/Alaska Native	100	34	36	30
		Percentage at or above *basic*		
Total	69	75	71	56
White	80	85	81	69
Black	42	49	43	30
Hispanic	52	58	52	40
Asian/Pacific Islander	81	86	81	64
American Indian/Alaska Native	53	62	56	41

*Total includes other race/ethnicity categories not separately shown.
Note: Race categories exclude persons of Hispanic origin. Detail may not sum to totals because of rounding.

SOURCE: Angelina KewalRamani et al., "Table 15. Percentage Distribution of 8th-Graders and Percentage at or above *Basic* on the NAEP Mathematics Assessment, by Race/Ethnicity and Number of Days Absent from School in the Past Month: 2005," in *Status and Trends in the Education of Racial and Ethnic Minorities*, U.S. Department of Education, National Center for Education Statistics, Institute of Education Sciences, September 2007, http://nces.ed.gov/pubs2007/2007039.pdf (accessed December 13, 2007)

much more than participation of non-Hispanic white students. For example, the participation of Hispanic students increased by 213%, the participation of African-American students increased by 177%, and the participation of Native American students increased by 124%. However, the NCES explains in *High School Coursetaking: Findings from the Condition of Education 2007* (June 2007, http://nces.ed.gov/programs/coe/2007/analysis/2007065.pdf) that even though the average scores of non-Hispanic white and Asian-American students remained relatively stable during this period, at 3.0 and 3.1, respectively, the scores of other minority students declined. This lack of preparation for college coursework could affect these students' acceptance to and success in college.

GRADE POINT AVERAGE. Most groups of minority students, except for Asian-American students, are at a disadvantage when applying to college because of low grades in high school. In *College-Bound Seniors 2007*, the College Board notes that in 2007 the average grade point average (GPA) of most minority groups who took the Scholastic Assessment Test (SAT) was lower than 3.33, the average GPA of all students who took the SAT. The average GPA of African-American students was 0.33 lower than the average GPA, the average of Puerto Rican

can be awarded for a qualifying score of 3.0 or better on a five-point scale. Between 1997 and 2005 the number of students taking AP examinations increased by 111%. (See Table 3.11.) Participation of minority students increased

TABLE 3.7

Percentage distribution of high school graduates, by highest level of science course completed and race/ethnicity, 2004

| | | | | | Advanced academic level | | |
Characteristic	No science*	Low academic level	General biology	Total	Chemistry I or physics I	Chemistry I and physics I	Chemistry II, physics II, and/ or advanced biology
Total	**0.6**	**5.6**	**25.4**	**68.4**	**33.3**	**17.1**	**18.1**
Race/ethnicity							
White	0.5	5.0	23.9	70.7	32.1	18.2	20.3
Black	0.9	5.0	31.2	63.0	39.8	12.4	10.8
Hispanic	0.7	8.3	30.9	60.2	35.9	15.5	8.8
Asian/Pacific Islander	0.5	3.0	12.8	83.7	25.9	19.1	38.8
American Indian	#	10.3	41.9	47.8	28.2	12.3	7.3

#Rounds to zero.
*Graduates in this category may have taken some science courses, but these courses are not defined as science courses according to the classification used in this analysis.
Note: The distribution of graduates in the various levels of science courses was determined by the level of the most academically advanced course they had completed. Graduates may have completed advanced levels of courses without having taken courses at lower levels. Race categories exclude persons of Hispanic ethnicity. Detail may not sum to totals because of rounding.

SOURCE: Adapted from Michael Planty, Stephen Provasnik, and Bruce Daniel, "Table SA-7. Percentage Distribution of High School Graduates, by Highest Level of Science Course Completed and Selected Characteristics: 2004," in *High School Coursetaking: Findings from The Condition of Education 2007*, U.S. Department of Education, National Center for Education Statistics, June 2007, http://nces.ed.gov/programs/coe/2007/analysis/2007065.pdf (accessed December 13, 2007)

TABLE 3.8

Percentage distribution of high school graduates, by highest level of mathematics course completed and race/ethnicity, 2004

| | | | | Middle academic | | | Advanced academic | | | |
Characteristic	No mathematics[b]	Non-academic	Low academic	Total	Algebra/ geometry	Algebra II	Total	Trigonometry/ Algebra III	Precalculus	Calculus
Total	**0.6**	**1.8**	**3.0**	**44.6**	**18.7**	**25.9**	**50.0**	**17.6**	**18.5**	**13.9**
Race/ethnicity										
White	0.5	1.6	2.6	41.0	16.9	24.0	54.3	18.2	20.1	16.0
Black	1.3	1.8	3.8	51.3	19.8	31.5	41.7	22.9	14.0	4.7
Hispanic	0.3	2.5	4.2	58.6	27.0	31.6	34.3	13.0	14.5	6.8
Asian/Pacific Islander	0.4	0.3	1.5	28.7	11.3	17.5	69.1	12.5	23.1	33.4
American Indian	2.4[a]	8.5	4.5	62.9	22.8	40.1	21.8	8.9	7.2	5.6

#Rounds to zero.
[a]Interpret data with caution (estimates are unstable).
[b]Students in this category may have taken some mathematics courses, but these courses are not defined as mathematics courses according to the classification used in this analysis.
Note: The distribution of graduates among the various levels of mathematics courses was determined by the level of the most academically advanced course they had completed. Graduates may have completed advanced levels of courses without having taken courses at lower levels. Academic levels are labeled according to the most commonly known course at that level; courses with different names or on topics of different but similar academic difficulty may be included under these rubrics. Race categories exclude persons of Hispanic ethnicity. Detail may not sum to totals because of rounding.

SOURCE: Adapted from Michael Planty, Stephen Provasnik, and Bruce Daniel, "Table SA-8. Percentage Distribution of High School Graduates, by Highest Level of Mathematics Course Completed and Selected Characteristics: 2004," in *High School Coursetaking: Findings from The Condition of Education 2007*, U.S. Department of Education, National Center for Education Statistics, June 2007, http://nces.ed.gov/programs/coe/2007/analysis/2007065.pdf (accessed December 13, 2007)

students was 0.2 lower, the average of Mexican-American students was 0.1 lower, and the average of other Hispanic students was 0.15 lower. Only Native American students narrowed the gap between their average GPA and the overall average GPA from 1997 to 2007.

Asian-American students' average GPA remained higher than the average GPA of all students and higher than the GPA of non-Hispanic white students in 2007— Asian-American students' GPAs were 0.12 higher than the average, whereas non-Hispanic white students' GPAs were 0.07 higher than the average. However, the gap between Asian-American and non-Hispanic white students' average GPAs actually narrowed between 1997 and 2007.

SAT and ACT Scores

Students wishing to enter most colleges and universities in the United States must take the SAT or the ACT Assessment (formerly the American College Test). These are standardized tests intended to measure verbal and

TABLE 3.9

Percentage distribution of high school graduates, by type of English course taken and race/ethnicity, 2004

Characteristic	No English[b]	Low academic level[c]	Regular English (no low or honors) courses	Advanced academic level[a]			
				Total	Less than 50 percent of courses	50–74 percent of courses	75–100 percent of courses
Total	**0.7**	**10.8**	**55.9**	**32.7**	**9.2**	**7.6**	**15.9**
Race/ethnicity							
White	0.6	7.5	56.5	35.4	9.5	8.3	17.6
Black	0.5	15.4	60.2	23.9	8.3	6.2	9.4
Hispanic	1.3	21.1	52.8	24.9	8.5	5.3	11.1
Asian/Pacific Islander	0.1	13.2	43.6	43.1	9.0	8.1	26.0
American Indian	1.0*	16.1	61.7	21.2	2.9	1.6	16.8

*Interpret data with caution (estimates are unstable).
[a]Includes graduates who completed a general English course classified as "below grade level" if they completed a greater percentage of "honors" courses than "below grade level" courses.
[b]Indicates that student transcript records did not list any recognized English courses; however, these graduates may have studied some English. If graduates took only English as a second language (ESL) courses for credit, they would be listed in this category.
[c]Low academic level courses include all general English courses classified as "below grade level." Graduates may have taken a general English course classified as regular or "honors" and be classified in the low academic level if the percentage of "below grade level" courses completed was the plurality of courses completed.
Note: For each graduate, the percentages of completed courses classified as "below level," "at grade level," and "honors" were calculated. (Not all graduates completed 4 years of English.) After the percentage of graduates at each level had been calculated, the percentage of graduates who fit the category requirement for each level was determined. Race categories exclude persons of Hispanic ethnicity. Detail may not sum to totals because of rounding.

SOURCE: Adapted from Michael Planty, Stephen Provasnik, and Bruce Daniel, "Table SA-11. Percentage Distribution of High School Graduates, by Type of English Course Taken and Selected Characteristics: 2004," in *High School Coursetaking: Findings from The Condition of Education 2007*, U.S. Department of Education, National Center for Education Statistics, June 2007, http://nces.ed.gov/programs/coe/2007/analysis/2007065.pdf (accessed December 13, 2007)

TABLE 3.10

Percentage distribution of high school graduates, by highest level of foreign language course completed and race/ethnicity, 2004

Characteristic	None	Year 1 or less	Year 2	Advanced academic level			
				Year 3 or higher	Year 3	Year 4	Advanced placement (AP)
Total	**15.5**	**16.1**	**33.9**	**34.5**	**19.1**	**10.1**	**5.4**
Race/ethnicity							
White	14.1	15.6	33.0	37.2	20.6	11.4	5.3
Black	15.9	22.5	42.0	19.6	13.3	5.5	0.8
Hispanic	20.4	14.6	32.3	32.8	15.1	7.8	10.0
Asian/Pacific Islander	10.8	12.3	26.4	50.5	27.2	14.2	9.1
American Indian	41.6	19.4	23.9	15.1	9.3	5.3	0.5

Note: Foreign language coursetaking based upon classes in Amharic (Ethiopian), Arabic, Chinese (Cantonese or Mandarin), Czech, Dutch, Finnish, French, German, Greek (Classical or Modern), Hawaiian, Hebrew, Italian, Japanese, Korean, Latin, Norse (Norwegian), Polish, Portuguese, Russian, Spanish, Swahili, Swedish, Turkish, Ukrainian, or Yiddish. Some graduates in each category also studied more than one foreign language. The distribution of graduates among the various levels of foreign language courses was determined by the level of the most academically advanced course they completed. Graduates who had completed courses in different languages were counted according to the highest level course completed. Graduates may have completed advanced levels of courses without having taken courses at lower levels. Race categories exclude persons of Hispanic ethnicity. Detail may not sum to totals because of rounding.

SOURCE: Adapted from Michael Planty, Stephen Provasnik, and Bruce Daniel, "Table SA-12. Percentage Distribution of High School Graduates, by Highest Level of Foreign Language Course Completed and Selected Characteristics: 2004," in *High School Coursetaking: Findings from The Condition of Education 2007*, U.S. Department of Education, National Center for Education Statistics, June 2007, http://nces.ed.gov/programs/coe/2007/analysis/2007065.pdf (accessed December 13, 2007)

mathematical ability to determine readiness for college-level work. Most students take the SAT. Performance on the SAT is measured in three areas, each on a scale of two hundred to eight hundred: critical reading, mathematics, and a written essay portion that was added to the SAT in 2005.

Historically, minority students have not scored as well on the SAT as non-Hispanic white students, but gains have been made by some groups since 1997. The College Board indicates in *College-Bound Seniors 2007* that in 2007 the average score for the critical reading portion of the SAT among non-Hispanic whites was 527, compared to 514 for Asians and Pacific Islanders, 487 for Native Americans and Alaskan Natives, and 433 for African-Americans. Among Hispanic subgroups, Mexican-Americans averaged 455 on the verbal portion of the test, Puerto Ricans averaged 459,

TABLE 3.11

Number and percent change of students taking Advanced Placement (AP) examinations, by race/ethnicity, 1997–2005

Race/ethnicity	1997	1998	1999	2000	2001	2002	2003	2004	2005	Percent change 1997 to 2005
Total*	566,720	618,257	685,981	747,922	820,880	913,251	998,329	1,081,102	1,197,439	111
White	371,606	403,553	445,880	504,600	549,065	607,816	660,225	702,489	762,548	105
Total minority*	154,046	170,054	194,557	225,825	250,230	280,276	315,046	350,425	398,243	159
Black	24,469	27,054	31,023	36,158	40,078	45,271	51,160	57,001	67,702	177
Hispanic	47,626	53,627	62,853	74,852	86,018	98,495	114,246	130,042	148,960	213
Asian/Asian American	63,528	68,109	75,875	85,756	92,762	102,653	111,704	121,038	135,815	114
American Indian/Alaska Native	2,520	2,761	3,136	3,584	3,472	3,896	4,530	4,974	5,654	124
Missing	41,068	44,650	45,544	17,497	21,585	25,159	23,058	28,188	36,648	−11

*Total includes other race/ethnicity categories not separately shown.
Note: Data reported are for all students who completed an AP exam. The College Board collects racial/ethnic information based on the categories American Indian/Alaska Native; Asian/Asian American; Black/Afro-American; Latino: Chicano/Mexican, Puerto Rican, other Latino; white; and other. Hispanic refers to the sum of all Latino subgroups. Race categories exclude persons of Hispanic ethnicity.

SOURCE: Michael Planty, Stephen Provasnik, and Bruce Daniel, "Table 3. Number and Percent Change of Students Taking Advanced Placement (AP) Examinations, by Race/Ethnicity: 1997–2005," in *High School Coursetaking: Findings from The Condition of Education 2007*, U.S. Department of Education, National Center for Education Statistics, June 2007, http://nces.ed.gov/programs/coe/2007/analysis/2007065.pdf (accessed December 13, 2007)

and the rest of the Hispanic subgroups combined for an average of 459. The College Board states that the average critical reading scores for minority groups improved overall from 1997 to 2007. Asian-Americans experienced the largest increase, from 496 to 514. Native Americans' average scores also improved, from 475 to 487. Mexican-Americans scored 455, and Puerto Ricans scored 459, up from 451 and 454, respectively, in 1997. Whites witnessed a smaller increase from 526 in 1997 to 527 in 2007. African-Americans' average score decreased by one point between 1997 and 2007, from 434 to 433. Likewise, other Hispanics' average score also decreased, from 512 in 1997 to 497 in 2007.

According to the College Board, mathematics scores were better in 2007 than they were in 1997 for all minority groups except other Hispanics. In 2007 Asians and Pacific Islanders scored the highest by far on the math portion of the test, with an average score of 578, up from 560 in 1997. Non-Hispanic whites scored an average of 534, up from 526 in 1997. Native Americans and Alaskan Natives scored 494, up from 475 in 1997. Mexican-Americans scored 466, and Puerto Ricans scored 454, up from 458 and 447, respectively, in 1997. African-Americans scored 429, up from 423 in 1997. Other Hispanics dropped from 468 in 1997 to 463 in 2007.

The writing portion of the SAT was a relatively new part of the test in 2007, having only been added by the College Board in 2005. In 2007 non-Hispanic whites and Asian-Americans did best on this portion of the test, at 518 and 513, respectively. Native Americans averaged 473, Mexican-Americans and other Hispanics both averaged 450, Puerto Ricans averaged 447, and African-Americans scored an average of 425.

Minority College Attendance

Generally, minority enrollment in colleges and universities has grown ever since racial and ethnic enrollment statistics were first reported in 1976. Even though these gains are encouraging, they must be viewed in the context of overall participation rates in higher education and degree completion rates.

In 2004, 60.3% of Asians and Pacific Islanders aged eighteen to twenty-four were enrolled in colleges and universities, the largest proportion of all race and ethnic groups, compared to 41.7% of white, non-Hispanic young adults aged eighteen to twenty-four. (See Figure 3.12.) Other minority groups had significantly lower enrollment rates. About one-third (31.8%) of African-Americans, 24.7% of Hispanics, and 24.4% of Native Americans and Alaskan Natives in this age group were enrolled in colleges and universities.

Earning a Bachelor's Degree

College participation rates are telling, but so, too, are college completion rates. A number of students begin college, only to drop out before receiving a bachelor's degree. In 2005 only 17.7% of African-Americans between the ages of twenty-five and twenty-nine had earned a bachelor's degree or higher. (See Figure 3.10.) Among Hispanics in this age group, only 12% had received a bachelor's degree or higher. Among Asian-Americans in this age group, 49.2% had received a bachelor's degree or higher—the highest completion rate of any race or ethnic group.

College completion rates among Asian-Americans and Hispanics vary according to their country of origin. Among Hispanics aged twenty-five to twenty-nine in 2005, those who traced their roots to South America

FIGURE 3.12

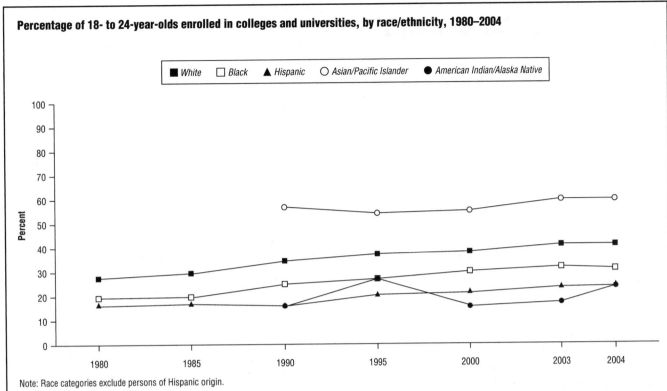

Percentage of 18- to 24-year-olds enrolled in colleges and universities, by race/ethnicity, 1980–2004

■ *White* □ *Black* ▲ *Hispanic* ○ *Asian/Pacific Islander* ● *American Indian/Alaska Native*

Note: Race categories exclude persons of Hispanic origin.

SOURCE: Angelina KewalRamani et al., "Figure 23.3. Percentage of 18- to 24-Year-Olds Enrolled in Colleges and Universities, by Race/Ethnicity: Selected Years, 1980–2004," in *Status and Trends in the Education of Racial and Ethnic Minorities*, U.S. Department of Education, National Center for Education Statistics, Institute of Education Sciences, September 2007, http://nces.ed.gov/pubs2007/2007039.pdf (accessed December 13, 2007)

had the highest completion rate, at 30.7%. (See Table 3.12.) Almost one out of five (18%) Dominicans in this age group had a bachelor's degree, and 16.4% of Puerto Ricans had a bachelor's degree. Not even one out of ten Hispanics who traced their roots to Mexico (8.3%) or Central America (8.6%) had earned a bachelor's degree by age twenty-nine.

Among those of Asian origin, twenty-five- to twenty-nine-year-olds who traced their roots to India had the highest percentage of bachelor's degrees, whereas those who traced their roots to Vietnam had the lowest percentage. Four out of five (80%) Indians in this age group had bachelor's degrees, compared to 71.4% of Chinese, 67.2% of Koreans, 57% of Japanese, 42% of Filipinos, and 37.7% of Vietnamese. (See Table 3.12.) However, the percentage of those who traced their roots to Vietnam who held bachelor's degrees was still more than twice as high as the percentage of African-Americans in the same age group with bachelor's degrees.

Affirmative Action in Higher Education

In the landmark 1978 affirmative action case *Regents of the University of California v. Bakke* (438 US 265), the Supreme Court allowed race and ethnicity to be considered in college admissions in the interest of racial and ethnic diversity on U.S. college campuses. This led many schools to take special steps to boost the number of minorities that they admitted, a process commonly called affirmative action.

Over time, many people came to see affirmative action as a negative policy. Their reasons varied, but a common complaint was that affirmative action allowed some minority students to get into colleges even when their test scores and high school grades were below what those colleges would accept from non-Hispanic white students. In June 1996 Pete Wilson (1933–), the governor of California, urged California voters to support the California Civil Rights Initiative (Proposition 209), a proposal to eliminate affirmative action in higher-education enrollment. In November 1996 California voters approved Proposition 209, prohibiting public universities from considering race and ethnicity when deciding on admissions. Sheila O'Rourke of the University of California (UC) reports in "Strategies for Achieving Faculty Diversity at the University of California in a Post-Proposition 209 Legal Climate" (2002, http://www.oma.umn.edu/kof/pdf/209.pdf) that in 1997, the last year that UC considered race and ethnicity in its admissions process, 17.9% of the students who were admitted were from underrepresented minority groups (Native Americans, African-Americans, and Hispanics).

TABLE 3.12

Number and percentage of persons ages 25 to 29 with bachelor's degree or higher, by race/ethnicity with Hispanic and Asian subgroups, 2005

Race/ethnicity and subgroup	Number	Percentage
Total*	5,391,000	28.0
White	3,834,000	33.3
Black	407,000	17.2
Hispanic	440,000	11.3
Mexican	217,000	8.3
Puerto Rican	50,000	16.4
Dominican	17,000	18.0
Central American	32,000	8.6
South American	61,000	30.7
Other Hispanic or Latino	63,000	20.1
Asian	606,000	61.5
Asian Indian	211,000	80.0
Chinese	146,000	71.4
Filipino	65,000	42.0
Japanese	29,000	57.0
Korean	68,000	67.2
Vietnamese	34,000	37.7
Other Asian	54,000	44.1
Native Hawaiian/Pacific Islander	3,000!	12.8!
American Indian/Alaska Native	17,000	12.0

!Interpret data with caution.
*Total includes other race/ethnicity categories not separately shown.
Note: Race categories exclude persons of Hispanic origin. Detail may not sum to totals because of rounding.

SOURCE: Angelina KewalRamani et al., "Table 26.2. Number and Percentage of Persons Age 25 to 29 with Bachelor's Degree or Higher, by Race/ Ethnicity with Hispanic and Asian Subgroups: 2005," in *Status and Trends in the Education of Racial and Ethnic Minorities*, U.S. Department of Education, National Center for Education Statistics, Institute of Education Sciences, September 2007, http://nces.ed.gov/pubs2007/2007039.pdf (accessed December 13, 2007)

In 1998, the first year of admissions after Proposition 209 went into effect, the proportion of underrepresented minorities dropped to 15.5%.

In *Hopwood v. Texas* (78 F.3d 932, 1996), the Fifth Circuit Court of Appeals unanimously ruled that the University of Texas (UT) School of Law was discriminating against non-Hispanic white students by using race and ethnicity as a factor in admissions. Four non-Hispanic white applicants charged that less-qualified African-American and Hispanic students had been accepted instead of them because of racial preference on the part of UT. The appeals court ruled that colleges could not give preferences to minority students, even for what it called "the wholesome practice of correcting perceived racial imbalance in the student body." In the opinion of the appeals court, "any consideration of race or ethnicity by the law school for the purpose of achieving a diverse student body is not a compelling interest under the Fourteenth Amendment." The *Hopwood* decision applied to all public universities in Texas, Louisiana, and Mississippi. In Texas, Attorney General Dan Morales (1956–) applied the admissions ruling to include financial aid and scholarships.

This decision negatively affected the number of underrepresented minority students at the UT School of Law. According to Lydia Lum, in "Minority Rolls Cut by Hopwood" (*Houston Chronicle*, September 1997), in 1997, following the decision affecting the law school, out of five hundred incoming students, only four African-American students and twenty-six Mexican-Americans were enrolled, down from thirty-one African-Americans and forty-two Mexican-Americans the previous year. At the undergraduate level, public universities throughout Texas also saw a drop in minority applications. Texas A&M University registered nearly 15% fewer Hispanics and 23% fewer African-Americans that year.

PUBLIC UNIVERSITIES RESPOND. In 1998 the UT system became the first public university to grant automatic admission to first-time freshmen based on class rank. Under Texas Education Code 51.803, students who graduate in the top 10% of their class from an accredited Texas high school are guaranteed admission to UT. Because some high schools have large minority populations, state officials hoped that more minority students would be admitted to state universities. After initial declines in minority enrollment, UT announced in early 2003 that Hispanic enrollment had returned to the pre-*Hopwood* level and that African-American enrollment was nearing its 1996 level.

In March 1999 UC regents approved a similar admission policy called Eligibility in the Local Context (ELC). UC Davis notes in "Freshman Eligibility in the Local Context" (2000, http://eaop.ucdavis.edu/images/ELC.pdf) that under the ELC, students graduating in the top 4% of their class in California high schools are eligible for admission to one of UC's undergraduate campuses. The ELC was implemented starting with freshmen applicants in the fall of 2001.

Supreme Court Affirms Racial Preferences

In June 2003 the Supreme Court made two separate rulings on the admission practices at the University of Michigan's undergraduate college and its law school. The undergraduate college used a point system in an effort to achieve diversity in the student body, awarding twenty points on a scale of 150 to African-Americans, Hispanics, and Native Americans. The Court rejected this system, maintaining that it was too broad and too much like a quota, and ruling that it violated the equal protection clause in the Fourteenth Amendment of the U.S. Constitution. By contrast, the University of Michigan law school weighed race and ethnicity along with a number of other admissions factors. The Court deemed this approach legal in *Grutter v. Bollinger* (539 U.S. 306, 2003), because it furthered "a compelling interest in obtaining the educational benefits that flow from a diverse student body." As a result, the Court upheld the concept of race-conscious admissions, but the nuanced approach to admissions that the Court found acceptable left the door open for further lawsuits. Even though smaller schools can devote more time and attention to individual applicants, larger institutions still face the problem of how to use race and ethnicity as a factor in screening many applications without assigning a numerical value to an individual's minority status.

Views of Educational Opportunities for African-Americans

African-Americans are less likely than whites to say that their children have the same opportunity as white children to get a good education. Lydia Saad of the Gallup Organization notes in *The Black-White Educational Opportunities Widely Seen as Equal* (July 2, 2007, http://www.gallup.com/poll/28021/BlackWhite-Educational-Opportunities-Widely-Seen-Equal.aspx) that in 2007, 49% African-Americans believed their children "have as good a chance as white children" of receiving a good education. (See Figure 3.13.) This figure had declined from a high of 68% in 1990. However, a large majority of non-Hispanic whites (80%) and Hispanics (73%) believed that African-American children "have as good a chance" as their white peers to get a good education.

This racial divide in perceptions of educational opportunities for African-American children continued into discussions of higher education. In *Blacks Convinced Discrimination Still Exists in College Admission Process* (August 24, 2007, http://www.gallup.com/poll/28507/Blacks-Convinced-Discrimination-Still-Exists-College-Admission-Process.aspx), Frank Newport of the Gallup Organization reports on a 2007 poll, in which respondents were asked: "If two equally qualified students, one white and one black, applied to a major U.S. college or university, who do you think would have the better chance of being accepted to the college—the white student, the black student—or would they have the same chance?" Nearly half (48%) of non-Hispanic white respondents believed that the two students would have the same chance, another quarter (26%) believed the African-American student would have the better chance, and one out of five (20%) believed the white student would have the better chance. (See Table 3.13.) African-Americans responded differently. Only 28% believed the two students would have the same chance, whereas six out of ten (61%) believed the white student would have the better chance. Only one out of twenty (5%) African-American respondents believed the African-American student would have the better chance for college admission. Newport notes that African-Americans who themselves had a college education felt most strongly that the white student would have the advantage.

Tribal Colleges

Special postsecondary institutions, collectively known as tribal colleges, were established to prepare Native American and Alaskan Native students with the skills most needed on

FIGURE 3.13

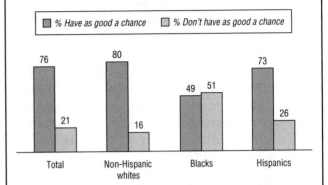

Public opinion on whether black children have as good a chance as white children to get a good education, 2007

IN GENERAL, DO YOU THINK THAT BLACK CHILDREN HAVE AS GOOD A CHANCE AS WHITE CHILDREN IN YOUR COMMUNITY TO GET A GOOD EDUCATION, OR DON'T YOU THINK THEY HAVE AS GOOD A CHANCE?

SOURCE: Lydia Saad, "In General, Do You Think That Black Children Have As Good a Chance As White Children in Your Community to Get a Good Education, or Don't You Think They Have As Good a Chance?" in *Black-White Educational Opportunities Widely Seen As Equal*, The Gallup Organization, July 2, 2007, http://www.gallup.com/poll/28021/BlackWhite-Educational-Opportunities-Widely-Seen-Equal.aspx?version=print (accessed January 16, 2008). Copyright © 2008 by The Gallup Organization. Reproduced by Permission of The Gallup Organization.

TABLE 3.13

Public opinion on whether a white student or a black student has a better chance of being accepted into college, 2003, 2005, and 2007

IF TWO EQUALLY QUALIFIED STUDENTS, ONE WHITE AND ONE BLACK, APPLIED TO A MAJOR U.S. COLLEGE OR UNIVERSITY, WHO DO YOU THINK WOULD HAVE THE BETTER CHANCE OF BEING ACCEPTED TO THE COLLEGE—[ROTATED: THE WHITE STUDENT, THE BLACK STUDENT]—OR WOULD THEY HAVE THE SAME CHANCE?

	White student	Black student	Same chance	No opinion
Total	%	%	%	%
2007 Jun 4–24	29	22	43	6
2005 Jun 6–25	29	20	47	4
2003 Jun 12–18	31	29	36	4
Non-Hispanic whites				
2007 Jun 4–24	20	26	48	6
2005 Jun 6–25	21	24	50	5
2003 Jun 12–15	24	34	38	4
Blacks				
2007 Jun 4–24	61	5	28	6
2005 Jun 6–25	64	4	29	3
2003 Jun 12–18	67	5	24	4

SOURCE: Frank Newport, "If Two Equally Qualified Students, One White and One Black, Applied to a Major U.S. College or University, Who Do You Think Would Have the Better Chance of Being Accepted to the College—[ROTATED: the White Student, the Black Student]—or Would They Have the Same Chance?" in *Blacks Convinced Discrimination Still Exists in College Admission Process*, The Gallup Organization, August 24, 2007, http://www.gallup.com/poll/28507/Blacks-Convinced-Discrimination-Still-Exists-College-Admission-Process.aspx?version=print (accessed January 16, 2008). Copyright © 2008 by The Gallup Organization. Reproduced by Permission of The Gallup Organization.

reservations, while at the same time preserving their culture. Usually situated in areas where the students cannot otherwise pursue education beyond high school without leaving the community, these colleges all offer associate's degrees. In addition, some offer bachelor's and master's degrees.

Tribal colleges offer courses ranging from teaching and nursing to secretarial skills and computer science that meet the needs of specific communities. Besides tribal languages, traditional subjects are a part of the curricula. According to the American Indian Higher Education Consortium, in *Tribal Colleges: An Introduction* (February 1999, http://www.aihec.org/documents/Research/intro.pdf), an example is a traditional tribal literature class offered by Bay Mills Community College in Brimley, Michigan, "only in the winter term because the stories are supposed to be told when snow is on the ground."

Freeman and Fox report that in the fall of 2002, 15,837 students were enrolled in tribal colleges—82.2% of them were Native American or Alaskan Native. Eight percent of all Native American or Alaskan Native college students were enrolled in tribally controlled colleges. Rising enroll-

ment figures suggest these schools do meet the unique needs of Native American students. Enrollment in tribally controlled colleges increased at a faster rate between 1997 and 2002 (32%) than did Native American and Alaskan Native enrollment in college generally (16%).

Black Colleges and Universities

Stephen Provasnik and Linda L. Shafer of the Education Statistics Services Institute indicate in *Historically Black Colleges and Universities, 1976 to 2001* (September 2004, http://nces.ed.gov/pubs2004/2004062.pdf) that 118 historically black colleges and universities exist in the United States. The state with the largest number of historically black colleges (eighteen) is Alabama. Georgia has twelve institutions, North Carolina and Mississippi each have eleven, while another ten are located in Texas. The NCES reports in "Fall Enrollment in Degree-Granting Historically Black Colleges and Universities, by Type and Control of Institution and Race/Ethnicity of Student: Selected Years, 1976–2004" (June 2006, http://nces.ed.gov/surveys/Annual Reports/historicallyblack.asp) that in 2004, 269,208 minority students, 257,545 of them African-American, were enrolled in these institutions.

CHAPTER 4
MINORITIES IN THE LABOR FORCE

A HISTORICAL PERSPECTIVE

Members of minority groups have always been an important part of the U.S. labor force. In many instances groups were allowed, or even encouraged, to immigrate to the United States to fill specific labor needs. Perhaps the most obvious example is the involuntary immigration of Africans, who provided slave labor for southern plantations as early as the seventeenth century. Later, Asians and Hispanics were employed to mine resources, farm land, and build railroads.

African-Americans

Since 1619, with the arrival of the first slave ships to North American shores, African-Americans have been part of the labor force. Even though most worked as unpaid slaves on southern plantations, a few were allowed to work for pay to purchase their freedom and that of their families, an effort that often took many years. Besides laboring on farms and in households, some enslaved people developed talents in masonry, music, or other skills and were hired out by their owners.

On January 1, 1863, during the Civil War (1861–1865), Abraham Lincoln (1809–1965) issued the Emancipation Proclamation. This freed all slaves in the Confederacy, although Confederate states did not recognize the authority of the Union government and African-Americans in the South remained enslaved. The proclamation did not free slaves held in Northern states where slavery remained legal. On January 31, 1865, Congress passed the Thirteenth Amendment, which abolished slavery in the entire United States; it was ratified after the war. However, when the period of Reconstruction (1865–1877) came to an end, many southern states enacted "black codes," which were new laws that restricted the freedom of African-Americans living in the South. These codes included provisions that forbade African-Americans from leaving their jobs without

permission. African-Americans in the South labored under these codes for decades.

The Library of Congress (LOC) explains in "African Immigration" (May 9, 2005, http://memory.loc.gov/learn/features/immig/african.html) that because the best job prospects were in urban areas in the North, and because the obstacles created by racial discrimination were the least burdensome there, hundreds of thousands of African-Americans left their rural southern homes and migrated north and west before and during World War I (1914–1918) in search of unskilled work in factories and homes. During the 1940s arms production for World War II (1939–1945) again attracted hundreds of thousands of African-Americans to the North, bringing about a moderate increase in the number of African-American workers in these factories. These migrations of African-Americans from the South to the North following both world wars were the largest movements of people within the United States in the country's history and did much to influence its future.

Asian-Americans

In "Chinese and Westward Expansion" (May 23, 2003, http://memory.loc.gov/ammem/award99/cubhtml/theme1.html), the LOC notes that Chinese immigrants came to the United States not only because of the gold rush in California but also to work on railroads, on farms, and in construction and manufacturing. Between 1886 and 1911 more than four hundred thousand Japanese people immigrated to the United States, often to work on the rapidly expanding sugarcane plantations in Hawaii or the fruit and vegetable farms in California. However, the LOC explains in "Japanese Immigration" (February 2, 2004, http://memory.loc.gov/learn/features/immig/japanese.html) that in the Gentleman's Agreement of 1907 President Theodore Roosevelt (1858–1919) and the Japanese government agreed to stop the flow of Japanese workers to the United States by withholding passports, thus cutting the flow to a trickle.

The most recent wave of Asians came to the United States in the 1970s and 1980s, when hundreds of thousands of refugees were admitted from Vietnam, Cambodia, Thailand, and Laos following the Vietnam War (1954–1975). The Southeast Asia Resource Action Center reports in "Southeast Asian Communities" (2008, http://www.searac.org/commun.html) that the first wave of refugees came from Vietnam when Saigon fell to the North Vietnamese Communists in April 1975. Over a hundred thousand Vietnamese people who had worked for the U.S. military during the war fled Vietnam for the United States, where they were resettled in communities around the nation. Subsequent waves of refugees fled Vietnam legally and illegally over the decades. The largest number of Vietnamese now live in Southern California, Washington, D.C., Texas, Washington, Pennsylvania, Minnesota, Massachusetts, New York, and Illinois. Cambodian refugees fled the Communist Khmer Rouge government to Thailand and were then resettled in other countries such as the United States. Laotian and Hmong refugees from the Communist government established in Laos after the fall of South Vietnam also fled to refugee camps in Thailand and were then resettled in the United States.

Hispanics

Many Hispanics can trace their roots to the time when the southwestern states were still a part of Mexico. However, the ancestors of most Hispanics arrived after Mexico surrendered much of its territory following its defeat in the Mexican-American War (1846–1848). The U.S. policy toward Hispanic workers (mainly from Mexico) has alternately encouraged and discouraged immigration, reflecting the nation's changing needs for labor. In "Mexican Immigration" (April 20, 2005, http://memory.loc.gov/learn/features/immig/mexican.html), the LOC states that before the start of the twentieth century, when there was little demand in the Southwest for Mexican labor, Mexicans moved back and forth across completely open borders to work in mines, on ranches, and on railroads.

However, as the Southwest began to develop and as Asian immigration slowed, the demand for Mexican labor increased. The LOC reports that between 1910 and 1930 the number of Mexican immigrants in the United States tripled, from two hundred thousand to six hundred thousand. The need for Mexican labor was so great that during World War I the Immigration and Naturalization Service exempted many Mexicans from meeting most immigration conditions, such as head taxes (paying a small amount to enter the country) and literacy requirements. Even though legal immigration rose, a large amount of illegal immigration also occurred. Historians estimate that during the 1920s there

were as many illegal as legal Mexican immigrants in the country.

During the Great Depression of the 1930s, the LOC explains that when jobs became scarce, many Americans believed the nation's unemployment situation was significantly compounded by illegal aliens working in the United States. As a result, hundreds of thousands of Mexican immigrants, both legal immigrants and illegal aliens, were repatriated (sent back) to Mexico.

When World War II began in Europe in 1939, the United States needed workers to help in its role as supplier to the Allied countries, primarily Great Britain. When the lure of better-paying factory jobs brought many rural workers to the city, the nation looked to Mexico to fill the need for agricultural workers. The Bracero Program (1942–1964) permitted entry of Mexican farm workers on a temporary contractual basis with U.S. employers. Even though the program was considered an alternative to illegal immigration, it likely contributed to it because there were more workers who wanted to participate in the program than there were openings. According to the LOC, more than five million Mexican immigrants came to the United States during and after the war as part of the Bracero Program, and hundreds of thousands stayed.

Marc Perry et al. of the U.S. Census Bureau estimate in *Evaluating Components of International Migration: Legal Migrants* (December 2001, http://www.census.gov/population/www/documentation/twps0059.html) that more than one million undocumented Hispanics entered the United States in the early 1980s. A major downturn in the Mexican economy led to a surge in Mexican immigrants, and several hundred thousand other Hispanics arrived from Central America, most notably from El Salvador and Guatemala, to escape bloody civil wars and repressive regimes. Overall, Hispanics accounted for approximately one out of every three legal immigrants to the United States during this period. In 1986 the Immigration Reform and Control Act gave more than two million Mexicans legal status in the United States. Since that time, Hispanics from Cuba, Central and South America, and Mexico have continued to enter the United States, legally and illegally.

"GET TOUGH" POLICY. To stem the flow of undocumented workers, a "get tough" policy was initiated in 1994, but in the opinion of critics the money spent on installing infrared sensors, cameras, and stadium-level lighting along the Mexican border was essentially wasted. Instead of crossing at more populated and better-secured areas, illegal immigrants crossed into the United States through mountains and deserts, facing dangerous conditions, and many have died as a result. In September 2006 Congress passed a bill authorizing the construction of a seven-hundred-mile fence along the U.S.-Mexican border in California, Arizona, New Mexico, and Texas, and the installation of a high-tech surveillance system to keep illegal Mexican immigrants from crossing into the United States. Jonathan Weisman reports in "With Senate Vote, Congress Passes Border Fence Bill" (*Washington Post*, September 30, 2006) that the fence itself is expected to cost $6 billion to construct. Critics charge that the fence, as planned, will be impossible to construct across the rugged terrain and the borders of the Tohono O'odham Nation, which opposed the bill.

Even though arrests of illegal aliens along the southwestern border increased, enforcement in the workplace was rare. In fact, the U.S. economy became so dependent on a pool of low-wage workers that mass deportation of undocumented workers was not a realistic option. In "Temporary Worker Program Is Explained" (*Washington Post*, October 19, 2005), Darryl Fears and Michael A. Fletcher state that in January 2004 President George W. Bush (1946–) proposed a guest-worker program that grants a three-year work permit to millions of undocumented workers. This permit is renewable for at least three more years, with a chance to apply for a green card to gain permanent residency. In addition, workers in other countries can apply for work permits to take jobs that no U.S. citizen wants. As of 2008 the administration's guest-worker program faced opposition from both Republicans and Democrats. Republican officeholders in states with small Hispanic populations were not supportive, and Democrats were quick to point out that the proposal offered no increased chance for permanent residency status, let alone citizenship. Undocumented workers were also split on the proposal. Even though they welcomed the chance to visit their home countries without fear of being unable to return to the United States, they were also wary of providing information about themselves to the government, fearful that they could more easily be deported once their permits expired.

Brian Naylor notes in "Bill Giving Children Path to Citizenship Blocked" (National Public Radio, October 24, 2007) that the debate on immigration heated up in 2007. Lawmakers debated legislation that would have allowed an estimated 1.1 million young people who had been brought to the United States when they were younger than fifteen to have worked toward eventual citizenship by attending college or serving in the military. The U.S. Senate blocked a final vote on the Development, Relief, and Education for Alien Minors Act in October 2007. Opponents called it an "amnesty bill," whereas proponents argued that many of these children do not even remember their home countries and should have the opportunity to become productive U.S. citizens.

LABOR FORCE PARTICIPATION AND UNEMPLOYMENT

Participation in the labor force means that a person is either employed or actively seeking employment. Those who are not looking for work because they are "going to school" or "unable to work" are not considered part of the labor force. The labor force increases with the long-term growth of the population. It responds to economic forces and social trends, and its size changes with the seasons.

To be classified as unemployed, a person must:

- Not have worked in the week specified for the survey
- Have actively sought work sometime during the four weeks preceding the survey
- Be currently available to take a suitable job

In November 2007, 1.4 million (8.4%) African-Americans in the civilian labor force were unemployed, an unemployment rate that was twice that of the white population. (See Table 4.1.) More than 1.2 million (5.7%) Hispanics in the civilian labor force were unemployed. (See Table 4.2.) The lowest unemployment rate was among Asians and Pacific Islanders. Approximately 262,000 (3.6%) Asian-Americans in the civilian labor force were unemployed in November 2007. (See Table 4.1.)

African-Americans

Historically, African-American workers have participated in the labor force in larger proportions than whites, primarily because African-American women were more likely to be working than their white counterparts. However, the increased entry of white women into the labor force since the 1970s has narrowed the gap between the two races. The U.S. Department of Labor (February 7, 2003, http://www.bls.gov/webapps/legacy/cpsatab2.htm) reports that in November 1972, 26.1 million (42.6%) white women participated in the labor force, compared to 3.6 million (51.8%) African-American women. By November 2007, 54.2 million (60.2%) white women over age twenty were in the civilian labor force, which was still proportionately lower than the 8.7 million (63.3%) African-American women over age twenty who participated in the labor force. (See Table 4.1.)

Conversely, the labor force participation rate of African-American men twenty years and older has declined since the 1970s. The Labor Department notes that in November 1972, 4.3 million (78.1%) African-American men twenty years and older were in the civilian labor force; in November 2007, 7.8 million (70.9%) were in the labor force. (See Table 4.1.) In comparison, 44.3 million (81.7%) white men were employed in November 1972; in November 2007, 65.5 million (76.4%) white men twenty years and older were in the civilian labor force. The overall participation rate for all African-Americans (men and women) was 63.1% (17.4 million) in November 2007, compared to a participation rate of 66.4% (125.4 million) among all non-Hispanic whites.

TABLE 4.1

Employment status of the civilian population, by race, sex, and age, 2006–07

[Numbers in thousands]

Employment status race, sex, and age	Not seasonally adjusted			Seasonally adjusted[a]					
	Nov. 2006	Oct. 2007	Nov. 2007	Nov. 2006	July 2007	Aug. 2007	Sept. 2007	Oct. 2007	Nov. 2007
White									
Civilian noninstitutional population	186,988	188,813	188,956	186,988	188,312	188,479	188,644	188,813	188,956
Civilian labor force	124,635	125,228	125,615	124,536	124,966	124,593	125,245	125,109	125,427
Participation rate	66.7	66.3	66.5	66.6	66.4	66.1	66.4	66.3	66.4
Employed	119,995	120,424	120,665	119,636	119,747	119,349	119,948	119,875	120,209
Employment-population ratio	64.2	63.8	63.9	64.0	63.6	63.3	63.6	63.5	63.6
Unemployed	4,640	4,804	4,951	4,900	5,219	5,243	5,297	5,233	5,218
Unemployment rate	3.7	3.8	3.9	3.9	4.2	4.2	4.2	4.2	4.2
Not in labor force	62,353	63,585	63,341	62,452	63,346	63,887	63,399	63,705	63,529
Men, 20 years and over									
Civilian labor force	64,972	65,337	65,552	64,935	65,224	65,018	65,202	65,230	65,504
Participation rate	76.6	76.2	76.4	76.6	76.3	76.0	76.2	76.1	76.4
Employed	62,895	63,143	63,307	62,712	62,768	62,556	62,646	62,748	63,091
Employment-population ratio	74.2	73.7	73.8	73.9	73.5	73.1	73.2	73.2	73.5
Unemployed	2,077	2,194	2,245	2,223	2,456	2,462	2,556	2,482	2,413
Unemployment rate	3.2	3.4	3.4	3.4	3.8	3.8	3.9	3.8	3.7
Women, 20 years and over									
Civilian labor force	53,879	54,355	54,539	53,594	53,922	53,961	54,209	54,093	54,214
Participation rate	60.4	60.4	60.5	60.1	60.0	60.0	60.3	60.1	60.2
Employed	52,066	52,476	52,645	51,700	51,957	51,978	52,300	52,149	52,250
Employment-population ratio	58.3	58.3	58.4	57.9	57.9	57.8	58.1	57.9	58.0
Unemployed	1,813	1,878	1,893	1,893	1,965	1,983	1,909	1,944	1,964
Unemployment rate	3.4	3.5	3.5	3.5	3.6	3.7	3.5	3.6	3.6
Both sexes, 16 to 19 years									
Civilian labor force	5,785	5,536	5,525	6,008	5,820	5,614	5,834	5,785	5,709
Participation rate	44.7	42.3	42.2	46.4	44.6	43.0	44.6	44.2	43.6
Employed	5,034	4,805	4,712	5,223	5,022	4,816	5,002	4,979	4,868
Employment-population ratio	38.9	36.7	36.0	40.4	38.5	36.9	38.3	38.1	37.2
Unemployed	751	731	812	784	797	798	832	807	840
Unemployment rate	13.0	13.2	14.7	13.1	13.7	14.2	14.3	13.9	14.7
Black or African American									
Civilian noninstitutional population	27,193	27,627	27,666	27,193	27,498	27,541	27,584	27,627	27,666
Civilian labor force	17,489	17,520	17,481	17,444	17,645	17,523	17,493	17,422	17,457
Participation rate	64.3	63.4	63.2	64.2	64.2	63.6	63.4	63.1	63.1
Employed	16,021	16,085	16,027	15,950	16,229	16,175	16,077	15,938	15,993
Employment-population ratio	58.9	58.2	57.9	58.7	59.0	58.7	58.3	57.7	57.8
Unemployed	1,469	1,435	1,454	1,494	1,416	1,349	1,416	1,484	1,464
Unemployment rate	8.4	8.2	8.3	8.6	8.0	7.7	8.1	8.5	8.4
Not in labor force	9,704	10,107	10,184	9,749	9,854	10,018	10,090	10,204	10,208
Men, 20 years and over									
Civilian labor force	7,831	7,896	7,930	7,778	7,987	7,955	7,884	7,814	7,897
Participation rate	71.6	71.0	71.2	71.1	72.2	71.8	71.0	70.3	70.9
Employed	7,220	7,274	7,316	7,170	7,383	7,411	7,303	7,178	7,281
Employment-population ratio	66.0	65.4	65.7	65.5	66.7	66.9	65.8	64.6	65.4
Unemployed	611	622	613	608	604	545	581	636	616
Unemployment rate	7.8	7.9	7.7	7.8	7.6	6.8	7.4	8.1	7.8
Women, 20 years and over									
Civilian labor force	8,814	8,863	8,789	8,798	8,880	8,808	8,852	8,838	8,776
Participation rate	64.6	64.0	63.4	64.4	64.4	63.8	64.0	63.8	63.3
Employed	8,177	8,243	8,161	8,152	8,274	8,241	8,235	8,203	8,160
Employment-population ratio	59.9	59.5	58.8	59.7	60.0	59.7	59.5	59.2	58.8
Unemployed	637	620	627	647	605	567	618	635	616
Unemployment rate	7.2	7.0	7.1	7.4	6.8	6.4	7.0	7.2	7.0

Even though unemployment rates rise and fall with the strength of the economy, for several decades the unemployment rates for African-Americans have been twice the rates for whites. Often having fewer marketable skills and less education than whites, besides facing long-standing discrimination in the labor force, African-Americans are more likely to remain unemployed for longer periods, especially during a recession. As a result, they are more likely to be labeled as "long-term unemployed" (those without work for at least twenty-seven weeks).

In November 2007 the unemployment rate for African-American men twenty years and older (616,000, or 7.8%) was more than twice that of white men of the same age (2.4 million, or 3.7%). (See Table 4.1.) African-American

TABLE 4.1

Employment status of the civilian population, by race, sex, and age, 2006–07 [CONTINUED]

[Numbers in thousands]

	Not seasonally adjusted			Seasonally adjusted[a]					
Employment status race, sex, and age	Nov. 2006	Oct. 2007	Nov. 2007	Nov. 2006	July 2007	Aug. 2007	Sept. 2007	Oct. 2007	Nov. 2007
Both sexes, 16 to 19 years									
Civilian labor force	844	761	763	868	778	760	757	770	784
Participation rate	32.5	28.6	28.7	33.4	29.4	28.7	28.6	29.0	29.5
Employed	624	568	549	629	572	523	539	558	553
Employment-population ratio	24.0	21.4	20.7	24.2	21.6	19.7	20.3	21.0	20.8
Unemployed	220	192	214	239	206	237	218	212	231
Unemployment rate	26.1	25.3	28.0	27.6	26.5	31.2	28.8	27.6	29.5
Asian									
Civilian noninstitutional population	10,214	10,719	10,731	b	b	b	b	b	b
Civilian labor force	6,779	7,069	7,222	b	b	b	b	b	b
Participation rate	66.4	65.9	67.3	b	b	b	b	b	b
Employed	6,565	6,806	6,960	b	b	b	b	b	b
Employment-population ratio	64.3	63.5	64.9	b	b	b	b	b	b
Unemployed	214	263	262	b	b	b	b	b	b
Unemployment rate	3.2	3.7	3.6	b	b	b	b	b	b
Not in labor force	3,435	3,650	3,509	b	b	b	b	b	b

[a]The population figures are not adjusted for seasonal variation; therefore, identical numbers appear in the unadjusted and seasonally adjusted columns.
[b]Data not available.
Note: Estimates for the above race groups will not sum to totals because data are not presented for all races. Beginning in January 2007, data reflect revised population controls used in the household survey.

SOURCE: "Table A-2. Employment Status of the Civilian Population by Race, Sex, and Age," in *The Employment Situation: November 2007,* U.S. Department of Labor, Bureau of Labor Statistics, December 7, 2007, http://www.bls.gov/news.release/pdf/empsit.pdf (accessed December 17, 2007)

women aged twenty and older (616,000, or 7%) had nearly twice the unemployment rate of white women twenty years and older (1.9 million, or 3.6%).

Hispanics

The Bureau of Labor Statistics (BLS) began maintaining annual employment data on Hispanics in 1973. In November 2007, 21.9 million (68.8%) Hispanics were employed or actively looking for work. (See Table 4.2.) As of the third quarter of 2007, Mexican-Americans had the highest overall participation rate among the three largest Hispanic groups in the United States. More than two out of three Mexican-Americans participated in the civilian labor force (13.9 million, or 69.7%), followed by Puerto Ricans (1.6 million, 59.9%) and Cuban-Americans (876,000, or 59.8%). (See Table 4.3.) Men twenty years and older in all three groups had a much higher labor force participation rate than did women of the same age. This difference in labor force participation rates was especially pronounced for Mexican-Americans. Among Mexican-Americans, 8.2 million (86.6%) men and nearly 4.9 million (58%) women participated in the labor force. Among Cuban-Americans, 464,000 (69%) men and 389,000 (55.2%) women participated in the labor force. Among Puerto Ricans, 766,000 (68.8%) men and 758,000 (57.5%) women participated in the labor force.

The unemployment rate for Hispanics in November 2007 was 5.7% (1.2 million). (See Table 4.3.) The unemployment rate varies among Hispanic people depending on the country of origin. In the third quarter of 2007 the Puerto Rican–origin population had the highest rate of unemployment at 8.4% (136,000). Cuban-Americans had a much lower unemployment rate (49,000 people, for a rate of 5.6%), and Mexican-Americans had the lowest unemployment rate of the Hispanic subgroups at 5.3% (738,000). The unemployment rate for all Hispanic groups had risen significantly from the third quarter of 2006, when it was 5.3%.

Asian-Americans

In November 2007, 7.2 million Asian-Americans aged sixteen and older were in the civilian labor force, for a labor force participation rate of 67.3%. (See Table 4.1.) In 2006, the most recent year for which detailed data are available, 3 million (60.4%) Asian-American women and 3.5 million (78.3%) Asian-American men aged twenty and older were in the labor force. (See Table 4.4.) In that year, a higher percentage of Asian-American men aged twenty and older were participating in the labor force than either white men (64.5 million, or 76.4%) or African-American men (7.7 million, or 71.1%). Among women aged twenty and older, a higher percentage of African-American women (8.7 million, or 64.2%) were participating in the labor force than were Asian-American women (3 million, or 60.4%). However, both groups of minority women were participating in the labor force at rates higher than white women (53.3 million, or 59.9%) in that year.

Unemployment figures for Asians and Pacific Islanders are similar to those for non-Hispanic whites. In November

TABLE 4.2

Employment status of the Hispanic population by sex and age, 2006–07

[Numbers in thousands]

Employment status, sex, and age	Not seasonally adjusted			Seasonally adjusted[a]					
	Nov. 2006	Oct. 2007	Nov. 2007	Nov. 2006	July 2007	Aug. 2007	Sept. 2007	Oct. 2007	Nov. 2007
Hispanic or Latino ethnicity									
Civilian noninstitutional population	30,508	31,714	31,809	30,508	31,423	31,520	31,617	31,714	31,809
Civilian labor force	21,048	21,811	21,937	20,994	21,602	21,795	21,901	21,775	21,895
Participation rate	69.0	68.8	69.0	68.8	68.7	69.1	69.3	68.7	68.8
Employed	20,006	20,656	20,701	19,953	20,331	20,599	20,654	20,563	20,656
Employment-population ratio	65.6	65.1	65.1	65.4	64.7	65.4	65.3	64.8	64.9
Unemployed	1,042	1,155	1,236	1,042	1,271	1,196	1,247	1,212	1,239
Unemployment rate	5.0	5.3	5.6	5.0	5.9	5.5	5.7	5.6	5.7
Not in labor force	9,460	9,903	9,872	9,513	9,821	9,725	9,716	9,939	9,914
Men, 20 years and over									
Civilian labor force	12,127	12,509	12,592	b	b	b	b	b	b
Participation rate	85.2	84.5	84.8	b	b	b	b	b	b
Employed	11,664	11,937	12,023	b	b	b	b	b	b
Employment-population ratio	82.0	80.6	81.0	b	b	b	b	b	b
Unemployed	463	571	569	b	b	b	b	b	b
Unemployment rate	3.8	4.6	4.5	b	b	b	b	b	b
Women, 20 years and over									
Civilian labor force	7,839	8,205	8,246	b	b	b	b	b	b
Participation rate	58.4	58.9	59.0	b	b	b	b	b	b
Employed	7,437	7,811	7,760	b	b	b	b	b	b
Employment-population ratio	55.4	56.1	55.6	b	b	b	b	b	
Unemployed	402	394	485	b	b	b	b	b	b
Unemployment rate	5.1	4.8	5.9	b	b	b	b	b	b
Both sexes, 16 to 19 years									
Civilian labor force	1,081	1,098	1,100	b	b	b	b	b	b
Participation rate	38.0	36.8	36.8	b	b	b	b	b	b
Employed	904	907	918	b	b	b	b	b	b
Employment-population ratio	31.8	30.4	30.7	b	b	b	b	b	b
Unemployed	177	190	182	b	b	b	b	b	b
Unemployment rate	16.4	17.3	16.5	b	b	b	b	b	b

[a]The population figures are not adjusted for seasonal variation; therefore, identical numbers appear in the unadjusted and seasonally adjusted columns.
[b]Data available.
Note: Persons whose ethnicity is identified as Hispanic or Latino may be of any race. Beginning in January 2007, data reflect revised population controls used in the household survey.

SOURCE: "Table A-3. Employment Status of the Hispanic or Latino Population by Sex and Age," in *The Employment Situation: November 2007*, U.S. Department of Labor, Bureau of Labor Statistics, December 7, 2007, http://www.bls.gov/news.release/pdf/empsit.pdf (accessed December 17, 2007)

2007 the unemployment rate for Asians and Pacific Islanders was 3.6% (262,000), slightly lower than the unemployment rate of 4.2% (5.2 million) for the white population. (See Table 4.1.) The low rate of unemployment among Asians and Pacific Islanders can be attributed, in part, to their high educational attainment and their commitment to small family businesses.

Older Asians and Pacific Islanders tend to work longer because of the strong work ethic in Asian cultures and frequently because of economic need. Often, they are employed in family businesses that do not offer retirement benefits. Depending on the time of their immigration and their work history, Asians and Pacific Islanders aged sixty-five and older may not be entitled to adequate Social Security benefits. Also, some may have immigrated under circumstances that prevented them from retaining any wealth they might have accumulated in their native lands.

Native Americans and Alaskan Natives

Gathering accurate statistical data on the labor force participation rates of Native Americans is difficult. They are often counted as "other" in BLS and Census Bureau data, making specific information hard to obtain. In addition, the concepts that guide the assessment of labor force participation nationally are considered to be inappropriate for Native American population groups. According to Judith Kleinfeld and John A. Kruse, in "Native Americans in the Labor Force: Hunting for an Accurate Measure" (*Monthly Labor Review*, July 1982), because few jobs are available on many reservations, adults do not actively seek work—but to exclude these individuals from the statistics on the labor force results in a serious underestimation of unemployment of Native Americans.

In *We the People: American Indians and Alaska Natives in the United States* (February 2006, http://www.census.gov/prod/2006pubs/censr-28.pdf), Stella U. Ogunwole of the Cen-

TABLE 4.3

Employment status of the Mexican, Puerto Rican, and Cuban population, by sex and age, 2006–07

[Numbers in thousands]

Employment status, sex, and age	Hispanic or Latino ethnicity							
	Total[a]		Mexican		Puerto Rican		Cuban	
	III 2006	III 2007	III 2006	III 2007	III 2006	III 2007	III 2006	III 2007
Total								
Civilian noninstitutional population	30,232	31,520	19,091	19,985	2,602	2,701	1,345	1,465
Civilian labor force	20,697	21,781	13,205	13,921	1,521	1,619	779	876
Percent of population	68.5	69.1	69.2	69.7	58.4	59.9	57.9	59.8
Employed	19,608	20,549	12,555	13,183	1,395	1,483	746	827
Unemployed	1,090	1,232	650	738	126	136	34	49
Unemployment rate	5.3	5.7	4.9	5.3	8.3	8.4	4.3	5.6
Not in labor force	9,535	9,738	5,885	6,064	1,082	1,082	566	589
Men, 16 years and over								
Civilian noninstitutional population	15,542	16,226	10,021	10,457	1,215	1,250	668	721
Civilian labor force	12,492	13,043	8,262	8,606	797	816	463	478
Percent of population	80.4	80.4	82.5	82.3	65.6	65.2	69.3	66.4
Employed	11,908	12,404	7,897	8,225	735	746	447	453
Unemployed	583	639	365	381	62	69	16	26
Unemployment rate	4.7	4.9	4.4	4.4	7.8	8.5	3.4	5.3
Not in labor force	3,050	3,183	1,759	1,851	419	434	205	242
Men, 20 years and over								
Civilian noninstitutional population	14,106	14,714	9,072	9,440	1,088	1,114	626	672
Civilian labor force	11,864	12,428	7,837	8,172	748	766	452	464
Percent of population	84.1	84.5	86.4	86.6	68.7	68.8	72.3	69.0
Employed	11,394	11,913	7,547	7,874	698	709	438	439
Unemployed	470	515	290	298	50	58	14	25
Unemployment rate	4.0	4.1	3.7	3.6	6.6	7.5	3.1	5.4
Not in labor force	2,242	2,286	1,235	1,268	340	348	173	208
Women, 16 years and over								
Civilian noninstitutional population	14,691	15,293	9,070	9,528	1,387	1,451	677	745
Civilian labor force	8,206	8,738	4,943	5,315	724	803	316	398
Percent of population	55.9	57.1	54.5	55.8	52.2	55.4	46.7	53.4
Employed	7,699	8,145	4,658	4,958	660	736	299	375
Unemployed	506	592	285	357	64	67	18	23
Unemployment rate	6.2	6.8	5.8	6.7	8.9	8.3	5.6	5.8
Not in labor force	6,485	6,555	4,127	4,213	663	647	361	347
Women, 20 years and over								
Civilian noninstitutional population	13,314	13,847	8,153	8,535	1,256	1,319	627	705
Civilian labor force	7,714	8,234	4,618	4,953	677	758	306	389
Percent of population	57.9	59.5	56.6	58.0	53.9	57.5	48.8	55.2
Employed	7,287	7,724	4,386	4,655	622	702	289	367
Unemployed	428	510	232	297	55	56	17	23
Unemployment rate	5.5	6.2	5.0	6.0	8.1	7.4	5.5	5.8
Not in labor force	5,600	5,613	3,535	3,582	579	561	321	316
Both sexes, 16 to 19 years								
Civilian noninstitutional population	2,813	2,959	1,866	2,010	259	267	92	88
Civilian labor force	1,119	1,118	751	796	96	95	21	23
Percent of population	39.8	37.8	40.3	39.6	37.2	35.4	22.8	25.8
Employed	927	912	622	653	75	72	18	22
Unemployed	192	206	129	143	21	23	2	1
Unemployment rate	17.1	18.4	17.1	17.9	22.2	24.0	b	b
Not in labor force	1,693	1,840	1,115	1,214	162	173	71	66

[a]Includes persons of Central or South American origin and of other Hispanic or Latino ethnicity, not shown separately.
[b]Data not shown where base is less than 60,000.
Note: Persons whose ethnicity is identified as Hispanic or Latino may be of any race. Beginning in January 2007, data reflect revised population controls used in the household survey.

SOURCE: "Table D-12. Employment Status of the Hispanic or Latino Population by Sex, Age, and Detailed Ethnic Group," in *Employment and Earnings*, U.S. Department of Labor, Bureau of Labor Statistics, 2007, http://www.bls.gov/web/cpseed12.pdf (accessed December 19, 2007)

sus Bureau indicates that in 2000, 33.5% of Native Americans and Alaskan Natives lived in "American Indian areas"—that is, reservations or trust lands. In *American Indian Population and Labor Force Report, 2003* (2003, http://www.doi.gov/bia/laborforce/2003LaborForceReportFinalAll.pdf), the Bureau of Indian Affairs notes that in 2003 unemployment rates varied greatly among reservations. The highest rates were in the

Native Village of Point Hope (98%), Beaver Village (89%), the Knik Tribe (89%), Arctic Village (88%), the Native Village of Tyonek (88%), and Douglas (87%). In contrast, the Nightmute (3%), Anchorage (8%), and Newhalen Village (8%) had single-digit unemployment rates. Regardless, many tribes had unemployment rates well over 50%. The overall unemployment rate was 49% in 2003.

TABLE 4.4

Employment status of the civilian noninstitutional population, by sex, age, and race, 2005–06

[Numbers in thousands]

Employment status, sex, and age	Total 2005	Total 2006	White 2005	White 2006	Black or African American 2005	Black or African American 2006	Asian 2005	Asian 2006
Total								
Civilian noninstitutional population	226,082	228,815	184,446	186,264	26,517	27,007	9,842	10,155
Civilian labor force	149,320	151,428	122,299	123,834	17,013	17,314	6,503	6,727
Percent of population	66.0	66.2	66.3	66.5	64.2	64.1	66.1	66.2
Employed	141,730	144,427	116,949	118,833	15,313	15,765	6,244	6,522
Unemployed	7,591	7,001	5,350	5,002	1,700	1,549	259	205
Unemployment rate	5.1	4.6	4.4	4.0	10.0	8.9	4.0	3.0
Not in labor force	76,762	77,387	62,148	62,429	9,504	9,693	3,339	3,427
Men, 16 years and over								
Civilian noninstitutional population	109,151	110,605	90,027	91,021	11,882	12,130	4,679	4,827
Civilian labor force	80,033	81,255	66,694	67,613	7,998	8,128	3,500	3,621
Percent of population	73.3	73.5	74.1	74.3	67.3	67.0	74.8	75.0
Employed	75,973	77,502	63,763	64,883	7,155	7,354	3,359	3,511
Unemployed	4,059	3,753	2,931	2,730	844	774	141	110
Unemployment rate	5.1	4.6	4.4	4.0	10.5	9.5	4.0	3.0
Not in labor force	29,119	29,350	23,334	23,408	3,884	4,002	1,178	1,206
Men, 20 years and over								
Civilian noninstitutional population	100,835	102,145	83,556	84,466	10,659	10,864	4,361	4,515
Civilian labor force	76,443	77,562	63,705	64,540	7,600	7,720	3,419	3,535
Percent of population	75.8	75.9	76.2	76.4	71.3	71.1	78.4	78.3
Employed	73,050	74,431	61,255	62,259	6,901	7,079	3,292	3,437
Unemployed	3,392	3,131	2,450	2,281	699	640	127	98
Unemployment rate	4.4	4.0	3.8	3.5	9.2	8.3	3.7	2.8
Not in labor force	24,392	24,584	19,851	19,927	3,060	3,144	942	980
Women, 16 years and over								
Civilian noninstitutional population	116,931	118,210	94,419	95,242	14,635	14,877	5,163	5,328
Civilian labor force	69,288	70,173	55,605	56,221	9,014	9,186	3,002	3,106
Percent of population	59.3	59.4	58.9	59.0	61.6	61.7	58.2	58.3
Employed	65,757	66,925	53,186	53,950	8,158	8,410	2,885	3,011
Unemployed	3,531	3,247	2,419	2,271	856	775	118	95
Unemployment rate	5.1	4.6	4.4	4.0	9.5	8.4	3.9	3.1
Not in labor force	47,643	48,037	38,814	39,021	5,621	5,691	2,161	2,222
Women, 20 years and over								
Civilian noninstitutional population	108,850	109,992	88,200	88,942	13,377	13,578	4,864	5,027
Civilian labor force	65,714	66,585	52,643	53,286	8,610	8,723	2,923	3,038
Percent of population	60.4	60.5	59.7	59.9	64.4	64.2	60.1	60.4
Employed	62,702	63,834	50,589	51,359	7,876	8,068	2,812	2,953
Unemployed	3,013	2,751	2,054	1,927	734	656	111	85
Unemployment rate	4.6	4.1	3.9	3.6	8.5	7.5	3.8	2.8
Not in labor force	43,136	43,407	35,557	35,656	4,768	4,854	1,941	1,989
Both sexes, 16 to 19 years								
Civilian noninstitutional population	16,398	16,678	12,690	12,856	2,481	2,565	616	613
Civilian labor force	7,164	7,281	5,950	6,009	803	871	160	154
Percent of population	43.7	43.7	46.9	46.7	32.4	34.0	26.0	25.1
Employed	5,978	6,162	5,105	5,215	536	618	140	132
Unemployed	1,186	1,119	845	794	267	253	20	22
Unemployment rate	16.6	15.4	14.2	13.2	33.3	29.1	12.4	14.0
Not in labor force	9,234	9,397	6,739	6,847	1,677	1,694	456	459

Note: Estimates for the above race groups (white, black or African American, and Asian) do not sum to totals because data are not presented for all races. Beginning in January 2006, data reflect revised population controls used in the household survey.

SOURCE: "5. Employment Status of the Civilian Noninstitutional Population by Sex, Age, and Race," in *Employment and Earnings*, U.S. Department of Labor, Bureau of Labor Statistics, 2007, http://www.bls.gov/cps/cpsaat5.pdf (accessed December 19, 2007)

In many cases reservations do not generate the jobs necessary to support Native American families. Even when Native Americans are employed, the Bureau of Indian Affairs notes that fully a third (32%) of employed individuals earn wages below the poverty guidelines. This is a major reason that the leadership on Native American reservations has been so willing to introduce or expand casino gambling on their reservations. William N. Evans and Julie H. Topoleski of the University of Maryland note in *The Social and Economic Impact of Native American Casinos* (August 7, 2002, http://www.bsos.umd.edu/econ/evans/wpapers/evans_topoleski_casinos.pdf) that the 310 gaming operations run by more than 200 tribes have increased employment by 26%, while increasing tribal population by about 12% (as Native Americans who left the reservation in search of jobs elsewhere return), resulting in an increase in employment to population ratio of about 12%. In addition, the proportion of adults who work but earn wages below the poverty line decreased by 14%. In "Lands of Opportunity: Social and Economic Effects of Tribal Gaming on Localities" (*Policy Matters*, vol. 1, no. 4, summer 2007), Mindy Marks and Kate Spilde Contreras of the University of California, Riverside, come to similar conclusions regarding tribal gaming in California, noting that the economic benefits often help the people most in need. The researchers note that "tribal governments with gaming are concentrating employment opportunity in areas that are economically worse off than areas without gaming reservations."

DISCRIMINATORY EMPLOYMENT PRACTICES

Under Title VII of the Civil Rights Act of 1964, employers may not intentionally use race, skin color, age, gender, religious beliefs, or national origin as the basis for decisions relating to almost any aspect of the employment relationship, including hiring. Despite this law, African-Americans, Hispanics, and other minority groups do suffer from discriminatory hiring practices as well as other race- and ethnicity-based obstacles to finding employment.

In one of the highest profile workplace discrimination cases in recent years, civil rights attorneys filed a class action lawsuit on June 17, 2003, against Abercrombie & Fitch, one of the nation's largest clothing retailers, for discriminating against people of Hispanic, Asian, and African-American descent. The young adults were represented by the Mexican American Legal Defense and Education Fund, the Asian Pacific American Legal Center, and the National Association for the Advancement of Colored People's Legal Defense and Educational Fund. In "Lieff Cabraser and Civil Rights Organizations Announce Abercrombie & Fitch Charged with Employment Discrimination in Federal Class Action Lawsuit" (June 17, 2003, http://www .afjustice.com/press_release_01.htm), Thomas A. Saenzof the Mexican American Legal Defense and Educational Fund is quoted as saying: "Through means both subtle and direct, Abercrombie has consistently reinforced to its store managers that they must recruit and maintain an overwhelmingly white workforce." AFjustice.com indicates in the press release "$40 Million Payment, Detailed Plan for Diversity in Employment Discrimination Suit against Retail Giant Abercrombie & Fitch" (November 16, 2004, http://www.afjustice.com/press_release_02.htm) that the lawsuit was settled in November 2004, requiring the company to pay $40 million to the applicants and employees who charged the company with discrimination as well as to comply with provisions related to the recruitment, hiring, job assignment, training, and promotion of minority employees. Even though this was a prominent case brought to court, discriminatory employ-

ment practices are difficult to prosecute effectively and remain pervasive in the United States.

In another important case, the federal government filed a lawsuit in 2006 against a medical clinic in California because a manager used racial code words, including "reggin," which Barbara Feder Ostrov reports in "Discrimination at Work Growing Subtle" (*San Jose Mercury News*, August 12, 2006) was the "infamous racial slur spelled backward." An African-American file clerk was fired from her job after she complained about the racial slurs. The case underscored the changing nature of racial and ethnic discrimination in the workplace, as methods of intimidation become more subtle. This kind of subtle discrimination does not always lead to lawsuits. In fact, the Level Playing Field Institute reports in *The Cost of Employee Turnover Due Solely to Unfairness in the Workplace* (2007, http://www .lpfi.org/docs/cl-executive-summary.pdf) that each year two million professionals and managers leave their jobs because they are "pushed out by cumulative small comments, whispered jokes and not-so-funny emails."

Equal Employment Opportunity Commission

On May 17, 2000, the U.S. Equal Employment Opportunity Commission (EEOC) issued new guidelines to facilitate the settlement of federal-sector discrimination complaints, including claims brought under Title VII. Under the administration of Chairperson Ida L. Castro (1953–), the EEOC sought to reform its complaint process for federal employees. The new directive authorizes federal agencies to enter into settlement of bias claims, including monetary payment.

In fiscal year 2006 the EEOC received 27,238 charges under Title VII alleging race-based discrimination. (See Table 4.5.) That same year, the EEOC resolved 25,992 charges (some of these cases were carried over from the previous year). Of those, 3,039 (11.7%) were settled, with payments totaling $61.4 million to the charging parties. The percent of cases settled was up substantially since 1997, when only 3.3% were settled. In 2006 another 1,016 (3.9%) of the claims were found to have reasonable cause; 292 (1.1%) of these were charges with reasonable cause closed after successful conciliation and 724 (2.8%) of them were charges with reasonable cause closed after unsuccessful conciliation. Another 1,177 (4.5%) cases were withdrawn by the charging party on receipt of desired benefits ("withdrawals with benefits"). In other words, over fifty-five hundred cases of racial discrimination were found to have reasonable cause or were settled or withdrawn after the employer admitted culpability and submitted to a monetary settlement. Countless other incidents of racial discrimination in the workplace are never brought to the attention of the EEOC. Instead, victims suffer silently or leave their places of employment, as found by the Level Playing Field Institute Survey.

TABLE 4.5

Race-based charges filed and resolved under Title VII of the Civil Rights Act of 1964, fiscal years 1997–2006

[Total number of charge receipts filed and resolved under Title VII alleging race-based discrimination]

	FY 1997	FY 1998	FY 1999	FY 2000	FY 2001	FY 2002	FY 2003	FY 2004	FY 2005	FY 2006
Receipts	29,199	28,820	28,819	28,945	28,912	29,910	28,526	27,696	26,740	27,238
Resolutions	36,419	35,716	35,094	33,188	32,077	33,199	30,702	29,631	27,411	25,992
Resolutions by type										
Settlements	1,206	1,460	2,138	2,802	2,549	3,059	2,890	2,927	2,801	3,039
	3.30%	4.10%	6.10%	8.40%	7.90%	9.20%	9.40%	9.90%	10.20%	11.70%
Withdrawals with benefits	912	823	1,036	1,150	1,203	1,200	1,125	1,088	1,167	1,177
	2.50%	2.30%	3.00%	3.50%	3.80%	3.60%	3.70%	3.70%	4.30%	4.50%
Administrative closures	8,395	7,871	7,213	5,727	5,626	5,043	4,759	4,261	3,674	3,436
	23.10%	22.00%	20.60%	17.30%	17.50%	15.20%	15.50%	14.40%	13.40%	13.20%
No reasonable cause	24,988	24,515	23,148	21,319	20,302	21,853	20,506	20,166	18,608	17,324
	68.60%	68.60%	66.00%	64.20%	63.30%	65.80%	66.80%	68.10%	67.90%	66.70%
Reasonable cause	918	1,047	1,559	2,190	2,397	2,044	1,422	1,189	1,161	1,016
	2.50%	2.90%	4.40%	6.60%	7.50%	6.20%	4.60%	4.00%	4.20%	3.90%
Successful conciliations	248	287	382	529	691	580	392	330	377	292
	0.70%	0.80%	1.10%	1.60%	2.20%	1.70%	1.30%	1.10%	1.40%	1.10%
Unsuccessful conciliations	670	760	1,177	1,661	1,706	1,464	1,030	859	784	724
	1.80%	2.10%	3.40%	5.00%	5.30%	4.40%	3.40%	2.90%	2.90%	2.80%
Merit resolutions	3,036	3,330	4,733	6,142	6,149	6,303	5,437	5,204	5,129	5,232
	8.30%	9.30%	13.50%	18.50%	19.20%	19.00%	17.70%	17.60%	18.70%	20.10%
Monetary benefits (millions)*	$41.80	$32.20	$53.20	$61.70	$86.50	$81.10	$69.60	$61.10	$76.50	$61.40

*Does not include monetary benefits obtained through litigation.

Notes: The total of individual percentages may not always sum to 100% due to rounding. Equal Employment Opportutunity Commission (EEOC) total workload includes charges carried over from previous fiscal years, new charge receipts and charges transferred to EEOC from Fair Employment Practice Agencies (FEPAs). Resolution of charges each year may therefore exceed receipts for that year because workload being resolved is drawn from a combination of pending, new receipts and FEPA transfer charges rather than from new charges only.

SOURCE: "Race-Based Charges, FY 1997–FY 2006," in *Enforcement Statistics and Litigation*, U.S. Equal Employment Opportunity Commission, Office of Research, Information, and Planning, January 31, 2007, http://www.eeoc.gov/stats/race.html (accessed December 19, 2007)

Views of Economic Opportunities

Non-Hispanic whites are much more likely than African-Americans and Hispanics to believe that members of minority groups have equal job opportunities in the United States. In *Whites, Minorities Differ in Views of Economic Opportunities in U.S.* (July 10, 2006, http://www.gallup.com/poll/23617/Whites-Minorities-Differ-Views-Economic-Opportunities-US.aspx), Joseph Carroll of the Gallup Organization reports on a June 2006 poll that asked the question: "Do you feel that racial minorities in this country have equal job opportunities as whites, or not?" Carroll notes that there were stark differences in the responses of non-Hispanic whites and members of minority groups. Over half (53%) of non-Hispanic whites surveyed believed members of minority groups have equal job opportunities. (See Figure 4.1.) By contrast, only a third (34%) of Hispanics surveyed believed this was true, down significantly from 46% in June 2001. Only 17% of African-Americans surveyed believed the job opportunities for minorities are equal to those of whites, down from 23% the previous year but basically unchanged from 2001.

WORKFORCE PROJECTIONS FOR 2016

In 2006 the percent of the workforce of Hispanic origin (13.7%) was higher than the percent of the workforce that was African-American (11.4%). (See Table 4.6.)

FIGURE 4.1

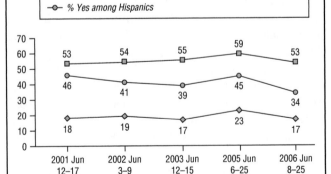

Public opinion on equal job opportunities, selected years 2001–06

DO YOU FEEL THAT RACIAL MINORITIES IN THIS COUNTRY HAVE JOB OPPORTUNITIES EQUAL TO WHITES, OR NOT?

SOURCE: Joseph Carroll, "Do You Feel That Racial Minorities in This Country Have Equal Job Opportunities As Whites, or Not?" in *Whites, Minorities Differ in Views of Economic Opportunities in U.S.*, The Gallup Organization, July 10, 2006, http://www.gallup.com/poll/23617/Whites-Minorities-Differ-Views-Economic-Opportunities-US.aspx?version=print (accessed January 16, 2008). Copyright © 2008 by The Gallup Organization. Reproduced by Permission of The Gallup Organization.

TABLE 4.6

Civilian labor force, by age, sex, race, and ethnicity, 1986, 1996, 2006, and projected 2016

[Numbers in thousands]

Group	Level				Change			Percent change			Annual growth rate			Percent distribution			
	1986	1996	2006	2016	1986–96	1996–2006	2006–16	1986–96	1996–2006	2006–16	1986–96	1996–2006	2006–16	1986	1996	2006	2016
Total, 16 years and older	117,834	133,943	151,428	164,232	16,109	17,485	12,804	13.7	13.1	8.5	1.3	1.2	0.8	100.0	100.0	100.0	100.0
Age, years																	
16 to 24	23,367	21,183	22,394	20,852	–2,184	1,211	–1,542	–9.3	5.7	–6.9	–1.0	.6	–.7	19.8	15.8	14.8	12.7
25 to 54	79,563	96,786	103,566	106,026	17,223	6,780	2,460	21.6	7.0	2.4	2.0	.7	.2	67.5	72.3	68.4	64.6
55 and older	14,904	15,974	25,468	37,354	1,070	9,494	11,886	7.2	59.4	46.7	.7	4.8	3.9	12.6	11.9	16.8	22.7
Sex																	
Men	65,422	72,087	81,255	87,781	6,665	9,168	6,526	10.2	12.7	8.0	1.0	1.2	.8	55.5	53.8	53.7	53.4
Women	52,413	61,857	70,173	76,450	9,444	8,316	6,277	18.0	13.4	8.9	1.7	1.3	.9	44.5	46.2	46.3	46.6
Race																	
White	101,801	113,108	123,834	130,665	11,307	10,726	6,831	11.1	9.5	5.5	1.1	.9	.5	86.4	84.4	81.8	79.6
Black	12,654	15,134	17,314	20,121	2,480	2,180	2,807	19.6	14.4	16.2	1.8	1.4	1.5	10.7	11.3	11.4	12.3
Asian	3,379	5,701	6,727	8,741	2,322	1,026	2,014	68.7	18.0	29.9	5.4	1.7	2.7	2.9	4.3	4.4	5.3
All other groups[1]	—	—	3,553	4,705	—	—	1,152	—	—	32.4	—	—	2.8	—	—	2.3	2.9
Ethnicity																	
Hispanic origin	8,076	12,774	20,694	26,889	4,698	7,920	6,195	58.2	62.0	29.9	4.7	4.9	2.7	6.9	9.5	13.7	16.4
Other than Hispanic origin	109,758	121,169	130,734	137,343	11,411	9,565	6,609	10.4	7.9	5.1	1.0	.8	.5	93.1	90.5	86.3	83.6
White non-Hispanic	94,027	100,915	104,629	106,133	6,888	3,714	1,504	7.3	3.7	1.4	.7	.4	.1	79.8	75.3	69.1	64.6
Age of baby boomers	22 to 40	32 to 50	42 to 60	52 to 70													

*The "all other groups" category includes (1) those classified as being of multiple racial origin and (2) the race categories of (2a) American Indian and Alaska Native and (2b) Native Hawaiian and other Pacific Islanders. Dash indicates no data collected for category.

SOURCE: Mitra Toossi, "Table 1. Civilian Labor Force, by Age, Sex, Race, and Ethnicity, 1986, 1996, 2006, and Projected 2016," in "Labor Force Projections to 2016: More Workers in Their Golden Years," *Monthly Labor Review*, November 2007, http://www.bls.gov/opub/mlr/2007/11/art3full.pdf (accessed December 19, 2007)

In addition, more Hispanics than African-Americans or non-Hispanic whites will enter the workforce through 2016, causing the group to make up an increasingly larger part of the workforce. The number of African-Americans in the labor force is expected to increase 16.2% during this period, whereas the number of non-Hispanic whites is expected to increase by only 1.4%. However, the number of Hispanics in the workforce is expected to increase by 29.9%. Hispanics are expected to make up 16.4% of the labor force by 2016, up from 13.7% in 2006. The growth of Hispanics in the workforce can be attributed to higher birth rates among that group as well as increased immigration.

Asian-Americans are another fast-growing group in the labor force. The proportion of Asian-Americans in the workforce is expected to increase at the same rate as Hispanics (29.9%) between 2006 and 2016, and Asian-Americans are expected to make up 5.3% of the labor force by 2016. (See Table 4.6.) As with most other minority groups, increases reflect continued high immigration and higher fertility rates among some minority populations.

As noted earlier, the non-Hispanic white labor force is expected to grow more slowly than the overall labor force in the coming decade; the non-Hispanic white proportion of the workforce will decrease from 69.1% in 2006 to 64.6% by 2016. (See Table 4.6.) As recently as 1986, non-Hispanic whites made up nearly four-fifths (79.8%) of the workforce. This decrease is due to a relatively low immigration rate of non-Hispanic whites to the United States, projected lower birth rates among the majority group than among minority populations, and declining labor force participation by non-Hispanic white men, a reflection of the aging of the white male labor force.

OCCUPATIONS
African-Americans and Jobs

African-Americans are much less likely than whites or Asian-Americans to hold the jobs requiring the most education and paying the highest salaries—those in management, professional, and related occupations. In 2006, 15.8 million African-Americans accounted for 10.9% of the civilian labor force aged sixteen and older, up slightly from the previous year. (See Table 4.7.) Only 27% of employed African-Americans held management, professional, or related occupations, compared to 35.5% of white (including many Hispanic) workers. Women of both races were more likely to hold these positions, but only 31.1% of African-American women were managers or professionals, compared to 38.9% of white women. The proportion of African-Americans who held these positions had risen slightly from the previous year.

African-Americans are much more likely than whites to work in the poorly paid service occupations. In 2006, 24.1% of African-Americans worked in service occupa-

tions, up from 23.9% the previous year. (See Table 4.7.) By contrast, 15.4% of white Americans worked in service occupations in 2006.

Any growth in professional employment for African-Americans has generally occurred in fields at the lower end of the earnings scale. The BLS notes in *Employment and Earnings* (2006, http://www.bls.gov/cps/cpsa2006.pdf) that 23.2% of all licensed practical and vocational nurses were African-American in 2006, but only 10.9% of registered nurses, 5.2% of physicians and surgeons, and 3.1% of dentists were African-American. The same pattern holds true for management positions. Even though 15% of social service and community service managers and 14.2% of education administrators were African-American in 2006, only 3.7% of construction managers, 3.1% of chief executives, and 2.9% of engineering managers were African-American.

In 2006 most African-Americans were concentrated in the management, professional, and related occupations (27%), sales and office occupations (25.7%), and service occupations (24.1%). (See Table 4.7.) Few African-Americans were employed in production, transportation, and material moving occupations (16.4%) or natural resources, construction, and maintenance occupations (6.8%). However, African-Americans were underrepresented in management, professional, and related occupations, as 34.9% of the total workforce is employed in these occupations, and overrepresented in the production, transportation, and material moving occupations, as 12.6% of the general population is employed in these occupations. African-Americans are also overrepresented in the service occupations (24.1%, vs. 16.5% of the general population).

Hispanics and Jobs

Overall, Hispanics are less likely than African-Americans to hold professional and technical positions. In 2006 only 17% of employed Hispanics held management, professional, and related occupations, compared to 27% of African-Americans. (See Table 4.7.) The largest percentage of Hispanics worked in service occupations (23.7%) and sales and office occupations (21.2%). Like African-Americans, Hispanics, except for Cuban-Americans who came to this country in 1959 following the Cuban revolution, are concentrated primarily in low-paying, low-skill jobs.

In 2006, 19.6 million Hispanics worked, making up 13.6% of the workforce. (See Table 4.7.) According to the BLS, in *Employment and Earnings*, Hispanics were concentrated in low-paying jobs and were underrepresented in management, professional, and related occupations, where they held only 6.6% of the available jobs in 2006. Hispanics were overrepresented in service occupations, making up 19.5% of the service workforce, and were concentrated in the lowest-paying occupations in this industry. They made

TABLE 4.7

Employed persons by occupation, race, Hispanic ethnicity, and sex, 2005–06

[Percent distribution]

Occupation, race, and Hispanic or Latino ethnicity	Total		Men		Women	
	2005	2006	2005	2006	2005	2006
Total						
Total, 16 years and over (thousands)	**141,730**	**144,427**	**75,973**	**77,502**	**65,757**	**66,925**
Percent	100.0	100.0	100.0	100.0	100.0	100.0
Management, professional, and related occupations	34.7	34.9	32.0	32.2	37.9	38.1
Management, business, and financial operations occupations	14.4	14.7	15.5	15.9	13.2	13.3
Professional and related occupations	20.3	20.2	16.6	16.2	24.6	24.8
Service occupations	16.3	16.5	13.0	13.1	20.2	20.4
Sales and office occupations	25.4	25.0	17.4	17.1	34.6	34.2
Sales and related occupations	11.6	11.5	11.0	10.9	12.3	12.2
Office and administrative support occupations	13.8	13.5	6.4	6.2	22.4	22.0
Natural resources, construction, and maintenance occupations	10.8	11.0	19.3	19.5	1.1	1.1
Farming, fishing, and forestry occupations	.7	.7	1.0	1.0	.3	.3
Construction and extraction occupations	6.5	6.6	11.7	11.9	.4	.4
Installation, maintenance, and repair occupations	3.7	3.7	6.6	6.6	.3	.4
Production, transportation, and material moving occupations	12.7	12.6	18.3	18.1	6.3	6.2
Production occupations	6.6	6.5	8.6	8.4	4.3	4.3
Transportation and material moving occupations	6.1	6.1	9.7	9.7	2.0	2.0
White						
Total, 16 years and over (thousands)	**116,949**	**118,833**	**63,763**	**64,883**	**53,186**	**53,950**
Percent	100.0	100.0	100.0	100.0	100.0	100.0
Management, professional, and related occupations	35.5	35.5	32.7	32.6	38.8	38.9
Management, business, and financial operations occupations	15.1	15.4	16.3	16.7	13.6	13.8
Professional and related occupations	20.4	20.1	16.3	15.9	25.2	25.2
Service occupations	15.2	15.4	12.1	12.2	19.0	19.3
Sales and office occupations	25.4	25.1	17.2	17.0	35.1	34.8
Sales and related occupations	11.9	11.8	11.3	11.3	12.5	12.4
Office and administrative support occupations	13.5	13.3	5.9	5.7	22.6	22.4
Natural resources, construction, and maintenance occupations	11.6	11.8	20.4	20.7	1.1	1.1
Farming, fishing, and forestry occupations	.8	.7	1.1	1.1	.4	.3
Construction and extraction occupations	7.0	7.1	12.4	12.7	.4	.5
Installation, maintenance, and repair occupations	3.9	3.9	6.9	6.9	.3	.4
Production, transportation, and material moving occupations	12.3	12.2	17.7	17.6	5.9	5.8
Production occupations	6.4	6.4	8.4	8.3	4.0	4.0
Transportation and material moving occupations	5.9	5.9	9.3	9.2	1.9	1.8
Black or African American						
Total, 16 years and over (thousands)	**15,313**	**15,765**	**7,155**	**7,354**	**8,158**	**8,410**
Percent	100.0	100.0	100.0	100.0	100.0	100.0
Management, professional, and related occupations	26.0	27.0	21.0	22.3	30.4	31.1
Management, business, and financial operations occupations	9.5	9.8	8.9	9.7	10.0	10.0
Professional and related occupations	16.5	17.2	12.1	12.6	20.4	21.1
Service occupations	23.9	24.1	20.0	20.4	27.3	27.3
Sales and office occupations	26.3	25.7	18.3	18.1	33.4	32.3
Sales and related occupations	9.8	9.5	8.5	8.0	11.0	10.9
Office and administrative support occupations	16.5	16.2	9.8	10.2	22.4	21.4
Natural resources, construction, and maintenance occupations	7.1	6.8	14.2	13.5	.9	1.0
Farming, fishing, and forestry occupations	.3	.3	.5	.4	.2	.2
Construction and extraction occupations	4.2	4.0	8.6	8.1	.3	.3
Installation, maintenance, and repair occupations	2.6	2.6	5.0	5.0	.4	.5
Production, transportation, and material moving occupations	16.7	16.4	26.5	25.7	8.0	8.3
Production occupations	7.6	7.3	10.2	9.7	5.3	5.2
Transportation and material moving occupations	9.1	9.1	16.3	16.0	2.7	3.1

up 26.8% of janitors and building cleaners, 37.2% of maids and housekeepers, and 40.9% of grounds maintenance workers. They also made up 21.1% of the food preparation and serving occupations—30.5% of dining room and cafeteria attendants and bartender helpers, 31.6% of cooks, and 36.7% of dishwashers. However, they made up only 15% of first-line supervisors of food preparation and serving workers and 9.4% of bartenders.

Significant occupational differences exist among Hispanic subgroups. When it comes to job outlook, Cuban-origin Hispanics have traditionally done better in securing higher-paying jobs, as these immigrants are often well educated. In 2006, 227,000 out of 778,000 (29.2%) Cuban-Americans in the workforce held professional or managerial positions. (See Table 4.8.) In contrast, 375,000 out of 1.5 million (25.3%) Puerto Ricans in the workforce and 1.8 million out of 12.5 million (14.7%) Mexican-Americans in the workforce held professional or managerial positions. Mexican-Americans were more likely to work in service occupations (3 million, or 23.9%) than in other occupations, especially in

TABLE 4.7

Employed persons by occupation, race, Hispanic ethnicity, and sex, 2005–06 [CONTINUED]

[Percent distribution]

Occupation, race, and Hispanic or Latino ethnicity	Total		Men		Women	
	2005	2006	2005	2006	2005	2006
Asian						
Total, 16 years and over (thousands)	6,244	6,522	3,359	3,511	2,885	3,011
Percent	100.0	100.0	100.0	100.0	100.0	100.0
Management, professional, and related occupations	46.4	47.3	48.0	48.7	44.5	45.7
Management, business, and financial operations occupations	15.7	15.8	15.9	16.9	15.6	14.5
Professional and related occupations	30.7	31.6	32.1	31.8	29.0	31.2
Service occupations	15.7	15.8	13.6	13.4	18.2	18.5
Sales and office occupations	23.3	22.4	18.7	18.2	28.7	27.3
Sales and related occupations	11.6	11.8	11.2	11.9	11.9	11.6
Office and administrative support occupations	11.7	10.7	7.4	6.3	16.8	15.7
Natural resources, construction, and maintenance occupations	4.4	4.4	7.6	7.6	.7	.7
Farming, fishing, and forestry occupations	.2	.2	.2	.3	.3	.2
Construction and extraction occupations	1.7	1.7	3.1	3.0	.1	.3
Installation, maintenance, and repair occupations	2.5	2.4	4.4	4.3	.3	.3
Production, transportation, and material moving occupations	10.1	10.1	12.1	12.1	7.9	7.7
Production occupations	7.3	7.0	7.9	7.1	6.7	6.7
Transportation and material moving occupations	2.8	3.1	4.2	4.9	1.2	1.0
Hispanic or Latino ethnicity						
Total, 16 years and over (thousands)	18,632	19,613	11,337	11,887	7,295	7,725
Percent	100.0	100.0	100.0	100.0	100.0	100.0
Management, professional, and related occupations	17.0	17.0	13.6	13.7	22.4	22.1
Management, business, and financial operations occupations	7.1	7.5	6.6	7.1	7.9	8.3
Professional and related occupations	9.9	9.5	7.0	6.6	14.4	13.9
Service occupations	23.8	23.7	19.5	19.2	30.5	30.6
Sales and office occupations	21.5	21.2	14.0	13.7	33.0	32.7
Sales and related occupations	9.4	9.4	7.5	7.3	12.3	12.6
Office and administrative support occupations	12.1	11.8	6.6	6.4	20.7	20.2
Natural resources, construction, and maintenance occupations	19.1	19.8	30.0	31.3	2.0	2.2
Farming, fishing, and forestry occupations	2.1	1.9	2.8	2.6	1.0	1.0
Construction and extraction occupations	13.1	14.2	21.2	22.9	.7	.9
Installation, maintenance, and repair occupations	3.8	3.7	6.0	5.9	.3	.3
Production, transportation, and material moving occupations	18.6	18.3	22.9	22.1	12.1	12.3
Production occupations	10.1	9.9	11.1	10.4	8.5	9.0
Transportation and material moving occupations	8.6	8.4	11.8	11.7	3.6	3.3

Note: Estimates for the above race groups (white, black or African American, and Asian) do not sum to totals because data are not presented for all races. In addition, persons whose ethnicity is identified as Hispanic or Latino may be of any race and, therefore, are classified by ethnicity as well as by race. Beginning in January 2006, data reflect revised population controls used in the household survey.

SOURCE: "10. Employed Persons by Occupation, Race, Hispanic or Latino Ethnicity, and Sex," in *Employment and Earnings*, U.S. Department of Labor, Bureau of Labor Statistics, 2007, http://www.bls.gov/cps/cpsaat10.pdf (accessed December 19, 2007)

food preparation and serving occupations and building and grounds cleaning and maintenance occupations. Puerto Ricans were more likely to work in sales and office occupations (407,000, or 27.4%) than in other occupations.

Asian-Americans and Jobs

The higher educational attainment of many Asian-Americans has resulted in a greater proportion of them working in higher-paying jobs than do other racial and ethnic groups. In 2006 almost half (47.3%) of all Asians and Pacific Islanders worked in management, professional, and related occupations—15.8% in management, business, and financial operations occupations and 31.6% in professional and related occupations. (See Table 4.7.) In comparison, only 35.5% of whites worked in these occupations. Asian-Americans were the next most likely to work in sales and office occupations (22.4%) and service occupations (15.8%), although they were

underrepresented in both. In *Employment and Earnings*, the BLS indicates that even though only 4.5% of the workforce was of Asian origin, 6.1% of managers and professionals were Asian-American, and they were especially overrepresented among computer software engineers (26.9%), computer hardware engineers (26.5%), and computer programmers (18.1%)—three highly paid occupations.

However, the BLS reports that in 2006 Asians and Pacific Islanders were underrepresented in natural resources, construction, and maintenance occupations (1.8%) and in installation, maintenance, and repair operations (3%). Even though only 4.3% of service workers were Asian-Americans, 45.5% of miscellaneous personal appearance workers were Asian-Americans—reflecting the large number of Asians and Pacific Islanders, particularly women, who work in nail salons and other personal care establishments.

TABLE 4.8

Employed Hispanic workers by sex, occupation, class of workers, full- or part-time status, and detailed ethnic group, 2005–06

[In thousands]

| | Hispanic or Latino ethnicity | | | | | | | |
| | Total[a] | | Mexican | | Puerto Rican | | Cuban | |
Category	2005	2006	2005	2006	2005	2006	2005	2006
Sex								
Total, 16 years and over	18,632	19,613	11,887	12,477	1,492	1,484	730	778
Men	11,337	11,887	7,526	7,863	788	782	429	452
Women	7,295	7,725	4,361	4,614	704	702	301	326
Occupation								
Management, professional, and related occupations	3,174	3,337	1,687	1,830	360	375	215	227
Management, business, and financial operations occupations	1,330	1,477	728	837	136	138	94	96
Management occupations	924	1,084	499	613	94	96	65	76
Business and financial operations occupations	406	393	230	223	42	42	30	21
Professional and related occupations	1,844	1,860	958	993	224	237	120	131
Computer and mathematical occupations	172	159	75	71	26	24	15	10
Architecture and engineering occupations	170	167	84	80	16	13	11	20
Life, physical, and social science occupations	63	59	34	33	6	10	6	1
Community and social services occupations	209	184	105	96	35	35	11	11
Legal occupations	111	93	60	52	11	12	8	5
Education, training, and library occupations	557	591	327	357	60	66	24	31
Arts, design, entertainment, sports, and media occupations	195	214	99	110	25	23	16	21
Healthcare practitioner and technical occupations	367	394	174	194	45	54	29	34
Service occupations	4,434	4,649	2,859	2,978	335	320	95	121
Healthcare support occupations	426	410	241	203	52	46	12	17
Protective service occupations	300	301	173	166	48	53	11	19
Food preparation and serving related occupations	1,518	1,608	1,081	1,140	86	78	22	29
Building and grounds cleaning and maintenance occupations	1,605	1,712	1,047	1,127	92	91	38	29
Personal care and service occupations	584	618	316	343	57	52	11	26
Sales and office occupations	4,000	4,154	2,380	2,435	427	407	199	200
Sales and related occupations	1,742	1,839	1,040	1,090	153	150	92	97
Office and administrative support occupations	2,258	2,314	1,340	1,345	274	257	107	103
Natural resources, construction, and maintenance occupations	3,552	3,893	2,616	2,818	140	147	102	107
Farming, fishing, and forestry occupations	394	382	364	356	3	—	1	2
Construction and extraction occupations	2,450	2,790	1,805	2,024	73	82	61	63
Installation, maintenance, and repair occupations	709	721	447	438	64	64	40	42
Production, transportation, and material moving occupations	3,473	3,580	2,346	2,416	231	235	119	123
Production occupations	1,875	1,936	1,328	1,362	106	114	45	49
Transportation and material moving occupations	1,597	1,645	1,018	1,055	125	122	74	74
Class of worker								
Agriculture:								
Wage and salary workers	409	410	377	375	3	1	1	3
Self-employed workers	14	18	9	12	2	1	—	—
Unpaid family workers	—	—	—	—	—	—	—	—
Nonagricultural industries:								
Wage and salary workers	17,180	18,043	10,855	11,363	1,439	1,424	673	722
Government	1,813	1,829	1,121	1,160	235	225	73	79
Private industries	15,367	16,214	9,733	10,204	1,203	1,199	599	643
Private households	276	263	156	143	6	8	5	4
Other industries	15,092	15,950	9,577	10,060	1,197	1,191	594	639
Self-employed workers	1,019	1,130	641	719	49	57	56	51
Unpaid family workers	10	12	6	8	—	1	—	1
Full- or part-time status[b]								
Full-time workers	15,997	16,943	10,233	10,822	1,268	1,269	664	696
Part-time workers	2,636	2,669	1,654	1,655	225	215	67	82

[a]Includes persons of Central or South American origin and of other Hispanic or Latino ethnicity, not shown separately.
[b]Employed persons are classified as full- or part-time workers based on their usual weekly hours at all jobs regardless of the number of hours they are at work during the reference week. Persons absent from work also are classified according to their usual status.
Note: Persons whose ethnicity is identified as Hispanic or Latino may be of any race. Beginning in January 2006, data reflect revised population controls used in the household survey. Dash indicates no data or data that do not meet publication criteria.

SOURCE: "13. Employed Hispanic or Latino Workers by Sex, Occupation, Class of Worker, Full- or Part-Time Status, and Detailed Ethnic Group," in *Employment and Earnings*, U.S. Department of Labor, Bureau of Labor Statistics, 2007, http://www.bls.gov/cps/cpsaat13.pdf (accessed December 19, 2007)

Native Americans and Alaskan Natives and Jobs

As stated previously, detailed data on Native American and Alaskan Native workers are difficult to obtain. However, the EEOC keeps some basic data on job patterns for minorities in private industry that includes Native Americans and Alaskan Natives as a separate category. In 2005 Native Americans made up only 0.6% of the total workforce. (See Table 4.9.) They made up

TABLE 4.9

Occupational employment in private industry, by race, ethnicity, sex, and industry, 2005

[210,866 units]

Racial/ ethnic group and sex	Total employment	Officials and managers	Professionals	Technicians	Sales workers	Office and clerical workers	Craft workers	Operatives	Laborers	Service workers
						Participation rate				
All employees	100	100	100	100	100	100	100	100	100	100
Men	52.3	64.6	47.4	52	43.9	21	88.6	74.2	66.5	41.9
Women	47.7	35.4	52.6	48	56.1	79	11.4	25.8	33.5	58.1
White	68.5	83.6	78.3	72.8	70.8	67.8	74.3	62.2	49.6	53.2
Men	36.2	54.9	37.6	38.7	32.4	13.5	66.9	47.5	33.3	20.7
Women	32.2	28.7	40.7	34.1	38.4	54.3	7.4	14.7	16.3	32.5
Minority	31.5	16.4	21.7	27.2	29.2	32.2	25.7	37.8	50.4	46.8
Men	16.1	9.7	9.8	13.3	11.6	7.5	21.8	26.7	33.2	21.1
Women	15.5	6.7	11.9	13.9	17.6	24.7	3.9	11.1	17.2	25.6
Black	14.1	6.7	7.3	12.6	13.8	17	9.7	17.4	18.8	23.5
Men	6.4	3.5	2.4	4.9	5	3.4	7.9	12.1	12.4	9.3
Women	7.7	3.2	4.8	7.7	8.7	13.6	1.8	5.3	6.4	14.1
Hispanic	11.9	5.4	4.4	7.7	10.9	10.5	12.5	15.8	27.3	18.4
Men	6.8	3.4	2.1	4.4	4.6	2.7	11.1	11.7	18.3	9.6
Women	5.1	2	2.3	3.2	6.3	7.8	1.4	4.1	9.1	8.8
Asian American	5	4	9.7	6.4	3.8	4.1	2.7	3.9	3.5	4.1
Men	2.6	2.5	5.1	3.7	1.7	1.2	2	2.4	2	1.8
Women	2.4	1.4	4.6	2.7	2.1	2.9	0.6	1.5	1.5	2.2
American Indian	0.6	0.4	0.4	0.6	0.7	0.6	0.8	0.7	0.8	0.9
Men	0.3	0.3	0.2	0.3	0.3	0.2	0.7	0.5	0.5	0.4
Women	0.3	0.1	0.2	0.3	0.4	0.4	0.1	0.2	0.3	0.5

SOURCE: Adapted from "Occupational Employment in Private Industry by Race/Ethnic Group/Sex and by Industry, United States,2005," in *Job Patterns for Minorities and Women in Private Industry*, U.S. Equal Employment Opportunity Commission, January 2007, http://www.eeoc.gov/stats/jobpat/2005/national .html (accessed December 20, 2007).

only 0.4% of all officials and managers and only 0.4% of professionals. However, Native Americans and Alaskan Natives were overrepresented among sales workers (0.7%), craft workers (0.8%), and operatives (0.7%).

MINORITIES AND THE FEDERAL GOVERNMENT

Traditionally, non-Hispanic white men have held most of the higher-level positions in the federal government. Along with cabinet members, who are selected by the president, these high-level officials wield the power in federal government. This holds true for many agencies, including the Federal Bureau of Investigation, the U.S. Immigration and Customs Enforcement, and the U.S. Customs and Border Protection.

In *Federal Equal Opportunity Recruitment Program, FY 2006* (January 2007, http://www.opm.gov/feorpreports/ 2006/feorp2006.pdf), the U.S. Office of Personnel Management finds that for fiscal year 2006 minorities were overrepresented in the government workforce with one exception: Hispanics were significantly underrepresented in federal jobs. African-Americans represented 17.6% of the federal workforce in 2006, but only 10.1% of the total civilian labor force. Asians and Pacific Islanders represented 5.2% of the federal workforce, but only 4.2% of the total civilian workforce. Native Americans represented 1.9% of the federal workforce, but only 0.6% of the total civilian labor force. Hispanics represented 7.6% of the federal workforce, but 12.8% of the total civilian workforce in 2006.

Even though minorities are generally overrepresented in the government workforce, they are underrepresented at the senior pay grades. For example, African-Americans made up 17.6% of the federal workforce in 2006 but were overrepresented at the lowest pay grades. In September 2006 more than one out of four (26.7%) employees in the lowest positions—General Schedule and Related (GSR) grades one through four—were African-American. Another 26% of GSR five through eight, 16.2% of GSR nine through twelve, 11.6% of GSR thirteen through fifteen, and just 6.7% of the senior pay levels were African-American. Asians and Pacific Islanders were also underrepresented at the senior pay levels, but less so than African-Americans, representing 6.1% of GSR one-through-four pay levels and only 3.3% of the senior pay level. Hispanics represented 8.3% of GSR one-through-four pay levels and only 3.7% of senior pay levels. Native Americans represented 5% of the GSR one-through-four pay levels and only 0.9% of the senior pay levels.

A major contributor to this situation is time. It takes about twenty years to rise to the top of any organization. In the late 1980s few people of color held any management positions in the federal government. Another possible factor is partiality or discrimination. Some lower-level government employees believe they have been deprived of promotions because of their gender or race and have filed bias complaints.

MINORITIES IN BUSINESS

The Census Bureau indicates in *2002 Survey of Business Owners: Advance Report on Characteristics of Employer Business Owners: 2002* (February 2, 2005, http://www.census.gov/econ/census02/sbo/sboadvance.htm) that in 2002—the year for which most data are available—the overwhelming majority of business owners in the United States were white, non-Hispanic individuals. All minority groups except Asian-Americans were underrepresented among business owners when compared to their presence in the U.S. residential population aged twenty-five and older. Only 6.8% of business owners were of Hispanic origin, even though the U.S. population was 11.1% Hispanic. (See Table 4.10.) African-Americans represented only 5.2% of business owners, even though 11.6% of the U.S. population was African-American. Only 0.9% of business owners were Native American or Alaskan Native, compared to 1.3% of the U.S. population. Only Asian-Americans, who represented 4.8% of business owners, were overrepresented in comparison with their presence in the U.S. population (4.4%). Minorities were even more underrepresented among business owners who owned firms with paid employees.

Minority Women-Owned Businesses

According to the Census Bureau, 28.2% of business owners in 2002 were women. (See Table 4.10.) The Center for Women's Business Research reports in *Businesses Owned by Women of Color in the United States, 2006: A Fact Sheet* (2007, http://www.cfwbr.org/assets/619_wom enofcoloroverviewwebco.pdf) that between 1997 and 2006 the number of businesses that were majority owned (51% or more) by women of color grew by 119.7%. By 2006 there were nearly 2.1 million firms majority owned by minority women in the United States. (See Figure 4.2.) In 2006 one out of five (21.4%) of all privately held, women-owned businesses in the United States were owned by minority women. These businesses generated over $161 billion in sales in 2006. Most of the firms (80.1%) were in the service industry.

Of the nearly 2.1 million businesses owned by minority women in 2006, 770,396 (36.9%) were owned by African-American women, 745,246 (35.7%) were owned by Hispanic women, 436,751 (20.9%) were owned by Asian-American women, 119,198 (5.7%) were owned by Native American and Alaskan Native women, and 15,258 (0.7%) were owned by Native Hawaiian or Pacific Islander

TABLE 4.10

Business ownership by gender, Hispanic origin, and race, 2002

Employer status by gender, Hispanic or Latino origin, and race	All firms	
	Number	Percent
All firms*	22,974,655	X
Female-owned	6,489,259	28.2
Male-owned	13,184,033	57.4
Equally male-/female-owned	2,693,360	11.7
Publicly held and other firms whose owners' characteristics are indeterminate	494,399	2.2
Hispanic or Latino	1,573,464	6.8
Not Hispanic or Latino	20,793,392	90.5
White	19,899,839	86.6
Black	1,197,567	5.2
American Indian and Alaska Native	201,387	0.9
Asian	1,103,587	4.8
Native Hawaiian and other Pacific Islander	28,948	0.1
Firms with paid employees	5,524,784	X
Female-owned	916,657	16.6
Male-owned	3,524,969	63.8
Equally male-/female-owned	717,961	13.0
Publicly held and other firms whose owners' characteristics are indeterminate	352,720	6.4
Hispanic or Latino	199,542	3.6
Not Hispanic or Latino	4,960,246	89.8
White	4,712,119	85.3
Black	94,518	1.7
American Indian and Alaska Native	24,498	0.4
Asian	319,468	5.8
Native Hawaiian and other Pacific Islander	3,693	0.1
Firms with no paid employees	17,449,871	X
Female-owned	5,572,602	31.9
Male-owned	9,659,064	55.4
Equally male-/female-owned	1,975,399	11.3
Publicly held and other firms whose owners' characteristics are indeterminate	141,679	0.8
Hispanic or Latino	1,373,922	7.9
Not Hispanic or Latino	15,833,146	90.7
White	15,187,720	87.0
Black	1,103,049	6.3
American Indian and Alaska Native	176,889	1.0
Asian	784,118	4.5
Native Hawaiian and other Pacific Islander	25,255	0.1

*Includes firms with paid employees and firms with no paid employees.
X Not applicable.

SOURCE: Adapted from "Table A. Comparison of Business Ownership for Respondent Firms to All U.S. Firms by Gender, Hispanic or Latino Origin, and Race: 2002," in *Characteristics of Businesses: 2002*, U.S. Census Bureau, September 27, 2006, http://www.census.gov/csd/sbo/cbsummary-offindings.htm (accessed December 19, 2007)

women. (See Table 4.11.) Firms owned by Native Hawaiian or Pacific Islander women experienced the greatest growth between 1997 and 2006 (190.2%). There was also a triple-digit growth in the number of firms owned by African-American women (147%), American Indian or Alaskan Native women (122.5%), and Hispanic women (121.3%). Firms owned by Asian-American women achieved a more modest growth of 80.4%.

Minority Set-Aside Programs under Increasing Attack

Many levels of government, including the federal government, have set-aside programs that award a certain percentage of contracts to minority- and women-owned businesses. These programs were developed to remedy

FIGURE 4.2

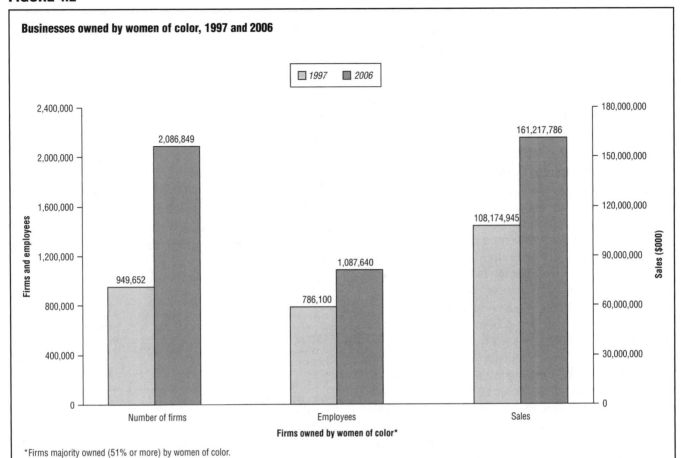

Businesses owned by women of color, 1997 and 2006

◻ *1997* ◼ *2006*

Firms and employees (left axis) / *Sales ($000)* (right axis)

Number of firms: 949,652 / 2,086,849
Employees: 786,100 / 1,087,640
Sales: 108,174,945 / 161,217,786

Firms owned by women of color*

*Firms majority owned (51% or more) by women of color.

SOURCE: "Businesses Majority Owned by Women of Color Number 2.1 Million, Employ Nearly 1.1 Million, and Generate More Than $161 Billion in Sales Nationwide," in *Businesses Owned by Women of Color in the United States, 2006: A Fact Sheet*, Center for Women's Business Research, 2007, http://www .cfwbr.org/assets/619_womenofcoloroverviewwebco.pdf (accessed December 19, 2007)

the effects of past discrimination and to address the difficulties these firms faced in competing with larger, more established firms for government contracts. Minority businesses are often newer and smaller and have difficulty competing with older, larger businesses that know the process and can afford to make lower bids. Acquiring government contracts can be involved and confusing for businesses unfamiliar with the process. Governments, especially the federal government, are often slow to pay their bills, so businesses frequently have to borrow money to bridge the gap between the delivery of goods and services that must be paid for and the time it takes the government to pay them.

Even though the U.S. Supreme Court has not yet declared the use of racial classifications unconstitutional, it has ruled them suspect and subject to strict judicial scrutiny. As a result, set-aside programs came under increasing attack in the 1990s and early 2000s.

In *City of Richmond v. Croson County* (488 US 469, 1989), the Supreme Court struck down a Richmond, Virginia, city ordinance that reserved 30% of city-financed construction contracts for minority-owned businesses. The Court ruled that the ordinance violated equal protection because there was no "specific" and "identified" evidence of past discrimination, "public or private," against the Richmond Minority Business Enterprise in city contracting. The majority opinion, written by Justice Sandra Day O'Connor (1930–), also noted that the city had failed to "narrowly tailor" the remedy to accomplish any objective other than "outright racial balancing." The opinion further stated that it was a "completely unrealistic" assumption that a 30% assignment to minority business enterprises in a particular trade would be a fair representation of the community.

In a similar case, Adarand Constructors, a white-owned company, sued the government, claiming the company failed to receive a government contract because racial preferences had violated the owner's right to equal protection under the Fifth Amendment. In 1989 the U.S. Department of Transportation awarded a contract for a federal highway project to a construction firm, which in turn subcontracted the job to a Disadvantaged Business Enterprise in compliance with the Subcontractor Compensation Clause. In *Adarand Constructors, Inc. v. Peña* (515 US 200, 1995), the Supreme Court

TABLE 4.11

Private businesses owned by minority women, by race/ethnicity, 2006

	2006		Firms owned by women of color	
	Firms owned by women of color	Firms owned by men of color	% Change 1997–2006	% Share of firms owned by all persons of color
Total U.S.				
Number of firms	2,086,849	2,924,438	119.7	39.8
Employment	1,087,640	3,596,053	38.4	21.0
Sales ($000)	161,217,786	587,431,727	49.0	20.4
By race/ethnicity				
African American or Black				
Number of firms	770,396	731,102	147.0	48.2
Employment	202,712	560,429	20.4	24.3
Sales ($000)	29,026,442	77,571,218	69.9	26.3
Asian American				
Number of firms	436,751	807,908	80.4	33.3
Employment	536,839	1,587,452	77.2	22.5
Sales ($000)	73,548,748	273,057,184	56.7	19.6
Hispanic or Latino				
Number of firms	745,246	1,202,331	121.3	36.9
Employment	277,683	1,285,947	18.6	16.2
Sales ($000)	45,933,840	212,272,420	33.3	17.0
American Indian or Alaska Native				
Number of firms	119,198	160,441	122.5	43.0
Employment	61,645	139,950	−17.3	31.2
Sales ($000)	7,716,663	20,476,507	−9.6	25.8
Native Hawaiian or Pacific Islander				
Number of firms	15,258	22,657	190.2	38.4
Employment	8,761	22,275	40.9	29.0
Sales ($000)	818,387	4,054,397	−30.0	14.6

Note: Ownership refers to majority (51% or more) ownership.

SOURCE: "Majority-Owned, Privately-Held Firms Owned by Women of Color in the U.S., 2006," in *Businesses Owned by Women of Color in the United States, 2006: A Fact Sheet*, Center for Women's Business Research, 2007, http://www.cfwbr.org/assets/619_womenofcoloroverviewwebco.pdf (accessed December 19, 2007)

expressed doubt in the validity of the affirmative action programs, based on the Surface Transportation and Uniform Relocation Assistance Act of 1987 that channeled $10 billion a year in construction contracts to women- and minority-owned businesses. The Court, citing the need for stricter and narrower standards in determining racial preferences when awarding contracts, returned the case to the district court for review.

These Supreme Court decisions have brought many set-aside programs under scrutiny. In June 2000 a federal court in *Associated General Contractors of Ohio v. Sandra A. Drabnik* decided that the Ohio state program to set-aside 5% of state construction projects for minority-owned businesses was unconstitutional. Even though that court had upheld the state's program in 1983, subsequent U.S. Supreme Court decisions required the federal court to apply a more stringent standard of judicial review, no longer allowing legislatures to use "implicit factfinding of discrimination" to justify racial preferences and affirmative action programs such as set-asides.

NATIVE AMERICAN CASINOS—A MATTER OF SELF-RULE

The Indian Gaming Regulatory Act of 1988 gives tribes "the exclusive right to regulate gaming on Indian lands if the gaming activity is not specifically prohibited by federal law and is conducted within a State which does not, as a matter of criminal law and public policy, prohibit such gaming activity." The law requires that only tribes, not individuals, run gaming operations. The tribes do not need state approval for class-two casinos, which are supposedly bingo halls but which in many cases have slot machine parlors that skirt the law. Class-three casinos offer slots, roulette, craps, and poker, and they require state approval. Thus, governors make deals with tribes, granting class-three approval in exchange for a share of the profits going to the state treasury. With many states facing severe budget problems, tribal gaming has become an attractive source of revenue. As a result, tribal gaming has gained considerable political influence. The Tribal Law and Policy Institute reports in "Native Gaming Resources" (May 30, 2007, http://www.tribal-institute.org/lists/gaming.htm) that in 2008, 224 out of 562 federally recognized Indian tribes were engaged in gaming. How much has tribal gaming helped the Native American population as a whole?

In "Wheel of Misfortune" (*Time*, December 8, 2002), Donald L. Barlett and James B. Steele provide a scathing and controversial review of tribal gaming. According to Barlett and Steele, when tribal gaming emerged in the late

1980s "in a frenzy of cost cutting and privatization, Washington perceived gaming on reservations as a cheap way to wean tribes from government handouts, encourage economic development and promote tribal self-sufficiency." However, the 1988 Gaming Act "was so riddled with loopholes, so poorly written, so discriminatory and subject to such conflicting interpretations that 14 years later, armies of high-priced lawyers are still debating the definition of a slot machine." Barlett and Steele maintain that only a handful of tribal gaming establishments, those operating close to major population centers, are successful, whereas the overwhelming majority are either too small or too remote in location: "Casinos in California, Connecticut and Florida—states with only 3% of the Indian population—haul in 44% of all revenue." Barlett and Steele state that in 2002 "290 Indian casinos in 28 states pulled in at least $12.7 billion in revenue. Of that sum, . . . the casinos kept more than $5 billion as profit. That would place overall Indian gaming among *Fortune* magazine's 20 most profitable U.S. corporations." However, "just 39 casinos generated $8.4 billion. In short, 13% of the casinos accounted for 66% of the take."

Also controversial was the authenticity of the tribes involved in gaming. According to Barlett and Steele, leaders of tribes involved in gaming "are free to set their own whimsical rules for admission, without regard to Indian heritage. They may exclude rivals, potential whistle-blowers and other legitimate claimants. The fewer tribe members, the larger the cut for the rest. Some tribes are booting out members, while others are limiting membership." Moreover, many "long-defunct tribes and extended families" have attempted to gain congressional certification to become involved in tribal gaming. In New York state some tribes that are not even recognized as New York tribes, including tribes from Oklahoma and Wisconsin, have teamed with area developers to buy land in the Catskills and elsewhere in the state in hopes of building casinos. They are opposed, however, by local communities—as well as by Donald Trump (1946–)—who fear further competition to casinos operating in Atlantic City, New Jersey.

By contrast, Anne Merline McCulloch argues in "The Politics of Indian Gaming: Tribe/State Relations and American Federalism" (*Publius*, vol. 24, no. 3, 1994) that revenues from gambling casinos have helped spur economic development on reservations and allowed Native Americans to reassert tribal sovereignty. She states that "Native American tribes have looked to gambling as a means to achieve the economic autonomy

requisite for tribal sovereignty, and to improve the lives and the health of their members through employment. The immediate effect of Indian gaming seems to have done just that." In "The Economic Impact of Native American Gaming: Cost-Benefit Analysis of the Mashantucket Pequot Tribal Nation" (2002, http://www.econ.ilstu.edu/uauje/PDF's/issue2002/LisaBorromeo.pdf), a study of gaming on the Mashantucket Pequot Tribal Nation, Lisa Borromeo of George Washington University backs up McCulloch's claims. Borromeo notes that "Indian gaming appears to be the most successful strategy in turning around 150 years of failed attempts by United States government to aid American Indians, by providing a means to self-sufficiency for Tribal nations." The casinos employ large numbers of Native Americans, and with the profits from casinos, the tribes are building schools and community centers; financing education trust funds, local government, and new businesses; and putting in water and sewer systems on reservation lands.

Proponents of tribal gaming point to a number of success stories. Marks and Spilde Contreras find that in 2007 tribal gaming reduced poverty and improved employment and income in the communities near the casinos in California. The Oneidas of Wisconsin took advantage of a bingo hall to lower the tribe's unemployment rate in the early 1990s and used proceeds to build an elementary school and subsidize a Head Start program. The Suquamish in Washington used gambling profits to buy back former reservation land. Even though only a handful of tribal casinos generate large revenues, even those operations that break even create jobs that benefit many Native Americans. Tribes not able to take advantage of gambling can also benefit from revenue-sharing programs, such as the one set up in California. The California Nations Indian Gaming Association reports in the press release "California's Gaming Tribes Share More Than $200 Million with Other Tribes" (November 17, 2005, http://www.cniga.com/media/pressrelease_detail.php?id=73) that in 2005, sixty-one tribes with gaming compacts shared profits with 70 qualifying tribes.

Much of the growth in tribal gaming, which is outpacing both Atlantic City and Las Vegas, Nevada, is due to the expansion of facilities into full-fledged resorts. Wary that the future might see the curtailment in revenues, some tribes are looking to diversify by investing proceeds into nongaming businesses, thereby establishing an economic base independent of gambling. To counter adverse publicity regarding tribal gaming, the National Indian Gaming Association has launched a public relations effort: the United Tribal Public Relations Campaign.

CHAPTER 5

MONEY, INCOME, AND POVERTY STATUS

Income greatly influences where people live, what they eat, how they dress, what cars they drive or transportation they take, and what schools their children can attend. How much money and income people have is usually determined by their occupation, which is often directly related to their level of education. Racial and ethnic backgrounds can play a big role in all these factors as well.

INCOME DIFFERENCES
All Households

A household consists of a person or people who occupy the same housing unit and may have just one person (the householder who owns or rents the house). It may also consist of related family members (family household) or unrelated people (nonfamily household).

The median income (half of all households earned more and half earned less) of U.S. households in 2006, including money income before taxes but excluding the value of noncash benefits such as food stamps, Medicare, Medicaid, public housing, and employer-provided benefits, was $48,201, up from $47,845 the year before. (See Table 5.1.) This median income varied substantially between races and ethnic groups. The median income of non-Hispanic white households was $52,423, considerably higher than that of Hispanic households ($37,781) and African-American households ($31,969). However, non-Hispanic white income was significantly less than the median household income of Asian-Americans ($64,238). Some of the reasons for these income disparities are discussed in this chapter.

Married-Couple Households

In 2006 there were 58.9 million married-couple households in the United States, representing 75.2% of all family households. (See Table 5.1.) Married couples tend to have a higher household income than single householders do, because often both the husband and wife work outside of the home. In 2006 married-couple households had a median income of $69,716. The median income for female-headed households with no husband present was substantially lower, at $31,818—less than half the median income of married-couple households. The median income for male-headed households with no wife present was also lower than the married-couple median but substantially higher than the female-headed households, at $47,078.

Per Capita Income

Per capita income is figured by dividing the total (aggregate or composite) national income by the total population. This means that if all the nation's earnings were divided equally among every man, woman, and child, each person would receive this amount. The per capita figure is often used to compare the wealth of countries. It can also be used to compare the wealth of minority groups within countries. In 2006 the per capita income for non-Hispanic whites in the United States was $30,431, which was about the same as the per capita income of Asian-Americans ($30,474). (Table 5.1.) African-Americans and Hispanics had significantly lower per capital incomes, at $17,902 and $15,421, respectively. In fact, the per capita income for Asian-Americans and non-Hispanic whites was almost twice that of Hispanics.

Minority Incomes

HISPANIC INCOME. Even though Table 5.1 shows that Hispanic households earned an average median income of $37,781 in 2006, up from $37,146 in 2005, the financial situation among Hispanic subgroups tends to vary. The U.S. Census Bureau notes in *The Hispanic Population in the United States: 2006* (October 5, 2007, http://www.census.gov/population/www/socdemo/hispanic/cps2006.html) that in 2006 a third (33.6%) of Hispanic households had money

TABLE 5.1

Median household and per capita income by selected characteristics, 2005 and 2006

[Income in 2006 dollars. Households and people as of March of the following year.]

Characteristic	2005 Median income (dollars)		2006 Median income (dollars)		Percentage change in real median income (2006 less 2005)
	Number (thousands)	Estimate	Number (thousands)	Estimate	Estimate
Households					
All households	114,384	47,845	116,011	48,201	0.7
Type of household					
Family households	77,402	59,156	78,425	59,894	1.2
Married-couple	58,179	68,233	58,945	69,716	2.2
Female householder, no husband present	14,093	31,655	14,416	31,818	0.5
Male householder, no wife present	5,130	48,289	5,063	47,078	−2.5
Nonfamily households	36,982	28,222	37,587	29,083	3.1
Female householder	20,230	23,432	20,249	23,876	1.9
Male householder	16,753	35,164	17,338	35,614	1.3
Race[a] and Hispanic origin of householder					
White	93,588	50,146	94,705	50,673	1.1
White, not Hispanic	82,003	52,449	82,675	52,423	—
Black	14,002	31,870	14,354	31,969	0.3
Asian	4,273	63,097	4,454	64,238	1.8
Hispanic origin (any race)	12,519	37,146	12,973	37,781	1.7
Nativity of householder					
Native	99,579	48,435	100,603	49,074	1.3
Foreign born	14,806	43,418	15,408	43,943	1.2
Naturalized citizen	6,990	51,670	7,210	51,440	−0.4
Not a citizen	7,815	37,945	8,198	39,497	4.1
Earnings of full-time, year-round workers					
Men with earnings	61,500	42,743	63,055	42,261	−1.1
Women with earnings	43,351	32,903	44,663	32,515	−1.2
Per capita income[b]					
Total[a]	293,834	25,857	296,824	26,352	1.9
White	235,903	27,365	237,892	27,821	1.7
White, not Hispanic	195,893	29,895	196,252	30,431	1.8
Black	36,965	17,427	37,369	17,902	2.7
Asian	12,599	28,227	13,194	30,474	8.0
Hispanic origin (any race)	43,168	14,958	44,854	15,421	3.1

—Represents or rounds to zero.

[a]Federal surveys now give respondents the option of reporting more than one race. Therefore, two basic ways of defining a race group are possible. A group such as Asian may be defined as those who reported Asian and no other race (the race-alone or single-race concept) or as those who reported Asian regardless of whether they also reported another race (the race-alone-or-in-combination concept). This table shows data using the first approach (race alone). The use of the single-race population does not imply that it is the preferred method of presenting or analyzing data. The Census Bureau uses a variety of approaches. About 2.6 percent of people reported more than one race in Census 2000. Data for American Indians and Alaska Natives, Native Hawaiians and other Pacific Islanders, and those reporting two or more races are not shown separately in this table.

[b]Per capita income is the mean income computed for every man, woman, and child in a particular group. It is derived by dividing the total income of a particular group by the total population in that group (excluding patients or inmates in institutional quarters).

SOURCE: Adapted from Carmen DeNavas-Walt, Bernadette D. Proctor, and Jessica Smith, "Table 1. Income and Earnings Summary Measures by Selected Characteristics: 2005 and 2006," in *Income, Poverty, and Health Insurance Coverage in the United States: 2006*, U.S. Census Bureau, August 2007, http://www.census.gov/prod/2007pubs/p60-233.pdf (accessed December 20, 2007).

income under $25,000 a year, compared to only 23.7% of non-Hispanic white households. Nearly a third (31.1%) of Hispanic families earned under $25,000 per year, compared to only 14% of non-Hispanic white households.

Among the Hispanic subgroups, however, the Census Bureau indicates that the yearly earnings outlook was best for Hispanic families of Cuban and South American origin. About one out of five Cuban family households (22.7%) and South American family households (21.9%) earned under $25,000 per year in 2006, compared to 34.7% of Puerto Rican family households, 33% of Mexican families, and 23.9% of Central American families. Even though only 18.2% of Hispanic families earned $75,000 per year or more, 28.6% of Cuban families and 25.7% of South American families did. Only 16.1% of Mexican families, 19.6% of Puerto Rican families, and 16.8% of Central American families earned $75,000 a year or more in 2006.

Hispanic incomes are relatively low for a variety of reasons, including language barriers and discrimination in the workplace. However, the lack of educational attainment is a major reason for low Hispanic incomes. In *U.S. Hispanic Population: 2006* (October 2007, http://www.census.gov/population/socdemo/hispanic/cps2006/

CPS_Powerpoint_2006.pdf), the Census Bureau indicates that in 2006, 24.4% of all Hispanics aged twenty-five and older had less than a ninth-grade education, another 16.3% did not have a high school diploma, and only 12.4% had a bachelor's degree or more.

AFRICAN-AMERICAN INCOME. African-Americans had the lowest median income in 2006 by far, at $31,969. The next lowest median income was that of Hispanics, at $37,781. As shown earlier, households headed by an unmarried adult have substantially lower incomes than do married-couple households. This puts African-Americans at a disadvantage. Among those over age fifteen, African-Americans are far more likely than whites, Hispanics, or Asians and Pacific Islanders to have never married. According to the Census Bureau, in *America's Families and Living Arrangements: 2006* (March 27, 2007, http://www.census.gov/population/www/socdemo/hh-fam/cps2006.html), 45.4% of African-Americans aged fifteen and older had never been married in 2006, compared to 35.2% of Hispanics, 31.5% of Asians, and 25.4% of non-Hispanic whites.

However, the differences in marriage rates do not explain the entire discrepancy between household incomes of non-Hispanic whites and African-Americans. Married-couple African-American households have lower incomes than married-couple non-Hispanic white households; African-American female- and male-headed households also have lower incomes than comparable non-Hispanic white households. The Census Bureau states in *The Black Population in the United States: March 2004* (March 29, 2006, http://www.census.gov/population/www/socdemo/race/ppl-186.html) that in 2003, the most recent year for which detailed income data by race and type of household are available, 16.9% of African-American married-couple households with money income had incomes of less than $25,000 per year, compared to only 11.6% of non-Hispanic white married-couple households. Only 29.9% of African-American married-couple households had incomes of $75,000 and over, whereas 43% of non-Hispanic white married-couple households had incomes this high. Even though the average income of all households headed by a female householder was substantially lower than the average income of married-couple households, fully 57.2% of households headed by single African-American women had incomes of less than $25,000 per year in 2003, compared to 38.7% of households headed by single, non-Hispanic white women. Lower educational attainment as well as discrimination in the workforce are two additional factors that may work together to lower the incomes of African-American households.

ASIAN AND PACIFIC ISLANDER INCOME. Conversely, Asian-American households tend to have higher incomes than comparable non-Hispanic white households. In *The*

Asian Alone Population in the United States: March 2004 (March 19, 2006, http://www.census.gov/population/www/socdemo/race/ppl-184.html), the Census Bureau reports that among married-couple households in 2003, even though a higher proportion of Asian-Americans had incomes of less than $25,000 per year (15%) than did non-Hispanic whites (11.6%), a higher proportion of Asian-Americans had incomes of more than $75,000 per year (45.3%) than did non-Hispanic whites (43%). In addition, Asian-American female householders were decidedly better off than their non-Hispanic white counterparts. Among these female-headed households, 37.5% of Asians had incomes of less than $25,000, compared to 38.7% of non-Hispanic whites. On the other end of the scale, 15.2% of female-headed Asian households had incomes of $75,000 and more per year, compared to only 11.2% of female-headed, non-Hispanic white households.

POVERTY STATUS OF MINORITIES

Every year the Census Bureau establishes poverty thresholds that determine the distribution of different welfare benefits. In 2006 the poverty threshold ranged from $9,669 for people aged sixty-five and older who lived alone, to $44,649 for a family with nine or more members. (See Table 5.2.) A family of four (two adults and two children) was considered poor if it had an income below the poverty threshold of $20,444, whereas a family headed by a single adult with three children was considered poor if it had an income below the poverty threshold of $20,516. In 2006, 36.5 million people, or 12.3% of the population, were in poverty. (See Figure 5.1.) Both the number of people in poverty and the poverty rate steadily rose from 2000 to 2004 before leveling off between 2005 and 2006.

In 2006, 24.3% of African-Americans and 20.6% of Hispanics lived in poverty. Asian-Americans had a relatively low rate of poverty, at 10.3%, although it was still higher than the poverty rate of non-Hispanic whites (8.2%). (See Table 5.3.) According to Carmen DeNavas-Walt, Bernadette D. Proctor, and Jessica Smith of the Census Bureau, in *Income, Poverty, and Health Insurance Coverage in the United States: 2006* (August 2007, http://www.census.gov/prod/2007pubs/p60-233.pdf), the poverty rate for non-Hispanic whites, African-Americans, and Asian-Americans was statistically unchanged from 2005.

The poverty rate varies among Hispanic subgroups. The Census Bureau notes in *Hispanic Population in the United States* that in 2006, 25.3% of Puerto Ricans lived below the poverty line, compared to 23.8% of Mexicans and 17.5% of Central Americans. Cubans and South Americans had the lowest poverty rates, at 10.7% and 12%, respectively. Cubans and South Americans tend to be better educated than other Hispanic subgroups, which partially explains the income disparities between the groups.

TABLE 5.2

Poverty thresholds, by size of family and number of related children under 18 years, 2006

Size of family unit	Weighted average thresholds	Related children under 18 years								
		None	One	Two	Three	Four	Five	Six	Seven	Eight or more
One person (unrelated individual)	10,294									
Under 65 years	10,488	10,488								
65 years and over	9,669	9,669								
Two people	13,167									
Householder under 65 years	13,569	13,500	13,896							
Householder 65 years and over	12,201	12,186	13,843							
Three people	16,079	15,769	16,227	16,242						
Four people	20,614	20,794	21,134	20,444	20,516					
Five people	24,382	25,076	25,441	24,662	24,059	23,691				
Six people	27,560	28,842	28,957	28,360	27,788	26,938	26,434			
Seven people	31,205	33,187	33,394	32,680	32,182	31,254	30,172	28,985		
Eight people	34,774	37,117	37,444	36,770	36,180	35,342	34,278	33,171	32,890	
Nine people or more	41,499	44,649	44,865	44,269	43,768	42,945	41,813	40,790	40,536	38,975

SOURCE: "Poverty Thresholds 2006," in *Poverty*, U.S. Census Bureau, Housing and Household Economics Statistics Division, January 2008, http://www.census.gov/hhes/www/poverty/threshld/thresh06.html (accessed December 20, 2007)

FIGURE 5.1

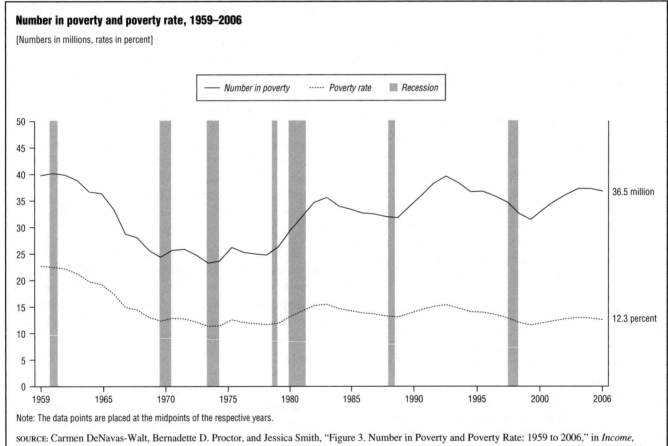

Number in poverty and poverty rate, 1959–2006

[Numbers in millions, rates in percent]

Note: The data points are placed at the midpoints of the respective years.

SOURCE: Carmen DeNavas-Walt, Bernadette D. Proctor, and Jessica Smith, "Figure 3. Number in Poverty and Poverty Rate: 1959 to 2006," in *Income, Poverty, and Health Insurance Coverage in the United States: 2006*, U.S. Census Bureau, August 2007, http://www.census.gov/prod/2007pubs/p60-233.pdf (accessed December 20, 2007)

Depth of Poverty

Even though measuring the proportions of people in various groups who are above and below the poverty threshold provides one measure of poverty, it does not account for levels of poverty. Some people below the poverty level are moderately poor, whereas others are extremely poor. Some households with incomes above the poverty threshold are just above it and barely scraping

TABLE 5.3

People and families in poverty by selected characteristics, 2005 and 2006

[Numbers in thousands. People as of March of the following year.]

Characteristic	Below poverty in 2005		Below poverty in 2006		Change in poverty (2006 less 2005)[a]	
	Number	Percentage	Number	Percentage	Number	Percentage
People						
Total	**36,950**	**12.6**	**36,460**	**12.3**	**−490**	**−0.3**
Family status						
In families	26,068	10.8	25,915	10.6	−153	−0.2
Householder	7,657	9.9	7,668	9.8	11	−0.1
Related children under 18	12,335	17.1	12,299	16.9	−37	−0.2
Related children under 6	4,784	20.0	4,830	20.0	46	—
In unrelated subfamilies	456	37.4	567	41.5	111	4.1
Reference person	181	35.9	229	40.4	48	4.6
Children under 18	270	39.7	323	44.9	53	5.2
Unrelated individuals	10,425	21.1	9,977	20.0	−448	−1.1
Male	4,315	17.9	4,388	17.8	73	−0.1
Female	6,111	24.1	5,589	22.2	−522	−1.9
Race[b] and Hispanic origin						
White	24,872	10.6	24,416	10.3	−456	−0.3
White, not Hispanic	16,227	8.3	16,013	8.2	−214	−0.1
Black	9,168	24.9	9,048	24.3	−120	−0.7
Asian	1,402	11.1	1,353	10.3	−49	−0.9
Hispanic origin (any race)	9,368	21.8	9,243	20.6	−126	−1.1
Age						
Under 18 years	12,896	17.6	12,827	17.4	−69	−0.2
18 to 64 years	20,450	11.1	20,239	10.8	−211	−0.3
65 years and older	3,603	10.1	3,394	9.4	−210	−0.7
Nativity						
Native	31,080	12.1	30,790	11.9	−290	−0.2
Foreign born	5,870	16.5	5,670	15.2	−200	−1.3
Naturalized citizen	1,441	10.4	1,345	9.3	−96	−1.1
Not a citizen	4,429	20.4	4,324	19.0	−105	−1.3
Region						
Northeast	6,103	11.3	6,222	11.5	119	0.2
Midwest	7,419	11.4	7,324	11.2	−95	−0.2
South	14,854	14.0	14,882	13.8	28	−0.2
West	8,573	12.6	8,032	11.6	−541	−1.0
Metropolitan status						
Inside metropolitan statistical areas	30,098	12.2	29,283	11.8	−815	0.5
Inside principal cities	15,966	17.0	15,336	16.1	−630	−0.9
Outside principal cities	14,132	9.3	13,947	9.1	−185	−0.2
Outside metropolitan statistical areas[c]	6,852	14.5	7,177	15.2	325	0.6
Work Experience						
All workers (16 years and older)	9,340	6.0	9,181	5.8	−159	−0.2
Worked full-time, year-round	2,894	2.8	2,906	2.7	12	−0.1
Not full-time, year-round	6,446	12.8	6,275	12.6	−170	−0.2
Did not work at least 1 week	16,041	21.8	15,715	21.1	−327	−0.6

by. The ratio of income to poverty compares a family's income with its poverty threshold, providing one way to measure how poor a family actually is.

Table 5.4 shows people 0.50 over the poverty threshold (extreme poverty), people between 0.50 and 1.00 of the poverty threshold (below poverty, but above extreme poverty), and people between 1.00 and 1.25 of the poverty threshold (low income) by race and Hispanic origin. In 2006 more than one out of ten (10.9%) African-Americans lived on incomes under 0.50 of the poverty threshold, compared to 7.7% of Hispanics, 5.1% of Asian-Americans, and only 3.5% of non-Hispanic whites. In other words, a far

greater proportion of African-Americans live in extreme poverty than people from other racial and ethnic backgrounds. In addition, families with children under age six were much more likely than other families to live in extreme poverty in 2006.

Children Living in Poverty

In 2005 Hispanic and African-American children were more than three times as likely to live in poverty than non-Hispanic white children. One out of three (34%) African-American children and 28% of Hispanic children lived in poverty, whereas 10% of white, non-Hispanic children

TABLE 5.3

People and families in poverty by selected characteristics, 2005 and 2006 [CONTINUED]

[Numbers in thousands. People as of March of the following year.]

Characteristic	Below poverty in 2005		Below poverty in 2006		Change in poverty (2006 less 2005)[a]	
	Number	Percentage	Number	Percentage	Number	Percentage
Families						
Total	7,657	9.9	7,668	9.8	11	−0.1
Type of family						
Married-couple	2,944	5.1	2,910	4.9	−34	−0.1
Female householder, no husband present	4,044	28.7	4,087	28.3	43	−0.4
Male householder, no wife present	669	13.0	671	13.2	2	0.2

—Represents or rounds to zero.

[a]Details may not sum to totals because of rounding.

[b]Federal surveys now give respondents the option of reporting more than one race. Therefore, two basic ways of defining a race group are possible. A group such as Asian may be defined as those who reported Asian and no other race (the race-alone or single-race concept) or as those who reported Asian regardless of whether they also reported another race (the race-alone-or-in-combination concept). This table shows data using the first approach (race alone). The use of the single-race population does not imply that it is the preferred method of presenting or analyzing data. The Census Bureau uses a variety of approaches. Information on people who reported more than one race, such as white *and* American Indian and Alaska Native or Asian and black or African American, is available from Census 2000 through American FactFinder. About 2.6 percent of people reported more than one race in Census 2000. Data for American Indians and Alaska Natives, Native Hawaiians and other Pacific Islanders, and those reporting two or more races are not shown separately.

[c]The "outside metropolitan statistical areas" category includes both micropolitan statistical areas and territory outside of metropolitan and micropolitan statistical areas.

SOURCE: Carmen DeNavas-Walt, Bernadette D. Proctor, and Jessica Smith, "Table 3. People and Families in Poverty by Selected Characteristics: 2005 and 2006," in *Income, Poverty, and Health Insurance Coverage in the United States: 2006*, U.S. Census Bureau, August 2007, http://www.census.gov/prod/2007pubs/p60-233.pdf (accessed December 20, 2007)

---

lived in poverty. (See Table 5.5.) In families headed by married couples, only 5% of white, non-Hispanic children lived in poverty. The African-American poverty rate of children living in married-couple families was significantly lower than for all African-American children, at 13%, but more than double the poverty rate of non-Hispanic white children in married-couple families. Hispanic children living in married-couple families did not have as significant a drop in their poverty rates; 20% of Hispanic children living with married parents lived in poverty. Children were particularly at risk in households headed by a single female. One out of two Hispanic (50%) and African-American (50%) children living in female-headed families lived in poverty. One out of three (33%) non-Hispanic white children living in female-headed families lived in poverty.

African-American children were also much more likely to live in extreme poverty than non-Hispanic white children in 2005. Seventeen percent of African-American children lived in families with incomes below 50% of the poverty threshold, compared to 11% of Hispanic children and only 4% of white, non-Hispanic children. (See Table 5.5.) More than one out of four African-American children (26%) and Hispanic children (28%) living in female-householder families lived in extreme poverty, compared to 15% of white, non-Hispanic children living in female-householder families.

The National School Lunch Program provides free or reduced-price meals to children from low-income families. Sometimes eligibility for the program is used as a rough guide to family income. Angelina KewalRamani et al. note in *Status and Trends in the Education of Racial and Ethnic Minorities* (September 2007, http://nces .ed.gov/pubs2007/2007039.pdf) that nationwide, 41% of all fourth graders were eligible for free or reduce-price lunches in 2005. The percentages of African-American (70%) and Hispanic (73%) fourth graders who were eligible for these lunches were three times the percentage of non-Hispanic white students who were eligible (24%), and a high proportion of Native American students were also eligible (65%). A third (33%) of Asian and Pacific Islander fourth graders were eligible for the reduced-price lunches.

The percent of students eligible for the National School Lunch Program also varied by where they lived. African-American and Hispanic students who lived in a central city (75% and 79%, respectively) or a rural area (78% and 72%, respectively) were more likely than students who lived in the suburbs or a large town (60% and 66%, respectively) to be eligible for a free or reduced-price lunch. (See Table 5.6.) Asian-American students were the most likely to be eligible if they lived in a central city, where 42% were eligible, rather than in the suburbs or a rural area, where only 25% were eligible. Native Americans who lived in rural areas, including reservations, were the most likely to be eligible for the program. Almost three-quarters (73%) of Native Americans in rural areas, compared to a little over half of Native Americans in central cities (57%) or suburban areas (52%), were eligible.

The Haves and Have-Nots

African-Americans, Hispanics, and non-Hispanic whites view the reality of income and poverty rate differentials between races and ethnic groups differently. In *Whites,*

TABLE 5.4

People with income below specified ratios of their poverty thresholds, by selected characteristics, 2006

[Numbers in thousands]

| Characteristic | Total | Income-to-poverty ratio | | | | | |
| | | Under 0.50 | | Under 1.00 | | Under 1.25 | |
		Number	Percent	Number	Percent	Number	Percent
All people	**296,450**	**15,447**	**5.2**	**36,460**	**12.3**	**49,688**	**16.8**
Age							
Under 18 years	73,727	5,508	7.5	12,827	17.4	17,051	23.1
18 to 24 years	28,405	2,612	9.2	5,047	17.8	6,475	22.8
25 to 34 years	39,868	2,185	5.5	4,920	12.3	6,628	16.6
35 to 44 years	42,762	1,618	3.8	4,049	9.5	5,506	12.9
45 to 54 years	43,461	1,464	3.4	3,399	7.8	4,566	10.5
55 to 59 years	18,221	666	3.7	1,468	8.1	2,002	11.0
60 to 64 years	13,970	482	3.4	1,357	9.7	1,822	13.0
65 years and older	36,035	914	2.5	3,394	9.4	5,638	15.6
Race[a] and Hispanic origin							
White	237,619	9,987	4.2	24,416	10.3	34,290	14.4
White, not Hispanic	196,049	6,917	3.5	16,013	8.2	22,432	11.4
Black	37,306	4,057	10.9	9,048	24.3	11,463	30.7
Asian	13,177	668	5.1	1,353	10.3	1,854	14.1
Hispanic (any race)	44,784	3,455	7.7	9,243	20.6	12,922	28.9
Family status							
In families	245,199	10,341	4.2	25,915	10.6	35,810	14.6
Householder	78,454	3,156	4.0	7,668	9.8	10,531	13.4
Related children under 18	72,609	5,143	7.1	12,299	16.9	16,451	22.7
Related children under 6	24,204	2,231	9.2	4,830	20.0	6,291	26.0
Unrelated subfamilies	1,367	327	23.9	567	41.5	666	48.7
Unrelated individuals	49,884	4,779	9.6	9,977	20.0	13,213	26.5
Male	24,674	2,268	9.2	4,388	17.8	5,661	22.9
Female	25,210	2,511	10.0	5,589	22.2	7,552	30.0

[a]Federal surveys now give respondents the option of reporting more than one race. Therefore, two basic ways of defining a race group are possible. A group such as Asian may be defined as those who reported Asian and no other race (the race-alone or single-race concept) or as those who reported Asian regardless of whether they also reported another race (the race-alone-or-in-combination concept). This table shows data using the first approach (race alone). The use of the single-race population does not imply that it is the preferred method of presenting or analyzing data. The Census Bureau uses a variety of approaches. About 2.6 percent of people reported more than one race in Census 2000. Data for American Indians and Alaska Natives, Native Hawaiians and other Pacific Islanders, and those reporting two or more races are not shown separately.
Note: Details may not sum to totals because of rounding.

SOURCE: Carmen DeNavas-Walt, Bernadette D. Proctor, and Jessica Smith, "Table 4. People with Income below Specified Ratios of Their Poverty Thresholds by Selected Characteristics: 2006," in *Income, Poverty, and Health Insurance Coverage in the United States: 2006*, U.S. Census Bureau, August 2007, http://www.census.gov/prod/2007pubs/p60-233.pdf (accessed December 20, 2007)

Minorities Differ in Views of Economic Opportunities in U.S. (July 10, 2006, http://www.gallup.com/poll/23617/Whites-Minorities-Differ-Views-Economic-Opportunities-US.aspx), Joseph Carroll of the Gallup Organization indicates that when asked whether racial minorities in the nation have equal job opportunities to whites, over half (53%) of non-Hispanic whites surveyed said racial minorities have equal job opportunities. However, 34% of Hispanics and just 17% of African-Americans believed their job opportunities are equal to those of whites.

A Gallup poll finds that in 2006 African-Americans were much more likely than non-Hispanic whites to believe that American society is divided into two groups: the haves and have-nots. Two-thirds (67%) of African-Americans answered that society is divided, whereas only 42% of non-Hispanic whites did. (See Figure 5.2.) What is surprising, considering Hispanics' experience of lower income and higher poverty rates than non-Hispanic

whites in the United States, Hispanics were less likely than non-Hispanic whites to answer that society is divided into the haves and have-nots. Only 31% of Hispanics believed society is divided, whereas 64% said they do not think the United States is divided in this way.

In "The Optimistic Immigrant: Among Latinos, the Recently Arrived Have the Most Hope for the Future" (May 30, 2006, http://pewresearch.org/pubs/28/the-optimistic-immigrant), Gabriel Escobar of the Pew Research Center points out what has been a historic truism in American society: that first-generation immigrants to the United States expect their children to have better opportunities than they have at present. Escobar notes that "Hispanics in general, and Hispanic immigrants in particular, are more inclined than blacks or whites to take an upbeat view about one of the most enduring tenets of the American dream—the idea that each generation will do better in life than the one that preceded it." Part of the

TABLE 5.5

Percentage of related children under age 18 living below selected poverty levels, by age, family structure, race, and Hispanic origin, selected years, 1980–2005

Characteristic	1980	1985	1990	1995	2000	2001	2002	2003	2004	2005
Below 100% poverty										
Related children[a]										
Children in all families, total	18	20	20	20	16	16	16	17	17	17
Related children ages 0–5	20	23	23	24	18	18	19	20	20	20
Related children ages 6–17	17	19	18	18	15	15	15	16	16	16
White, non-Hispanic	11	12	12	11	9	9	9	9	10	10
Back	42	43	44	42	31	30	32	34	33	34
Hispanic[b]	33	40	38	39	28	27	28	29	29	28
Children in married-couple families, total	—	—	10	10	8	8	9	9	9	9
Related children ages 0–5	—	—	12	11	9	9	10	10	10	10
Related children ages 6–17	—	—	10	9	8	7	8	8	8	8
White, non-Hispanic	—	—	7	6	5	5	5	5	5	5
Black	—	—	18	13	9	10	12	11	13	13
Hispanic[b]	—	—	27	28	21	20	21	21	21	20
Children in female-householder families, no husband present, total	51	54	53	50	40	39	40	42	42	43
Related children ages 0–5	65	66	66	62	50	49	49	53	53	53
Related children ages 6–17	46	48	47	45	36	35	36	37	37	38
White, non-Hispanic	—	—	40	34	28	29	29	31	32	33
Black	65	67	65	62	49	47	48	50	49	50
Hispanic[b]	65	72	68	66	50	49	48	51	52	50
Below 50% poverty										
Related children[a]										
Children in all families, total	7	8	8	8	6	7	7	7	7	7
Related children ages 0–5	—	—	10	10	8	8	8	10	9	9
Related children ages 6–17	—	—	7	7	6	6	6	6	6	6
White, non-Hispanic	—	—	4	3	3	3	3	4	4	4
Black	17	22	22	20	15	16	15	17	17	17
Hispanic[b]	—	—	14	16	9	10	11	11	10	11
Children in married-couple families, total	—	—	3	3	2	2	2	2	3	2
Related children ages 0–5	—	—	3	3	2	3	3	3	3	3
Related children ages 6–17	—	—	2	3	2	2	2	2	2	2
White, non-Hispanic	—	—	2	1	2	2	2	1	2	1
Black	—	—	4	3	3	3	3	4	4	5
Hispanic[b]	—	—	7	9	4	5	5	5	4	5
Children in female-householder families, no husband present, total	—	—	28	24	19	20	20	22	22	22
Related children ages 0–5	—	—	37	34	28	28	28	31	31	29
Related children ages 6–17	—	—	23	19	15	17	16	17	18	19
White, non-Hispanic	—	—	19	13	12	13	12	15	15	15
Black	—	—	37	32	24	27	25	27	27	26
Hispanic[b]	—	—	32	33	25	26	26	25	28	28

—Not available.

[a]A related child is a person ages 0–17 who is related to the householder by birth, marriage, or adoption, but is not the householder or the householder's spouse.

[b]Persons of Hispanic origin may be of any race.

Note: The 2004 data have been revised to reflect a correction to the weights in the 2005 Annual Social and Economic Supplements Data for 1999, 2000, and 2001 use Census 2000 population controls. Data for 2000 onward are from the expanded Current Population Survey sample. The poverty level is based on money income and does not include noncash benefits, such as food stamps. Poverty thresholds reflect family size and composition and are adjusted each year using the annual average consumer price index level. The average poverty threshold for a family of four was $19,971 in 2005. The levels shown here are derived from the ratio of the family's income to the family's poverty threshold.

SOURCE: Adapted from "Table ECON 1.A. Child Poverty: Percentage of All Children and Related Children Ages 0–17 Living below Selected Poverty Levels by Selected Characteristics, Selected Years 1980–2005," in *America's Children: Key National Indicators of Well-Being, 2007*, Federal Interagency Forum on Child and Family Statistics, July 2007, http://www.childstats.gov/pdf/ac2007/appendices.pdf (accessed December 27, 2007)

explanation for this positive view lies in the general optimism of immigrants. Immigrants take on the challenge to move to an entirely new country because they strongly believe in their hopes for the future.

GOVERNMENT PROGRAMS

Because minorities are disproportionately poor, they have long accounted for a major portion of the welfare rolls across the United States. The U.S. government offers various forms of assistance to people living with economic hardship. Some of these programs are federally run, and others are run at the state level. In many cases states run federally mandated government programs, which can make tracking them complicated.

In 1996 Congress enacted the Personal Responsibility and Work Opportunity Reconciliation Act to reform the welfare system. The primary goal of the legislation was to get as many people as possible into the paid labor force and off welfare rolls. The law set limits on how long people could receive welfare benefits. Aid to Families with Dependent Children, a guaranteed assistance program for low-income families, was eliminated and replaced with the

TABLE 5.6

Percentage of 4th-graders eligible for free or reduced-price lunch, by school location and race/ethnicity, 2005

Race/ethnicity	Total	10 percent or less	11–25 percent	26–50 percent	51–75 percent	More than 75 percent
Total*	100	15	16	26	21	22
White	100	21	23	32	19	5
Black	100	4	6	18	24	48
Hispanic	100	4	6	16	24	49
Asian/Pacific Islander	100	27	19	21	16	16
American Indian/Alaska Native	100	4	8	21	31	36

*Total includes other race/ethnicity categories not separately shown.
Note: To be eligible for the National School Lunch Program, a student must be from a household with an income at or below 185 percent of the poverty level for reduced-price lunch or at or below 130 percent of the poverty level for free lunch. Race categories exclude persons of Hispanic origin. Detail may not sum to totals because of rounding.

SOURCE: Angelina KewalRamani et al., "Figure 7.4. Percentage of 4th-Graders Eligible for Reduced-Price Lunch, by School Location and Race/Ethnicity: 2005," in *Status and Trends in the Education of Racial and Ethnic Minorities*, U.S. Department of Education, National Center for Education Statistics, Institute of Education Sciences, September 2007, http://nces.ed.gov/pubs2007/2007039.pdf (accessed December 13, 2007)

FIGURE 5.2

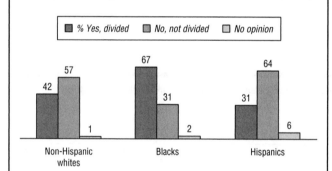

Public opinion on whether "haves" and "have-nots" exist in American society, June 2006

SOME PEOPLE THINK OF AMERICAN SOCIETY AS DIVIDED INTO TWO GROUPS—THE 'HAVES' AND 'HAVE-NOTS'—WHILE OTHERS THINK IT'S INCORRECT TO HINK OF AMERICA THAT WAY. DO YOU, YOURSELF, THINK OF AMERICA AS DIVIDED INTO HAVES AND HAVE-NOTS, OR DON'T YOU THINK OF AMERICA THAT WAY?

SOURCE: Joseph Carroll, "Some People Think of American Society As Divided into Two Groups—the 'Haves' and 'Have-Nots'—While Others Think It's Incorrect to Think of America That Way. Do You, Yourself, Think of America As Divided into Haves and Have-Nots, or Don't You Think of America That Way?" in *Whites, Minorities Differ in Views of Economic Opportunities in U.S.*, The Gallup Organization, July 10, 2006, http://www.gallup.com/poll/23617/Whites-Minorities-Differ-Views-Economic-Opportunities-US.aspx?version=print (accessed January 16, 2008). Copyright © 2008 by The Gallup Organization. Reproduced by Permission of The Gallup Organization.

Temporary Assistance for Needy Families (TANF) program in 1996. The House Committee on Ways and Means (March 6, 2007, http://waysandmeans.house.gov/hearings .asp?formmode=printfriendly&id=5582) reports that the number of families receiving welfare had dropped from 4.4 million in August 1996 to 1.7 million families in September 2006, a decrease of 60%.

The U.S. Department of Health and Human Services indicates that in 2004, 32.4% of all African-Americans received some portion of their total annual family income

from means-tested assistance programs, which include TANF, Supplementary Security Income, and food stamps. (See Table 5.7.) One out of five (22.6%) Hispanics received means-tested assistance. Only 10.1% of non-Hispanic whites received such assistance. Moreover, 10% African-Americans received more than half of their total annual family income from means-tested assistance programs, compared to only 5.2% of Hispanics and only 2.2% of non-Hispanic whites.

Therefore, African-Americans are the most likely to receive means-tested assistance, especially food stamps—14% of African-Americans received food stamps in 2004, compared to 8.2% of Hispanics and 4.3% of non-Hispanic whites. (See Table 5.8.) In addition, African-Americans are more likely than non-Hispanic whites or Hispanics to receive assistance from multiple programs. While a quarter of African-Americans received means-tested assistance in 2004, 5.7% of them received both TANF and food stamps, compared to 2.8% of Hispanics and 0.7% of non-Hispanic whites.

The high number of female-headed families in the African-American community may be part of the explanation for the high rate of means-tested assistance receipt. More than four out of ten (42.6%) individuals in female-headed families received means-tested assistance in 2004, compared to only 8.6% of individuals in married-couple families. (See Table 5.7.) In addition, individuals in female-headed families were the most likely to receive more than half of the annual family income from these programs—13.8% did so, compared to only 1% of individuals living in married-couple families. These numbers suggest that it is particularly difficult for single women with children to make ends meet without turning to government programs for assistance.

In spite of the work requirements of the welfare law, earnings contributed substantially less to the total family income of African-American families than they did to

TABLE 5.7

Percentage of total family income from means-tested assistance programs, by race/ethnicity and age, 2004

	0%	> 0% and <= 25%	> 25% and <= 50%	> 50% and <= 75%	> 75% and <= 100%	Total > 50%
All persons	85.0	8.8	2.5	1.1	2.5	3.7
Racial/ethnic categories						
Non-Hispanic white	89.9	6.4	1.5	0.7	1.5	2.2
Non-Hispanic black	67.6	16.2	6.1	2.9	7.1	10.0
Hispanic	77.4	13.4	4.1	1.8	3.4	5.2
Age categories						
Children ages 0–5	75.4	12.6	5.0	2.6	4.5	7.1
Children ages 6–10	77.8	11.6	4.6	2.2	3.8	6.0
Children ages 11–15	79.6	11.3	4.0	1.9	3.2	5.1
Women ages 16–64	85.0	8.9	2.4	1.1	2.6	3.7
Men ages 16–64	88.4	7.6	1.6	0.5	1.9	2.4
Adults ages 65 and over	90.0	6.2	1.6	0.8	1.5	2.2
Family categories						
Persons in married-couple families	91.4	6.3	1.3	0.4	0.7	1.0
Persons in female-headed families	57.4	19.9	9.0	4.8	9.0	13.8
Persons in male-headed families	78.1	14.4	3.6	1.5	2.5	4.0
Unrelated individuals	87.3	7.0	1.2	0.5	4.0	4.5

Note: Means-tested assistance includes Temporary Assistance for Needy Families (TANF), Supplemental Security Income (SSI) and food stamps. Total >50% with more than 50 percent of their total annual family income from these means-tested programs. Income includes cash income and the value of food stamps. Spouses are not present in the female-headed and male-headed family categories. Persons of Hispanic ethnicity may be of any race. Beginning in 2002, estimates for whites and blacks are for persons reporting a single race only. Persons who reported more than one race are included in the total for all persons but are not shown under any race category. Due to small sample size, American Indians/Alaska Natives, Asians and Native Hawaiians/other Pacific Islanders are included in the total for all persons but are not shown separately.

SOURCE: Gil Crouse, Sarah Douglas, and Susan Hauan, "Table IND 1a. Percentage of Total Annual Family Income from Means-Tested Assistance Programs by Race/Ethnicity and Age: 2004," in *Indicators of Welfare Dependence, Annual Report to Congress, 2007*, U.S. Department of Health and Human Services, 2007, http://aspe.hhs.gov/hsp/Indicators07/ch2.pdf (accessed January 2, 2008)

TABLE 5.8

Percentage of population receiving assistance from Temporary Assistance for Needy Families (TANF), Food Stamps (FS), and/or Supplemental Security Income (SSI), by race/ethnicity and age, 2004

	Any receipt	One program only			Two programs	
		TANF	FS	SSI	TANF & FS	FS & SSI
All persons	10.3	0.2	6.1	1.2	1.6	1.1
Racial/ethnic categories						
Non-Hispanic white	6.8	0.1	4.3	0.9	0.7	0.8
Non-Hispanic black	24.9	0.5	14.0	1.9	5.7	2.8
Hispanic	14.3	0.5	8.2	1.7	2.8	1.2
Age categories						
Children ages 0–5	20.2	0.6	12.1	0.6	6.2	0.7
Children ages 6–10	17.8	0.5	11.5	0.7	4.5	0.6
Children ages 11–15	15.8	0.5	10.1	0.9	3.6	0.7
Women ages 16–64	9.5	0.1	6.0	1.0	1.3	1.1
Men ages 16–64	6.6	0.1	4.0	1.2	0.3	0.9
Adults ages 65 and over	7.9	0.0	2.3	3.1	0.0	2.5
Family categories						
Persons in married-couple families	4.9	0.1	3.1	0.7	0.5	0.4
Persons in female-headed families	33.0	0.6	19.3	2.7	7.9	2.5
Persons in male-headed families	13.7	0.4	7.5	2.2	2.3	1.3
Unrelated individuals	9.7	0.0	5.2	1.7	0.0	2.8

Note: Categories are mutually exclusive. SSI receipt is based on individual receipt; AFDC/TANF (Aid to Families with Dependent Children/Temporary Assistance for Needy Families) and food stamp receipt are based on the full recipient unit. In practice, individuals do not tend to receive both AFDC/TANF and SSI; hence, no individual receives benefits from all three programs. The percentage of individuals receiving assistance from any one program in an average month (shown here) is lower than the percentage residing in families receiving assistance at some point over the course of a year. Spouses are not present in the female-headed and male-headed family categories. Persons of Hispanic ethnicity may be of any race. Beginning in 2002, estimates for whites and blacks are for persons reporting a single race only. Persons who reported more than one race are included in the total for all persons but are not shown under any race category. Due to small sample size, American Indians/Alaska Natives, Asians and Native Hawaiians/other Pacific Islanders are included in the total for all persons but are not shown separately.

SOURCE: Gil Crouse, Sarah Douglas, and Susan Hauan, "Table IND 5a. Percentage of Population Receiving Assistance from Multiple Programs (TANF, Food Stamps, SSI), by Race/Ethnicity and Age: 2004," in *Indicators of Welfare Dependence, Annual Report to Congress, 2007*, U.S. Department of Health and Human Services, 2007, http://aspe.hhs.gov/hsp/Indicators07/ch2.pdf (accessed January 2, 2008)

TABLE 5.9

Percentage of total family income from various sources, by poverty status and race/ethnicity, 2004

	<50% poverty	<100% of poverty	<200% of poverty	200% + of poverty	All individuals
All persons					
TANF, SSI and food stamps	58.4	31.1	10.4	0.2	1.2
Earnings	25.7	48.2	67.2	86.8	84.9
Other income	15.9	20.7	22.4	13.0	13.9
Racial/ethnic categories					
Non-Hispanic white					
TANF, SSI and food stamps	49.0	27.9	7.9	0.1	0.6
Earnings	29.6	44.1	61.4	85.8	84.3
Other income	21.5	28.0	30.7	14.1	15.1
Non-Hispanic black					
TANF, SSI and food stamps	69.8	43.4	18.5	0.5	4.2
Earnings	17.0	36.6	60.3	87.3	81.8
Other income	13.2	20.0	21.2	12.1	14.0
Hispanic					
TANF, SSI and food stamps	56.5	24.5	9.0	0.5	2.6
Earnings	31.5	64.0	81.1	92.1	89.4
Other income	12.0	11.5	9.9	7.4	8.0

Note: Total income is total annual family income, including the value of food stamps. Other income is non-means-tested, non-earnings income such as child support, alimony, pensions, Social Security benefits, interest and dividends. Poverty status categories are not mutually exclusive. Spouses are not present in the female-headed and male-headed family categories. Persons of Hispanic ethnicity may be of any race. Beginning in 2002, estimates for whites and blacks are for persons reporting a single race only. Persons who reported more than one race are included in the total for all persons but are not shown under any race category. Due to small sample size, American Indians/Alaska Natives, Asians and Native Hawaiians/other Pacific Islanders are included in the total for all persons but are not shown separately. TANF is Temporary Assistance for Needy Families. SSI is Supplemental Security Income.

SOURCE: Adapted from Gil Crouse, Sarah Douglas, and Susan Hauan, "Table IND 1c. Percentage of Total Annual Family Income from Various Sources, by Poverty Status, Race/Ethnicity and Age: 2004," in *Indicators of Welfare Dependence, Annual Report to Congress, 2007*, U.S. Department of Health and Human Services, 2007, http://aspe.hhs.gov/hsp/Indicators07/ch2.pdf (accessed January 2, 2008)

non-Hispanic white or Hispanic families in 2004. Among families in poverty, earnings contributed only 36.6% of the total family income of African-American families, but 44.1% of the total family income of non-Hispanic white families and 64% of the total family income of Hispanic families. (See Table 5.9.) Among families in extreme poverty, earnings contributed only 17% of the total family income of African-American families, but 29.6% of the total family income of non-Hispanic white families and 31.5% of the total family income of Hispanic families.

The TANF program has been criticized since its inception in 1996. Critics maintain that success cannot be measured by the drop in the number of recipients. Caseloads initially decreased simply because the eligibility requirements were stiffened. As a result, many immigrants, especially Hispanics who were working poor, were denied aid, adversely affecting their children, who were U.S. citizens. Moreover, the type of work available to individuals on welfare was generally low paying, offering no health insurance or other benefits, and doing little to lift welfare-to-work participants above the poverty level. So, despite falling numbers of TANF recipients, rising poverty levels perhaps provide a more telling portrayal of the program's progress. (See Figure 5.1 and Table 5.3.)

CHAPTER 6
HEALTH

The demographic profiles of African-Americans, Hispanics, Asian-Americans, Pacific Islanders, Native Americans, and Alaskan Natives differ considerably from those of the majority population in the United States. Because a high percentage of minorities live in urban areas, they are exposed to a greater number of environmental hazards, including pollution, traffic hazards, substandard and/or overcrowded housing, and crime. Occupational risks are also greater for minorities because a greater percentage of them are employed in potentially dangerous jobs. Poverty, which is experienced disproportionately by African-Americans, Hispanics, and Native Americans and Alaskan Natives, leads to poor nutrition, poor housing conditions, and poor access to health care. In addition, the amount of stress involved in facing daily discrimination and changing cultural environments as well as the lack of resources for solving stressful situations can play a critical role in the mental and physical health of minority groups.

As a whole, Hispanics enjoy better health on a variety of measures than do non-Hispanic whites, despite Hispanics' disadvantaged position, higher poverty rates, lower educational attainment, and the obstacles to health care that they encounter. This is most likely due in part to the fact that Hispanics in the United States are younger than the non-Hispanic white population. According to the U.S. Census Bureau, in *The Hispanic Population in the United States: 2006* (October 5, 2007, http://www.census .gov/population/www/socdemo/hispanic/cps2006.html), 34.3% of the Hispanic population is under eighteen years in 2006, compared to just 21.9% of the non-Hispanic white population. Conversely, only 5.4% of Hispanics were aged sixty-five or older, compared to 14.7% of non-Hispanic whites. The median (average) age of Hispanics in 2005 was twenty-seven, compared to a median age of forty for non-Hispanic whites. (See Table 6.1.)

In *The Hispanic Population in the United States: March 2002* (June 2003, http://www.census.gov/prod/

2003pubs/p20-545.pdf), Roberto R. Ramirez and G. Patricia de la Cruz of the Census Bureau explain that this age differential is partly due to the higher fertility rate of Hispanics and partly to their recent immigration status—younger people tend to immigrate. In 2002, 40.2% of Hispanics in the United States were foreign born. In addition, first-generation immigrants tend to have more children than do other Americans. In 2005 the median age of native-born Hispanics was only seventeen, compared to a median age of thirty-five for foreign-born Hispanics, which was still lower than the median age of the non-Hispanic white population. (See Table 6.1.)

HEALTH CARE
Quality of Care

In *2006 National Healthcare Disparities Report* (December 2006, http://www.ahrq.gov/qual/nhdr06/nhdr06 report.pdf), the U.S. Department of Health and Human Services (HHS) defines quality health care as "doing the right thing, at the right time, in the right way, for the right people—and having the best possible results." Quality health care is defined as care that is effective, safe, and timely, as well as equitable—meaning that the care does not vary in quality because of personal characteristics such as race or ethnicity.

The HHS focuses on twenty-two core measures of quality and six core measures of access to care to compare the health care received across racial and ethnic groups. It finds that minorities consistently receive a poorer quality of care than non-Hispanic whites. In 2006 African-Americans received poorer quality of care than whites for about 73% of the quality measures, Native Americans and Alaskan Natives for about 41% of quality measures, and Asian-Americans for about 32% of the quality measures. (See Figure 6.1.) Hispanics received lower quality of care than non-Hispanic whites for about 77% of the quality measures. The health-care

TABLE 6.1

Median age by sex, race and ethnicity, 2005

	Total	Male	Female
Hispanic	27	26	27
Native born	17	16	18
Foreign born	35	34	36
White alone, not Hispanic	40	39	41
Black alone, not Hispanic	31	29	33
Asian alone, not Hispanic	35	34	35
Other, not Hispanic	24	22	25
Total	**36**	**35**	**37**

SOURCE: "Table 6. Median Age by Sex, Race and Ethnicity: 2005," in *A Statistical Portrait of Hispanics at Mid-Decade*, Pew Hispanic Center, September 2006, http://pewhispanic.org/files/other/middecade/Table-6.pdf (accessed January 4, 2007)

gap appears to be growing; according to the HHS, in *2004 National Healthcare Disparities Report* (December 2004, http://www.qualitytools.ahrq.gov/disparitiesreport/2004/documents/nhdr2004.pdf), these disparities were more pronounced in 2006 than they had been in 2004.

Access to Care

In *2006 National Healthcare Disparities Report*, the HHS also measures access to health care, finding that minorities, particularly those of low socioeconomic status, face barriers to accessing health care that make receiving basic health services a struggle. Access is measured in several ways, including ability to get into the health-care system, to get care within the health-care system, and to find providers to meet their needs.

The HHS finds that in 2006 Native Americans and Alaskan Natives had worse access to care than did whites for about 17% of the access measures, African-Americans for about 33% of access measures, and Asian-Americans for about 33% of access measures. (See Figure 6.2.) Hispanics had worse access to care than non-Hispanic whites for a staggering 83% of access measures. Part of these differences in access to care for minority groups had to do with socioeconomics; people below the poverty level had worse access to care than did high-income people (family incomes above 400% of the poverty level) for every one of the access measures.

The HHS notes that the change in disparities in core access measures varied greatly by race and ethnic group in 2006. Even though 80% of disparities in access to care were improving for Native Americans and 60% of disparities in access to care were improving for African-Americans and Asian-Americans, only 20% of disparities in access to care were improving for Hispanics. Likewise, no core access measures were worsening for Native Americans; 20% were worsening for Asian-Americans, and 40% were worsening for African-Americans. However, fully 80% of core access measures were worsening

FIGURE 6.1

Percent of minority groups that experienced better, same, or poorer quality of care compared with reference groups, 2006

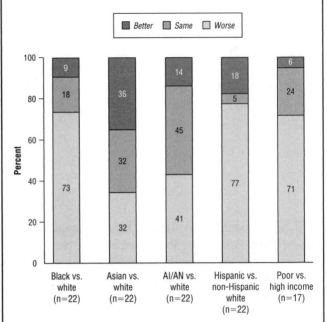

Better = Population received better quality of care than the reference group.
Same = Population and reference group received about the same quality of care.
Worse = Population received poorer quality of care than reference group.
Key: AI/AN = American Indian or Alaska Native.
Note: "Asian" includes "Asian or Pacific Islander" (API) when information is not collected separately for each group. Data presented are the most recent data available. Totals may not add to 100% due to rounding.
n = Sample size.

SOURCE: "Figure H.1. Core Quality Measures for Which Members of Selected Group Experienced Better, Same, or Poorer Quality of Care Compared with Reference Group," in *National Healthcare Disparities Report*, 2006, U.S. Department of Health and Human Services, Agency for Healthcare Research and Quality, June 2007, http://www.ahrq.gov/qual/nhdr06/nhdr06high.pdf (accessed January 4, 2008)

for Hispanics. African-Americans' access to their primary care provider and ability to pay for health care were getting worse. Hispanics were increasingly uninsured, had worse access to their primary care provider, and were getting less likely to have access to a source of ongoing health care.

HEALTH INSURANCE. Lack of health insurance is one formidable barrier to receiving health care. Carmen DeNavas-Walt, Bernadette D. Proctor, and Jessica Smith of the Census Bureau indicate in *Income, Poverty, and Health Insurance Coverage in the United States: 2006* (August 2007, http://www.census.gov/prod/2007pubs/p60-233.pdf) that the number of uninsured Americans rose to its highest level ever in 2006, when forty-seven million people were uninsured. Lack of insurance coverage is a significant barrier to getting basic health-care services. The HHS, in *2006 National Healthcare Disparities Report*, emphasizes that uninsured people are more likely to die early and to have a poor health status because it is more difficult for

FIGURE 6.2

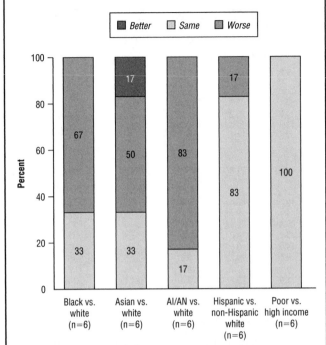

Percent of minority groups that experienced better, same, or worse access to care compared with reference groups, 2006

Better = Population received better quality of care than the reference group.
Same = Population and reference group received about the same quality of care.
Worse = Population received poorer quality of care than reference group.
Key: AI/AN = American Indian or Alaska Native.
Note: "Asian" includes "Asian or Pacific Islander" (API) when information is not collected separately for each group. Data presented are the most recent data available. Totals may not add to 100% due to rounding.
n = Sample size.

SOURCE: "Figure H.2. Core Access Measures for Which Members of Selected Group Experienced Better, Same, or Worse Access to Care Compared with Reference Group," in *National Healthcare Disparities Report, 2006*, U.S. Department of Health and Human Services, Agency for Healthcare Research and Quality, December 2006, http://www.ahrq.gov/qual/nhdr06/nhdr06high.pdf (accessed January 4, 2008)

TABLE 6.2

People without health insurance coverage, by race and Hispanic origin, 2004–06

[Numbers in thousands]

| Race[a] and Hispanic origin | 3-year average 2004–2006[b] | |
	Number Estimate	Percentage Estimate
All races	45,102	15.3
White	34,151	14.5
White, not Hispanic	20,875	10.7
Black	7,174	19.4
American Indian and Alaska Native	748	31.4
Asian	2,036	16.1
Native Hawaiian and other Pacific Islander	139	21.7
Hispanic origin (any race)	14,187	32.7

[a]Federal surveys now give respondents the option of reporting more than one race. Therefore, two basic ways of defining a race group are possible. A group such as Asian may be defined as those who reported Asian and no other race (the race-alone or single-race concept) or as those who reported Asian regardless of whether they also reported another race (the race-alone-or-in-combination concept). This table shows data using the first approach (race alone). The use of the single-race population does not imply that it is the preferred method of presenting or analyzing data. About 2.6 percent of people reported more than one race in Census 2000.
[b]The 2004 and 2005 data have been revised since originally published.

SOURCE: Carmen DeNavas-Walt, Bernadette D. Proctor, and Jessica Smith, "Table 7. People without Health Insurance Coverage by Race and Hispanic Origin Using 3-Year Average: 2004 to 2006," in *Income, Poverty, and Health Insurance Coverage in the United States: 2006*, U.S. Census Bureau, August 2007, http://www.census.gov/prod/2007pubs/p60-233.pdf (accessed December 20, 2007)

the uninsured to get health care and therefore they are diagnosed at later disease stages.

Between 2004 and 2006 members of minority groups were much less likely to carry health insurance coverage than were their white, non-Hispanic counterparts. On average during this period, 32.7% of Hispanics, 31.4% of Native Americans and Alaskan Natives, 21.7% of Native Hawaiians and Other Pacific Islanders, 19.4% of African-Americans, and 16.1% of Asian-Americans lacked coverage. (See Table 6.2.) In comparison, only 10.7% of non-Hispanic whites lacked health insurance coverage during this period.

Those minorities who do have health insurance are more likely than non-Hispanic whites to be covered by government programs rather than by private health insurance. In 2005 members of all minority groups except

Asian-Americans were more likely to be covered by Medicaid (the federally funded health-care program for low-income people) than were non-Hispanic whites. In that year Medicaid covered 8.5% of non-Hispanic whites and 8.2% of Asian-Americans. (See Table 6.3.) However, Medicaid covered 24.9% of African-Americans, 24.2% of Native Americans and Alaskan Natives, and 22.9% of Hispanics. Among Hispanics, Puerto Ricans were the most likely (31.9%) and Cubans were the least likely (17.7%) to be covered by Medicaid. The large proportion of minorities on Medicaid is in part explained by eligibility requirements; only poor and low-income people qualify, and members of these groups are disproportionately poor. However, Benjamin Le Cook notes in "Effect of Medicaid Managed Care on Racial Disparities in Health Care Access" (*Health Services Research*, vol. 42, no. 1, February 2007) that because Medicaid reimburses physicians at lower rates than do private insurance plans, fewer and fewer doctors accept it, thereby erecting further barriers for those covered by Medicaid to receiving adequate health care.

Nearly all people aged sixty-five and older are covered by health insurance largely due to Medicare (the federally funded health-care program for senior citizens). However, a much higher proportion of minorities are additionally covered by Medicaid, whereas non-Hispanic

TABLE 6.3

Medicaid coverage among persons under 65 years of age, by race/ethnicity, selected years, 1984–2005

[Data are based on household interviews of a sample of the civilian noninstitutionalized population]

Characteristic	1984	1989	1995	1997[a]	2000	2002	2003	2004(1)[b]	2004(2)[b]	2005[b]
					Number in millions					
Total[c]	14.0	15.4	26.6	22.9	23.2	29.4	30.9	31.1	31.6	33.2
					Percent of population					
Total[c]	6.8	7.2	11.5	9.7	9.5	11.8	12.3	12.3	12.5	12.9
Race[d]										
White only	4.6	5.1	8.9	7.4	7.1	9.3	10.4	10.2	10.4	11.0
Black or African American only	20.5	19.0	28.5	22.4	21.2	23.2	23.7	24.5	24.9	24.9
American Indian or Alaska Native only	28.2*	29.7	19.0	19.6	15.1	21.1	18.5	18.0	18.4	24.2
Asian only	8.7*	8.8*	10.5	9.6	7.5	9.8	8.0	9.6	9.8	8.2
Native Hawaiian or other Pacific Islander only	—	—	—	—	*	*	*	*	*	*
2 or more races	—	—	—	—	19.1	21.6	23.5	19.0	19.3	22.0
Hispanic origin and race[d]										
Hispanic or Latino	13.3	13.5	21.9	17.6	15.5	20.8	21.8	21.9	22.5	22.9
Mexican	12.2	12.4	21.6	17.2	14.0	20.2	21.7	21.9	22.4	23.0
Puerto Rican	31.5	27.3	33.4	31.0	29.4	29.0	31.0	28.5	29.1	31.9
Cuban	4.8*	7.7*	13.4	7.3	9.2	14.9	13.8	17.9	17.9	17.7
Other Hispanic or Latino	7.9	11.1	18.2	15.3	14.5	19.6	19.3	19.9	20.8	19.7
Not Hispanic or Latino	6.2	6.6	10.2	8.7	8.5	10.3	10.6	10.5	10.7	11.1
White only	3.7	4.2	7.1	6.1	6.1	7.7	8.0	7.8	7.9	8.5
Black or African American only	20.7	19.0	28.1	22.1	21.0	23.2	23.4	24.1	24.6	24.8

*Estimates are considered unreliable.
— Data not available.
[a]Starting with 1997 data, the National Health Interview Survey (NHIS) was redesigned, and changes to the questions on health insurance coverage were made.
[b]Beginning in quarter 3 of the 2004 NHIS, persons under 65 years with no reported coverage were asked explicitly about Medicaid coverage. Estimates were calculated without and with the additional information from this question in the columns labeled 2004(1) and 2004(2), respectively, and estimates were calculated with the additional information in 2005.
[c]Includes all other races not shown separately and, in 1984 and 1989, with unknown poverty level.
[d]The race groups, white, black, American Indian or Alaska Native, Asian, Native Hawaiian or other Pacific Islander, and 2 or more races, include persons of Hispanic and non-Hispanic origin. Persons of Hispanic origin may be of any race. Starting with 1999 data, race-specific estimates are tabulated according to the 1997 revisions to the Standards for the Classification of Federal Data on Race and Ethnicity and are not strictly comparable with estimates for earlier years. The five single-race categories plus multiple-race categories shown in the table conform to the 1997 standards. Starting with 1999 data, race-specific estimates are for persons who reported only one racial group; the category 2 or more races includes persons who reported more than one racial group. Prior to 1999, data were tabulated according to the 1977 standards with four racial groups and the Asian only category included Native Hawaiian or other Pacific Islander. Estimates for single-race categories prior to 1999 included persons who reported one race or, if they reported more than one race, identified one race as best representing their race. Starting with 2003 data, race responses of other race and unspecified multiple race were treated as missing, and then race was imputed if these were the only race responses. Almost all persons with a race response of other race were of Hispanic origin.
Notes: Medicaid includes other public assistance through 1996. Starting with 1997 data, state-sponsored health plan coverage is included as Medicaid coverage. Starting with 1999 data, coverage by the State Children's Health Insurance Program (SCHIP) is included as Medicaid coverage. In 2005, 10.2% of persons under 65 years of age were covered by Medicaid, 1.3% by state-sponsored health plans, and 1.5% by SCHIP.

SOURCE: Adapted from "Table 138. Medicaid Coverage among Persons under 65 Years of Age, by Selected Characteristics: United States, Selected Years 1984–2005," in *Health, United States, 2007. With Chartbook on Trends in the Health of Americans*, U.S. Department of Health and Human Services, Centers for Disease Control and Prevention, National Center for Health Statistics, 2007, http://www.cdc.gov/nchs/data/hus/hus07.pdf (accessed January 4, 2008)

whites tend to be covered by private insurance. For example, in 2005 only 6.1% of non-Hispanic whites aged sixty-five and older were covered by Medicaid, compared to 23.6% of African-Americans and 29.2% of Hispanics. (See Table 6.4.) In 2005 non-Hispanic whites aged sixty-five and older were covered either by an employer-sponsored plan (39.5%) or by a Medigap plan (29.1%), both of which are forms of private health insurance. In contrast, 27.9% of African-Americans and 18.6% of Hispanics were covered by an employer-sponsored plan and 9.5% and 11.1%, respectively, were covered by a Medigap plan.

DOCTOR VISITS. Another measure of a group's access to care is the number of doctor visits made annually. Since the 1980s, as more outpatient clinics and other outreach health facilities have opened, Americans have had increased opportunities to seek medical help. However, in 2005 members of minority groups were more likely than non-Hispanic whites to have made no visits to a doctor's office or emergency room in the previous twelve months. In that year, 24% of Hispanics, 21.6% of Asian-Americans, 20.5% of Native Americans and Alaskan Natives, and 16% of African-Americans made no visits to health-care providers. (See Table 6.5.) By contrast, only 13.1% of non-Hispanic whites made no health-care visits in that year. In part, this disparity can be explained by the disproportionate number of minorities who are poor or low income; these groups were more likely than non-low income people to make no visits to a doctor's office or an emergency room in 2005.

INDIAN HEALTH SERVICE. Federal funding for Native American health care is provided through the Indian Health Service (IHS; November 6, 2007, http://www.ihs.gov/PublicInfo/PublicAffairs/Welcome_Info/IHSintro.asp),

TABLE 6.4

Health insurance coverage for persons 65 years of age and over, according to type of coverage and race/ethnicity, selected years, 1992–2005

[Data are based on household interviews of a sample of the civilian noninstitutionalized population]

Characteristic	Medicare risk Health Maintenance Organization[a]					Medicaid[b]				
	1992	1995	2000	2004	2005	1992	1995	2000	2004	2005
Age	Number in millions									
65 years and over	1.1	2.6	5.9	4.5	4.6	2.7	2.8	2.7	3.2	3.2
	Percent of population									
65 years and over	3.9	8.9	19.3	14.3	14.5	9.4	9.6	9.0	10	10.1
65–74 years	4.2	9.5	20.6	13.9	13.9	7.9	8.8	8.5	9.3	9.9
75–84 years	3.7	8.3	18.5	15.1	15.3	10.6	9.6	8.9	10.3	9.9
85 years and over	*	7.3	16.3	13.6	13.9	16.6	13.6	11.2	12.5	11.9
Race and Hispanic origin										
White, not Hispanic or Latino	3.6	8.4	18.4	13.0	13.2	5.6	5.4	5.1	6.0	6.1
Black, not Hispanic or Latino	*	7.9	20.7	15.9	17.1	28.5	30.3	23.6	24.7	23.6
Hispanic	*	15.5	27.5	28.0	27.2	39.0	40.5	28.7	27.2	29.2

Characteristic	Employer-sponsored plan[c]					Medigap[d]				
	1992	1995	2000	2004	2005	1992	1995	2000	2004	2005
Age	Number in millions									
65 years and over	12.5	11.3	10.7	11.5	11.6	9.9	9.5	7.6	7.8	8.2
	Percent of population									
65 years and over	42.8	38.6	35.2	36.6	36.4	33.9	32.5	25.0	24.8	25.7
65–74 years	46.9	41.1	36.6	38.4	38.1	31.4	29.9	21.7	22.1	23.2
75–84 years	38.2	37.1	35.0	36.1	35.5	37.5	35.2	27.8	26.5	27.3
85 years and over	31.6	30.2	29.4	31.0	31.8	38.3	37.6	31.1	30.4	30.8
Race and Hispanic origin										
White, not Hispanic or Latino	45.9	41.3	38.6	39.6	39.5	37.2	36.2	28.3	28.2	29.1
Black, not Hispanic or Latino	25.9	26.7	22.0	28.0	27.9	13.6	10.2	7.5	8.5	9.5
Hispanic	20.7	16.9	15.8	19.5	18.6	15.8	10.1	11.3	9.2	11.1

Characteristic	Medicare fee-for-service only or other[e]				
	1992	1995	2000	2004	2005
Age	Number in millions				
65 years and over	2.9	3.1	3.5	4.5	4.3
	Percent of population				
65 years and over	9.9	10.5	11.5	14.3	13.3
65–74 years	9.7	10.7	12.6	16.3	14.9
75–84 years	10.1	9.9	9.9	12.1	11.9
85 years and over	10.8	11.3	12.1	12.5	11.6
Race and Hispanic origin					
White, not Hispanic or Latino	7.7	8.7	9.6	13.2	12.2
Black, not Hispanic or Latino	26.7	25.0	26.1	22.9	21.9
Hispanic	18.3	17.1	16.7	16.2	13.9

*Sample cell size is 50 or fewer.
[a]Enrollee has Medicare risk Health Maintenance Organization (HMO) regardless of other insurance.
[b]Enrolled in Medicaid and not enrolled in a Medicare risk HMO.
[c]Private insurance plans purchased through employers (own, current, or former employer, family business, union, or former employer or union of spouse) and not enrolled in a Medicare risk HMO or Medicaid.
[d]Supplemental insurance purchased privately or through organizations such as the American Association of Retired Persons (AARP) or professional organizations, and not enrolled in a Medicare risk HMO, Medicaid, or employer-sponsored plan.
[e]Medicare fee-for-service only or other public plans (except Medicaid).
Notes: Insurance categories are mutually exclusive.

SOURCE: Adapted from "Table 140. Health Insurance Coverage for Persons 65 Years of Age and over, by Type of Coverage and Selected Characteristics: United States, Selected Years 1992–2005," in *Health, United States, 2007. With Chartbook on Trends in the Health of Americans*, U.S. Department of Health and Human Services, Centers for Disease Control and Prevention, National Center for Health Statistics, 2007, http://www.cdc.gov/nchs/data/hus/hus07.pdf (accessed January 4, 2008)

whose mission is "to raise the physical, mental, social, and spiritual health of American Indians and Alaska Natives to the highest level." Delivery of health care to Native Americans is complicated by the lack of services and the long distances that sometimes must be traveled to receive care. Alaskan Natives are often able to get preventive medical care only by flying to a medical facility, and, even though transportation costs are covered for emergency care, they

TABLE 6.5

Health care visits to doctor offices, emergency departments, and home visits within the past 12 months, by race/ethnicity, health insurance, and poverty level, 1997, 2004, and 2005

[Data are based on household interviews of a sample of the civilian noninstitutionalized population]

| | Number of health care visits[a] | | | | | | | | | | | |
| | None | | | 1–3 visits | | | 4–9 visits | | | 10 or more visits | | |
Characteristic	1997	2004	2005	1997	2004	2005	1997	2004	2005	1997	2004	2005
Race[b, c]												
White only	16.0	16.0	15.2	46.1	45.4	46.0	23.9	24.8	24.9	14.0	13.8	14.0
Black or African American only	16.8	15.8	16.0	46.1	47.0	47.5	23.2	24.6	23.6	13.9	12.6	12.9
American Indian or Alaska Native only	17.1	17.7	20.5	38.0	41.7	36.6	24.2	25.0	29.4	20.7	15.5	13.4
Asian only	22.8	20.8	21.6	49.1	51.5	49.5	19.7	19.7	20.5	8.3	8.1	8.5
Native Hawaiian or other Pacific Islander only		*	*	—	*	*	—	*	*	—	*	*
2 or more races	—	13.6	15.6	—	42.9	37.9	—	26.2	26.7	—	17.3	19.9
Hispanic origin and race[b, c]												
Hispanic or Latino	24.9	26.7	24.0	42.3	41.8	42.4	20.3	20.6	21.7	12.5	10.9	11.9
Mexican	28.9	29.7	26.7	40.8	41.0	41.7	18.5	18.9	20.5	11.8	10.4	11.1
Not Hispanic or Latino	15.4	14.2	13.9	46.7	46.5	46.8	24.0	25.2	25.2	13.9	14.1	14.0
White only	14.7	13.5	13.1	46.6	46.1	46.7	24.4	25.7	25.7	14.3	14.7	14.6
Black or African American only	16.9	15.6	16.0	46.1	47.3	47.5	23.1	24.6	23.6	13.8	12.5	12.9
Hispanic origin and race and percent of poverty level[b, c]					Percent distribution							
Hispanic or Latino												
Below 100%	30.2	31.6	28.1	34.8	35.0	37.4	19.9	19.6	19.8	15.0	13.9	14.7
100%–less than 200%	28.7	30.5	27.8	39.7	39.3	39.0	20.4	19.4	22.2	11.2	10.9	11.1
200% or more	18.9	21.5	19.4	48.8	47.0	47.1	20.4	22.2	22.7	11.9	9.2	10.8
Not Hispanic or Latino												
White only												
Below 100%	17.0	16.2	16.6	38.3	37.5	36.4	23.9	25.4	27.4	20.9	20.9	19.7
100%–less than 200%	17.3	16.7	17.6	44.1	43.2	42.2	22.2	23.4	23.2	16.3	16.7	17.0
200% or more	13.8	12.7	11.8	48.2	47.4	48.7	24.9	26.1	26.0	13.1	13.8	13.6
Black or African American only												
Below 100%	17.4	15.9	17.9	38.5	40.9	40.2	23.4	25.7	24.5	20.7	17.5	17.4
100%–less than 200%	18.8	18.1	16.2	43.7	44.5	47.1	22.9	23.8	24.0	14.5	13.7	12.7
200% or more	15.6	14.3	15.2	51.7	51.3	50.4	22.7	24.4	23.4	10.0	10.0	11.0
Health insurance status prior to interview[e, f]												
Under 65 years												
Insured continuously all 12 months	14.1	13.4	12.4	49.2	49.4	50.1	23.6	24.6	24.5	13.0	12.7	12.9
Uninsured for any period up to 12 months	18.9	20.0	18.9	46.0	45.7	45.1	20.8	21.9	22.1	14.4	12.3	13.8
Uninsured more than 12 months	39.0	43.9	43.6	41.4	41.3	40.1	13.2	10.0	12.1	6.4	4.8	4.2

*Estimates are considered unreliable.
— Data not available.
[a]This table presents a summary measure of health care visits to doctor offices, emergency departments, and home visits during a 12-month period.
[b]Estimates are age-adjusted to the year 2000 standard population using six age groups: Under 18 years, 18–44 years, 45–54 years, 55–64 years, 65–74 years, and 75 years and over.
[c]The race groups, white, black, American Indian or Alaska Native, Asian, Native Hawaiian or other Pacific Islander, and 2 or more races, include persons of Hispanic and non-Hispanic origin. Persons of Hispanic origin may be of any race. Starting with 1999 data, race-specific estimates are tabulated according to the 1997 Revisions to the Standards for the Classification of Federal Data on Race and Ethnicity and are not strictly comparable with estimates for earlier years. The five single-race categories plus multiple-race categories shown in the table conform to the 1997 standards. Starting with 1999 data, race-specific estimates are for persons who reported only one racial group; the category 2 or more races includes persons who reported more than one racial group. Prior to 1999, data were tabulated according to the 1977 standards with four racial groups and the Asian only category included Native Hawaiian or other Pacific Islander. Estimates for single-race categories prior to 1999 included persons who reported one race or, if they reported more than one race, identified one race as best representing their race. Starting with 2003 data, race responses of other race and unspecified multiple race were treated as missing, and then race was imputed if these were the only race responses. Almost all persons with a race response of other race were of Hispanic origin.
[d]Percent of poverty level is based on family income and family size and composition using U.S. Census Bureau poverty thresholds. Missing family income data were imputed for 25%-29% of persons in 1997–1998 and 32%-35% in 1999–2005.
[e]Estimates for persons under 65 years of age are age-adjusted to the year 2000 standard population using four age groups: Under 18 years, 18–44 years, 45 -54 years, and 55–64 years of age.
[f]Health insurance categories are mutually exclusive. Persons who reported both Medicaid and private coverage are classified as having private coverage. Starting in 1997, Medicaid includes state-sponsored health plans and State Children's Health Insurance Program (SCHIP). In addition to private and Medicaid, the insured category also includes military plans, other government-sponsored health plans, and Medicare, not shown separately. Persons not covered by private insurance, Medicaid, SCHIP, public assistance (through 1996), state-sponsored or other government-sponsored health plans (starting in 1997), Medicare, or military plans are considered to have no health insurance coverage. Persons with only Indian Health Service coverage are considered to have no health insurance coverage.
Note: In 1997, the National Health Interview Survey questionnaire was redesigned.

SOURCE: Adapted from "Table 82. Health Care Visits to Doctor Offices, Emergency Departments, and Home Visits within the Past 12 Months, by Selected Characteristics: United States, 1997, 2004, and 2005," in *Health, United States, 2007. With Chartbook on Trends in the Health of Americans*, U.S. Department of Health and Human Services, Centers for Disease Control and Prevention, National Center for Health Statistics, 2007, http://www.cdc.gov/nchs/data/hus/hus07.pdf (accessed January 4, 2008)

are not provided for routine care. The HHS indicates in *2006 National Healthcare Disparities Report* that nationwide about 45% of Native Americans rely on the IHS to provide access to health care.

Many Native American tribes have invested some of the money earned from casinos to improve health services. For example, the Pueblo of Sandia (2000, http://www.sandiapueblo.nsn.us/health_and_social_services.html) in New Mexico built a multimillion-dollar medical complex. This new complex saves the residents the long drives to distant clinics that provide medical and dental care through the IHS. The center includes examination rooms, dental rooms, and state-of-the-art equipment. There is an adjacent wellness and education center that houses a gymnasium, a weight room, and aquatic therapy facilities.

PREGNANCY AND BIRTH
Prenatal Care

The importance of early prenatal care cannot be over-emphasized, as doctors are now better able to detect, and often correct, potential problems early in pregnancy. Every pregnant woman should receive prenatal care, and the National Center for Health Statistics (NCHS) believes the United States is capable of guaranteeing that more than 90% of pregnant women receive prenatal care during the first trimester of pregnancy.

In 2004, 83.9% of all women in the United States received prenatal care during their first trimester of pregnancy, but that percentage was significantly lower among some minority groups. (See Table 6.6.) Almost nine out of ten non-Hispanic white women (88.9%) and Asian and Pacific Islander women (85.6%) received prenatal care during their first trimester. By contrast, only 77.5% of Hispanic women, 76.4% of African-American women, and 69.9% of Native American women did so. It is worthy of note, however, that despite the low rates of first-trimester prenatal care among Hispanic women in general, Cuban women had among the highest rates of prenatal care of all racial and ethnic groups, at 86.6%.

Births and Fertility

Of the nearly 4.3 million births in 2006, 2.3 million were to non-Hispanic white mothers, 1 million were to Hispanic mothers, 617,220 were to African-American mothers, 239,829 were to Asian and Pacific Islander mothers, and 47,494 were to Native American mothers. (See Table 6.7.) However, the birth rate (live births per one thousand population in a specified group) was highest among Hispanics (23.4), followed by Asians and Pacific Islanders and African-Americans (both had a birth rate of 16.5) and Native Americans (14.8). Non-Hispanic whites had the lowest birthrate, at 11.6 per 1,000 population.

The fertility rate refers to the number of live births per one thousand women aged fifteen to forty-four in a specified group. In 2006 Hispanic women had the highest fertility rate (101.5), followed by African-American women (70.6), Asian and Pacific Islander women (67.2), and Native American women (62.8) (See Table 6.7.). Non-Hispanic white women had the lowest fertility rate, at 59.5. Even though Hispanic women had the highest fertility rate, it varied among Hispanics from different countries of origin. According to Joyce A. Martin et al. of the Centers for Disease Control and Prevention (CDC), in "Births: Final Data for 2004" (*National Vital Statistics Reports*, vol. 55, no. 1, September 29, 2006), in 2004, the most recent year for which data are available, women of Mexican origin had the highest fertility rate (106.8) among Hispanics, whereas Cuban women had the lowest (53.2).

Low Birth Weight and Infant Mortality

In "Explaining the 2001–02 Infant Mortality Increase: Data from the Linked Birth/Infant Death Data Set" (*National Vital Statistics Reports*, vol. 53, no. 12, January 24, 2005), Marian F. MacDorman et al. of the CDC explain that moderately low birth weight is defined as being equal to 1,500 to 2,499 grams (3.3 to 5.5 pounds). Very low birth weight is less than fifteen hundred grams. Low-birth-weight babies, as well as premature babies (born before thirty-seven weeks of gestation), often suffer serious health problems and encounter developmental problems later in life. In 2002 the infant mortality rate for low-birth-weight infants was twenty-five times that for infants born weighing twenty-five hundred grams or more.

The percentage of babies born with low birth weights increased between 1990 and 2004. According to the CDC, 7% of babies born in 1990 weighed less than twenty-five hundred grams, compared to 8.1% of babies born in 2004. (See Table 6.8.) In 2004 African-Americans were almost twice as likely as non-Hispanic whites to have low-birth-weight babies. In that year, 13.4% of non-Hispanic African-American babies were born with low birth weights, whereas 7.9% of Asian and Pacific Islander babies, 7.5% of Native American or Alaskan Native babies, 7.2% of non-Hispanic white babies, and 6.8% of Hispanic babies were born with low birth weights. The percentage of very low-birth-weight live births also increased during this period, from 1.3% in 1990 to 1.5% in 2004. Again, African-American mothers (3.1%) faced twice the risk of having a very low-birth-weight baby than did all mothers (1.5%).

The infant mortality rate (rate of deaths before one year of age) increased in 2002 for the first time in more than forty years, from 6.9 infant deaths per 1,000 live births in 2000 to 7 infant deaths per 1,000 live births in 2002. (See Table 6.9.) This increase was due primarily to an increase in the number of births of very low-birth-weight

TABLE 6.6

Prenatal care for live births, according to detailed race and Hispanic origin of mother, selected years, 1970–2004

[Data are based on birth certificates]

Prenatal care, race, and Hispanic origin of mother	1970	1975	1980	1985	1990	1995	2000	2002	2003ᵃ	43 reporting areas 2003ᵇ	2004ᵃ
Prenatal care began during 1st trimester						Percent of live birthsᶜ					
All races	68.0	72.4	76.3	76.2	75.8	81.3	83.2	83.7	84.1	84.0	83.9
White	72.3	75.8	79.2	79.3	79.2	83.6	85.0	85.4	85.7	85.5	85.4
Black or African American	44.2	55.5	62.4	61.5	60.6	70.4	74.3	75.2	75.9	76.1	76.4
American Indian or Alaska Native	38.2	45.4	55.8	57.5	57.9	66.7	69.3	69.8	70.8	70.6	69.9
Asian or Pacific Islanderᵈ	—	—	73.7	74.1	75.1	79.9	84.0	84.8	85.4	85.4	85.6
Chinese	71.8	76.7	82.6	82.0	81.3	85.7	87.6	87.2	—	—	—
Japanese	78.1	82.7	86.1	84.7	87.0	89.7	91.0	90.5	—	—	—
Filipino	60.6	70.6	77.3	76.5	77.1	80.9	84.9	85.4	—	—	—
Hawaiian	—	—	68.8	67.7	65.8	75.9	79.9	78.1	—	—	—
Other Asian or Pacific Islander	—	—	67.4	69.9	71.9	77.0	82.5	83.9	—	—	—
Hispanic or Latinoᵉ	—	—	60.2	61.2	60.2	70.8	74.4	76.7	77.5	77.3	77.5
Mexican	—	—	59.6	60.0	57.8	69.1	72.9	75.7	76.5	76.9	77.2
Puerto Rican	—	—	55.1	58.3	63.5	74.0	78.5	79.9	81.2	80.3	79.9
Cuban	—	—	82.7	82.5	84.8	89.2	91.7	92.0	92.1	86.5	86.6
Central and South American	—	—	58.8	60.6	61.5	73.2	77.6	78.7	79.2	78.1	77.6
Other and unknown Hispanic or Latino	—	—	66.4	65.8	66.4	74.3	75.8	76.7	77.0	77.5	78.1
Not Hispanic or Latino:ᵉ											
White	—	—	81.2	81.4	83.3	87.1	88.5	88.6	89.0	89.1	88.9
Black or African American	—	—	60.8	60.2	60.7	70.4	74.3	75.2	75.9	76.2	76.5
Prenatal care began during 3rd trimester or no prenatal care											
All races	7.9	6.0	5.1	5.7	6.1	4.2	3.9	3.6	3.5	3.6	3.6
White	6.3	5.0	4.3	4.8	4.9	3.5	3.3	3.1	3.0	3.1	3.2
Black or African American	16.6	10.5	8.9	10.2	11.3	7.6	6.7	6.2	6.0	5.9	5.7
American Indian or Alaska Native	28.9	22.4	15.2	12.9	12.9	9.5	8.6	8.0	7.6	7.7	7.9
Asian or Pacific Islanderᵈ	—	—	6.5	6.5	5.8	4.3	3.3	3.1	3.1	3.1	3.0
Chinese	6.5	4.4	3.7	4.4	3.4	3.0	2.2	2.1	—	—	—
Japanese	4.1	2.7	2.1	3.1	2.9	2.3	1.8	2.1	—	—	—
Filipino	7.2	4.1	4.0	4.8	4.5	4.1	3.0	2.8	—	—	—
Hawaiian	—	—	6.7	7.4	8.7	5.1	4.2	4.7	—	—	—
Other Asian or Pacific Islander	—	—	9.3	8.2	7.1	5.0	3.8	3.5	—	—	—
Hispanic or Latinoᵉ	—	—	12.0	12.4	12.0	7.4	6.3	5.5	5.3	5.3	5.4
Mexican	—	—	11.8	12.9	13.2	8.1	6.9	5.8	5.6	5.5	5.5
Puerto Rican	—	—	16.2	15.5	10.6	5.5	4.5	4.1	3.7	3.9	3.9
Cuban	—	—	3.9	3.7	2.8	2.1	1.4	1.3	1.3	2.9	2.9
Central and South American	—	—	13.1	12.5	10.9	6.1	5.4	4.9	4.7	4.9	5.1
Other and unknown Hispanic or Latino	—	—	9.2	9.4	8.5	6.0	5.9	5.3	5.4	5.6	5.5
Not Hispanic or Latino:ᵉ											
White	—	—	3.5	4.0	3.4	2.5	2.3	2.2	2.1	2.1	2.2
Black or African American	—	—	9.7	10.9	11.2	7.6	6.7	6.2	6.0	5.9	5.7

—Data not available.

ᵃReporting areas that have adopted the 2003 revision of the U.S. Standard Certificate of Live Birth are excluded because prenatal care data based on the 2003 revision are not comparable with data based on the 1989 and earlier revisions of the U.S. Standard Certificate of Live Birth. In 2003, Pennsylvania and Washington adopted the 2003 revision; in 2004, Florida, Idaho, Kentucky, New Hampshire, New York State (excluding New York City), South Carolina, and Tennessee adopted the 2003 Revision.

ᵇData for 2003 are limited to the 43 reporting areas using the 1989 revision of the U.S. Standard Certificate of Live Birth in 2004 and are provided for comparison with 2004.

ᶜExcludes live births where trimester when prenatal care began is unknown.

ᵈStarting with 2003 data, estimates are not shown for Asian or Pacific Islander subgroups during the transition from single race to multiple race reporting.

ᵉPrior to 1993, data from states lacking an Hispanic-origin item on the birth certificate were excluded. Data for non-Hispanic white and non-Hispanic black women for years prior to 1989 are not nationally representative and are provided for comparison with Hispanic data.

Notes: Data are based on the 1989 and earlier revisions of the U.S. Standard Certificate of Live Birth. Data for 1970 and 1975 exclude births that occurred in states not reporting prenatal care. The race groups, white, black, American Indian or Alaska Native, and Asian or Pacific Islander, include persons of Hispanic and non-Hispanic origin. Persons of Hispanic origin may be of any race. Starting with 2003 data, some states reported multiple-race data. The multiple-race data for these states were bridged to the single-race categories of the 1977 Office of Management and Budget standards for comparability with other states. Interpretation of trend data should take into consideration changes in reporting areas and immigration. Data for additional years are available.

SOURCE: "Table 7. Prenatal Care for Live Births, by Detailed Race and Hispanic Origin of Mother, United States, Selected Years, 1970–2004," in *Health, United States, 2007. With Chartbook on Trends in the Health of Americans*, U.S. Department of Health and Human Services, Centers for Disease Control and Prevention, National Center for Health Statistics, 2007, http://www.cdc.gov/nchs/data/hus/hus07.pdf (accessed January 4, 2008)

babies. The rate then decreased to 6.8 infant deaths per 1,000 lives births in both 2003 and 2004. In 2004 non-Hispanic African-Americans suffered the highest rate of infant mortality, with 13.6 infant deaths per 1,000 live births. This rate was more than double the rate of 5.7 infant deaths per 1,000 live births for non-Hispanic whites. Native

Americans and Alaskan Natives also had a relatively high rate of infant deaths, at 8.4 per 1,000 live births. Hispanic women (5.5 deaths per 1,000 live births) and Asian and Pacific Islander women (4.7 deaths per 1,000 live births) had the lowest infant mortality rates of any racial or ethnic group.

TABLE 6.7

Total births and percentage of births with selected demographic characteristics, by race and Hispanic origin of mother, 2005–06

[Data for 2006 are based on a continous file of records received from the states. Birth rates are live births per 1,000 population in the specified group. Fertility rates are live births per 1,000 women aged 15–44 years in the specified group. Total fertility rates are sums of birth rates for 5-year age groups in the specified group, multiplied by 5.]

Race and Hispanic origin of mother	Number		Birth rate		Fertility rate		Total fertility rate		Percent of births to unmarried women	
	2006	2005	2006	2005	2006	2005	2006	2005	2006	2005
All races and origins[a]	4,265,996	4,138,349	14.2	14.0	68.5	66.7	2,101.0	2,053.5	38.5	36.9
Non-Hispanic white[b]	2,309,833	2,279,768	11.6	11.5	59.5	58.3	1,864.0	1,839.5	26.6	25.3
Non-Hispanic black[b]	617,220	583,759	16.5	15.7	70.6	67.2	2,114.5	2,019.0	70.7	69.9
American Indian or Alaska Native total[b, c]	47,494	44,813	14.8	14.2	62.8	59.9	1,819.5	1,750.0	64.6	63.5
Asian or Pacific Islander total[b, c]	239,829	231,108	16.5	16.5	67.2	66.6	1,908.0	1,889.0	16.3	16.2
Hispanic[d]	1,039,051	985,505	23.4	23.1	101.5	99.4	2,958.5	2,885.0	49.9	48.0

[a]Includes Hispanic origin not stated.

[b]Race and Hispanic origin are reported separately on birth certificates. Persons of Hispanic origin may be of any race. Race categories are consistent with the 1977 Office of Management and Budget (OMB) standards. Twenty-three states reported multiple-race data for 2006. The multiple-race data for these states were bridged to the single-race categories of the 1977 OMB standards for comparability with other states.

[c]Data for persons of Hispanic origin are included in the data for each race group according to the person's reported race.

[d]Includes all persons of Hispanic origin of any race.

SOURCE: Brady E. Hamilton, Joyce A. Martin, and Stephanie J. Ventura, "Table 1. Total Births and Percentage of Births with Selected Demographic Characteristics, by Race and Hispanic Origin of Mother: United States, Final 2005 and Preliminary 2006," in "Births: Preliminary Data for 2006," *National Vital Statistics Reports*, vol. 56, no. 7, December 5, 2007, http://www.cdc.gov/nchs/data/nvsr/nvsr56/nvsr56_07.pdf (accessed December 9, 2007)

According to the Pew Hispanic Center, in the fact sheet "Hispanic Health: Divergent and Changing" (January 2002, http://pewhispanic.org/files/factsheets/1.pdf), the connection between low income and educational attainment and high infant mortality seems to be more complicated than previously thought. Hispanics, who suffer higher poverty rates and lower educational attainment than do non-Hispanic whites, have a consistently lower infant mortality rate. Researchers speculate that greater social support, less high-risk behavior, and dietary factors may explain the differences. However, as Hispanic immigrants begin to adopt the lifestyle of the American mainstream, experts worry that the health of this population will decline and the infant mortality rates will rise.

Other research showing that even professional, middle-class, educated African-American women have a higher risk than their white counterparts of having low-birth-weight babies complicates the view of low birth weight as a result of low incomes and low educational attainment. Ziba Kashef indicates in "Persistent Peril: Why African American Babies Have the Highest Infant Mortality Rate in the Developed World" (*RaceWire*, February 2003) that "researchers have found that even when they control for such varied factors as poverty, housing, employment, medical risk, abuse, social support and so on, 90 percent of the differences in birth weight between black and white moms remains unaccounted for." As a result, some experts have begun to look at factors such as the health of the mother's mother as well as chronic emotional stress resulting from living in a racist society to explain the poorer birth outcomes of African-American mothers.

DISEASES AND MINORITY POPULATIONS

Cancer

Cancer is the uncontrolled multiplication and spread of abnormal cells and can lead to death if unchecked. Cancer incidence varies according to racial and ethnic background. Risk factors such as occupation, use of tobacco and alcohol, sexual and reproductive behaviors, and nutritional and dietary habits influence the development of cancer. Cancer screening, treatment, and mortality rates also vary by race and ethnicity.

African-Americans have both the highest cancer incidence and the highest cancer mortality rates of all racial and ethnic groups, whereas the cancer incidence and mortality rates of other minority groups are relatively low. The Surveillance, Epidemiology, and End Results (SEER) Program of the National Cancer Institute (NCI) is the most authoritative source of information on cancer incidence, mortality, and survival in the United States. L. A. G. Ries et al. of the NCI report in *SEER Cancer Statistics Review, 1975–2004* (2007, http://seer.cancer.gov/csr/1975_2004/) that the incidence rates of all cancers between 2000 and 2004 were 504.1 per 100,000 African-Americans, down 1% annually between 1995 and 2004; 477.5 per 100,000 whites, down 0.5% annually between 1995 and 2004; 356 per 100,000 Hispanics, down 0.7% annually between 1995 and 2004; 314.9 per 100,000 Asians and Pacific Islanders, down 0.6% annually between 1995 and 2004; and 297.6 per 100,000 Native Americans and Alaskan Natives, down 1% annually between 1995 and 2004. (See Table 6.10.) The mortality rates of all cancers between 2000 and 2004 were 238.8 per

TABLE 6.8

Low-birthweight live births, by detailed race, Hispanic origin, and smoking status of mother, selected years 1970–2004

[Data are based on birth certificates]

Birthweight, race and Hispanic origin of mother, and smoking status of mother	1970	1975	1980	1985	1990	1995	1999	2000	2002	2003	2004
Low birthweight (less than 2,500 grams)					**Percent of live births[a]**						
All races	7.93	7.38	6.84	6.75	6.97	7.32	7.62	7.57	7.82	7.93	8.08
White	6.85	6.27	5.72	5.65	5.70	6.22	6.57	6.55	6.80	6.94	7.07
Black or African American	13.90	13.19	12.69	12.65	13.25	13.13	13.11	12.99	13.29	13.37	13.44
American Indian or Alaska Native	7.97	6.41	6.44	5.86	6.11	6.61	7.15	6.76	7.23	7.37	7.45
Asian or Pacific Islander[b]	—	—	6.68	6.16	6.45	6.90	7.45	7.31	7.78	7.78	7.89
Chinese	6.67	5.29	5.21	4.98	4.69	5.29	5.19	5.10	5.52	—	—
Japanese	9.03	7.47	6.60	6.21	6.16	7.26	7.95	7.14	7.57	—	—
Filipino	10.02	8.08	7.40	6.95	7.30	7.83	8.30	8.46	8.61	—	—
Hawaiian	—	—	7.23	6.49	7.24	6.84	7.69	6.76	8.14	—	—
Other Asian or Pacific Islander	—	—	6.83	6.19	6.65	7.05	7.76	7.67	8.16	—	—
Hispanic or Latino[c]	—	—	6.12	6.16	6.06	6.29	6.38	6.41	6.55	6.69	6.79
Mexican	—	—	5.62	5.77	5.55	5.81	5.94	6.01	6.16	6.28	6.44
Puerto Rican	—	—	8.95	8.69	8.99	9.41	9.30	9.30	9.68	10.01	9.82
Cuban	—	—	5.62	6.02	5.67	6.50	6.80	6.49	6.50	7.04	7.72
Central and South American	—	—	5.76	5.68	5.84	6.20	6.38	6.34	6.53	6.70	6.70
Other and unknown Hispanic or Latino	—	—	6.96	6.83	6.87	7.55	7.63	7.84	7.87	8.01	7.78
Not Hispanic or Latino:[c]											
White	—	—	5.69	5.61	5.61	6.20	6.64	6.60	6.91	7.04	7.20
Black or African American	—	—	12.71	12.62	13.32	13.21	13.23	13.13	13.39	13.55	13.74
Cigarette smoker[d]	—	—	—	—	11.25	12.18	12.06	11.88	12.15	12.40	12.54
Nonsmoker[d]	—	—	—	—	6.14	6.79	7.21	7.19	7.48	7.66	7.79
Very low birthweight (less than 1,500 grams)											
All races	1.17	1.16	1.15	1.21	1.27	1.35	1.45	1.43	1.46	1.45	1.48
White	0.95	0.92	0.90	0.94	0.95	1.06	1.15	1.14	1.17	1.17	1.20
Black or African American	2.40	2.40	2.48	2.71	2.92	2.97	3.14	3.07	3.13	3.07	3.07
American Indian or Alaska Native	0.98	0.95	0.92	1.01	1.01	1.10	1.26	1.16	1.28	1.30	1.28
Asian or Pacific Islander[b]	—	—	0.92	0.85	0.87	0.91	1.08	1.05	1.12	1.09	1.14
Chinese	0.80	0.52	0.66	0.57	0.51	0.67	0.68	0.77	0.74	—	—
Japanese	1.48	0.89	0.94	0.84	0.73	0.87	0.86	0.75	0.97	—	—
Filipino	1.08	0.93	0.99	0.86	1.05	1.13	1.41	1.38	1.31	—	—
Hawaiian	—	—	1.05	1.03	0.97	0.94	1.41	1.39	1.55	—	—
Other Asian or Pacific Islander	—	—	0.96	0.91	0.92	0.91	1.09	1.04	1.17	—	—
Hispanic or Latino[c]	—	—	0.98	1.01	1.03	1.11	1.14	1.14	1.17	1.16	1.20
Mexican	—	—	0.92	0.97	0.92	1.01	1.04	1.03	1.06	1.06	1.13
Puerto Rican	—	—	1.29	1.30	1.62	1.79	1.86	1.93	1.96	2.01	1.96
Cuban	—	—	1.02	1.18	1.20	1.19	1.49	1.21	1.15	1.37	1.30
Central and South American	—	—	0.99	1.01	1.05	1.13	1.15	1.20	1.20	1.17	1.19
Other and unknown Hispanic or Latino	—	—	1.01	0.96	1.09	1.28	1.32	1.42	1.44	1.28	1.27
Not Hispanic or Latino:[c]											
White	—	—	0.87	0.91	0.93	1.04	1.15	1.14	1.17	1.18	1.20
Black or African American	—	—	2.47	2.67	2.93	2.98	3.18	3.10	3.15	3.12	3.15
Cigarette smoker[d]	—	—	—	—	1.73	1.85	1.91	1.91	1.88	1.92	1.88
Nonsmoker[d]	—	—	—	—	1.18	1.31	1.43	1.40	1.45	1.44	1.47

—Data not available.

[a]Excludes live births with unknown birthweight. Percent based on live births with known birthweight.

[b]Starting with 2003 data, estimates are not shown for Asian or Pacific Islander subgroups during the transition from single race to multiple race reporting.

[c]Prior to 1993, data from states lacking a Hispanic-origin item on the birth certificate were excluded. Data for non-Hispanic white and non-Hispanic black women for years prior to 1989 are not nationally representative and are provided for comparison with Hispanic data.

[d]Percent based on live births with known smoking status of mother and known birthweight. Data from states that did not require the reporting of mother's tobacco use during pregnancy on the birth certificate are not included. Reporting area for tobacco use increased from 43 states and the District of Columbia (DC) in 1989 to 49 states and DC in 2000–2002. Data for 2003 and 2004 exclude states that implemented the 2003 revision of the U.S. Standard Certificate of Live Birth: Pennsylvania and Washington (in 2003), Florida, Idaho, Kentucky, New Hampshire, New York State (excluding New York City), Pennsylvania, South Carolina, Tennessee, and Washington (in 2004). Tobacco use data based on the 2003 revision are not comparable with data based on the 1989 revision of the U.S. Standard Certificate of Live Birth. California has never required reporting of tobacco use during pregnancy.

Notes: The race groups, white, black, American Indian or Alaska Native, and Asian or Pacific Islander, include persons of Hispanic and non-Hispanic origin. Persons of Hispanic origin may be of any race. Starting with 2003 data, some states reported multiple-race data. The multiple-race data for these states were bridged to the single-race categories of the 1977 Office of Management and Budget standards for comparability with other states should take into consideration expansion of reporting areas and immigration. Data for additional years are available.

SOURCE: "Table 13. Low-Birthweight Live Births, by Detailed Race, Hispanic Origin, and Smoking Status of Mother: United States, Selected Years, 1970–2004," in *Health, United States, 2007. With Chartbook on Trends in the Health of Americans*, U.S. Department of Health and Human Services, Centers for Disease Control and Prevention, National Center for Health Statistics, 2007, http://www.cdc.gov/nchs/data/hus/hus07.pdf (accessed January 4, 2008)

100,000 African-Americans, down 1.8% annually between 1995 and 2004; 190.7 per 100,000 whites, down 1.1% annually between 1995 and 2004; 160.4 per 100,000 Native Americans and Alaskan Natives, down 0.3% annually between 1995 and 2004; 129.1 per 100,000 Hispanics, down 1.3% annually between 1995 and 2004; and 115.5 per 100,000 Asians and Pacific Islanders, down 1.8% annually between 1995 and 2004. (See Table 6.11.)

TABLE 6.9

Infant, neonatal, and postneonatal mortality rates, by detailed race and Hispanic origin of mother, selected years, 1983–2004

[Data are based on linked birth and death certificates for infants]

Race and Hispanic origin of mother	1983[a]	1985[a]	1990[a]	1995[b]	2000[b]	2002[b]	2003[b]	2004[b]
	Infant[c] deaths per 1,000 live births							
All mothers	10.9	10.4	8.9	7.6	6.9	7.0	6.8	6.8
White	9.3	8.9	7.3	6.3	5.7	5.8	5.7	5.7
Black or African American	19.2	18.6	16.9	14.6	13.5	13.8	13.5	13.2
American Indian or Alaska Native	15.2	13.1	13.1	9.0	8.3	8.6	8.7	8.4
Asian or Pacific Islander[d]	8.3	7.8	6.6	5.3	4.9	4.8	4.8	4.7
Chinese	9.5	5.8	4.3	3.8	3.5	3.0	—	—
Japanese	5.6*	6.0*	5.5*	5.3*	4.5*	4.9*	—	—
Filipino	8.4	7.7	6.0	5.6	5.7	5.7	—	—
Hawaiian	11.2	9.9*	8.0*	6.5*	9.0	9.6	—	—
Other Asian or Pacific Islander	8.1	8.5	7.4	5.5	4.8	4.7	—	—
Hispanic or Latino[e, f]	9.5	8.8	7.5	6.3	5.6	5.6	5.6	5.5
Mexican	9.1	8.5	7.2	6.0	5.4	5.4	5.5	5.5
Puerto Rican	12.9	11.2	9.9	8.9	8.2	8.2	8.2	7.8
Cuban	7.5	8.5	7.2	5.3	4.6	3.7	4.6	4.6
Central and South American	8.5	8.0	6.8	5.5	4.6	5.1	5.0	4.6
Other and unknown Hispanic or Latino	10.6	9.5	8.0	7.4	6.9	7.1	6.7	6.7
Not Hispanic or Latino								
White[f]	9.2	8.6	7.2	6.3	5.7	5.8	5.7	5.7
Black or African American[f]	19.1	18.3	16.9	14.7	13.6	13.9	13.6	13.6
	Neonatal[c] deaths per 1,000 live births							
All mothers	7.1	6.8	5.7	4.9	4.6	4.7	4.6	4.5
White	6.1	5.8	4.6	4.1	3.8	3.9	3.9	3.8
Black or African American	12.5	12.3	11.1	9.6	9.1	9.3	9.2	8.9
American Indian or Alaska Native	7.5	6.1	6.1	4.0	4.4	4.6	4.5	4.3
Asian or Pacific Islander[d]	5.2	4.8	3.9	3.4	3.4	3.4	3.4	3.2
Chinese	5.5	3.3	2.3	2.3	2.5	2.4	—	—
Japanese	3.7*	3.1*	3.5*	3.3*	2.6*	3.7*	—	—
Filipino	5.6	5.1	3.5	3.4	4.1	4.1	—	—
Hawaiian	7.0*	5.7*	4.3*	4.0*	6.2*	5.6*	—	—
Other Asian or Pacific Islander	5.0	5.4	4.4	3.7	3.4	3.3	—	—
Hispanic or Latino[e, f]	6.2	5.7	4.8	4.1	3.8	3.8	3.9	3.8
Mexican	5.9	5.4	4.5	3.9	3.6	3.6	3.8	3.7
Puerto Rican	8.7	7.6	6.9	6.1	5.8	5.8	5.7	5.3
Cuban	5.0*	6.2	5.3	3.6*	3.2*	3.2*	3.4	2.8*
Central and South American	5.8	5.6	4.4	3.7	3.3	3.5	3.6	3.4
Other and unknown Hispanic or Latino	6.4	5.6	5.0	4.8	4.6	5.1	4.7	4.7
Not Hispanic or Latino								
White[f]	5.9	5.6	4.5	4.0	3.8	3.9	3.8	3.7
Black or African American[f]	12.0	11.9	11.0	9.6	9.2	9.3	9.3	9.1
	Postneonatal[c] deaths per 1,000 live births							
All mothers	3.8	3.6	3.2	2.6	2.3	2.3	2.2	2.3
White	3.2	3.1	2.7	2.2	1.9	1.9	1.9	1.9
Black or African American	6.7	6.3	5.9	5.0	4.3	4.5	4.3	4.3
American Indian or Alaska Native	7.7	7.0	7.0	5.1	3.9	4.0	4.2	4.2
Asian or Pacific Islander[d]	3.1	2.9	2.7	1.9	1.4	1.4	1.4	1.5
Chinese	4.0	2.5*	2.0*	1.5*	1.0*	0.7*	—	—
Japanese	*	2.9*	*	*	*	*	—	—
Filipino	2.8*	2.7	2.5	2.2	1.6	1.7	—	—
Hawaiian	4.2*	4.3*	3.8*	*	*	4.0*	—	—
Other Asian or Pacific Islander	3.0	3.0	3.0	1.9	1.4	1.4	—	—
Hispanic or Latino[e, f]	3.3	3.2	2.7	2.1	1.8	1.8	1.7	1.7
Mexican	3.2	3.2	2.7	2.1	1.8	1.8	1.7	1.7
Puerto Rican	4.2	3.5	3.0	2.8	2.4	2.4	2.5	2.5
Cuban	2.5*	2.3*	1.9*	1.7*	*	*	*	1.7*
Central and South American	2.6	2.4	2.4	1.9	1.4	1.6	1.4	1.2
Other and unknown Hispanic or Latino	4.2	3.9	3.0	2.6	2.3	2.0	1.9	2.0
Not Hispanic or Latino								
White[f]	3.2	3.0	2.7	2.2	1.9	1.9	1.9	2.0
Black or African American[f]	7.0	6.4	5.9	5.0	4.4	4.6	4.3	4.5

Ries et al. state that more whites survived five years after diagnosis of invasive cancer than did African-Americans. Two-thirds (65.8%) of whites survived five years, compared to only 56.4% of African-Americans. Much of this difference in survival can be attributed to later diagnosis of cancer in African-Americans because of lower screening rates and less access to health care. Among the most diagnosed cancers for all groups in the United States are breast cancer, prostate cancer, lung and bronchus cancer, and colon and rectum cancer. These cancers are examined in more detail in the following sections.

TABLE 6.9

Infant, neonatal, and postneonatal mortality rates, by detailed race and Hispanic origin of mother, selected years, 1983–2004 [CONTINUED]

[Data are based on linked birth and death certificates for infants]

Race and Hispanic origin of mother	1983–1985[a, g]	1986–1988[a, g]	1989–1991[a, g]	1995–1997[b, g]	1999–2001[b, g]	2002–2004[b, g]
			Infant[c] deaths per 1,000 live births			
All mothers	10.6	9.8	9.0	7.4	6.9	6.9
White	9.0	8.2	7.4	6.1	5.7	5.7
Black or African American	18.7	17.9	17.1	14.1	13.6	13.5
American Indian or Alaska Native	13.9	13.2	12.6	9.2	9.1	8.6
Asian or Pacific Islander[d]	8.3	7.3	6.6	5.1	4.8	4.8
Chinese	7.4	5.8	5.1	3.3	3.2	—
Japanese	6.0	6.9	5.3	4.9	4.0	—
Filipino	8.2	6.9	6.4	5.7	5.7	—
Hawaiian	11.3	11.1	9.0	7.0	7.8	—
Other Asian or Pacific Islander	8.6	7.6	7.0	5.4	4.9	—
Hispanic or Latino[e, f]	9.2	8.3	7.5	6.1	5.6	5.6
Mexican	8.8	7.9	7.2	5.9	5.4	5.5
Puerto Rican	12.3	11.1	10.4	8.5	8.4	8.1
Cuban	8.0	7.3	6.2	5.3	4.5	4.3
Central and South American	8.2	7.5	6.6	5.3	4.8	4.9
Other and unknown Hispanic or Latino	9.8	9.0	8.2	7.1	6.7	6.8
Not Hispanic or Latino						
White[f]	8.8	8.1	7.3	6.1	5.7	5.7
Black or African American[f]	18.5	17.9	17.2	14.2	13.7	13.7
			Neonatal[c] deaths per 1,000 live births			
All mothers	6.9	6.3	5.7	4.8	4.6	4.6
White	5.9	5.2	4.7	4.0	3.8	3.8
Black or African American	12.2	11.7	11.1	9.4	9.2	9.2
American Indian or Alaska Native	6.7	5.9	5.9	4.4	4.5	4.5
Asian or Pacific Islander[d]	5.2	4.5	3.9	3.3	3.2	3.3
Chinese	4.3	3.3	2.7	2.1	2.1	—
Japanese	3.4	4.4	3.0	2.8	2.6	—
Filipino	5.3	4.5	4.0	3.7	4.0	—
Hawaiian	7.4	7.1	4.8	4.5	4.9	—
Other Asian or Pacific Islander	5.5	4.7	4.2	3.5	3.3	—
Hispanic or Latino[e, f]	6.0	5.3	4.8	4.0	3.8	3.9
Mexican	5.7	5.0	4.5	3.8	3.6	3.7
Puerto Rican	8.3	7.2	7.0	5.7	5.9	5.6
Cuban	5.9	5.3	4.6	3.7	3.1	3.1
Central and South American	5.7	4.9	4.4	3.7	3.3	3.5
Other and unknown Hispanic or Latino	6.1	5.8	5.2	4.6	4.4	4.9
Not Hispanic or Latino						
White[f]	5.7	5.1	4.6	4.0	3.8	3.8
Black or African American[f]	11.8	11.4	11.1	9.4	9.2	9.2
			Postneonatal[c] deaths per 1,000 live births			
All mothers	3.7	3.5	3.3	2.5	2.3	2.2
White	3.1	3.0	2.7	2.1	1.9	1.9
Black or African American	6.4	6.2	6.0	4.7	4.4	4.4
American Indian or Alaska Native	7.2	7.3	6.7	4.8	4.5	4.1
Asian or Pacific Islander[d]	3.1	2.8	2.6	1.8	1.6	1.4
Chinese	3.1	2.5	2.4	1.2	1.1	—
Japanese	2.6	2.5	2.2	2.1	1.4*	—
Filipino	2.9	2.4	2.3	2.1	1.7	—
Hawaiian	3.9	4.0	4.1	2.5*	2.9	—
Other Asian or Pacific Islander	3.1	2.9	2.8	1.9	1.6	—

BREAST CANCER. Even though a smaller proportion of African-American women (111.9 per 100,000) were diagnosed with breast cancer than were white women (128.5 per 100,000) between 1975 and 2004, a higher proportion of African-American women (35.1 per 100,000) died of the disease than did white women (30.1 per 100,000). (See Figure 6.3.) For years experts assumed that the difference in mortality rates was due to poor health care and late treatment for African-American women. However, the Dr. Susan Love Research Foundation explains in "African American Women and Breast Cancer" (2006, http://www.susanlovemd.com/pdfs/african_american_bc.pdf) that African-American women may be more susceptible to a more deadly form of the cancer. Tumors from African-American women have been found to contain more actively dividing cells than tumors from white women. The tumor cells in African-American women also lack hormone receptors, another indicator of a poor prognosis. After peaking in the early 1990s, the death rate from breast cancer for African-American women had shown some improvement by 2004. (See Figure 6.3.)

Hispanics, Asians and Pacific Islanders, and Native Americans and Alaskan Natives are less likely to be diagnosed with breast cancer or to die from breast cancer than either whites or African-Americans. The incidence

94 Health

Minorities

TABLE 6.9

Infant, neonatal, and postneonatal mortality rates, by detailed race and Hispanic origin of mother, selected years, 1983–2004 [CONTINUED]

[Data are based on linked birth and death certificates for infants]

Race and Hispanic origin of mother	1983–1985[a, g]	1986–1988[a, g]	1989–1991[a, g]	1995–1997[b, g]	1999–2001[b, g]	2002–2004[b, g]
Hispanic or Latino[e, f]	3.2	3.0	2.7	2.1	1.8	1.7
Mexican	3.2	2.9	2.7	2.1	1.8	1.7
Puerto Rican	4.0	3.9	3.4	2.8	2.5	2.4
Cuban	2.2	2.0	1.6	1.5	1.4	1.2
Central and South American	2.5	2.6	2.2	1.7	1.5	1.4
Other and unknown Hispanic or Latino	3.7	3.2	3.0	2.5	2.3	2.0
Not Hispanic or Latino						
White[f]	3.1	3.0	2.7	2.2	1.9	1.9
Black or African American[f]	6.7	6.5	6.1	4.8	4.5	4.5

—Data not available.

*Estimates are considered unreliable. Rates preceded by an asterisk are based on fewer than 50 deaths in the numerator. Rates not shown are based on fewer than 20 deaths in the numerator.
[a]Rates based on unweighted birth cohort data.
[b]Rates based on a period file using weighted data.
[c]Infant (under 1 year of age), neonatal (under 28 days), and postneonatal (28 days–11 months).
[d]Starting with 2003 data, estimates are not shown for Asian or Pacific Islander subgroups during the transition from single race to multiple race reporting.
[e]Persons of Hispanic origin may be of any race.
[f]Prior to 1995, data shown only for states with an Hispanic-origin item on their birth certificates.
[g]Average annual mortality rate.
Notes: The race groups white, black, American Indian or Alaska Native, and Asian or Pacific Islander include persons of Hispanic and non-Hispanic origin. Starting with 2003 data, some states reported multiple-race data. The multiple-race data for these states were bridged to the single-race categories of the 1977 Office of Management and Budget standards for comparability with other states. National linked files do not exist for 1992–1994. Data for additional years are available.

SOURCE: "Table 19. Infant, Neonatal, and Postneonatal Mortality Rates, by Detailed Race and Hispanic Origin of Mother: United States, Selected Years, 1983–2004," in *Health, United States, 2007. With Chartbook on Trends in the Health of Americans*, U.S. Department of Health and Human Services, Centers for Disease Control and Prevention, National Center for Health Statistics, 2007, http://www.cdc.gov/nchs/data/hus/hus07.pdf (accessed January 4, 2008)

rates of breast cancer between 2000 and 2004 were 48.6 per 100,000 Asians and Pacific Islanders, 48.1 per 100,000 Hispanics, and 37.6 per 100,000 Native Americans and Alaskan Natives. (See Table 6.10.) Between 2000 and 2004 the mortality rates of breast cancer were lowest for Asian and Pacific Islanders, at seven per one hundred thousand, despite their higher incidence rates. (See Table 6.11.) The mortality rate for Hispanics was highest of the three groups, at nine per one hundred thousand. Figure 6.3 shows the mortality rates of these three groups compared to those of African-American and white women.

PROSTATE CANCER. African-American men have a particularly high incidence of and mortality rate for prostate cancer. Between 1975 and 2004 the prostate cancer incidence rate among African-American men was 232.4 cases per 100,000 population, compared to a rate of only 147.9 cases per 100,000 population among whites. (See Figure 6.4.) During this same period African-American men averaged 68.4 deaths per 100,000 population from prostate cancer, compared to 31.1 deaths per 100,000 white men. Even though the incidence and mortality rates for prostate cancer decreased for both groups between the early 1990s and 2002, the incidence and mortality rates for African-American men remained higher than for all other races and ethnic groups.

Hispanics, Asians and Pacific Islanders, and Native Americans and Alaskan Natives have both lower rates of prostate cancer incidence and lower rates of prostate cancer mortality than do African-Americans or whites. (See Figure 6.4.) The incidence rates of prostate cancer between 2000 and 2004 were 60.8 per 100,000 Hispanics, 41.6 per 100,000 Asians and Pacific Islanders, and 30.1 per 100,000 Native Americans and Alaskan Natives. (See Table 6.10.) The mortality rate of prostate cancer was lowest for Asian and Pacific Islander males, at 4.6 per 100,000, despite their higher incidence rates. The mortality rates for Hispanic and Native American males were much higher at 8.3 per 100,000 and 8.4 per 100,000, respectively. (See Table 6.11.)

LUNG AND BRONCHUS CANCER. According to Ries et al., lung cancer is the deadliest cancer in the United States; the five-year survival rate for all races was only 15.7% of those diagnosed between 1996 and 2003. African-Americans have a particularly high incidence of lung cancer and mortality rate compared to other groups. Between 2000 and 2004 the lung cancer incidence rate among African-Americans was 76.6 cases per 100,000 population, compared to a rate of 65.7 cases per 100,000 non-Hispanic whites, 44 cases per 100,000 Native Americans and Alaskan Natives, 39.4 cases per 100,000 Asians and Pacific Islanders, and 33.3 per 100,000 Hispanics. (See Table 6.10.) Both the incidence and mortality rates for lung cancer decreased between 1995 and 2004, especially for Hispanics and African-Americans; however, the incidence and mortality rates for African-Americans remained substantially higher than for all other races and ethnic groups. (See Figure 6.5.)

TABLE 6.10

Cancer incidence rates and trends for the top 15 cancer sites[a], by race/ethnicity, 2000–04

Both sexes

All Races	Rate[b] 2000–2004	APC[c] 1995–2004
All sites	470.1	−0.6
Prostate[f]	73.9	0.3
Breast	69.6	−1.1
Lung and bronchus	64.5	−1.4
Colon and rectum	51.6	−1.5
Urinary bladder	21.1	0.0
Non-Hodgkin lymphoma	19.3	0.1
Melanoma of the skin	18.5	1.2
Kidney and renal pelvis	12.8	2.1
Corpus and uterus, ONS[f]	12.6	−1.0
Leukemia	12.3	−1.0
Pancreas	11.4	0.0
Oral cavity and pharynx	10.5	−1.5
Thyroid	8.5	5.3
Stomach	8.1	−1.5
Ovary[fh]	7.4	−1.3

White	Rate[b] 2000–2004	APC[c] 1995–2004
All sites	477.5	−0.5
Prostate[f]	71.6	0.4
Breast	71.5	−1.1
Lung and bronchus	65.7	−1.3
Colon and rectum	51.2	−1.6
Urinary bladder	23.0	0.1
Melanoma of the skin	21.6	1.8
Non-Hodgkin lymphoma	20.2	0.2
Kidney and renal pelvis	13.3	2.3
Corpus and uterus, ONS[f]	13.1	−1.2
Leukemia	12.8	−1.1
Pancreas	11.2	0.3
Oral cavity and pharynx	10.6	−1.3
Thyroid	8.9	5.7
Ovary[fh]	7.7	−1.4
Stomach	7.1	−1.4

Black	Rate[b] 2000–2004	APC[c] 1995–2004
All sites	504.1	−1.0
Prostate[f]	105.5	−1.1
Lung and bronchus	76.6	−1.6
Breast	68.0	−0.6
Colon and rectum	62.1	−0.4
Pancreas	15.0	−1.6
Non-Hodgkin lymphoma	14.6	0.2
Kidney and renal pelvis	14.3	1.4
Urinary bladder	12.6	0.7
Stomach	12.5	−2.9
Corpus and uterus, ONS[f]	11.3	1.3
Myeloma	11.3	−0.5
Oral cavity and pharynx	11.1	−3.0
Leukemia	10.2	−0.2
Liver & IBD[g]	7.6	3.3
Cervix uteri[f]	6.3	−5.0

Asian/Pacific Islander	Rate[b] 2000–2004	APC[c] 1995–2004
All sites	314.9	−0.6
Breast	48.6	0.1
Prostate[f]	41.6	−0.1
Colon and rectum	41.6	−1.2
Lung and bronchus	39.4	−0.7
Stomach	14.3	−3.0
Liver & IBD[g]	13.9	0.0
Non-Hodgkin lymphoma	13.2	0.2
Urinary bladder	9.2	0.2
Pancreas	9.0	0.0
Corpus and uterus, ONS[f]	8.8	0.2
Thyroid	8.5	2.3
Oral cavity and pharynx	7.9	−1.8
Leukemia	7.4	−1.1
Kidney and renal pelvis	6.3	1.1
Ovary[fh]	5.3	−0.2

American Indian/Alaska Native[d]	Rate[b] 2000–2004	APC[c] 1995–2004
All sites	297.6	−1.0
Lung and bronchus	44.0	−1.2
Colon and rectum	40.8	−0.5
Breast	37.6	−2.0
Prostate[f]	30.1	−2.7
Kidney and renal pelvis	14.7	1.4
Stomach	11.5	−0.2
Non-Hodgkin lymphoma	10.4	0.4
Liver & IBD[g]	9.7	0.2
Pancreas	9.2	−1.1
Corpus and uterus, ONS[f]	8.1	—
Oral cavity and pharynx	7.1	−3.5
Urinary bladder	7.0	—
Leukemia	6.4	1.1
Ovary[fh]	6.0	−3.4
Thyroid	5.3	0.5

Hispanic[e]	Rate[b] 2000–2004	APC[c] 1995–2004
All sites	356.0	−0.7
Prostate[f]	60.8	0.0
Breast	48.1	−1.0
Colon and rectum	39.3	−0.9
Lung and bronchus	33.3	−2.1
Non-Hodgkin lymphoma	16.5	−0.4
Kidney and renal pelvis	12.4	2.0
Stomach	12.3	−1.9
Urinary bladder	11.6	0.1
Pancreas	10.5	−1.1
Liver & IBD[g]	9.7	1.0
Leukemia	9.6	−1.6
Corpus and uterus, ONS[f]	9.4	0.6
Thyroid	7.5	4.4
Cervix uteri[f]	7.1	−3.8
Ovary[fh]	6.2	−0.6

COLON AND RECTUM CANCER. Colon and rectum cancer is the fourth-most frequently diagnosed cancer in the United States after prostate cancer, breast cancer, and lung and bronchus cancer; it is also the second-most deadly. African-Americans are diagnosed more frequently than other groups. Between 2000 and 2004 African-Americans had an incidence of 62.7 cases per 100,000 population, compared to a rate of 51.2 per 100,000 whites, 41.6 per 100,000 Asians and Pacific Islanders, 40.8 per 100,000 Native Americans and Alaskan Natives, and 39.3 per 100,000 Hispanics. (See Table 6.10.) African-Americans also had the highest mortality rate from colon and rectum

TABLE 6.10

Cancer incidence rates and trends for the top 15 cancer sites^a, by race/ethnicity, 2000–04 [CONTINUED]

—Statistic not shown. Rate based on less than 16 cases for the time interval. Trend based on less than 10 cases for at least one year within the time interval.
^aTop 15 cancer sites selected based on 2000–2004 age-adjusted rates for the race/ethnic group.
^bIncidence data used in calculating the rates are from the 17 SEER areas (San Francisco, Connecticut, Detroit, Hawaii, Iowa, New Mexico, Seattle, Utah, Atlanta, San Jose-Monterey, Los Angeles, Alaska Native Registry, rural Georgia, California excluding SF/SJM/LA, Kentucky, Louisiana and New Jersey). Rates are age-adjusted to the 2000 US standard Population (19 age groups-Census P25-1130).
^cThe APC is the annual percent change over the time interval. Incidence data used in calculating the trends are from 13 areas (San Francisco, Connecticut, Detroit, Hawaii, Iowa, New Mexico, Seattle, Utah, Atlanta, San Jose-Monterey, Los Angeles, Alaska Native Registry and rural Georgia). Trends are based on rates age-adjusted to the 2000 US standard Population (19 age groups-Census P25-1130).
^dRates for American Indian/Alaska Native are based on the CHSDA (contract health service delivery area) counties.
^eHispanic is not mutually exclusive from whites, blacks, Asian/Pacific Islanders, and American Indians/Alaska Natives. Incidence data for Hispanics are based on NHIA and exclude cases from the Alaska Native Registry and Kentucky.
^fThe rates for sex-specific cancer sites are calculated using the population for both sexes combined.
^gIBD=Intrahepatic bile duct. ONS=Other nervous system.
^hOvary excludes borderline cases or histologies 8442, 8451, 8462, 8472, and 8473.

SOURCE: L.A.G. Ries et al., eds., "Table I-23. Age-Adjusted SEER Incidence Rates and Trends for the Top 15 Cancer Sites by Race/Ethnicity," in *SEER Cancer Statistics Review, 1975–2004*, National Cancer Institute, 2007, http://seer.cancer.gov/csr/1975_2004/results_merged/topic_inc_trends.pdf (accessed January 4, 2008)

cancer, at 26.7 deaths per 100,000, compared to 18.9 deaths per 100,000 whites, 17 deaths per 100,000 Native Americans and Alaskan Natives, 13.6 deaths per 100,000 Hispanics, and 12.3 deaths per 100,000 Asians and Pacific Islanders. (See Table 6.11.) Furthermore, even though both the incidence and mortality rates of colon and rectum cancer steadily decreased for whites between the mid-1980s and 2004, the incidence and mortality rates for African-Americans remained relatively constant. (See Figure 6.6.)

Heart Disease and Stroke

Heart disease includes coronary and hypertensive heart diseases and heart failure. According to the HHS, in *2006 National Healthcare Disparities Report*, each year approximately 13.2 million Americans suffer from coronary heart disease. About 7.2 million heart attacks occur each year, and 5 million Americans have heart failure.

Rates of heart disease vary considerably by race, with higher rates for African-Americans. Along with age, sex, and race, heredity is one of the risk factors for heart disease that cannot be changed. However, because of their higher rates of incidence of heart disease and stroke, African-Americans are encouraged to control other risk factors, including use of tobacco and alcohol, blood pressure and cholesterol levels, physical activity, weight, and stress.

HYPERTENSION. The American Heart Association (AHA) explains in *Heart Disease and Stroke Statistics: 2007 Update* (2007, http://circ.ahajournals.org/cgi/content/full/CIRCULATIONAHA.106.179918#FIG1179736) that the prevalence of hypertension, or high blood pressure, in both African-American men and women is significantly higher than in white men and women, whereas the prevalence of high blood pressure among Mexican-Americans of both sexes is comparable to that in the non-Hispanic white community. Among adults aged twenty and older, 32.5% of

non-Hispanic white males and 31.9% of non-Hispanic white females had high blood pressure in 2004, and 28.7% of Mexican-American males and 31.4% of Mexican-American females had high blood pressure. However, 42.6% of African-American males and 46.6% of African-American females had high blood pressure in that year. In fact, the AHA notes that the prevalence of high blood pressure among African-Americans in the United States is among the highest in the world. Compared to whites, African-Americans develop high blood pressure earlier in life and their average blood pressure is much higher. As a result, African-Americans had a 1.3 times greater rate of nonfatal stroke, a 1.8 times greater rate of fatal stroke, and a 1.5 times greater rate of death from heart disease than did whites in 2004. Native American and Alaskan Native adults were slightly less likely than non-Hispanic whites to have high blood pressure (23.9%), whereas Asian-Americans were much less likely to have high blood pressure (16.1%) than any other race or ethnic group.

DEATHS FROM HEART DISEASE. The NCHS notes in *Health, United States, 2007* (2007, http://www.cdc.gov/nchs/data/hus/hus07.pdf) that the death rate from heart disease was higher for males among all racial and ethnic groups, but that rate declined between 1990 and 2004 for all groups. African-American males had the highest death rate from heart disease in 2004, at 342.1 deaths per 100,000 people, down from 485.4 in 1990. Hispanic males (193.9), Native American and Alaskan Native males (182.7), and Asian and Pacific Islander males (146.5) all had lower death rates from heart disease than did non-Hispanic white males (268.7).

The NCHS reports that females die of heart disease at high rates as well, although not at the rate that males do. In 2004 African-American females had the highest death rate for heart disease of all racial and ethnic groups, at 236.5 per 100,000 people, down significantly from the

TABLE 6.11

Cancer mortality rates and trends for the top 15 cancer sites[a], by race/ethnicity, 2000–04

Both sexes

All Races	Rate[b] 2000–2004	APC[c] 1995–2004
All sites	192.7	−1.2
Lung and bronchus	54.7	−1.0
Colon and rectum	19.4	−2.2
Breast	14.5	−2.4
Pancreas	10.6	0.1
Prostate[f]	10.5	−3.6
Non-hodgkin lymphoma	7.6	−2.5
Leukemia	7.5	−0.8
Ovary[f]	5.0	−0.3
Liver & IBD[g]	4.9	1.7
Brain and ONS[g]	4.4	−1.0
Esophagus	4.4	0.3
Urinary bladder	4.3	−0.2
Stomach	4.2	−3.2
Kidney and renal pelvis	4.2	−0.4
Myeloma	3.7	−0.9

White	Rate[b] 2000–2004	APC[c] 1995–2004
All sites	190.7	−1.1
Lung and bronchus	55.0	−0.8
Colon and rectum	18.9	−2.3
Breast	14.1	−2.5
Pancreas	10.4	0.3
Prostate[f]	9.6	−3.5
Non-hodgkin lymphoma	7.9	−2.5
Leukemia	7.7	−0.7
Ovary[f]	5.2	−0.3
Brain and ONS[g]	4.8	−0.9
Urinary bladder	4.5	0.0
Liver & IBD[g]	4.5	1.7
Esophagus	4.3	1.2
Kidney and renal pelvis	4.3	−0.3
Stomach	3.7	−3.2
Myeloma	3.5	−0.8

Black	Rate[b] 2000–2004	APC[c] 1995–2004
All sites	238.8	−1.8
Lung and bronchus	62.0	−1.6
Colon and rectum	26.7	−1.5
Prostate[f]	21.9	−3.6
Breast	20.1	−1.7
Pancreas	13.8	−0.6
Stomach	8.2	−3.3
Myeloma	7.1	−1.4
Leukemia	6.7	−1.1
Liver & IBD[g]	6.5	1.3
Esophagus	6.0	−4.2
Non-hodgkin lymphoma	5.2	−2.4
Ovary[f]	4.5	0.0
Corpus and uterus, ONS[f]	4.3	0.4
Kidney and renal pelvis	4.1	−0.7
Oral cavity and pharynx	3.9	−3.8

Asian/Pacific Islander	Rate[b] 2000–2004	APC[c] 1995–2004
All sites	115.5	−1.8
Lung and bronchus	26.9	−1.4
Colon and rectum	12.3	−2.0
Liver & IBD[g]	10.6	−0.6
Stomach	8.0	−4.6
Pancreas	7.4	−0.2
Breast	7.0	−0.2
Non-hodgkin lymphoma	4.8	−2.1
Prostate[f]	4.6	−5.6
Leukemia	3.9	−1.9
Ovary[f]	2.7	0.8
Oral cavity and pharynx	2.3	−2.6
Brain and ONS[g]	2.0	0.5
Esophagus	1.8	−2.6
Urinary bladder	1.8	−0.1
Kidney and renal pelvis	1.7	−3.0

American Indian/Alaska Native[d]	Rate[b] 2000–2004	APC[c] 1995–2004
All sites	160.4	−0.3
Lung and bronchus	39.9	−0.1
Colon and rectum	17.0	−1.4
Breast	9.0	0.1
Liver & IBD[g]	8.4	2.2
Prostate[f]	8.4	−2.2
Pancreas	7.5	1.0
Stomach	7.2	−0.6
Kidney and renal pelvis	6.5	0.6
Non-hodgkin lymphoma	5.5	0.5
Leukemia	4.8	0.3
Ovary[f]	4.0	2.0
Myeloma	3.8	−2.0
Esophagus	3.8	4.5
Oral cavity and pharynx	2.5	−0.3
Cervix uteri[f]	2.2	−2.0

Hispanic[e]	Rate[b] 2000–2004	APC[c] 1995–2004
All sites	129.1	−1.3
Lung and bronchus	23.6	−1.6
Colon and rectum	13.6	−0.9
Breast	9.0	−2.6
Prostate[f]	8.3	−3.1
Pancreas	8.3	0.2
Liver & IBD[g]	7.6	1.4
Stomach	6.8	−2.1
Non-hodgkin lymphoma	5.7	−3.1
Leukemia	5.1	−1.2
Kidney and renal pelvis	3.6	0.5
Ovary[f]	3.4	0.3
Myeloma	3.1	−0.7
Brain and ONS[g]	2.8	−0.3
Urinary bladder	2.4	0.2
Esophagus	2.4	−2.2

1990 rate of 327.5. Non-Hispanic white females had the next highest death rate from heart disease, at 175.1. Hispanic females (130), Native American and Alaskan Native females (119.9), and Asian and Pacific Islander females (96.1) all had lower death rates from heart disease than did African-Americans and non-Hispanic whites. Death rates for all females from heart disease had declined since 1990.

Alzheimer's Disease

Alzheimer's disease is a progressive brain disorder that gradually destroys a person's memory and ability to

TABLE 6.11

Cancer mortality rates and trends for the top 15 cancer sites[a], by race/ethnicity, 2000–04 [CONTINUED]

—Statistic not shown. Rate based on less than 16 cases for the time interval. Trend based on less than 10 cases for at least one year within the time interval.
[a]Top 15 cancer sites selected based on 2000–2004 age-adjusted rates for the race/ethnic group.
[b]Mortality data used in calculating the rates are analyzed from a public use file provided by the National Center for Health Statistics (NCHS). Rates are age-adjusted to the 2000 US Std Population (19 age groups-Census P25-1130). The rates shown for sex-specific cancer sites are calculated using the population for both sexes combined.
[c]The APC is the annual percent change over the time interval. Mortality data used in calculating the trends are analyzed from a public use file provided by the National Center for Health Statistics (NCHS). Trends are based on rates age-adjusted to the 2000 US Std Population (19 age groups-Census P25-1130).
[d]Rates for American Indian/Alaska Native are based on the CHSDA (contract health service delivery area) counties.
[e]Hispanic is not mutually exclusive from whites, blacks, Asian/Pacific Islanders, and American Indians/Alaska Natives. The 2000–2004 Hispanic death rates do not include deaths from Minnesota, New Hampshire and North Dakota. The 1995–2004 Hispanic mortality trends do not include deaths from Maine, Minnesota, New Hampshire, North Dakota, and Oklahoma.
[f]The rates for sex-specific cancer sites are calculated using the population for both sexes combined.
[g]IBD=Intrahepatic bile duct. ONS=Other nervous system.

SOURCE: L.A.G. Ries et al.,eds., "Table I-26. Age-Adjusted U.S. Death Rates and Trends for the Top 15 Cancer Sites by Race/Ethnicity," in *SEER Cancer Statistics Review, 1975–2004*, National Cancer Institute, 2007, http://seer.cancer.gov/csr/1975_2004/results_merged/topic_ mor_trends.pdf (accessed January 4, 2008)

FIGURE 6.3

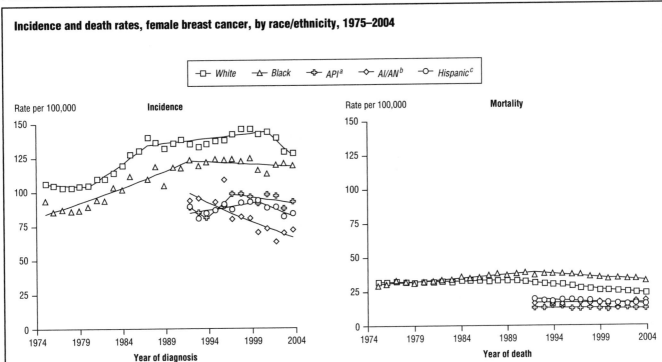

Incidence and death rates, female breast cancer, by race/ethnicity, 1975–2004

Notes: Rates are age-adjusted to the 2000 US standard population (19 age groups—Census P25-1103).
Regression lines are calculated using the Joinpoint Regression Program Version 3.0, April 2005, National Cancer Institute.
[a]API = Asian/Pacific Islander.
[b]AI/AN = American Indian/Alaska Native. Rates for American Indian/Alaska Native are based on the CHSDA (contract health service delivery area) counties.
[c]Hispanic is not mutually exclusive from whites, blacks, Asian/Pacific Islanders, and American Indians/Alaska Natives. Incidence data for Hispanics are based on NHIA and exclude cases from the Alaska Native Registry. Mortality data for Hispanics exclude cases from Connecticut, Maine, Maryland, Minnesota, New Hampshire, New York, North Dakota, Oklahoma, and Vermont.

SOURCE: L.A.G. Ries et al., eds., "SEER Incidence and U.S. Death Rates: Female Breast Cancer," in *SEER Cancer Statistics Review, 1975–2004*, National Cancer Institute, 2007, http://seer.cancer.gov/csr/1975_2004/results_merged/sect_04_breast.pdf (accessed January 4, 2008)

reason, communicate, and carry out daily activities. As it progresses, it also tends to affect personality and behavior and may result in anxiety, paranoia, and delusions or hallucinations. The disease can last from three to twenty years, and eventually the loss of brain function will cause death. Even though the underlying causes of Alzheimer's disease remain unclear, some research indicates that

minorities, particularly African-Americans, are at a greater risk of developing the disease.

In "The *APOE*-ε4 Allele and the Risk of Alzheimer Disease among African-Americans, Whites, and Hispanics" (*Journal of the American Medical Association*, vol. 279, no. 10, March 11, 1998), a study that was conducted between

FIGURE 6.4

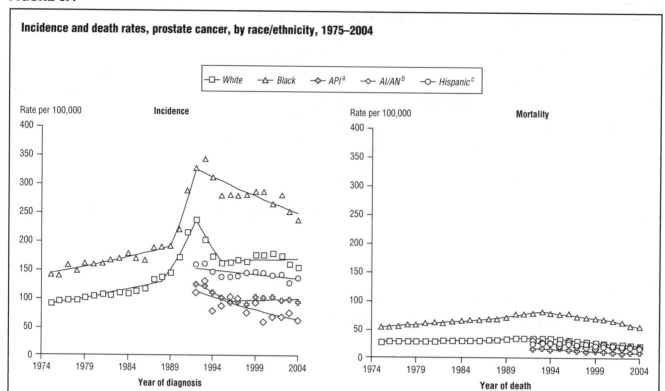

Incidence and death rates, prostate cancer, by race/ethnicity, 1975–2004

Notes: Rates are age-adjusted to the 2000 US standard population (19 age groups—Census P25-1103). Regression lines are calculated using the Joinpoint Regression Program Version 3.0, April 2005, National Cancer Institute.
[a]API=Asian/Pacific Islander.
[b]AI/AN=American Indian/Alaska Native. Rates for American Indian/Alaska Native are based on the CHSDA (contract health service delivery area) counties.
[c]Hispanic is not mutually exclusive from whites, blacks, Asian/Pacific Islanders, and American Indians/Alaska Natives. Incidence data for Hispanics are based on National Health Insurance Act (NHIA) and exclude cases from the Alaska Native Registry. Mortality data for Hispanics exclude cases from Connecticut, Maine, Maryland, Minnesota, New Hampshire, New York, North Dakota, Oklahoma, and Vermont.

SOURCE: L.A.G. Ries et al., eds., "SEER Incidence and U.S. Death Rates: Prostate Cancer," in *SEER Cancer Statistics Review, 1975–2004*, National Cancer Institute, 2007, http://seer.cancer.gov/csr/1975_2004/results_merged/sect_23_prostate.pdf (accessed January 4, 2008)

1991 and 1996, Ming-Xin Tang et al. indicate that African-Americans and Hispanics might be at greater risk for Alzheimer's disease than non-Hispanic whites. In 1992 scientists first discovered that people with the apolipoprotein E gene (*APOE-ϵ4*; approximately 25% of the total population) have a greater risk for developing the disease. However, Tang et al. show that the increased risk associated with the *APOE-ϵ4* gene applies only to non-Hispanic whites. The researchers find that African-Americans and a group of Hispanic-Americans, mainly from the Caribbean, who do not have the gene, are still at a greater risk for Alzheimer's disease than whites.

The researchers surveyed 1,079 elderly men and women and found that African-Americans who lacked the *APOE-ϵ4* gene were still four times more likely than whites to get Alzheimer's disease. Because the *APOE-ϵ4* could not account for the increased risk in African-Americans and Hispanics, researchers now believe that there are other genetic or environmental factors affecting minorities that increase their risk of developing Alzheimer's disease. None of the subjects of the study had

the disease when the study began, but 221 developed it by the time the study ended.

The Alzheimer's Association emphasizes in *African-Americans and Alzheimer's Disease: The Silent Epidemic* (2003, http://www.alz.org/national/documents/report_africanamericanssilentepidemic.pdf) that the prevalence of Alzheimer's disease among African-Americans is estimated to be 14% to 100% higher than among whites. Since the turn of the twenty-first century, discoveries of risk factors for Alzheimer's disease—hypertension and high cholesterol—have begun to provide some explanation for this increased risk, as these risk factors are disproportionately present in the African-American community. The Alzheimer's Association stresses the importance of getting effective medical therapies for vascular disease and its risk factors, as these drugs could potentially protect against Alzheimer's disease as well.

Diabetes

Diabetes is a chronic disease in which the body does not produce or use insulin properly, leading to cells being

FIGURE 6.5

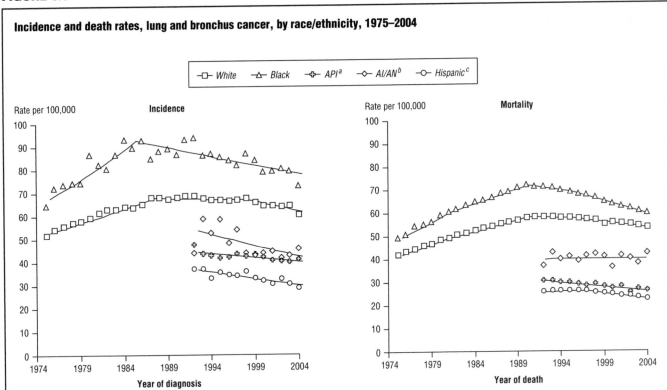

Incidence and death rates, lung and bronchus cancer, by race/ethnicity, 1975–2004

Notes: Rates are age-adjusted to the 2000 US standard population (19 age groups—Census P25-1103).
Regression lines are calculated using the Joinpoint Regression Program Version 3.0, April 2005, National Cancer Institute.
[a]API = Asian/Pacific Islander.
[b]AI/AN = American Indian/Alaska Native. Rates for American Indian/Alaska Native are based on the CHSDA (contract health service delivery area) counties.
[c]Hispanic is not mutually exclusive from whites, blacks, Asian/Pacific Islanders, and American Indians/Alaska Natives. Incidence data for Hispanics are based on National Health Insurance Act (NHIA) and exclude cases from the Alaska Native Registry. Mortality data for Hispanics exclude cases from Connecticut, Maine, Maryland, Minnesota, New Hampshire, New York, North Dakota, Oklahoma, and Vermont.

SOURCE: L.A.G. Ries et al., eds., "SEER Incidence and U.S. Death Rates: Lung and Bronchus Cancer, Both Sexes," in *SEER Cancer Statistics Review,* *1975–2004*, National Cancer Institute, 2007, http://seer.cancer.gov/csr/1975_2004/results_merged/sect_15_lung_bronchus.pdf (accessed January 4, 2008)

starved for sugar and often resulting in damage to the heart, kidneys, and eyes. According to the NCHS, in *Health, United States, 2007,* diabetes was the sixth-deadliest disease in the United States in 2004; in fact, the death rate due to diabetes is on the rise at the same time that the death rates due to other diseases such as cancer and heart disease are declining. In "Age-Adjusted Prevalence of Diagnosed Diabetes by Race/Ethnicity and Sex, United States, 1980–2005" (March 26, 2007, http://www.cdc.gov/diabetes/statistics/prev/national/figraceethsex.htm), the CDC reports that in 2005, 8% of African-American males and 8.3% of African-American females had been diagnosed with diabetes, 7.1% of Hispanic males and 7.5% of Hispanic females had diabetes, and 5.4% of non-Hispanic white males and 4.7% of white females had diabetes. However, the rates for all groups had risen since the year before.

Diabetes is a dangerous disease because it can cause many different complications, including heart disease, kidney failure, and loss of circulation in the extremities. The lack of circulation in the lower limbs can lead to infection of small wounds and gangrene, which can even-

tually require leg amputation. Diabetes requires effective management of hemoglobin A1c and lipids, as well as regular examination of eyes and feet and yearly influenza immunizations. However, the rates of receiving all three diabetic management services vary by race and ethnic group. The HHS explains in *2006 National Healthcare Disparities Report* that non-Hispanic whites were much more likely than either African-Americans or Hispanics to receive the recommended services between 2000 and 2003, although less than a majority of all groups had received the services in the past year. (See Figure 6.7.)

AIDS

The acquired immune deficiency syndrome (AIDS) is caused by a virus that affects the body's immune system, making it difficult to fight invasions from infection or other foreign substances. As a result, people infected with the AIDS virus are subject to a number of opportunistic infections, primarily *Pneumocystis carinii* pneumonia and Kaposi's sarcoma, a form of skin cancer. AIDS, which is caused by the human immunodeficiency

FIGURE 6.6

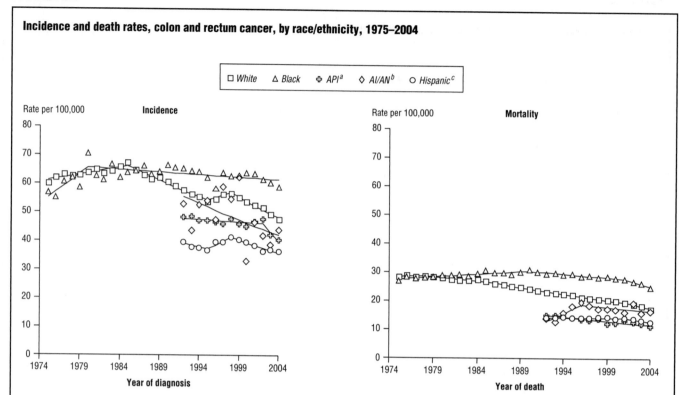

Incidence and death rates, colon and rectum cancer, by race/ethnicity, 1975–2004

Notes: Rates are age-adjusted to the 2000 US standard population (19 age groups—Census P25-1103).
Regression lines are calculated using the Joinpoint Regression Program Version 3.0, April 2005, National Cancer Institute.
[a]API = Asian/Pacific Islander.
[b]AI/AN = American Indian/Alaska Native. Rates for American Indian/Alaska Native are based on the CHSDA (contract health service delivery area) counties.
[c]Hispanic is not mutually exclusive from whites, blacks, Asian/Pacific Islanders, and American Indians/Alaska Natives. Incidence data for Hispanics are based on National Health Insurance Act (NHIA) and exclude cases from the Alaska Native Registry. Mortality data for Hispanics exclude cases from Connecticut, Maine, Maryland, Minnesota, New Hampshire, New York, North Dakota, Oklahoma, and Vermont.

SOURCE: "SEER Incidence and U.S. Death Rates: Colon and Rectum Cancer, Both Sexes," in *SEER Cancer Statistics Review, 1975–2004*, National Cancer Institute, 2007, http://seer.cancer.gov/csr/1975_2004/results_merged/sect_06_colon_rectum.pdf (accessed January 4, 2008)

FIGURE 6.7

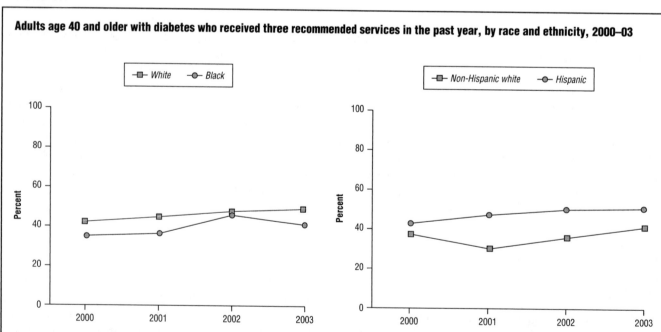

Adults age 40 and older with diabetes who received three recommended services in the past year, by race and ethnicity, 2000–03

SOURCE: Adapted from "Figure 2.4. Adults Age 40 and over with Diabetes Who Had Three Recommended Services for Diabetes in the Past Year, by Race, Ethnicity, Family Income, and Education, 2000–2003," in *National Healthcare Disparities Report, 2006*, U.S. Department of Health and Human Services, Agency for Healthcare Research and Quality, June 2007, http://www.ahrq.gov/qual/nhdr06/nhdr06chap2.pdf (accessed January 4, 2008)

FIGURE 6.8

Cases of HIV/AIDS among persons aged 13 and older, by year of diagnosis and race/ethnicity, 2001–05

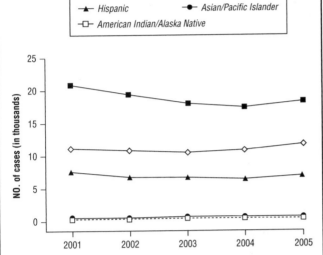

Note: Reported case counts have been adjusted for reporting delays.

SOURCE: "Cases of HIV/AIDS among Persons Aged 13 and Older, by Year of Diagnosis and Race/Ethnicity, 2001–2005—33 States with Confidential Name-Based HIV Infection Reporting," in *HIV/AIDS Surveillance Report 2005*, vol. 17, rev. ed., U.S. Department of Health and Human Services, Centers for Disease Control and Prevention, June 2007, http://www.cdc.gov/hiv/topics/surveillance/resources/reports/2005report/pdf/2005SurveillanceReport.pdf (accessed January 4, 2008)

TABLE 6.12

Estimated numbers of AIDS cases in children less than 13 years of age, by year of diagnosis and race/ethnicity, 2001–05

	Year of diagnosis					
	2001	2002	2003	2004	2005	Cumulative[a]
Race/ethnicity						
White, not Hispanic	13	14	12	6	6	1,613
Black, not Hispanic	85	72	46	31	46	5,631
Hispanic	23	16	11	9	13	1,738
Asian/Pacific Islander	1	1	0	1	1	54
American Indian/Alaska Native	0	1	0	1	0	32
Total[b]	**121**	**105**	**71**	**50**	**68**	**9,101**

Note: These numbers do not represent reported case counts. Rather, these numbers are point estimates, which result from adjustments of reported case counts. The reported case counts have been adjusted for reporting delays and for redistribution of cases in persons initially reported without an identified risk factor, but not for incomplete reporting.

[a]From the beginning of the epidemic through 2005.
[b]Includes children of unknown race or multiple races. Cumulative total includes 33 children of unknown race or multiple races. Because column totals were calculated independently of the values for the subpopulations, the values in each column may not sum to the column total.

SOURCE: Adapted from "Table 4. Estimated Numbers of AIDS Cases in Children <13 Years of Age, by Year of Diagnosis and Selected Characteristics, 2001–2005 and Cumulative—50 States and the District of Columbia," in *HIV/AIDS Surveillance Report 2005*, vol. 17, rev. ed., U.S. Department of Health and Human Services, Centers for Disease Control and Prevention, June 2007, http://www.cdc.gov/hiv/topics/surveillance/resources/reports/2005report/pdf/2005SurveillanceReport.pdf (accessed January 4, 2008)

virus (HIV), is not transmitted casually, but only through the transfer of bodily fluids, such as blood and semen. The CDC reports in the fact sheet "HIV and Its Transmission" (March 2007, http://www.cdc.gov/hiv/resources/factsheets/transmission.htm) that there are only four methods of transmission: contaminated blood, sexual transmission, contaminated syringes from intravenous drug use, and perinatal (around the time of birth) transmission from a mother to her child or through breast milk.

Minorities have been especially hard hit by the AIDS epidemic. (See Figure 6.8.) The HHS and CDC note in *HIV/AIDS Surveillance Report 2005* (June 2007, http://www.cdc.gov/hiv/topics/surveillance/resources/reports/2005report/pdf/2005SurveillanceReport.pdf) that of the estimated 475,871 people living with AIDS in 2005, 224,815 (47.2%) were African-Americans, 160,746 (33.8%) were non-Hispanic whites, and 81,389 (17.1%) were Hispanics. Asians and Pacific Islanders and Native Americans and Alaskan Natives were the least likely groups to be living with HIV/AIDS, at less than 1% (2,996 and 2,055, respectively) each.

In "Pregnancy and Childbirth: HIV/AIDS" (October 10, 2007, http://www.cdc.gov/hiv/topics/perinatal/), the CDC explains that children primarily get HIV in utero

from infected mothers. Far more AIDS cases have been diagnosed among African-American children than among children of other racial or ethnic backgrounds. Through 2005, 5,631 cases among African-American children, 1,738 among Hispanic children, and 1,613 among white, non-Hispanic children had been diagnosed. (See Table 6.12.) Only fifty-four cases had been diagnosed among Asian and Pacific Islander children, and only thirty-two had been diagnosed among Native American and Alaskan Native children. The use of antiretroviral drugs has greatly diminished the rate of infection of the children of HIV-positive mothers; the use of these drugs reduces the rate of transmission from about 25% to about 2%. The rate of diagnosis among African-American children dropped from eighty-five cases in 2001 to forty-six in 2005—a decrease of 45.9%. Cases among Hispanic children fell from twenty-three in 2001 to thirteen in 2005, a decrease of 43.5%. Cases among white, non-Hispanic children fell from thirteen in 2001 to six in 2005, a decrease of 53.8%.

The methods of transmission of HIV among the adolescent and adult population differ considerably by race. By 2005 white men with AIDS had overwhelmingly contracted the disease through homosexual contact; 73% had done so over the course of the epidemic, with the next-highest transmission method for this group being intravenous drug use, at 9%. (See Table 6.13.) Most Asian

TABLE 6.13

Male adult/adolescent AIDS cases by exposure category and race/ethnicity, reported through 2005

Transmission category	2005 No.	2005 %	Cumulative[a] No.	Cumulative[a] %
White, not Hispanic				
Male-to-male sexual contact	6,820	65	248,186	73
Injection drug use	831	8	31,275	9
Male-to-male sexual contact and injection drug use	799	8	30,401	9
Hemophilia/coagulation disorder	50	0	3,971	1
High-risk heterosexual contact[b]	344	3	7,454	2
Sex with injection drug user	68	1	2,249	1
Sex with person with hemophilia	0	0	35	0
Sex with HIV-infected transfusion recipient	1	0	177	0
Sex with HIV-infected person, risk factor not specified	275	3	4,993	1
Receipt of blood transfusion, blood components, or tissue	22	0	3,193	1
Other/risk factor not reported or identified	1,569	15	15,815	5
Total	**10,435**	**100**	**340,295**	**100**
Black, not Hispanic				
Male-to-male sexual contact	4,731	36	99,269	37
Injection drug use	2,059	16	82,233	30
Male-to-male sexual contact and injection drug use	596	4	21,260	8
Hemophilia/coagulation disorder	11	0	598	0
High-risk heterosexual contact[b]	1,958	15	28,104	10
Sex with injection drug user	224	2	6,675	2
Sex with person with hemophilia	3	0	34	0
Sex with HIV-infected transfusion recipient	8	0	218	0
Sex with HIV-infected person, risk factor not specified	1,723	13	21,177	8
Receipt of blood transfusion, blood components, or tissue	37	0	1,210	0
Other/risk factor not reported or identified	3,868	29	38,097	14
Total	**13,260**	**100**	**270,771**	**100**
Hispanic				
Male-to-male sexual contact	2,884	44	61,824	43
Injection drug use	1,213	19	45,068	32
Male-to-male sexual contact and injection drug use	293	4	10,390	7
Hemophilia/coagulation disorder	5	0	457	0
High-risk heterosexual contact[b]	740	11	10,301	7
Sex with injection drug user	93	1	2,325	2
Sex with person with hemophilia	0	0	11	0
Sex with HIV-infected transfusion recipient	4	0	119	0
Sex with HIV-infected person, risk factor not specified	643	10	7,846	6
Receipt of blood transfusion, blood components, or tissue	13	0	642	0
Other/risk factor not reported or identified	1,392	21	13,841	10
Total	**6,540**	**100**	**142,523**	**100**
Asian/Pacific Islander				
Male-to-male sexual contact	214	55	4,317	68
Injection drug use	18	5	312	5
Male-to-male sexual contact and injection drug use	12	3	261	4
Hemophilia/coagulation disorder	2	1	71	1
High-risk heterosexual contact[b]	44	11	356	6
Sex with injection drug user	0	0	55	1
Sex with person with hemophilia	0	0	1	0
Sex with HIV-infected transfusion recipient	0	0	9	0
Sex with HIV-infected person, risk factor not specified	44	11	291	5
Receipt of blood transfusion, blood components, or tissue	1	0	114	2
Other/risk factor not reported or identified	97	25	883	14
Total	**388**	**100**	**6,314**	**100**

TABLE 6.13

Male adult/adolescent AIDS cases by exposure category and race/ethnicity, reported through 2005 [CONTINUED]

Transmission category	2005 No.	2005 %	Cumulative[a] No.	Cumulative[a] %
American Indian/Alaska Native				
Male-to-male sexual contact	63	48	1,351	55
Injection drug use	20	15	388	16
Male-to-male sexual contact and injection drug use	19	15	426	17
Hemophilia/coagulation disorder	0	0	31	1
High-risk heterosexual contact[b]	11	8	109	4
Sex with injection drug user	4	3	34	1
Sex with person with hemophilia	0	0	0	0
Sex with HIV-infected transfusion recipient	0	0	3	0
Sex with HIV-infected person, risk factor not specified	7	5	72	3
Receipt of blood transfusion, blood components, or tissue	0	0	9	0
Other/risk factor not reported or identified	18	14	150	6
Total	**131**	**100**	**2,464**	**100**
Total cases				
Male-to-male sexual contact	14,819	48	416,232	54
Injection drug use	4,168	13	159,676	21
Male-to-male sexual contact and injection drug use	1,742	6	62,940	8
Hemophilia/coagulation disorder	68	0	5,142	1
High-risk heterosexual contact[b]	3,110	10	46,533	6
Sex with injection drug user	389	1	11,371	1
Sex with person with hemophilia	3	0	81	0
Sex with HIV-infected transfusion recipient	13	0	529	0
Sex with HIV-infected person, risk factor not specified	2,705	9	34,552	5
Receipt of blood transfusion, blood components, or tissue	73	0	5,190	1
Other/risk factor not reported or identified	6,976	23	69,095	9
Total	**30,956[c]**	**100**	**764,808[d]**	**100**

[a]Reported from the beginning of the epidemic through 2005.
[b]Heterosexual contact with a person known to have, or to be at high risk for, HIV infection.
[c]Includes 202 males of unknown race or multiple races.
[d]Includes 2,441 males of unknown race or multiple races.

SOURCE: "Table 19. Reported AIDS Cases for Male Adults and Adolescents, by Transmission Category and Race/Ethnicity, 2005 and Cumulative—United States and Dependent Areas," in *HIV/AIDS Surveillance Report 2005*, vol. 17, rev. ed., U.S. Department of Health and Human Services, Centers for Disease Control and Prevention, June 2007, http://www.cdc.gov/hiv/topics/surveillance/resources/reports/2005report/pdf/2005SurveillanceReport .pdf (accessed January 4, 2008).

contracted the disease through homosexual contact. Even though male-to-male sexual contact was the method of transmission for the plurality of African-American men with AIDS (37%) and Hispanic men with AIDS (43%), a significant proportion of African-American men (30%) and Hispanic men (32%) with AIDS contracted the disease through intravenous drug use. In addition, a sizeable portion of African-American men with AIDS had contracted the disease through heterosexual contact (10%).

Most women who had contracted AIDS through 2005 had done so through heterosexual contact or intravenous drug use. Non-Hispanic white women were about equally

and Pacific Islander men with AIDS (68%) and Native American and Alaskan Native men with AIDS (55%) also

TABLE 6.14

Female adult/adolescent AIDS cases by exposure category and race/ethnicity, reported through 2005

Transmission category	2005 No.	2005 %	Cumulative[a] No.	Cumulative[a] %
White, not Hispanic				
Injection drug use	506	28	14,519	40
Hemophilia/coagulation disorder	2	0	119	0
High-risk heterosexual contact[b]	749	42	15,094	42
Sex with injection drug user	188	10	5,536	15
Sex with bisexual male	60	3	1,779	5
Sex with person with hemophilia	6	0	325	1
Sex with HIV-infected transfusion recipient	7	0	336	1
Sex with HIV-infected person, risk factor not specified	488	27	7,118	20
Receipt of blood transfusion, blood components, or tissue	20	1	1,871	5
Other/risk factor not reported or identified	517	29	4,653	13
Total	**1,794**	**100**	**36,256**	**100**
Black, not Hispanic				
Injection drug use	1,130	16	37,977	35
Hemophilia/coagulation disorder	5	0	143	0
High-risk heterosexual contact[b]	3,079	44	46,642	43
Sex with injection drug user	367	5	13,184	12
Sex with bisexual male	115	2	2,190	2
Sex with person with hemophilia	6	0	117	0
Sex with HIV-infected transfusion recipient	12	0	266	0
Sex with HIV-infected person, risk factor not specified	2,579	37	30,885	28
Receipt of blood transfusion, blood components, or tissue	53	1	1,531	1
Other/risk factor not reported or identified	2,711	39	22,158	20
Total	**6,978**	**100**	**108,451**	**100**
Hispanic				
Injection drug use	371	19	12,407	36
Hemophilia/coagulation disorder	3	0	65	0
High-risk heterosexual contact[b]	990	51	16,964	49
Sex with injection drug user	175	9	6,293	18
Sex with bisexual male	46	2	782	2
Sex with person with hemophilia	1	0	45	0
Sex with HIV-infected transfusion recipient	7	0	130	0
Sex with HIV-infected person, risk factor not specified	761	39	9,714	28
Receipt of blood transfusion, blood components, or tissue	9	0	608	2
Other/risk factor not reported or identified	578	30	4,570	13
Total	**1,951**	**100**	**34,614**	**100**
Asian/Pacific Islander				
Injection drug use	9	11	124	12
Hemophilia/coagulation disorder	0	0	7	1
High-risk heterosexual contact[b]	37	44	524	52
Sex with injection drug user	4	5	112	11
Sex with bisexual male	0	0	79	8
Sex with person with hemophilia	0	0	4	0
Sex with HIV-infected transfusion recipient	1	1	23	2
Sex with HIV-infected person, risk factor not specified	32	38	306	30
Receipt of blood transfusion, blood components, or tissue	3	4	93	9
Other/risk factor not reported or identified	36	42	258	26
Total	**85**	**100**	**1,006**	**100**

TABLE 6.14

Female adult/adolescent AIDS cases by exposure category and race/ethnicity, reported through 2005 [CONTINUED]

Transmission category	2005 No.	2005 %	Cumulative[a] No.	Cumulative[a] %
American Indian/Alaska Native				
Injection drug use	15	28	267	42
Hemophilia/coagulation disorder	0	0	3	0
High-risk heterosexual contact[b]	24	44	264	41
Sex with injection drug user	8	15	101	16
Sex with bisexual male	0	0	26	4
Sex with person with hemophilia	0	0	2	0
Sex with HIV-infected transfusion recipient	0	0	5	1
Sex with HIV-infected person, risk factor not specified	16	30	130	20
Receipt of blood transfusion, blood components, or tissue	2	4	17	3
Other/risk factor not reported or identified	13	24	88	14
Total	**54**	**100**	**639**	**100**
Total cases				
Injection drug use	2,047	19	65,534	36
Hemophilia/coagulation disorder	11	0	340	0
High-risk heterosexual contact[b]	4,918	45	79,872	44
Sex with injection drug user	751	7	25,310	14
Sex with bisexual male	223	2	4,876	3
Sex with person with hemophilia	13	0	493	0
Sex with HIV-infected transfusion recipient	27	0	767	0
Sex with HIV-infected person, risk factor not specified	3,904	36	48,426	27
Receipt of blood transfusion, blood components, or tissue	87	1	4,144	2
Other/risk factor not reported or identified	3,881	35	31,879	18
Total	**10,944[c]**	**100**	**181,769[d]**	**100**

[a]From the beginning of the epidemic through 2005.
[b]Heterosexual contact with a person known to have, or to be at high risk for, HIV infection.
[c]Includes 82 females of unknown race or multiple races.
[d]Includes 803 females of unknown race or multiple races.

SOURCE: "Table 21. Reported AIDS Cases for Female Adults and Adolescents, by Transmission Category and Race/Ethnicity, 2005 and Cumulative—United States and Dependent Areas," in *HIV/AIDS Surveillance Report 2005*, vol. 17, rev. ed., U.S. Department of Health and Human Services, Centers for Disease Control and Prevention, June 2007, http://www.cdc.gov/hiv/topics/surveillance/resources/reports/2005report/pdf/2005SurveillanceReport.pdf (accessed January 4, 2008)

were more likely to contract the disease through heterosexual contact (43%) than they were through intravenous drug use (35%). Hispanic women were also slightly more likely to contract AIDS through heterosexual contact (49%) than through intravenous drug use (36%). Asian and Pacific Islander women were much more likely to contract AIDS through heterosexual contact (52%) than they were through intravenous drug use (12%).

African-Americans are extremely overrepresented in new diagnoses of HIV/AIDS each year. However, the disparities in the care that they received earlier in the epidemic seemed to have disappeared by 2003. In *2006 National Healthcare Disparities Report*, the HHS states that "without adequate treatment, as HIV disease progresses, CD4 cell counts fall and patients become increasingly susceptible to opportunistic infections."

likely to contract AIDS through heterosexual contact (42%) or intravenous drug use (40%) as were Native Americans and Alaskan Natives, 41% of whom contracted the disease through heterosexual contact and 42% of whom contracted the disease through intravenous drug use. (See Table 6.14.) African-American women

The HHS notes that the receipt of antiretroviral therapy (to prevent HIV-infected people from developing AIDS) and drug therapy to prevent *Pneumocystis carinii* pneumonia did not differ significantly by race or ethnicity in that year.

Sickle-Cell Anemia in African-Americans

In "Facts about Sickle Cell Disease" (2008, http://www.cdc.gov/ncbddd/sicklecell/faq_sicklecell.htm), the CDC explains that sickle-cell anemia, a hereditary disease that primarily strikes African-American people in the United States, is a blood disorder in which defective hemoglobin causes red blood cells to become sickle shaped, rather than round. This can create blockages in small arteries and can result in many problems, including chronic anemia, episodes of intense pain, strokes, and death. Scientists believe the genetic trait arose randomly in Africa and survived as a defense against malaria. The disease can be inherited only when both parents have the sickle-cell trait and the child inherits the defective gene from both parents. The CDC notes in "Health Care Professionals: Data and Statistics" (2008, http://www.cdc.gov/ncbddd/sicklecell/hcp_data.htm) that in 2008 one out of every twelve African-Americans was a carrier for sickle-cell anemia, and about one out of every five hundred African-American infants was born with it. Of the more than seventy thousand Americans who had sickle-cell anemia in 2008, most were of African descent. More than one thousand babies are born each year in the United States with the disease.

BEHAVIORS THAT THREATEN HEALTH
Cigarette Smoking

Nicotine is the drug in tobacco that causes addiction; cigarette smoking is the most popular method of taking nicotine in the United States. The National Institutes of Health indicates in the press release "Most Behaviors Preceding Major Causes of Preventable Death Have Begun by Young Adulthood" (January 11, 2006, http://www.nih.gov/news/pr/jan2006/nichd-11.htm) that tobacco use is the leading cause of preventable death in the United States. Smoking during pregnancy causes an increased risk of stillborn, premature birth, low birth weight, and sudden infant death syndrome. The tar in cigarettes increases the user's risk of lung cancer and other bronchial diseases, and the carbon monoxide in the smoke increases the chance of cardiovascular diseases.

In 2006 Native Americans and Alaskan Natives were more likely to smoke than any other group: 42.3% reported smoking in the past month, 48.9% in the past year, and 78.8% had smoked at some point in their lifetime. (See Table 6.15.) Non-Hispanic whites were the next most likely to smoke: 30.4% had smoked within the past month, 35.7% in the past year, and 72.8% in their lifetime. African-Americans were slightly more likely to smoke than Hispanics: 29.1% had smoked in the past month, compared to 24.4% of Hispanics; 32.9% had smoked in the past year, compared to 30.2% of Hispanics; and 60.2% had smoked in their lifetime, compared to 57.1% of Hispanics. Asian-Americans were the least likely to smoke; only 16% reported smoking in the past month, 20.7% in the past year, and 44.4% in their lifetime.

The Substance Abuse and Mental Health Services Administration reports in *Results from the 2004 National Survey on Drug Use and Health: National Findings* (2005, http://www.drugabusestatistics.samhsa.gov/NSDUH/2k4nsduh/2k4Results/2k4Results.pdf) that cigarette smoking is the most likely among those aged eighteen to twenty-five, regardless of race or ethnic group. Among this age group, whites are overwhelmingly more likely to smoke than their African-American or Hispanic counterparts. In 2004, 45.1% of eighteen- to twenty-five-year-old whites smoked, compared to 31.7% of Hispanics and 28.8% of African-Americans. However, the race and ethnic difference leveled off among smokers aged twenty-six and older. In 2004, 25.7% of African-Americans in this age group smoked, as did 25% of whites and 20.9% of Hispanics.

Diet and Nutrition

One reason that Asians and Pacific Islanders enjoy better health than other racial and ethnic groups is their diet. The typical Asian and Pacific Islander diet is low in fat and cholesterol. The staple food for many Asian-Americans is rice. The consumption of vegetables is relatively high, and pork and fish are also commonly eaten. Dairy products are used less frequently. The traditional sources of calcium are soybean curd, sardines, and green, leafy vegetables, all healthy sources of nutrients. As a result, Patricia M. Barnes, Patricia F. Adams, and Eve Powell-Griner of the CDC note in *Health Characteristics of the Asian Adult Population: United States, 2004–2006* (January 22, 2008, http://www.cdc.gov/nchs/data/ad/ad394.pdf) that Asian-Americans are more likely to be a healthy weight (59.3% of them are) than are non-Hispanic whites (39.7%), Hispanics (31.5%), African-Americans (29.7%), or Native Americans (28.6%).

The Healthy Eating Index is computed periodically by the U.S. Department of Agriculture's Center for Nutrition Policy and Promotion, and its most recent publication on diet quality is the *Report Card on the Diet Quality of African Americans* (July 1998, http://www.cnpp.usda.gov/Publications/NutritionInsights/Insight6.pdf). The center finds that of the various population subgroups, African-Americans have a particularly poor diet. Between 1994 and 1996, the period of the study, 28% of African-Americans had a poor diet, compared to 16% of whites. Fewer than 50% of African-Americans met the dietary recommendations for the consumption of grains, vegetables, fruits, milk, meat, total fat, saturated fat, or sodium.

TABLE 6.15

Tobacco product use by age, gender, and race/ethnicity, 2005 and 2006

Demographic characteristic	Time period					
	Lifetime		Past year		Past month	
	2005	2006	2005	2006	2005	2006
Total	70.8	70.7	34.9	35.0	29.4	29.6
Age						
12–17	30.7	29.7	21.2	20.8	13.1	12.9
18–25	72.3	71.8	54.3	54.0	44.3	43.9
26 or older	76.0	76.0	33.4	33.5	29.0	29.4
Gender						
Male	78.3	78.3	42.3	42.9	35.8	36.4
Female	63.8	63.5	28.0	27.4	23.4	23.3
Hispanic origin and race						
Not Hispanic or Latino	72.7	72.8	35.5	35.7	30.1	30.4
White	76.5	76.8	36.9	37.0	31.2	31.4
Black or African American	60.7	60.2	32.1	32.9	28.4	29.1
American Indian or Alaska Native	73.6	78.8	48.5	48.9	41.7	42.3
Native Hawaiian or other Pacific Islander	68.9	*	37.3	*	30.3	*
Asian	44.3	44.4	19.9	20.7	14.6	16.0
Two or more races	66.1	69.8	40.0	38.2	33.9	34.2
Hispanic or Latino	58.5	57.1	31.0	30.2	24.5	24.4

*Low precision; no estimate reported.
Note: Tobacco products include cigarettes, smokeless tobacco (i.e., chewing tobacco or snuff), cigars, or pipe tobacco. Tobacco product use in the past year excludes past year pipe tobacco use, but includes past month pipe tobacco use.

SOURCE: "Table 2.17B. Tobacco Product Use in Lifetime, Past Year, and Past Month among Persons Aged 12 or Older, by Demographic Characteristics: Percentages, 2005 and 2006," in *Results from the 2006 National Survey on Drug Use and Health: Detailed Tables*, U.S. Department of Health and Human Services, Substance Abuse and Mental Health Services Administration, Office of Applied Studies, September 2007, http://www.oas.samhsa.gov/NSDUH/2k6nsduh/tabs/Sect2peTabs17to21.pdf (accessed December 14, 2007)

The Native American diet has been negatively affected by the introduction of nonnative foods. Even though there are considerable tribal variations in diet, studies show that the less Native Americans eat of their traditional foods, the greater their levels of obesity and adult-onset diabetes. High carbohydrate, sodium, and saturated fat contents characterize the most current Native American diet. Also, the Native American diet is relatively low in meat and dairy products. Factors contributing to these eating habits include food availability, preference for nonnative food, and place of residence.

Drug Abuse

ALCOHOL. Alcohol depresses the central nervous system. The consumption of small amounts of alcohol can actually have a beneficial affect on the body. However, when consumed in larger amounts, alcohol impairs judgment and increases reaction time, can interfere with prescription and nonprescription medications in adverse ways, and can cause serious damage to developing fetuses. Chronic health consequences of excessive drinking include increased risk of liver cirrhosis, pancreatitis, certain types of cancer, high blood pressure, and psychological disorders. Addiction to alcohol is a chronic disease that is often progressive and sometimes fatal.

In 2006 Asian-Americans, Native Americans and Alaskan Natives, Hispanics, and African-Americans were all less likely to report having used alcohol in the past month than were non-Hispanic whites. The rate of binge alcohol use, defined as five or more drinks on one occasion in at least one day in the previous month, was lowest among Asian-Americans (11.8%) and African-Americans (19.1%), and Hispanics (23.9%) and Native Americans and Alaskan Natives (31%) had rates comparable to or higher than that of non-Hispanic whites (24.1%) in 2006. (See Table 6.16.) The rates of heavy alcohol use, defined as drinking five or more drinks on each of five or more days in the past thirty days, were highest among Native Americans and Alaskan Natives (9%) and non-Hispanic whites (7.8%). Hispanics (5.7%), African-Americans (4.6%), and Asian-Americans (2.4%) had the lowest rates of heavy alcohol use in 2006.

ILLICIT DRUG USE. According to the CDC, illicit drugs include marijuana/hashish, cocaine (including crack), heroin, hallucinogens (including LSD and PCP), inhalants, or any prescription-type psychotherapeutic drug used nonmedically. Illicit drug use is a particular problem in the Native American and Alaskan Native community, where rates of use in the past month, past year, and lifetime use were highest. In 2006 the rate of illicit drug use in the past month was highest for Native Americans and Alaskan Natives (13.7%) and lowest for Asian-Americans (3.6%) and Hispanics (6.9%). (See Table 6.17.) African-Americans (9.8%) and non-Hispanic whites (8.5%) reported similar

TABLE 6.16

Alcohol use, binge alcohol use, and heavy alcohol use in the past month among persons aged 12 or older, by age, gender, and race/ethnicity, 2005 and 2006

	Type of alcohol use					
	Alcohol use		Binge alcohol use		Heavy alcohol use	
Demographic characteristic	2005	2006	2005	2006	2005	2006
Total	51.8	50.9	22.7	23.0	6.6	6.9
Age						
12–17	16.5	16.6	9.9	10.3	2.4	2.4
18–25	60.9	61.9	41.9	42.2	15.3	15.6
26 or older	55.1	53.7	21.0	21.4	5.6	6.0
Gender						
Male	58.1	57.0	30.5	31.2	10.3	10.7
Female	45.9	45.2	15.2	15.2	3.1	3.3
Hispanic origin and race						
Not Hispanic or Latino	53.2	52.4	22.5	22.9	6.7	7.1
White	56.5	55.8	23.4	24.1	7.4	7.8
Black or African American	40.8	40.0	20.3	19.1	4.2	4.6
American Indian or Alaska Native	42.4	37.2	32.8	31.0	11.5	9.0
Native Hawaiian or other Pacific Islander	37.3	36.7	25.7	24.1	5.3	11.0
Asian	38.1	35.4	12.7	11.8	2.0	2.4
Two or more races	47.3	47.1	20.8	22.8	5.6	6.3
Hispanic or Latino	42.6	41.8	23.7	23.9	5.6	5.7

Note: Binge alcohol use is defined as drinking five or more drinks on the same occasion (i.e., at the same time or within a couple of hours of each other) on at least 1 day in the past 30 days. Heavy alcohol use is defined as drinking five or more drinks on the same occasion on each of 5 or more days in the past 30 days; all heavy alcohol users are also binge alcohol users.

SOURCE: "Table 2.42B. Alcohol Use, Binge Alcohol Use, and Heavy Alcohol Use in the Past Month among Persons Aged 12 or Older, by Demographic Characteristics: Percentages, 2005 and 2006," in *Results from the 2006 National Survey on Drug Use and Health: Detailed Tables*, U.S. Department of Health and Human Services, Substance Abuse and Mental Health Services Administration, Office of Applied Studies, September 2007, http://www.oas.samhsa.gov/NSDUH/2k6nsduh/tabs/Sect2peTabs37to46.pdf (accessed December 14, 2007)

rates of illicit drug use in the past month. Lifetime illicit drug use was also highest among Native Americans (58.8%), followed by non-Hispanic whites (49%), African-Americans (42.9%), Hispanics (35%), and Asian-Americans (23.7%).

LIFE EXPECTANCY AND DEATH
Life Expectancy

Women tend to live longer than men, and whites are likely to live longer than African-Americans. When comparing the life expectancies of African-American and white babies, African-American males born in 2004 had the shortest life expectancy of 69.5 years, whereas white females had the longest life expectancy of 80.8 years. (See Figure 6.9.) African-American females had a life expectancy of 76.3 years, and white males had a life expectancy of 75.7 years. The life expectancy of all groups at birth had risen since 1970, especially for African-Americans.

Age-adjusted death rates are measured per one hundred thousand in a specified population group. In 2004 African-Americans died at a higher rate than white Americans (1.3 African-Americans died for every 1 white death). (See Table 6.18.) Hispanics died at a lower rate than did non-Hispanic whites (0.7 Hispanics died for ever 1 non-Hispanic white death).

Leading Causes of Death

In 2004 heart disease was the leading cause of death among Americans, with 217 deaths per 100,000 of the population. Cancers (malignant neoplasms) were the second-leading cause of death, with 185.8 deaths per 100,000, followed by cerebrovascular diseases, which caused 50 deaths per 100,000. (See Table 6.18.) Chronic lower respiratory diseases and accidents rounded out the top-five leading causes of death that year, with 41.1 and 37.7 deaths per 100,000, respectively.

In *Health, United States, 2007*, the NCHS notes that in 2004 heart disease was the leading cause of death among every racial or ethnic group except for Asians and Pacific Islanders, who died more often from malignant neoplasms. That year, 74,225 (25.8%) African-Americans, 27,788 (22.7%) Hispanics, 2,598 (19.8%) Native Americans, and 9,960 (24.6%) Asians and Pacific Islanders died of heart disease. Cancer was the second-leading cause of death among most groups.

The NCHS reports that unintentional injuries, including automobile accidents, were particularly high in the Native American and Hispanic communities in 2004. In both, unintentional injuries were the third-leading cause of death. There were 1,520 Native American deaths and 10,408

TABLE 6.17

Illicit drug use by age, gender, and race/ethnicity, 2005 and 2006

	Time period					
	Lifetime		Past year		Past month	
Demographic characteristic	2005	2006	2005	2006	2005	2006
Total	46.1	45.4	14.4	14.5	8.1	8.3
Age						
12–17	27.7	27.6	19.9	19.6	9.9	9.8
18–25	59.2	59.0	34.2	34.4	20.1	19.8
26 or older	46.3	45.5	10.2	10.4	5.8	6.1
Gender						
Male	50.8	50.3	16.8	17.4	10.2	10.5
Female	41.6	40.9	12.1	11.8	6.1	6.2
Hispanic origin and race						
Not Hispanic or Latino	47.4	47.1	14.5	14.8	8.2	8.5
White	48.9	49.0	14.5	14.8	8.1	8.5
Black or African American	44.7	42.9	16.0	16.4	9.7	9.8
American Indian or Alaska Native	60.9	58.8	21.3	20.1	12.8	13.7
Native Hawaiian or other Pacific Islander	54.3	40.9	15.5	13.4	8.7	7.5
Asian	28.1	23.7	7.1	8.9	3.1	3.6
Two or more races	45.8	55.4	19.1	18.1	12.2	8.9
Hispanic or Latino	37.3	35.0	13.9	13.1	7.6	6.9

Note: Illicit drugs include marijuana/hashish, cocaine (including crack), heroin, hallucinogens, inhalants, or prescription-type psychotherapeutics used nonmedically.

SOURCE: "Table 1.19B. Illicit Drug Use in Lifetime, Past Year, and Past Month among Persons Aged 12 or Older, by Demographic Characteristics: Percentages, 2005 and 2006," in *Results from the 2006 National Survey on Drug Use and Health: Detailed Tables*, U.S. Department of Health and Human Services, Substance Abuse and Mental Health Services Administration, Office of Applied Studies, September 2007, http://www.oas.samhsa.gov/NSDUH/2k6nsduh/tabs/Sect1peTabs19to23.pdf (accessed December 14, 2007)

FIGURE 6.9

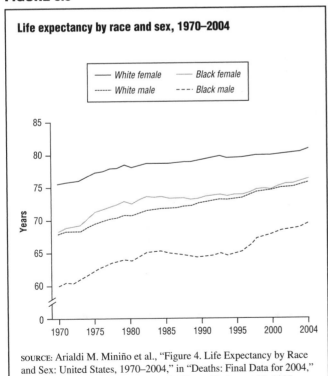

Life expectancy by race and sex, 1970–2004

- White female
- Black female
- White male
- Black male

SOURCE: Arialdi M. Miniño et al., "Figure 4. Life Expectancy by Race and Sex: United States, 1970–2004," in "Deaths: Final Data for 2004," *National Vital Statistics Reports*, vol. 55, no. 19, August 21, 2007, http://www.cdc.gov/nchs/data/nvsr/nvsr55/nvsr55_19.pdf (accessed December 9, 2007)

Hispanic deaths caused by these injuries. Suicide was the eighth-leading cause of death for both Native Americans and Asians and Pacific Islanders. Homicide ranked sixth among African-Americans and seventh among Hispanics.

HOMICIDE. The NCHS indicates in *Health, United States, 2007* that homicides are disproportionately high in the non-Hispanic African-American population, and the high homicide rate among African-Americans is one of the reasons African-American men in their twenties and thirties have a higher death rate than men this age in other ethnic and racial groups. In 2004, 6,839 African-American males were murdered. The highest rate of death by homicide was among African-American men aged twenty-five to thirty-four years (81.6 per 100,000), followed by African-American men aged fifteen to twenty-four (77.6 per 100,000) and African-American men aged thirty-five to forty-four (37.9 per 100,000). In comparison, there were 4.7 deaths per 100,000 white, non-Hispanic men aged fifteen to twenty-four, and 5.5 deaths per 100,000 white, non-Hispanic men aged twenty-five to thirty-four. However, the death rate by homicide for African-American men had dropped from a high of 78.2 per 100,000 in 1970 to 35.1 per 100,000 in 2004.

According to the NCHS, in 2004 Hispanics, like African-Americans, had a higher homicide rate than most other groups, particularly among youth. The death rate for Hispanic men aged fifteen to twenty-four years was

TABLE 6.18

Deaths by causes of death, race/ethnicity, and sex, 2004

[Death rates on an annual basis per 100,000 population: age-adjusted rates per 100,000 U.S. standard population.]

Rank[a]	Cause of death	Number	Percent of total deaths	2004 crude death rate	2004	2003 to 2004	Male to female	Black to white	Hispanic[b] to non-Hispanic white
—	All causes	2,397,615	100.0	816.5	800.8	−3.8	1.4	1.3	0.7
1	Diseases of heart	652,486	27.2	222.2	217.0	−6.6	1.5	1.3	0.7
2	Malignant neoplasms	553,888	23.1	188.6	185.8	−2.3	1.4	1.2	0.6
3	Cerebrovascular diseases	150,074	6.3	51.1	50.0	−6.5	1.0	1.5	0.8
4	Chronic lower respiratory diseases	121,987	5.1	41.5	41.1	−5.1	1.4	0.7	0.4
5	Accidents (unintentional injuries)	112,012	4.7	38.1	37.7	1.1	2.1	0.9	0.8
6	Diabetes mellitus	73,138	3.1	24.9	24.5	−3.2	1.3	2.2	1.5
7	Alzheimer's disease	65,965	2.8	22.5	21.8	1.9	0.7	0.8	0.6
8	Influenza and pneumonia	59,664	2.5	20.3	19.8	−10.0	1.4	1.1	0.9
9	Nephritis, nephrotic syndrome and nephrosis	42,480	1.8	14.5	14.2	−1.4	1.4	2.3	0.9
10	Septicemia	33,373	1.4	11.4	11.2	−3.4	1.2	2.2	0.8
11	Intentional self-harm (suicide)	32,439	1.4	11.0	10.9	0.9	4.0	0.4	0.5
12	Chronic liver disease and cirrhosis	27,013	1.1	9.2	9.0	−3.2	2.2	0.9	1.6
13	Essential (primary) hypertension and hypertensive renal disease	23,076	1.0	7.9	7.7	4.1	1.0	2.8	1.0
14	Parkinson's disease	17,989	0.8	6.1	6.1	−1.6	2.3	0.4	0.6
15	Assault (homicide)	17,357	0.7	5.9	5.9	−1.7	3.7	5.6	2.7
—	All other causes	414,674	17.3	141.2	—	—	—	—	—

—Category not applicable.
[a]Rank based on number of deaths.
[b]Data for Hispanic origin should be interpreted with caution because of inconsistencies between reporting Hispanic origin on death certificates and on censuses and surveys.

SOURCE: Arialdi M. Miniño et al., "Table C. Percentage of Total Deaths, Death Rates, Age-Adjusted Death Rates for 2004, Percentage Change in Age-Adjusted Death Rates from 2003 to 2004, and Ratio of Age-Adjusted Death Rates by Race and Sex for the 15 Leading Causes of Death for the Total Population in 2004: United States," in "Deaths: Final Data for 2004," *National Vital Statistics Reports*, vol. 55, no. 19, August 21, 2007, http://www.cdc.gov/nchs/data/nvsr/nvsr55/nvsr55_19.pdf (accessed December 9, 2007)

29.6 per 100,000, and for Hispanic men aged twenty-five to thirty-four it was 20.3 per 100,000. However, between 1990 and 2004 the homicide death rate among all Hispanic men dropped from 27.4 to 11.5 per 100,000.

HIV AND AIDS. The difference in the HIV/AIDS death rate among races and ethnic groups is staggering, with a much higher rate among African-Americans than any other group of Americans. In 2005, 8,562 African-Americans died from AIDS, compared to 5,006 non-Hispanic whites, 2,444 Hispanics, 97 Asians and Pacific Islanders, and 81 Native Americans. (See Table 6.19.) In *Health, United States, 2007*, the NCHS reports that the HIV/AIDS death rate for African-American males in 2004 was 29.2 per 100,000, compared to 8.2 per 100,000 Hispanic males, 4.3 per 100,000 Native American males, 3.1 per 100,000 non-Hispanic white males, and 1.2 per 100,000 Asian and Pacific Islander males. The death rate for African-American females in 2004 was also high, at 13 per 100,000, compared to 2.4 per 100,000 Hispanic females, 1.5 per 100,000 Native American females, and 0.6 per 100,000 non-Hispanic white females.

TABLE 6.19

Estimated numbers of deaths of persons with AIDS, by year of death and race/ethnicity, 2001–05

Data for 50 states and the District of Columbia	Year of death					
	2001	2002	2003	2004	2005	Cumulative*
Race/ethnicity						
White, not Hispanic	5,239	5,153	5,263	5,137	5,006	235,879
Black, not Hispanic	9,085	8,927	9,077	9,302	8,562	211,559
Hispanic	2,436	2,306	2,774	2,664	2,444	77,125
Asian/Pacific Islander	99	93	88	113	97	3,383
American Indian/Alaska Native	79	84	75	85	81	1,657

Note: These numbers do not represent reported case counts. Rather, these numbers are point estimates, which result from adjustments of reported case counts. The reported case counts have been adjusted for reporting delays and for redistribution of cases in persons initially reported without an identified risk factor, but not for incomplete reporting.
*From the beginning of the epidemic through 2005.

SOURCE: Adapted from "Table 7. Estimated Numbers of Deaths of Persons with AIDS, by Year of Death and Selected Characteristics, 2001–2005 and Cumulative—United States and Dependent Areas," in *HIV/AIDS Surveillance Report 2005*, vol. 17, rev. ed., U.S. Department of Health and Human Services, Centers for Disease Control and Prevention, June 2007, http://www.cdc.gov/hiv/topics/surveillance/resources/reports/2005report/pdf/2005SurveillanceReport.pdf (accessed January 4, 2008)

CHAPTER 7
CRIME

VICTIMIZATION OF MINORITIES

Certain groups in American society, including the poor, younger people, males, African-Americans, Hispanics, and residents of inner cities, are more likely to be victimized and are more vulnerable to violence than other groups. As discussed in other chapters of this book, African-Americans and Hispanics are more likely to be poor and to be unemployed than are non-Hispanic whites. These factors put minorities at an especially high risk of being victimized.

Violent Crimes

African-Americans are more likely than individuals of other races to be victims of violent crimes. In *Criminal Victimization, 2006* (December 2007, http://www.ojp.usdoj.gov/bjs/pub/pdf/cv06.pdf), Michael Rand and Shannan M. Catalano of the Bureau of Justice Statistics (BJS) report that in 2006, 32.7 per 1,000 African-Americans were victims of a violent crime, compared to 23.2 per 1,000 whites and 18.7 per 1,000 people of other races. (See Table 7.1.) People who reported they were two or more races had nearly twice the rate of violent victimization as did African-Americans, at 64.9 per 1,000 people. Data on the rate of violent victimization in the Hispanic community were not given in the 2006 report. The previous year, however, Catalano indicates in *Criminal Victimization, 2005* (September 2006, http://www.ojp.gov/bjs/pub/pdf/cv05.pdf) that 25 per 1,000 Hispanics were victims of a violent crime in 2005, compared to 20.6 per 1,000 non-Hispanics.

Catalano notes that even though minorities were particularly likely to be victimized, the rate of violent crimes in each racial and ethnic group declined significantly between 1993 and 2005. The rate of violent crimes committed against Hispanics had dropped 54.7%, the rate of violent crimes committed against African-Americans had dropped 59.9%, and the rate of violent crimes committed against people of other minority groups had dropped 65.1%.

The rates of violent crimes by type of crime show that minorities are more likely than non-Hispanic whites to be victims of some types of violent crime and about equally likely to be victims of other types of violent crime. In 2005 African-Americans were twice as likely as whites to be victims of aggravated assault (7.6 per 1,000 and 3.8 per 1,000, respectively) and of robbery (4.6 per 1,000 and 2.2 per 1,000, respectively). (See Table 7.2.) The rate of rape and sexual assault was three times higher among African-Americans than among whites (1.8 per 1,000 and 0.6 per 1,000, respectively), although rape and sexual assault data are unreliable because so many go unreported. The rates of aggravated assault were also higher among Hispanics than among non-Hispanics (5.9 per 1,000 and 4.1 per 1,000, respectively), as were the rates of robbery (4 per 1,000 and 2.4 per 1,000, respectively) and of rape and sexual assault (1.1 per 1,000 and 0.7 per 1,000). People who reported that they were multiracial were much more likely than any other group to be victims of simple assault (61.5 per 1,000), aggravated assault (16.6 per 1,000), or rape and sexual assault (3.8 per 1,000).

HOMICIDE. African-Americans are also more likely than people of other races to be victims of homicides. African-American males between the ages of eighteen and twenty-four had the highest homicide victimization rate in the last half of the twentieth century and into the twenty-first century. This proportion rose from 89.8 homicide victims per 100,000 population in 1976 to 102 homicide victims per 100,000 population in 2005, but the number had actually dropped since peaking at 183.5 in 1993. (See Table 7.3.) The homicide victimization rate among white men between the ages of eighteen and twenty-four had also risen, from 11.3 homicides per 100,000 population in 1976 to 12.2 homicides per 100,000 in 2005. Again, there was a spike in homicides among young white males in the early 1990s, with the victimization rate topping out at 18.2 in 1991. Among African-American and white women,

TABLE 7.1

Violent and property victimizations, by race of victim or race of head of household, 2006

Race of victim	Violent			Property		
	Population	Number	Rate[a]	Households	Number	Rate[a]
White only	201,524,080	4,682,980	23.2	96,382,970	15,016,110	155.8
Black only	29,980,370	980,400	32.7	14,819,970	2,721,330	183.6
Other race[b]	12,849,300	240,740	18.7	5,506,430	759,650	138.0
Two or more races[c]	2,936,460	190,590	64.9	1,243,070	311,720	250.8

[a]Victimization rates are per 1,000 persons age 12 or older or per 1,000 households.
[b]Includes American Indians, Eskimo, Asian Pacific Islander if only one of these races is given.
[c]Includes all persons of any race, indicating two or more races.

SOURCE: Michael Rand and Shannan Catalano, "Table 5. Violent and Property Victimizations, by Race of Victim or Race of Head of Household, 2006," in *Criminal Victimization, 2006*, U.S. Department of Justice, Bureau of Justice Statistics, December 2007, http://www.ojp.usdoj.gov/bjs/pub/pdf/cv06.pdf (accessed January 4, 2008)

TABLE 7.2

Rates of violent crime and personal theft, by gender, race, Hispanic origin, and age, 2005

Demographic characteristic of victim	Population	Victimizations per 1,000 persons age 12 or older						Personal theft
		Violent crimes						
		All	Rape/sexual assault	Robbery	Assault			
					Total	Aggravated	Simple	
Gender								
Male	118,937,730	25.5	0.1*	3.8	21.5	5.6	15.9	0.8
Female	125,555,710	17.1	1.4	1.4	14.3	3.1	11.2	1.0
Race								
White	200,263,410	20.1	0.6	2.2	17.2	3.8	13.4	0.9
Black	29,477,880	27.0	1.8	4.6	20.6	7.6	13.0	1.7
Other race	12,522,090	13.9	0.5*	3.0	10.4	2.5*	7.9	0.2*
Two or more races	2,230,050	83.6	3.8*	1.8*	78.0	16.6	61.5	0.0*
Hispanic origin								
Hispanic	31,812,270	25.0	1.1*	4.0	19.9	5.9	14.0	1.0*
Non-Hispanic	211,629,880	20.6	0.7	2.4	17.5	4.1	13.4	0.9
Age								
12–15	17,061,940	44.0	1.2*	3.5	39.3	8.7	30.6	1.3*
16–19	16,524,940	44.2	3.2	7.0	33.9	9.7	24.2	1.6*
20–24	20,363,570	46.9	1.1*	5.5	40.3	10.0	30.3	1.5*
25–34	39,607,310	23.6	0.7*	3.1	19.9	4.7	15.2	1.0
35–49	65,707,720	17.5	0.6*	1.9	15.0	3.2	11.8	1.0
50–64	50,164,650	11.4	0.6*	1.4	9.3	2.4	7.0	0.6*
65 or older	35,063,310	2.4	0.0*	0.6*	1.9	0.8*	1.1	0.4*

Note: The National Crime Victimization Survey (NCVS) includes as violent crime rape, sexual assault, robbery, and assault. Because the NCVS interviews persons about their victimizations, murder and manslaughter cannot be included. Racial and ethnic categories in 2005 are not comparable to categories used prior to 2003.
*Based on 10 or fewer sample cases.

SOURCE: Shannan M. Catalano, "Table 6. Rates of Violent Crime and Personal Theft, by Gender, Race, Hispanic Origin, and Age, 2005," in *Criminal Victimization, 2005*, U.S. Department of Justice, Bureau of Justice Statistics, September 2006, http://www.ojp.usdoj.gov/bjs/pub/pdf/cv05.pdf (accessed January 4, 2008)

the homicide victimization rate decreased in all age categories between 1976 and 2005.

Circumstances surrounding homicides vary from racial group to racial group. African-Americans are overrepresented as both victims and offenders in all types of homicide compared to their presence in the U.S. population as a whole, but they are also overrepresented compared to their already heightened representation among homicide victims in homicides involving drugs. Even though 46.9% of all homicide victims between 1976 and 2005 were African-American, they represented 61.6% of all victims of drug-related homicides. (See Table 7.4.) Conversely, African-Americans are underrepresented as victims among sex-related homicides (30.5%), workplace killings (12.2%), and gang-related homicides (39%). Approximately 50.9% of all victims killed by guns were African-American, whereas only 16.9% of all victims killed by poison were.

TABLE 7.3

Homicide victimization rates per 100,000 population by age, race, and gender, 1976–2005

	White male			Black male			White female			Black female		
	14–17	18–24	25+	14–17	18–24	25+	14–17	18–24	25+	14–17	18–24	25+
1976	3.7	11.3	9.8	24.2	89.8	97.2	2.1	4.2	3.0	6.3	25.1	19.3
1977	4.1	12.5	9.9	22.4	86.9	94.1	2.4	4.4	3.1	8.7	24.5	17.2
1978	4.7	13.3	10.4	21.9	86.4	90.3	2.5	4.4	3.1	7.6	23.7	16.5
1979	4.9	16.0	11.0	23.2	90.9	95.7	2.3	5.2	3.2	7.8	24.0	18.2
1980	5.1	16.2	11.4	26.3	96.7	94.8	2.6	5.3	3.3	6.8	23.5	17.1
1981	4.3	14.9	11.3	23.0	89.7	93.2	2.4	4.9	3.3	6.0	20.4	16.0
1982	4.0	13.9	10.4	22.3	82.6	79.5	1.9	5.2	3.3	7.5	17.7	14.4
1983	3.8	12.7	9.4	21.4	75.0	70.7	2.0	4.2	3.1	5.2	19.4	13.0
1984	3.5	11.9	9.1	18.4	68.0	64.6	2.1	5.1	3.0	6.4	18.2	12.4
1985	3.9	12.1	8.9	23.7	73.3	62.4	1.9	4.2	3.2	7.3	16.5	13.2
1986	4.1	13.3	9.0	26.8	87.9	70.2	2.3	4.7	3.1	6.5	19.7	14.1
1987	3.7	12.3	8.5	36.2	96.4	64.0	2.2	4.6	3.3	7.1	19.6	14.4
1988	3.9	12.3	8.1	43.3	109.5	69.2	2.2	4.5	3.0	7.2	20.8	14.8
1989	5.3	13.4	8.2	54.3	128.3	70.5	2.1	4.4	2.8	8.6	20.0	14.7
1990	7.5	16.7	8.7	59.0	151.0	74.4	2.5	4.0	2.9	10.3	20.5	14.3
1991	8.5	18.2	8.8	71.9	173.7	72.7	2.5	4.6	2.8	9.4	23.4	15.0
1992	9.0	17.4	8.4	67.3	171.8	67.6	2.4	4.4	2.8	12.8	20.8	14.4
1993	9.1	17.2	8.1	76.4	183.5	68.3	2.7	4.3	3.0	12.7	24.1	14.5
1994	8.7	17.8	7.7	71.6	176.2	64.3	2.0	3.8	2.6	10.0	20.7	13.7
1995	8.6	17.3	6.9	63.2	148.9	56.4	2.7	4.2	2.7	11.9	17.1	12.2
1996	7.9	15.4	6.5	52.2	138.2	50.0	2.0	3.3	2.4	8.9	15.4	11.3
1997	5.7	14.5	5.9	42.0	136.5	45.5	1.7	3.5	2.1	7.2	15.4	9.9
1998	5.7	14.5	5.3	32.8	117.4	40.6	1.9	3.4	2.2	5.9	14.3	9.3
1999	5.1	12.5	5.0	31.0	102.4	36.5	1.7	3.4	2.0	5.9	12.9	7.9
2000	4.1	12.1	4.7	25.8	100.6	38.1	1.4	2.9	2.0	4.5	13.5	7.6
2001	3.8	12.9	4.8	26.3	104.0	37.5	1.4	3.2	2.0	3.9	10.1	7.6
2002	3.6	12.7	4.8	22.6	102.5	39.0	1.5	2.9	1.9	6.1	11.8	7.4
2003	3.5	13.0	4.8	24.7	104.8	39.8	1.1	3.2	1.9	3.8	11.9	6.9
2004	4.0	12.0	4.9	25.8	95.6	38.3	1.1	2.9	1.9	3.7	9.7	6.6
2005	4.4	12.2	4.9	26.4	102.0	39.9	1.1	2.5	1.9	4.0	11.3	6.2

SOURCE: James Alan Fox and Marianne W. Zawitz, "Homicide Victimization Rates per 100,000 Population by Age, Race, and Gender," in *Homicide Trends in the United States*, U.S. Department of Justice, Bureau of Justice Statistics, July 2007, http://www.ojp.usdoj.gov/bjs/homicide/tables/varstab.htm (accessed January 4, 2008)

TABLE 7.4

Homicide type by race, 1976–2005

	Victims			Offenders		
	White	Black	Other	White	Black	Other
All homicides	50.9%	46.9%	2.1%	45.8%	52.2%	2.0%
Victim/offender relationship						
Intimate	56.6%	41.2%	2.2%	54.4%	43.4%	2.2%
Family	60.7%	36.9%	2.4%	59.2%	38.5%	2.3%
Infanticide	55.9%	41.6%	2.5%	55.4%	42.1%	2.5%
Eldercide	69.2%	29.1%	1.6%	54.5%	43.8%	1.6%
Circumstances						
Felony murder	54.7%	42.7%	2.6%	39.1%	59.3%	1.6%
Sex related	66.9%	30.5%	2.5%	54.7%	43.4%	1.9%
Drug related	37.4%	61.6%	.9%	33.9%	65.0%	1.1%
Gang related	57.5%	39.0%	3.5%	54.3%	41.2%	4.4%
Argument	48.6%	49.3%	2.1%	46.8%	51.1%	2.2%
Workplace	84.6%	12.2%	3.2%	70.5%	26.7%	2.8%
Weapon						
Gun homicide	47.2%	50.9%	1.9%	41.9%	56.4%	1.7%
Arson	58.9%	38.1%	2.9%	55.7%	42.0%	2.3%
Poison	80.6%	16.9%	2.5%	79.8%	18.4%	1.8%
Multiple victims or offenders						
Multiple victims	63.4%	33.2%	3.3%	55.7%	40.8%	3.5%
Multiple offenders	54.8%	42.5%	2.7%	44.6%	53.0%	2.4%

SOURCE: James Alan Fox and Marianne W. Zawitz, "Homicide Type by Race, 1976–2005," in *Homicide Trends in the United States*, U.S. Department of Justice, Bureau of Justice Statistics, July 2007, http://www.ojp.usdoj.gov/bjs/pub/pdf/htius.pdf (accessed January 4, 2008)

Most murders are intraracial. James Alan Fox and Marianne W. Zawitz report in *Homicide Trends in the United States* (July 11, 2007, http://www.ojp.usdoj.gov/bjs/pub/pdf/htius.pdf) that between 1976 and 2005 most murders of whites were perpetrated by whites (86%), whereas most murders of African-Americans were perpetrated by African-Americans (94%). A low proportion of African-American perpetrators kill white victims, whereas an even smaller percentage of white perpetrators kill African-Americans.

Property Crimes

In 2006 African-Americans were more likely than whites to be victims of property crime, whereas those who reported they were two or more races were the most likely to be victims of property crime. That year, 183.6 per 1,000 African-Americans were victims of property crime, compared to 155.8 per 1,000 whites and 138 per 1,000 people of another race, including Native Americans and Asians and Pacific Islanders. (See Table 7.1.) However, 250.8 per 1,000 people who reported they were multiracial were victims of property crime in 2006.

According to Catalano, the poorest members of society are paradoxically the most likely to be victimized by property crimes. In 2005, 200.6 per 1,000 households with annual incomes of less than $7,500 were victims of property crime. The rate of property crime declined as income rose; only 155.9 per 1,000 households with annual incomes between $50,000 and $74,999 were victims of property crime. Even though property crime rates rose to 171 per 1,000 households in the highest income bracket (over $75,000 per year), this rate was still substantially lower than among the lowest-income households. Those with the lowest incomes are often forced to live in the least safe areas and have the fewest resources with which to protect themselves from crime. Members of minority groups are disproportionately poor, and thus often vulnerable to these types of crimes.

Hate Crimes

The Hate Crime Statistics Act of 1990 required the U.S. attorney general to provide the "acquisition and publication of data about crimes that manifest prejudice based on race, religion, homosexuality or heterosexuality, or ethnicity." The Violent Crime and Law Enforcement Act of 1994 amended the Hate Crime Statistics Act to include crimes motivated by discrimination against people with physical and/or mental disabilities. For an offense to be considered a hate crime, law enforcement investigation must reveal sufficient evidence to lead to the conclusion that the offender's actions were motivated by his or her bias against a certain group. Therefore, data on hate crimes must be considered underreported, as many incidents and offenses motivated by bias go uncounted without sufficient

evidence concerning this motivation. Even though hate crimes can be perpetrated against members of majority groups, most hate crimes are directed at minorities: racial minorities, religious minorities, ethnic minorities, gay and lesbian people, or people with disabilities.

The hate crime data collection program counts one offense for each victim of crimes against people, but only one offense for each distinct crime against property, regardless of the number of victims—therefore, the number of victims is higher than the number of offenses. Of the 9,080 hate-bias offenses reported in 2006, 4,737 were racially motivated and 1,233 were motivated by ethnicity or national origin. (See Table 7.5.) Of the racially motivated incidents, 3,136 were committed against African-Americans and 1,008 were committed against whites. Another 230 were committed against Asians and Pacific Islanders, and 72 were committed against Native Americans. Of the offenses motivated by ethnicity or national origin, 770 were anti-Hispanic and 463 were directed against people of another ethnic minority.

The Intelligence Project (2007, http://www.splcenter.org/intel/intelreport/intrep.jsp) of the Southern Poverty Law Center in Montgomery, Alabama, a private organization that monitors hate groups and paramilitary organizations nationwide, reports that there were 888 active hate group chapters in 2007, up from 844 in 2006. These groups included racist groups such as chapters of the Ku Klux Klan, racist skinhead groups (a particularly violent element of the white supremacist movement), neo-Confederate groups (an alliance of southern heritage organizations that claims allegiance to the antebellum South), and others. The project also tracks black separatist groups that typically oppose integration and want separate institutions for African-Americans. Even though the project recognizes that this black racism is in part a response to centuries of white racism, it believes that a criterion for considering a group racist should be applied to all groups regardless of color. The Intelligence Project states that there were 207 neo-Nazi groups, 155 Ku Klux Klan chapters, 104 neo-Confederate groups, 90 racist skinhead groups, 81 black separatist groups, 36 Christian identity groups, and 69 other types of hate groups operating nationwide in 2007.

Crime at School

Even though students are less likely to be victimized at school than they are away from school, any crime at school, especially violent crimes, justifiably horrifies students and the community at large. In *Indicators of School Crime and Safety: 2007* (December 2007, http://nces.ed.gov/pubs2008/2008021.pdf), Rachel Dinkes, Emily Forrest Cataldi, and Wendy Lin-Kelly state that "any instance of crime or violence at school not only affects the individuals involved but also may disrupt the educational process and affect bystanders, the school itself, and the surrounding community."

TABLE 7.5

Hate-bias incidents, 2006

Bias motivation	Incidents	Offenses	Victims[a]	Known offenders[b]
Total	**7,722**	**9,080**	**9,652**	**7,330**
Single-bias incidents	7,720	9,076	9,642	7,324
Race:	4,000	4,737	5,020	3,957
Anti-white	890	1,008	1,054	1,074
Anti-black	2,640	3,136	3,332	2,437
Anti-American Indian/Alaskan Native	60	72	75	72
Anti-Asian/Pacific Islander	181	230	239	181
Anti-multiple races, group	229	291	320	193
Religion:	1,462	1,597	1,750	705
Anti-Jewish	967	1,027	1,144	362
Anti-Catholic	76	81	86	44
Anti-Protestant	59	62	65	35
Anti-Islamic	156	191	208	147
Anti-other religion	124	140	147	63
Anti-multiple religions, group	73	88	92	49
Anti-Atheism/Agnosticism/etc.	7	8	8	5
Sexual orientation:	1,195	1,415	1,472	1,380
Anti-male homosexual	747	881	913	914
Anti-female homosexual	163	192	202	154
Anti-homosexual	238	293	307	268
Anti-heterosexual	26	28	29	26
Anti-bisexual	21	21	21	18
Ethnicity/national origin:	984	1,233	1,305	1,209
Anti-Hispanic	576	770	819	802
Anti-other ethnicity/national origin	408	463	486	407
Disability:	79	94	95	73
Anti-physical	17	20	21	17
Anti-mental	62	74	74	56
Multiple-bias incidents[c]	2	4	10	6

[a]The term *victim* may refer to a person, business, institution, or society as a whole.
[b]The term *known offender* does not imply that the identity of the suspect is known, but only that an attribute of the suspect has been identified, which distinguishes him/her from an unknown offender.
[c]In a *multiple-bias incident*, two conditions must be met: (a) more than one offense type must occur in the incident and (b) at least two offense types must be motivated by different biases.

SOURCE: "Table 1. Incidents, Offenses, Victims, and Known Offenders by Bias Motivation, 2006," in *Hate Crime Statistics, 2006*, U.S. Department of Justice, Federal Bureau of Investigation, November 2007, http://www.fbi.gov/ucr/hc2006/table1.html (accessed January 4, 2008)

Racial and ethnic minorities are disproportionately affected by crimes at school. Dinkes, Cataldi, and Lin-Kelly indicate that all types of crimes (theft, violent, and serious violent) are the most likely to occur in urban, rather than in suburban or rural, schools. In 2005 the rate of school crime in urban schools was sixty-four per one thousand students, whereas the rate in suburban schools was fifty-five per one thousand students and the rate in rural schools was fifty per one thousand students. (See Figure 7.1.) The rate of violent crime was particularly high in urban schools, at thirty-four per one thousand students, compared to nineteen and twenty-one per one thousand students in suburban and rural schools, respectively.

According to Dinkes, Cataldi, and Lin-Kelly, urban students were also the most likely to report in 2005 that street gangs were present at school during the previous six months, and this proportion had risen since 2001. In 2005, 36% of urban students reported gangs were present at school, compared to 21% of suburban students and 16% of rural students. In 2001, 29% of urban students, 18% of suburban students, and 13% of rural students had reported that gangs were present at school. Gangs were particularly a problem for Hispanic students. Of urban students, 48% of Hispanic students reported street gangs were present at school, compared to 41% of African-American students and 23% of white students. (See Figure 7.2.)

Drugs were another serious problem at school. Dinkes, Cataldi, and Lin-Kelly note that "the availability of drugs on school property has a disruptive and corrupting influence on the school environment." In 2005, 25% of students reported that drugs had been made available to them on school property during the previous twelve months. (See Figure 7.3.) However, this percentage varied by race and ethnicity. Pacific Islanders (41%) were the most likely to have had drugs made available to them on school property during the previous twelve months, followed by Hispanics (34%), Native Americans, African-Americans, and whites (all at 24%). Asian-Americans (16%) were the least likely to have had drugs made available to them on school property during the past year.

Students were also made the target of hate-related words and saw hate-related graffiti at school all too often in 2005. Students were asked whether someone at school

FIGURE 7.1

Rate of student-reported nonfatal crimes against students ages 12–18 at school per 1,000 students, by type of crime and selected student characteristics, 2005

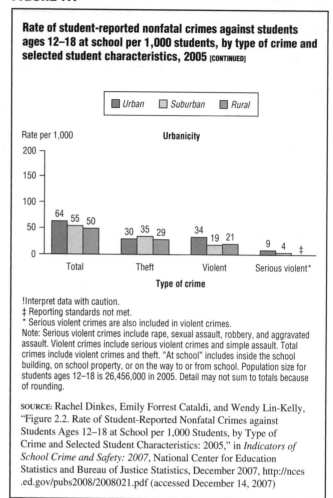

FIGURE 7.1

Rate of student-reported nonfatal crimes against students ages 12–18 at school per 1,000 students, by type of crime and selected student characteristics, 2005 [CONTINUED]

!Interpret data with caution.
‡ Reporting standards not met.
* Serious violent crimes are also included in violent crimes.
Note: Serious violent crimes include rape, sexual assault, robbery, and aggravated assault. Violent crimes include serious violent crimes and simple assault. Total crimes include violent crimes and theft. "At school" includes inside the school building, on school property, or on the way to or from school. Population size for students ages 12–18 is 26,456,000 in 2005. Detail may not sum to totals because of rounding.

SOURCE: Rachel Dinkes, Emily Forrest Cataldi, and Wendy Lin-Kelly, "Figure 2.2. Rate of Student-Reported Nonfatal Crimes against Students Ages 12–18 at School per 1,000 Students, by Type of Crime and Selected Student Characteristics: 2005," in *Indicators of School Crime and Safety: 2007*, National Center for Education Statistics and Bureau of Justice Statistics, December 2007, http://nces .ed.gov/pubs2008/2008021.pdf (accessed December 14, 2007)

had called them a derogatory word having to do with their race, ethnicity, religion, gender, sexual orientation, or disability and if they had seen any hate-inspired graffiti in the past six months at school. Eleven percent of all students had been the target of hate-related words in the past six months—particularly African-American students (15%). (See Figure 7.4.) More than a third (38%) of all students had seen hate-related graffiti at school; this varied little by race or ethnic group. Dinkes, Cataldi, and Lin-Kelly indicate that of all African-American students surveyed, 7% reported having been the target of hate-related words related to their race; among Hispanic students, 5.7% reported being targets of hate-related words related to their race and ethnicity. Students were more likely to report being targeted for their race (4.5%) and ethnicity (2.6%) than for any other reason, including religion, disability, gender, or sexual orientation.

MINORITIES AS OFFENDERS

African-Americans—particularly males—commit a higher number of offenses as a proportion of the population than do other groups. Between 1976 and 2005, 52.2% of murders were perpetrated by African-Americans. (See Table 7.4.) African-American males between the ages of fourteen and twenty-four made up a growing proportion of homicide offenders between 1976 and 2005. In 1994 African-American males between the ages of fourteen and twenty-four made up more than 30% of homicide offenders, but that number dropped somewhat by 2002 before rising again in 2005. (See Figure 7.5.)

The circumstances under which African-American and white homicide offenders committed their crimes vary by race. African-American offenders were the most likely to commit homicides related to illegal drug activity. Between 1976 and 2005, 65% of homicide offenders who had committed their crimes under drug-related circumstances were African-American. A high proportion of felony murders (deaths that occur during violent crimes such as burglary, sexual assault, or robbery) between these years were committed by African-Americans (59.3%) as well. (See Table 7.4.) By contrast, whites committed a disproportionate number of workplace murders (70.5%), sex-related murders (54.7%), and gang-related murders (54.3%). African-American offenders committed the majority of homicides

FIGURE 7.2

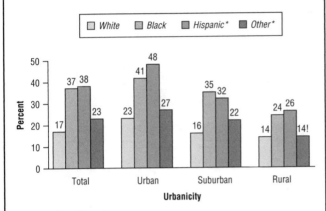

Percentage of students ages 12–18 who reported that gangs were present at school during the previous 6 months, by urbanicity and race/ethnicity, 2005

☐ White ☐ Black ■ Hispanic* ■ Other*

! Interpret data with caution.
*Other includes American Indian, Alaska Native, Asian or Pacific Islander, and more than one race. For this report, non-Hispanic students who identified themselves as more than one race were included in the other category. Respondents who identified themselves as being of Hispanic origin are classified as Hispanic, regardless of their race.
Note: All gangs, whether or not they are involved in violent or illegal activity, are included. "At school" includes the school building, on school property, on a school bus, or going to and from school. In 2005, the unit response rate for this survey did not meet National Center for Education Statistics' (NCES) statistical standards; therefore, interpret the data with caution. Population size for students ages 12–18 is 25,811,000 in 2005.

SOURCE: Rachel Dinkes, Emily Forrest Cataldi, and Wendy Lin-Kelly, "Figure 8.2. Percentage of Students Ages 12–18 Who Reported That Gangs Were Present at School during the Previous 6 Months, by Urbanicity and Race/Ethnicity: 2005," in *Indicators of School Crime and Safety: 2007*, National Center for Education Statistics and Bureau of Justice Statistics, December 2007, http://nces.ed.gov/pubs2008/2008021.pdf (accessed December 14, 2007).

FIGURE 7.3

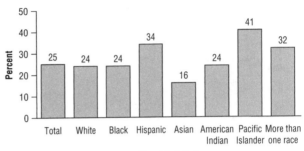

Percentage of students in grades 9–12 who reported that drugs were made available to them on school property during the previous 12 months, by race/ethnicity, 2005

*American Indian includes Alaska Native, black includes African American, Pacific Islander includes Native Hawaiian, and Hispanic includes Latino. Respondents who identified themselves as being of Hispanic origin are classified as Hispanic, regardless of their race.
Note: "On school property" was not defined for survey respondents. Population size from the Digest of Education Statistics, 2005 (NCES 2006-030) for students in grades 9–12 is 16,286,000 (projected) in 2005.

SOURCE: Rachel Dinkes, Emily Forrest Cataldi, and Wendy Lin-Kelly, "Figure 9.2. Percentage of Students in Grades 9–12 Who Reported That Drugs Were Made Available to Them on School Property during the Previous 12 Months, by Race/Ethnicity: 2005," in *Indicators of School Crime and Safety: 2007*, National Center for Education Statistics and Bureau of Justice Statistics, December 2007, http://nces.ed.gov/pubs2008/2008021.pdf (accessed December 14, 2007).

using guns (56.4%), and whites committed the majority of murders using arson (55.7%) and poison (79.8%).

Whites were more likely than African-Americans to commit homicide in the context of an intimate victim-offender relationship or family relationship. Between 1976 and 2005 whites committed 54.4% of homicides of intimate partners, whereas African-Americans committed 43.4%. (See Table 7.4.) During this same period, whites committed 59.2% of homicides of family members, whereas African-Americans committed 38.5% of these murders. Most of the perpetrators who killed elder family members (54.5%) or infants (55.4%) were white.

MINORITIES IN PRISONS AND JAILS

In June 2006 there were more African-American males in state and federal prisons and local jails than there were non-Hispanic white or Hispanic males. Of a total of 2 million incarcerated males, 836,800 were African-American, 718,100 were non-Hispanic white, and 426,900 were Hispanic. (See Table 7.6.) Young men between the ages of twenty and twenty-four made up the largest proportion of African-American males in the prison population.

The rate of incarceration for African-American males greatly exceeds the rates for non-Hispanic white and Hispanic males. In June 2006 the rate for African-Americans was 4,789 inmates for every 100,000 residents. (See Table 7.7.) This proportion was much higher than that among non-Hispanic whites, with 736 inmates for every 100,000 residents imprisoned in the same period. Among Hispanic men there were 1,862 inmates for every 100,000 residents, more than double the rate for non-Hispanic whites but much lower than the rate of imprisonment of African-Americans.

Even though non-Hispanic white women (95,300) outnumbered African-American women (68,800) in federal and state prisons and local jails in June 2006, African-American women were incarcerated at nearly four times the rate of non-Hispanic white women (358 per 100,000 residents and 94 per 100,000 residents, respectively). (See Table 7.6 and Table 7.7.) Hispanic women were incarcerated at a rate of 152 per 100,000 residents.

In "Minorities in the Criminal Justice System" (July 22, 2003, http://www.ncja.org/Content/NavigationMenu/PoliciesPractices/PolicyStatements/ArchivedPolicyStatements/default.htm), the National Criminal Justice Association (NCJA) discusses the overrepresentation of minorities among the ranks of offenders in the criminal justice system, noting that social factors play a role in this

FIGURE 7.4

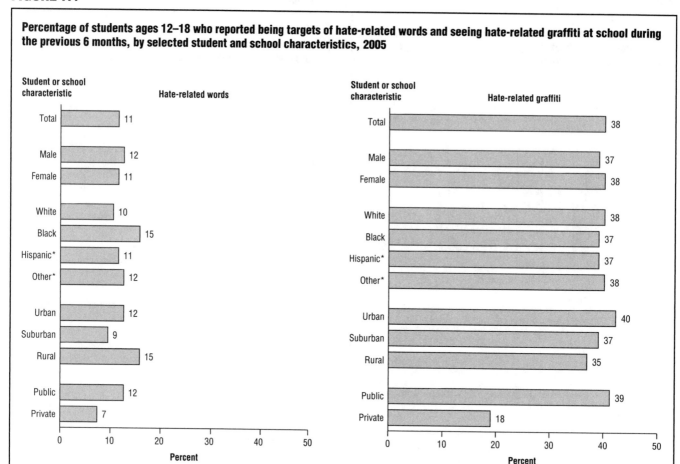

Percentage of students ages 12–18 who reported being targets of hate-related words and seeing hate-related graffiti at school during the previous 6 months, by selected student and school characteristics, 2005

*Other includes American Indian, Alaska Native, Asian or Pacific Islander, and more than one race. For this report, non-Hispanic students who identified themselves as more than one race were included in the other category. Respondents who identified themselves as being of Hispanic origin are classified as Hispanic, regardless of their race.

Note: "At school" includes the school building, on school property, on a school bus, or going to and from school. Hate-related refers to derogatory terms used by others in reference to students' personal characteristics. In 2005, the unit response rate for this survey did not meet National Center for Education Statistics' (NCES) statistical standards; therefore, interpret the data with caution. Population size for students ages 12–18 is 25,811,000 in 2005.

SOURCE: Rachel Dinkes, Emily Forrest Cataldi, and Wendy Lin-Kelly, "Figure 10.1. Percentage of Students Ages 12–18 Who Reported Being Targets of Hate-Related Words and Seeing Hate-Related Graffiti at School during the Previous 6 Months, by Selected Student and School Characteristics: 2005," in *Indicators of School Crime and Safety: 2007*, National Center for Education Statistics and Bureau of Justice Statistics, December 2007, http://nces.ed.gov/pubs2008/2008021.pdf (accessed December 14, 2007).

overrepresentation, including the lack of employment and educational opportunities, poor economic conditions, the lack of minority role models, and the negative portrayal of minorities in the media. Observing that an estimated 4.4% of white males will enter prison during their lifetime, compared to 16% of Hispanic males and 28% of African-American males, the NCJA resolves that state and local criminal justice policymakers must continually address minority-related criminal justice issues. Among these issues are the overrepresentation of minorities in both the juvenile and adult criminal justice populations and the underrepresentation of minorities in law enforcement, corrections, and legal professions; conscious and unconscious tensions between members of minority groups and law enforcement personnel; accurate reporting of hate crimes; racial profiling by law enforcement and its effects on community relations and prison crowding; racially biased effects of drug laws and enforcement

strategies; minorities' equal access to the court system; racially biased sentencing patterns; and unequal socioeconomic conditions.

In "Schools and Prisons: Fifty Years after *Brown v. Board of Education*" (2004, http://www.sentencingproject.org/Admin/Documents/publications/rd_brownvboard.pdf), Marc Mauer and Ryan Scott King of the Sentencing Project call attention to the dramatic rise in imprisonment in the African-American community after 1954. According to Mauer and King, this rise resulted from a punitive crime policy that disproportionately affects African-Americans. They note that the causes for the rising imprisonment rate of African-Americans include higher crime and imprisonment rates, the war on drugs, disparities in crack-cocaine and powder-cocaine sentencing policies, school-zone drug laws, three-strikes policies, inadequate defense resources for poor people, and zero-tolerance policies in schools.

FIGURE 7.5

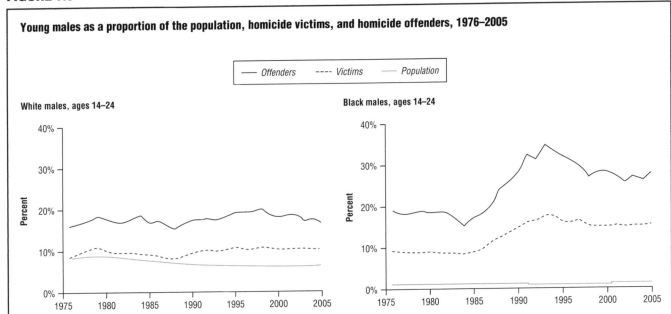

Young males as a proportion of the population, homicide victims, and homicide offenders, 1976–2005

SOURCE: James Alan Fox and Marianne W. Zawitz, "Young Males As a Proportion of the Population, Homicide Victims, and Homicide Offenders, 1976–2005," in *Homicide Trends in the United States*, U.S. Department of Justice, Bureau of Justice Statistics, July 2007, http://www.ojp.usdoj.gov/bjs/pub/pdf/htius.pdf (accessed January 4, 2008)

TABLE 7.6

Number of inmates in state or federal prisons and local jails, by gender, race, Hispanic origin, and age, June 30, 2006

	Males				Females			
	Total[a]	White[b]	Black/African American[b]	Hispanic/ Latino	Total[a]	White[b]	Black/African American[b]	Hispanic/ Latino
Total	2,042,100	718,100	836,800	426,900	203,100	95,300	68,800	32,400
18–19	75,600	24,800	33,000	15,300	4,900	2,000	1,600	1,200
20–24	365,700	111,100	160,000	84,900	29,600	13,900	9,300	5,900
25–29	359,300	103,700	156,200	90,800	30,300	13,700	10,100	5,600
30–34	328,300	109,600	132,400	78,000	36,000	16,800	12,100	6,000
35–39	298,700	110,900	120,500	58,300	39,800	18,900	13,800	5,600
40–44	262,600	107,200	103,000	43,200	32,000	15,100	11,700	4,200
45–54	257,400	105,100	101,000	41,500	24,600	11,700	8,700	3,100
55 or older	79,000	41,800	22,200	12,200	4,700	2,800	1,000	700

Note: Based on custody counts from the National Prisoner Statistics (NPS-1A) 2006 and the Annual Survey of Jails, 2006. Estimates by age were obtained from the Survey of Inmates in Local Jails, 2002, the National Corrections Reporting Program, 2003, and the Federal Justice Statistics Program (FJSP) for inmates on September, 30, 2003. Estimates were rounded to the nearest 100. Detailed categories exclude persons identifying with two or more races.
[a]Includes American Indians, Alaska Natives, Asians, Native Hawaiians, and other Pacific Islanders.
[b]Not Hispanic or Latino.

SOURCE: William J. Sabol, Todd D. Minton, and Paige M. Harrison, "Table 13. Number of Inmates in State or Federal Prisons and Local Jails, by Gender, Race, Hispanic Origin, and Age, June 30, 2006," in *Prison and Jail Inmates at Midyear 2006*, U.S. Department of Justice, Bureau of Justice Statistics, June 2007, http://www.ojp.usdoj.gov/bjs/pub/pdf/pjim06.pdf (accessed January 4, 2008)

Mauer and King state that "at current rates of incarceration, one of every three black males born today can expect to be imprisoned at some point in his lifetime. Whether or not one believes that current crime control policies are 'working' to reduce crime, such an outcome should be shocking to all Americans. Imposing a crime policy with such profound racial dynamics calls into question the nation's commitment to a free and democratic society."

In the policy statement "Racial Disparity in the Criminal Justice System" (July 29, 2007, http://www.ncja.org/Content/NavigationMenu/PoliciesPractices/PolicyStatements/Minorities.htm), the NCJA calls on all criminal justice professionals to seek out effective ways to reduce the over-representation of minorities in the criminal justice system. The policy also notes that minority professionals are underrepresented in the criminal justice system, contributing further to racial disparities.

TABLE 7.7

Number of inmates in state or federal prisons and local jails per 100,000 residents, by gender, race, Hispanic origin, and age, June 30, 2006

Number of inmates per 100,000 residents

	Males				Females			
	Total[a]	White[b]	Black/African American[b]	Hispanic/ Latino	Total[a]	White[b]	Black/African American[b]	Hispanic/ Latino
U.S. total	**1,384**	**736**	**4,789**	**1,862**	**134**	**94**	**358**	**152**
18–19	1,766	935	5,336	2,112	120	81	262	175
20–24	3,352	1,675	10,698	4,168	290	221	637	346
25–29	3,395	1,685	11,695	3,912	300	226	716	346
30–34	3,289	1,874	11,211	3,652	370	292	924	305
35–39	2,805	1,641	9,804	3,094	378	282	999	333
40–44	2,344	1,419	7,976	2,630	284	200	798	337
45–54	1,209	677	4,421	1,813	112	75	326	279
55 or older	256	170	869	543	12	9	28	141
								26

Note: Based on the U.S. resident population for July 1, 2006, by gender, race, Hispanic origin, and age. Detailed categories exclude persons identifying with two or more races.
[a]Includes American Indians, Alaska Natives, Asians, Native Hawaiians, and other Pacific Islanders.
[b]Not Hispanic or Latino.

SOURCE: William J. Sabol, Todd D. Minton, and Paige M. Harrison, "Table 14. Number of Inmates in State or Federal Prisons and Local Jails, per 100,000 Residents, by Gender, Race, Hispanic Origin, and Age, June 30, 2006," in *Prison and Jail Inmates at Midyear 2006*, U.S. Department of Justice, Bureau of Justice Statistics, June 2007, http://www.ojp.usdoj.gov/bjs/pub/pdf/pjim06.pdf (accessed January 4, 2008)

Parole and Probation

Because African-Americans account for the largest proportion of prison and jail inmates, it is no surprise that African-Americans also outnumber other racial and ethnic groups in the nation's parole system. The parole system grants inmates early release from prison with fewer rights than the general population and under monitored conditions.

Minorities are slightly underrepresented in the parole population compared to their presence in the prisons and jails as a whole. Of the 2 million prison and jail inmates in 2006, 836,800, or 40.9%, were African-American. (See Table 7.6.) However, only 39% of inmates paroled from state prisons were African-American. (See Table 7.8.) In the same year, 426,900 of the 2 million prisoners, or 20.9%, were Hispanic; only 18% of those on parole were Hispanic. By contrast, 718,100 of the 2 million prisoners, or 35.2%, were non-Hispanic whites, and 41% of those on parole were non-Hispanic white.

The proportion of non-Hispanic whites on probation, a system where people convicted of a crime are under supervision by a probation officer rather than incarcerated, is even more disproportionate to their representation in the criminal justice system. In 2006, 55% of probationers were non-Hispanic white, compared to the 35.2% of non-Hispanic whites who were in prisons and jails. (See Table 7.9.) Conversely, only 29% of probationers were African-American, whereas 40.9% of inmates were African-American; and 13% of probationers were Hispanic, whereas 20.9% of inmates were Hispanic. These numbers show that non-Hispanic white offenders are more likely than minority offenders to receive the more lenient sentence of probation.

TABLE 7.8

Characteristics of adults on parole, 1995, 2000, and 2006

Characteristic	1995	2000	2006
Total	**100%**	**100%**	**100%**
Gender			
Male	90%	88%	88%
Female	10	12	12
Race			
White*	34%	38%	41%
Black*	45	40	39
Hispanic or Latino	21	21	18
American Indian/Alaska Native*	1	1	1
Asian/Native Hawaiian/other Pacific Islander	--	--	1
Two or more races*	—	—	--
Status of supervision			
Active	78%	83%	84%
Inactive	11	4	4
Absconder	6	7	7
Supervised out of state	4	5	4
Financial conditions remaining	—	—	--
Other	--	1	2
Sentence length			
Less than 1 year	6%	3%	6%
1 year or more	94	97	94
Type of offense			
Violent	—	—	26%
Property	—	—	24
Drug	—	—	37
Public order	—	—	6
Other	—	—	6

Note: Each characteristic included persons of unknown type. Detail may not sum to total because of rounding.
--Less than 0.5%.
—Not available.
*Excludes persons of Hispanic origin.

SOURCE: Lauren E. Glaze and Thomas P. Bonczar, "Table 4. Characteristics of Adults on Parole, 1995, 2000, and 2006," in *Probation and Parole in the United States, 2006*, U.S. Department of Justice, Bureau of Justice Statistics, December 2007, http://www.ojp.usdoj.gov/bjs/pub/pdf/ppus06.pdf (accessed January 4, 2008)

TABLE 7.9

Characteristics of adults on probation, 1995, 2000, and 2006

Characteristic	1995	2000	2006
Total	100%	100%	100%
Gender			
Male	79%	78%	76%
Female	21	22	24
Race/Hispanic origin			
White*	53%	54%	55%
Black*	31	31	29
Hispanic or Latino	14	13	13
American Indian/Alaska Native*	1	1	1
Asian/Native Hawaiian/other Pacific Islander	--	1	1
Two or more races*	—	.—	--
Status of probation			
Direct imposition	48%	56%	58%
Split sentence	15	11	10
Sentence suspended	26	25	23
Imposition suspended	6	7	9
Other	4	1	1
Status of supervision			
Active	79%	76%	71%
Residential/other treatment program	—	—	1
Financial conditions remaining	—	—	2
Inactive	8	9	7
Absconder	9	9	9
Supervised out of state	2	3	3
Warrant status	—	—	6
Other	2	3	2
Type of offense			
Felony	54%	52%	49%
Misdemeanor	44	46	49
Other infractions	2	2	2
Most serious offense			
Sexual assault	—	—	3%
Domestic violence	—	—	4
Other assault	—	—	9
Burglary	—	—	5
Larceny/theft	—	—	13
Motor vehicle theft	—	—	1
Fraud	—	—	5
Drug law violations	—	24	27
Driving while intoxicated	16	18	16
Minor traffic offenses	—	6	6
Other	84	52	11

Note: Each characteristic includes persons of unknown type. Detail may not sum to total because of rounding.
--Less than 0.5%.
—Not available.
*Excludes persons of Hispanic origin.

SOURCE: Lauren E. Glaze and Thomas P. Bonczar, "Table 2. Characteristics of Adults on Probation, 1995, 2000, and 2006," in *Probation and Parole in the United States, 2006*, U.S. Department of Justice, Bureau of Justice Statistics, December 2007, http://www.ojp.usdoj.gov/bjs/pub/pdf/ppus06.pdf (accessed January 4, 2008)

Hispanics in the Criminal Justice System

Even though much attention has been given to the fact that African-Americans are disproportionately represented in the criminal justice system, a report released in 2002 by Michigan State University's Institute for Children, Youth, and Families points to a growing number of Hispanic youths being targeted by law enforcement. The report,

¿Dónde Está la Justicia? A Call to Action on Behalf of the Latino and Latina Youth in the U.S. Justice System (July 2002, http://www.buildingblocksforyouth.org/Full%20Report%20English.pdf) by Francisco A. Villarruel et al., finds that Hispanic youths are often treated more harshly than their white counterparts and suggests that the problem will only intensify because Hispanics are the fastest-growing minority group in the country.

In addition, Hispanics face harsher treatment in the federal court system. The Sentencing Project points out in "Hispanic Prisoners in the United States" (August 2003, http://www.sentencingproject.org/pdfs/1051.pdf) that Hispanic defendants are about one-third as likely as non-Hispanic defendants (22.7% versus 63.1%) to be released before their cases come to trial.

Minorities on Death Row

Tracy L. Snell of the BJS reports in *Capital Punishment, 2006* (December 2007, http://www.ojp.usdoj.gov/bjs/pub/html/cp/2006/cp06st.pdf) that in December 2006, 3,228 state and federal prisoners were incarcerated under the sentence of death. Whites made up 55.8% and African-Americans made up 41.9% of all death-row prisoners. (See Table 7.10.) Only 2.3% were of other races. Of those whose ethnicity was known, 11.1% were Hispanic.

Of those sentenced to death row in 2006, 62.6% were white and 36.5% were African-American. (See Table 7.10.) Hispanics made up 11.5% of those sentenced to death row in that year.

Racial Disparities in Sentencing

In 1984 the U.S. Sentencing Commission (USSC) set forth sentencing guidelines in the Sentencing Reform Act of 1984, which was designed to implement uniform sentencing practices that would eliminate disparities based on race. In November 2004 the USSC released *Fifteen Years of Guidelines Sentencing: An Assessment of How Well the Federal Criminal Justice System Is Achieving the Goals of Sentencing Reform* (http://www.ussc.gov/15_year/15_year_study_full.pdf), which evaluated the effectiveness of these practices. The USSC concludes that remaining disparity in sentencing is the result of sentencing rules and charging practices that have "institutionalized" disparity. In fact, variables such as mandatory minimums and plea bargaining have had "a greater adverse impact on Black offenders than did the factors taken into account by judges in the discretionary system . . . prior to guidelines implementation."

In *Racial Disparity in Sentencing: A Review of the Literature* (January 2005, http://www.sentencingproject.org/pdfs/disparity.pdf), Tushar Kansal of the Sentencing Project reviews the literature about the nature of this ongoing racial disparity. Kansal finds that in noncapital cases racially

TABLE 7.10

Demographic characteristics of prisoners under sentence of death, 2006

Characteristic	Percent of prisoners under sentence of death, 2006		
	Yearend	Admissions	Removals
Total	3,228	115	132
Gender			
Male	98.3%	95.7%	98.5%
Female	1.7	4.3	1.5
Race			
White	55.8%	62.6%	54.5%
Black	41.9	36.5	42.4
All other races*	2.3	0.9	3.0
Hispanic origin			
Hispanic	11.1%	11.5%	12.0%
Non-Hispanic	76.1	88.5	88.0
Number unknown	414	19	15
Education			
8th grade or less	13.9%	11.7%	20.5%
9th–11th grade	37.0	40.3	33.3
High school graduate/GED	40.0	40.3	35.9
Any college	9.0	7.8	10.3
Median	11th	11th	11th
Number unknown	486	38	15
Marital status			
Married	21.7%	17.7%	32.8%
Divorced/separated	20.6	22.9	17.6
Widowed	3.0	3.1	1.6
Never married	54.8	56.3	48.0
Number unknown	348	19	7

Note: Calculations are based on those cases for which data were reported. Detail may not add to total due to rounding.

*At yearend 2005, inmates of "other" races consisted of 31 American Indians, 34 Asians, and 12 self-identified Hispanics. During 2006, one Asian was admitted, and three American Indians and one self-identified Hispanic were removed.

SOURCE: Tracy L. Snell, "Table 5. Demographic Characteristics of Prisoners under Sentence of Death, 2006," in *Capital Punishment, 2006—Statistical Tables*, U.S. Department of Justice, Bureau of Justice Statistics, December 2007, http://www.ojp.usdoj.gov/bjs/pub/html/cp/2006/cp06st.pdf (accessed January 4, 2008)

discriminatory sentencing outcomes do exist, but that they are not uniform or extensive. Kansal notes that the following groups suffer harsher sentencing: young, African-American and Hispanic males, especially if unemployed; African-Americans convicted of harming white victims; and African-American and Hispanic defendants convicted of less serious (nonviolent) crimes. An examination of death-penalty cases finds that in most cases, if the murder victim was white, the defendant was more likely to receive the death sentence, and in the federal system, minority defendants, especially African-Americans, were more likely to receive a death sentence than were white defendants.

In "Criminal Sentencing Policies Disproportionately Hurt Black Americans, Mauer Says" (November 6, 2007, http://www.law.virginia.edu/html/news/2007_fall/mauer .htm), Shea Connelly reports on a talk that Marc Mauer of the Sentencing Project gave at Virginia Law School in 2007. Mauer identified the war on drugs as a prime causal agent in the disproportionate number of African-Americans who are incarcerated. He pointed out that communities with monetary resources do not deal with kids with drug problems through the criminal justice system, but through treatment programs. By contrast, poor communities often call on the police to deal with drug-abuse problems. Because minorities are disproportionately poor, the strict sentencing laws arising from the war on drugs have fallen heavily on them. Harsher penalties for the possession of crack cocaine, which is more common in low-income communities, as opposed to powder cocaine, which is more common in white and affluent communities, have also contributed heavily to the problem of racial disparities in the criminal justice system.

GANGS

Testifying before the U.S. Senate, Steven R. Wiley (April 23, 1997, http://www.hi-ho.ne.jp/taku77/refer/gang.htm) of the Federal Bureau of Investigation explained that law enforcement agencies define a street gang as a "group of people that form an allegiance based on various social needs and engage in acts injurious to public health and safety." Even though gangs have been involved with the drug trade for many years, gang-related deadly violence is more likely to come from territorial conflicts.

Gangs are often (but not always) racially or ethnically based. As a rule, ethnic gangs require that all members belong to a particular race or ethnic group. Erika Harrell of the BJS indicates in "Violence by Gang Members, 1993–2003" (June 2005, http://www.ojp.usdoj.gov/bjs/pub/pdf/vgm03.pdf) that between 1998 and 2003, 6% of all violent crimes were perpetrated by gang members.

The most frightening crime committed by gangs is murder. More than half of all gang-related homicides between 1976 and 2005 involved whites. (See Table 7.4.) Approximately 57.5% of gang-related homicide victims during this period were white (Hispanic or non-Hispanic), and 54.3% of offenders were also white. African-Americans were the victims of gang-related homicides 39% of the time, and 41.2% of offenders were African-American.

The National Youth Gang Center notes in *National Youth Gang Survey Analysis* (2008, http://www.iir.com/nygc/nygsa/) the following trends:

- Approximately 29% of the jurisdictions that city (populations of twenty-five hundred or more) and county law enforcement agencies serve experienced youth gang problems in 2004.

- Gang problems are highly prevalent in larger cities; specifically, 99% of law enforcement agencies serving cities with populations of one hundred thousand or more reported multiple years of gang problems.

- Gang problem prevalence rates in suburban and rural counties and smaller cities declined yearly from the mid-1990s through the early 2000s.

- Approximately half as many rural counties reported gang problems in 2005 compared to 1996.

Furthemore, violence by perceived gang members declined between 1993 and 2003. Harrell states that in 1994 violent victimizations by gang members peaked at about 1.1 million, then fell to 341,000 in 2003. During this eleven-year period, Hispanic victims were more likely than non-Hispanic white or African-American victims to perceive their attackers as gang members. The rate of violence by victim-perceived gang members was 5.7 per 1,000 Hispanics, 4.1 per 1,000 African-Americans, and 2.4 per 1,000 non-Hispanic whites over the entire period. However, homicides by gang members have not declined. In 1993, 5.6% of all homicides were gang related; in 2003, 6.5% of all homicides were gang related.

CHAPTER 8

POLITICAL PARTICIPATION

A truly postethnic America would be one in which the ethno-racial component in identity would loom less large than it now does in politics.

—David A. Hollinger, *Postethnic America: Beyond Multiculturalism* (1995)

David A. Hollinger's words point out the large divide between minority groups and the majority in the political life of the nation. Not only are there racial and ethnic divides in voter registration and voter turnout but also minority groups by and large cast their support behind Democratic candidates. In addition, only in the last twenty years of the twentieth century did minority candidates running for office achieve much success. By 2008, however, there was a viable African-American candidate for the Democratic nomination for president: Senator Barack Obama Jr. (1961–) from Illinois.

VOTER REGISTRATION

Minority groups have traditionally trailed behind whites when it comes to registering to vote and actually voting. In 1993 Congress enacted the National Voter Registration Act (NVRA), which became popularly known as the "Motor Voter Act," because it included provisions to enable driver's license applicants to simultaneously register to vote. In "Big Increase in New Voters" (October 15, 1997, http://www.cgi.cnn.com/ALLPOLITICS/1996/news/9610/15/motor.voter/), CNN reports that in the two years after the law went into effect (in January 1995) nine million people had registered to vote.

To be eligible to vote, a person must be a U.S. citizen and at least eighteen years of age. The U.S. Election Assistance Commission states in *The Impact of the National Voter Registration Act of 1993 on the Administration of Elections for Federal Office, 2005–2006* (June 30, 2007, http://www.eac.gov/) that in 2006 the voting-age population numbered 225.7 million. Of that number, 172.8 million (76.6%) were registered to vote, a 7.6% increase over the

number of registrants in the 2002 midterm elections. However, since the presidential elections in 2004, the number of registered voters had decreased from 176.2 million voters, reflecting a normal drop in registration after a presidential election, when states remove some nonvoters from the registration rolls. Each state determines for itself how long an individual may remain on the list of registered voters without voting.

In 2004 (a presidential election year) there were 151.4 million non-Hispanic whites aged eighteen and older living in the United States, and 148.2 million of them were citizens. (See Table 8.1.) Of this number, 111.3 million (75.1%) were registered to vote. Of the 24.9 million African-Americans aged eighteen and old, 23.3 million were citizens. Only sixteen million (68.7%) were registered to vote. Of the 9.3 million Asian-Americans aged eighteen and older, only 6.3 million were citizens. Of these, 3.2 million (51.8%) were registered to vote. Of the 27.1 million Hispanics aged eighteen and older, 16.1 million were citizens. Only 9.3 million (57.9%) were registered to vote.

Minority voter registration habits tend to vary by region. African-Americans in the Midwest are more likely to register to vote than African-Americans in other regions. The U.S. Census Bureau reports in *Voting and Registration in the Election of November 2004* (December 11, 2007, http://www.census.gov/population/www/socdemo/voting/cps2004.html) that 71.6% of African-American citizens in the Midwest were registered to vote in 2004, compared to 54.9% in the Northeast, 65.3% in the South, and 64.3% in the West.

Since the 1960s the number of minority registered voters in the South has increased. This increase is due in large part to the passage of the Civil Rights Act of 1964 and the Voting Rights Act of 1965. These laws removed voting restrictions and led to often volatile and dangerous voter registration campaigns conducted during the 1960s and 1970s. Before these changes many southern states

TABLE 8.1

Reported rates of voting and registration by sex, age, race and Hispanic origin, and nativity status, November 2004

[Numbers in thousands]

Characteristic	Total	Citizens Total	Citizens Registered Number	Citizens Registered Percent	Citizens Voted Number	Citizens Voted Percent	Registered Percent reported voted
Total, 18 years and older	**215,694**	**197,005**	**142,070**	**72.1**	**125,736**	**63.8**	**88.5**
Sex							
Men	103,812	94,147	66,406	70.5	58,455	62.1	88.0
Women	111,882	102,858	75,663	73.6	67,281	65.4	88.9
Race and Hispanic origin							
White alone	176,618	162,959	119,929	73.6	106,588	65.4	88.9
White alone, non-Hispanic	151,410	148,158	111,318	75.1	99,567	67.2	89.4
Black alone	24,910	23,346	16,035	68.7	14,016	60.0	87.4
Asian alone	9,291	6,270	3,247	51.8	2,768	44.1	85.2
Hispanic (any race)	27,129	16,088	9,308	57.9	7,587	47.2	81.5
Nativity status							
Total citizens	**197,005**	**197,005**	**142,070**	**72.1**	**125,736**	**63.8**	**88.5**
Native	183,880	183,880	134,039	72.9	118,693	64.5	88.6
Naturalized	13,125	13,125	8,030	61.2	7,042	53.7	87.7
Age							
18 to 24 years	27,808	24,898	14,334	57.6	11,639	46.7	81.2
25 to 34 years	39,003	32,842	21,690	66.0	18,285	55.7	84.3
35 to 44 years	43,130	38,389	27,681	72.1	24,560	64.0	88.7
45 to 54 years	41,589	39,011	29,448	75.5	26,813	68.7	91.1
55 years and older	64,164	61,865	48,918	79.1	44,438	71.8	90.8
65 to 74 years	18,363	17,759	14,125	79.5	13,010	73.3	92.1
75 years and older	16,375	15,933	12,581	79.0	10,915	68.5	86.8

SOURCE: Adapted from Kelly Holder, "Table B. Reported Rates of Voting and Registration by Selected Characteristics: 2004," in *Voting and Registration in the Election of November 2004*, U.S. Census Bureau, March 2006, http://www.census.gov/prod/2006pubs/p20-556.pdf (accessed January 4, 2008)

enforced poll taxes, charging citizens for the right to vote and knowing that many poor African-Americans could not afford to pay. Some southern states had "grandfather clauses" that permitted voting rights only to those whose grandfathers had been able to vote. Many elderly African-Americans were the grandchildren of slaves who had not been able to vote, so these clauses restricted their rights. Furthermore, because they did not have the right to vote, their own children and grandchildren were also prevented from voting under the grandfather clauses. It took more than laws to open voting booths to southern African-Americans—it took marches, demonstrations, and the loss of a number of lives.

The Census Bureau notes that Asian-Americans living in the West were the most likely to be registered to vote in 2004; still, only 38.2% were registered there. In the Northeast 32.1% of Asian-Americans were registered to vote, in the Midwest 31.7% were registered to vote, and in the South 30.5% were registered to vote. Hispanics were the most likely to be registered to vote if they lived in the Northeast, where 38.2% of Hispanics were registered to vote in 2004. Only 36% of Hispanics were registered in the South, 34.6% in the Midwest, and 31.6% in the West.

VOTER TURNOUT

Registering to vote is one thing, but actually going out to the polls on election day is another. Often, people will register to vote but fail to exercise their right to vote when the time comes.

Even though African-Americans are somewhat less likely to vote than whites, both groups are much more likely to vote than Hispanics and Asians and Pacific Islanders. In 2004, 67.2% of non-Hispanic white citizens voted, compared to 60% of African-American citizens, 47.2% of Hispanic citizens, and 44.1% of Asian-American citizens. (See Table 8.1.)

Just as African-Americans in the Midwest were more likely to be registered to vote in 2004, they were more likely to vote than African-Americans in other parts of the country. Two-thirds (66%) of African-American citizens in the Midwest voted that year. (See Figure 8.1.) The lowest turnout of African-American citizens was in the Northeast, where only 56.2% voted. Hispanic turnout was also best in the Midwest, where 51.3% of Hispanic citizens voted in 2004, whereas the lowest turnout of Hispanics was in the South, where only 45.5% voted. Asian-Americans living in the Midwest and West were the most likely to vote—45.7% of those living in the

FIGURE 8.1

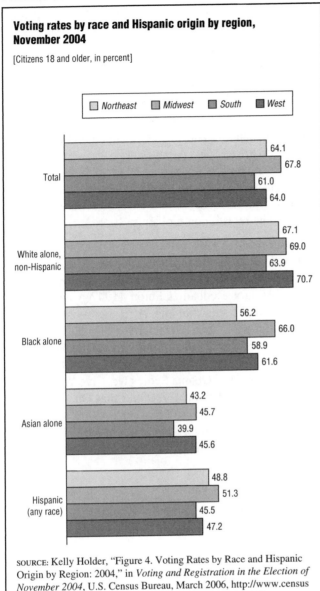

Voting rates by race and Hispanic origin by region, November 2004

[Citizens 18 and older, in percent]

Legend: Northeast · Midwest · South · West

Total
- 64.1
- 67.8
- 61.0
- 64.0

White alone, non-Hispanic
- 67.1
- 69.0
- 63.9
- 70.7

Black alone
- 56.2
- 66.0
- 58.9
- 61.6

Asian alone
- 43.2
- 45.7
- 39.9
- 45.6

Hispanic (any race)
- 48.8
- 51.3
- 45.5
- 47.2

SOURCE: Kelly Holder, "Figure 4. Voting Rates by Race and Hispanic Origin by Region: 2004," in *Voting and Registration in the Election of November 2004*, U.S. Census Bureau, March 2006, http://www.census.gov/prod/2006pubs/p20-556.pdf (accessed January 4, 2008)

FIGURE 8.2

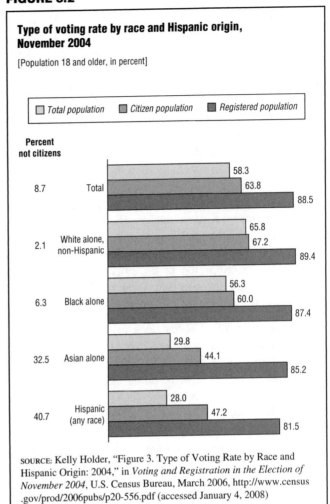

Type of voting rate by race and Hispanic origin, November 2004

[Population 18 and older, in percent]

Legend: Total population · Citizen population · Registered population

Percent not citizens

Total (8.7)
- 58.3
- 63.8
- 88.5

White alone, non-Hispanic (2.1)
- 65.8
- 67.2
- 89.4

Black alone (6.3)
- 56.3
- 60.0
- 87.4

Asian alone (32.5)
- 29.8
- 44.1
- 85.2

Hispanic (any race) (40.7)
- 28.0
- 47.2
- 81.5

SOURCE: Kelly Holder, "Figure 3. Type of Voting Rate by Race and Hispanic Origin: 2004," in *Voting and Registration in the Election of November 2004*, U.S. Census Bureau, March 2006, http://www.census.gov/prod/2006pubs/p20-556.pdf (accessed January 4, 2008)

Midwest and 45.6% of those living in the West voted in 2004—whereas the lowest turnout of Asian-Americans was in the South, at 39.9%.

A General Decline in Voting Participation

Since 1964 there has been a decline in the percentage of Americans who vote in presidential elections. The Census Bureau (November 1964, http://www.census.gov/population/socdemo/voting/p20-143/tab01.pdf; February 27, 2002, http://www.census.gov/population/socdemo/voting/p20-542/tab02.pdf) reports that in 1964, 69.3% of the voting-age population voted, compared to 54.7% in 2000. In 2004 this rate increased to 58.3%. (See Figure 8.2.) These figures include the resident voting-age population that is not eligible to vote, such as noncitizens.

A general decline in the proportion of Americans who vote was also seen across racial and ethnic groups. In *Historical Voting and Registration Reports* (October 16, 2007, http://www.census.gov/population/www/socdemo/voting/past-voting.html), the Census Bureau reports that only among non-Hispanic whites (who were counted separately from Hispanic whites starting in 1980) did the percentage of the voting-age population that votes rise; after dropping from 62.8% in 1980 to 60.4% in 2000, it rose to 65.8% in 2004. (See Figure 8.2.) In 1968, the first year that African-Americans were counted separately from other races, 57.6% of the African-American voting-age population voted. This percentage dropped to 53.5% in 2000, but rose again to 56.3% in 2004. Among Hispanics, 37.5% of the voting-age population voted in 1972, whereas in 2000 only 27.5% voted—and this percentage rose only slightly, to 28%, in 2004. The number of Asian-Americans who vote has been tracked only since the 1992 presidential election. In 1992, 27.3% of the Asian-American voting-age population voted, down to 25.4% in 2000 but up to 29.8% in 2004.

2000 Presidential Election

One reason the general decline in voting participation seems to have reversed somewhat in the 2004 presidential election was the close and controversial results of the 2000 presidential election. That election between George W. Bush (1946–), the Republican candidate and the governor of Texas, and Vice President Albert Gore Jr. (1948–), the Democratic candidate, was one of the most controversial presidential elections in history. The election remained undecided for five weeks, after the vote was too close to call and hinged on the number of ballots each candidate received in Florida. In several precincts ballots were recounted by hand, a project that sparked even more controversy as hole-punched ballots that were only partially punched through were viewed differently by different people. The election was eventually decided when the U.S. Supreme Court ruled that the recount would stop, and the election went to Bush, who was leading the recount vote in Florida at the time.

There were many accusations made of voting problems and irregularities in precincts throughout Florida that had large numbers of African-American voters. Following the election, the National Association for the Advancement of Colored People (NAACP) held hearings during which African-American residents of Florida testified about voter intimidation and irregularities such as polling places being moved and registered voters being told that they could not vote. Because African-Americans tend to vote for the Democratic Party, many groups charged that Gore would have won the election had the minority vote not been compromised. The complaints led the NAACP to file a lawsuit against the state of Florida over the election and resulted in widespread calls for election reform. Settling the lawsuit out of court in 2002, the state agreed to change voter registration procedures, improve maintenance of the list of eligible voters, better train poll workers, and improve communication between precincts and election headquarters.

Reasons for Not Voting

Age seems to affect one's likelihood to vote. Traditionally, the demographic group between the ages of eighteen and twenty-four has the lowest percentage of voters. This may partially explain the low voter turnout of Hispanics, because they are on average younger than other segments of the U.S. population. According to the Census Bureau, in *Voting and Registration in the Election of November 2004*, only 41.9% of young adults between the ages of eighteen and twenty-four voted in 2004. This percent was up from 32.3% in 2000, as reported by the Census Bureau (February 27, 2002, http://www.census.gov/population/socdemo/voting/p20-542/tab02.pdf). As citizens age, however, they are more likely to vote. In 2004, 52.2% of the voting-age population between the ages of twenty-five and forty-four voted, 66.6% of those between the ages of forty-five

and sixty-four voted, and 70.8% of those between the ages of sixty-five and seventy-four voted. The percent that voted was up in all age groups since 2000.

According to the Census Bureau, the number-one reason people gave for not voting in the 2004 presidential election was that they were too busy, an excuse given by 19.9% of registered nonvoters. (See Table 8.2.) Other leading reasons were illness or disability (15.4%), no interest (10.7%), dislike of candidates or campaign issues (9.9%), and out of town (9%). Asian-Americans were especially likely to state they were too busy to vote (31.5%), African-Americans were especially likely to say they did not know or refused to vote (13%), and Hispanics were especially likely to cite registration problems (10.9%).

Some evidence suggests that registration and voting rates will be up among minorities in the 2008 presidential election. In a fierce Democratic primary contest between Senator Hillary Rodham Clinton (1947–) and Obama, Obama had the edge among African-American voters. In a Gallup poll taken in January 2008, 57% of polled African-American democrats preferred Obama, whereas only 32% preferred Clinton. (See Figure 8.3.) Audie Cornish reports in "Obama Scores Decisive Win in South Carolina" (NPR, January 27, 2008) that Obama won the South Carolina primary on January 26, 2008, when Democrats turned out in unprecedented numbers. Four out of five African-American voters in that state said they voted for Obama.

AFRICAN-AMERICAN POLITICAL PARTICIPATION

Elected Officials

The number of African-Americans elected to public offices at all levels of the U.S. government has increased significantly since the 1980s. The largest gain has been in city and county offices, which include county commissioners, city council members, mayors, vice mayors, and aldermen/alderwomen. Obama became only the fifth African-American to serve in the U.S. Senate and only the third since the period of Reconstruction (1865–1877), when he was sworn in as a senator from Illinois on January 4, 2005. He had received international media coverage after delivering a stirring keynote address at the 2004 Democratic National Convention. In 2008 he won the Iowa caucus and was a front-runner in the race for the Democratic nomination for president, the first viable African-American presidential candidate in U.S. history.

African-Americans and Political Parties

According to the Pew Research Center for the People and the Press, in *Evenly Divided and Increasingly Polarized: The 2004 Political Landscape* (November 5, 2003, http://people-press.org/reports/pdf/196.pdf), African-Americans are the

TABLE 8.2

Reasons for not voting by sex, race and Hispanic origin, nativity status, and age, November 2004

[Numbers in thousands]

Characteristic	Total	Percent distribution of reasons for not voting											
		Too busy, conflicting schedule	Illness or disability	Other reason	Not interested	Did not like candidates or issues	Out of town	Don't know or refused	Registration problems	Forgot to vote	Inconvenient polling place	Transportation problems	Bad weather conditions
Total, 18 years and older	**16,334**	**19.9**	**15.4**	**10.9**	**10.7**	**9.9**	**9.0**	**8.5**	**6.8**	**3.4**	**3.0**	**2.1**	**0.5**
Sex													
Male	7,951	22.5	10.7	10.8	10.6	10.1	11.0	10.0	6.6	3.4	3.1	0.9	0.3
Female	8,383	17.4	19.8	10.9	10.7	9.7	7.1	7.2	7.0	3.5	2.9	3.3	0.6
Race and Hispanic origin													
White alone	13,341	19.4	15.6	10.9	10.8	10.6	9.4	7.9	6.8	3.4	3.0	1.9	0.4
White alone, non-Hispanic	11,752	18.9	16.2	10.8	10.8	11.1	9.9	7.6	6.2	3.0	3.2	1.9	0.5
Black alone	2,019	20.7	16.5	9.8	10.0	6.4	5.5	13.0	7.2	3.9	2.6	4.2	0.3
Asian alone	479	31.5	6.1	13.7	7.9	4.4	11.6	9.0	6.1	1.4	5.5	1.3	1.5
Hispanic (any race)	1,721	23.5	10.7	11.6	10.5	7.3	6.3	9.8	10.9	6.1	1.5	1.6	0.2
Nativity status													
Native	15,346	19.5	15.4	10.8	10.9	10.2	8.8	8.5	6.8	3.4	2.9	2.2	0.4
Naturalized	988	26.2	14.1	11.1	6.9	4.8	10.9	10.0	6.9	3.1	3.3	1.6	1.0
Age													
18 to 24 years	2,695	23.2	2.8	10.8	10.0	6.4	12.8	15.2	8.2	6.1	2.5	1.9	0.1
25 to 44 years	6,525	27.6	7.4	11.8	10.3	10.0	8.1	7.6	8.6	3.4	3.3	1.5	0.3
45 to 64 years	4,333	17.2	15.6	10.6	11.0	12.9	10.7	8.6	5.5	3.0	3.0	1.5	0.4
65 years and older	2,781	2.9	45.8	9.0	11.6	8.4	4.5	4.2	3.7	1.7	2.5	4.6	1.2

SOURCE: Adapted from Kelly Holder, "Table F. Reasons for Not Voting by Selected Characteristics: 2004," in *Voting and Registration in the Election of November 2004*, U.S. Census Bureau, March 2006, http://www.census.gov/prod/2006pubs/p20–556.pdf (accessed January 4, 2008)

FIGURE 8.3

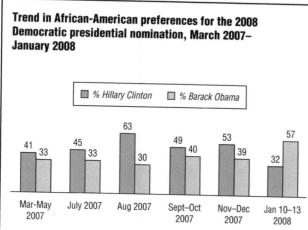

Trend in African-American preferences for the 2008 Democratic presidential nomination, March 2007– January 2008

SOURCE: Lydia Saad, "Trend in Black Preferences for the 2008 Democratic Presidential Nomination," in *Black Democrats Move into Obama's Column*, The Gallup Organization, January 15, 2008, http://www.gallup.com/poll/103756/Black-Democrats-Move-Into-Obamas-Column.aspx (accessed January 16, 2008). Copyright © 2008 by The Gallup Organization. Reproduced by Permission of The Gallup Organization.

strongest supporters of the Democratic Party. In 2003, 64% of African-Americans described themselves as Democrats, another 21% said they leaned toward the Democratic Party, and only 7% identified themselves as Republicans. Even though many Americans shifted toward the Republican Party after the terrorist attacks against the United States on September 11, 2001 (9/11), African-Americans did not. The Pew Research Center notes that across regions, socioeconomic groups, and ages, the preference for the Democratic Party among African-Americans is uniform; the most affluent African-Americans' party affiliation is almost identical to the least affluent, and the Democratic advantage is only slightly smaller among younger people.

The traditional African-American political goals, as presented by the thirteen original members of the Congressional Black Caucus (CBC; which was founded as the Democratic Select Committee in 1969), are to "promote the public welfare through legislation designed to meet the needs of millions of neglected citizens" (February 18, 2008, http://www.cbcfinc.org/About/CBC/index.html). In 2008 there were forty-three members of the CBC. The CBC encourages and seeks out African-American participation in government, especially as elected officials, to correct the ills of the disadvantaged, many of whom are minorities. Some African-Americans are turning away from this position and aligning themselves with the Republican Party, which believes in less government involvement.

As the African-American middle class continues to grow, party loyalties may change. Some younger professional African-Americans who may not have experienced pov-

erty or the deprivation of the inner cities may be attracted to the Republican Party platform of less government and lower taxes. A vast majority of African-Americans embraced the programs of President Lyndon B. Johnson's (1908–1973) Great Society and his war on poverty in the 1960s. In the twenty-first century a small minority believe that reliance on government has actually disempowered many African-Americans and other underprivileged people. For example, the African American Republican Leadership Council (2008, http://www.aarlc.org/issues/index.shtml) argues in favor of limited government, states that African-Americans "suffer the greatest losses under today's Social Security system," and charges that civil liberties groups who "represent entire groups or category of people" actually "strip away individual civil liberties and maintain power over those purportedly protected by these organization's leaders."

HISPANIC POLITICAL PARTICIPATION
Factors Contributing to Low Political Participation

There was a tremendous increase in the Hispanic population in the United States during the late twentieth century. According to the Census Bureau, in *National Population Estimates—Characteristics* (May 17, 2007, http://www.census.gov/popest/national/asrh/NC-EST2006-srh.html), by 2006, 44.3 million Hispanic people lived in the United States. However, the Hispanic community has not attained political power equal to its proportion of the population. Two characteristics of Hispanic demography help account for this. First, even though the Hispanic voting-age population grew during the 1970s and 1980s, Hispanics have a young population, with many in the eighteen- to twenty-four-year-old category—the age group that is the least likely to vote. In addition, a smaller proportion of Hispanics than of society as a whole are in the fifty-five and older category—the age group the most likely to vote. The second and perhaps more important characteristic is the issue of U.S. citizenship. In 2004, 40.7% Hispanics living in the United States were not U.S. citizens, thus eliminating over eleven million potential Hispanic voters. (See Table 8.1.)

Political Participation

Civil rights gains of the 1960s, such as the Twenty-fourth Amendment eliminating the poll tax, the extension of the Voting Rights Act of 1965 to the Southwest, and the elimination of the English literacy requirement, helped a number of Hispanics attain political office. During the 1970s both major political parties started wooing Hispanic voters and drafting Hispanic candidates. Advocacy groups, such as the Mexican American Legal Defense and Educational Fund, the Southwest Voter Registration Project, and the Puerto Rican Legal Defense and Educational Fund, were formed. All these groups helped develop the political influence of the Hispanic community.

The National Association of Latino Elected and Appointed Officials (NALEO; January 21, 2008, http://www.naleo.org/aboutnaleo.html) is a research, policy, and education organization comprising the nation's more than six thousand Latino officials. The organization's mission is to facilitate the integration of Latino immigrants into American society, to develop leadership abilities among Latino youth, and to support the nation's Latino elected and appointed officials. In 2004 the NALEO Educational Fund announced that it was collaborating with Univision Communications Inc. in a program aimed at mobilizing Hispanic voters throughout the United States. The "Voces del Pueblo" campaign included nonpartisan public service announcements on radio and television as well as voter education forums, phone contact, and targeted mailings. According to NALEO, in the press release "The NALEO Educational Fund and Univision Launch Effort to Mobilize Latino Electorate" (March 5, 2004, http://www.univision.net/corp/en/pr/Los_Angeles_05032004-2.html), Ivelisse Estrada of Univision is quoted as saying that "with the significant growth of the Latino population in the U.S. and the increasing number of Latinos registering to vote, the U.S. Hispanic community's ability to influence the course of our nation can no longer be ignored. Now more than ever, Latinos are demonstrating that they are key players on the political stage. With this campaign, we have the opportunity to listen to Latino voters and identify their concerns." The program was an attempt to mobilize Hispanic voters, in part by encouraging immigrants to become U.S. citizens, and develop the political influence of the Hispanic community. In "Univision Give Citizenship Drive an Unusual Life" (*Wall Street Journal*, May 10, 2007), Miriam Jordan reports that according to some observers, this citizenship drive might have significant effects on the outcome of the 2008 presidential race.

Hispanics and Political Parties

As a group, Hispanics have been important supporters of the Democratic Party. Like many other Americans in the aftermath of the terrorist attacks of 9/11, many Hispanics shifted their party affiliation to the Republican Party, although by 2007 that trend had reversed itself. Paul Taylor and Richard Fry of the Pew Research Center report in *Hispanics and the 2008 Election: A Swing Vote?* (December 6, 2007, http://pewhispanic.org/files/reports/83.pdf) that even though Democrats outnumbered Republicans among Hispanics by more than two to one in the 1990s, after 9/11 Democrats led by a smaller margin. In fact, Bush received an estimated 40% of the Hispanic vote in 2004, a record for a Republican presidential candidate.

However, between 2006 and 2007 the shift of Hispanic voters to the Republican Party reversed course. Taylor and Fry find that in 2006, 28% of Hispanics said they supported Republicans and 49% said they supported Democrats.

Within a year, only 23% of Hispanics called themselves Republicans and 57% called themselves Democrats. According to Taylor and Fry, more Hispanics believed the Democratic Party showed the greater concern for Latinos and thought the Democrats were doing a better job on the issue of illegal immigration. In addition, 41% of Hispanics surveyed believed the Bush administration's policies had been harmful to Latinos, whereas only 16% believed these policies had been helpful.

Taylor and Fry state that Hispanics have the potential to be a swing vote in helping decide the 2008 presidential election. Latino voters represented a sizeable share of the electorate in four of the six states that Bush carried by margins of five percentage points or fewer in the 2004 election: New Mexico, Florida, Nevada, and Colorado. In 2007 Hispanics made up 37.1% of the electorate in New Mexico, 13.6% of the electorate in Florida, 12.2% of the electorate in Nevada, and 12.3% of the electorate in Colorado. In addition, Hispanics might play a significant role in the selection of the Democratic candidate for president. Taylor and Fry indicate that in 2007, 59% of Hispanics favored Clinton, whereas only 15% supported Obama and 8% supported Bill Richardson (1947–), the governor of New Mexico.

RACE, ETHNICITY, AND ELECTORAL DISTRICTS

The design of electoral districts can have a tremendous impact on the political power of minorities. Depending on how the lines are drawn, an electoral district might have a large concentration of minorities, enhancing their political power, or minority populations may be split up between many electoral districts, weakening their political influence.

Designing electoral districts to favor one group over another is known as gerrymandering, named after the Massachusetts governor Elbridge Gerry (1744–1814), who became notorious for the salamander-shaped district he approved in 1812. In the first half of the twentieth century, gerrymandering was widely used as an attempt to prevent African-Americans and other minorities from gaining true political representation. Another practice was creating at-large districts, in which the entire population of a large area elected several representatives. The alternative, having several smaller districts each elect only one representative, allowed concentrated populations of minorities to elect their own representatives.

Under the requirements of the Voting Rights Act of 1965, jurisdictions with a history of systematic discrimination (such as a poll tax or literacy test) must create districts with majorities of African-Americans or Hispanics wherever the demographics warrant it. At the same time, they must avoid weakening existing "minority-majority" districts (i.e., districts "in which a majority of the population is a member of a specific minority group"). This law helped eliminate some districts that had been designed to favor whites. At the same time, however, it superseded the traditional criterion of compact districts and made for some oddly defined districts in the name of creating Hispanic- or African-American-majority districts.

Computerized Redistricting

Amy J. Douglas notes in *Real Choices/New Voices: How Proportional Representation Elections Could Revitalize American Democracy* (2002) that with computer software, gerrymandering in the twenty-first century has become highly sophisticated. Redistricters can now incorporate a variety of information—party registration, voting patterns, and ethnic makeup—from a variety of sources, including census data, property tax records, and old district lines. This information allows them to produce a number of potential scenarios in an instant. Contemporary gerrymandering techniques are called "packing" (concentrating a group of voters in the fewest number of districts); "cracking" (spreading a group of voters across districts); and "kidnapping" (remapping so that two incumbents from the same party are now located in the same district and vying for the same seat). Gerrymandering in the past was essentially self-correcting; by attempting to control as many districts as possible, parties risked losing, should a small percentage of voters shift allegiances. However, contemporary software has become so sophisticated, and politics have become so partisan, that the idea of self-correction is no longer applicable. As a result, few seats in the U.S. House of Representatives are now competitive, with incumbents enjoying a locked-in advantage that is almost impossible to overcome.

Challenges to Electoral Districting

Redistricting has become a major source of contention between Republicans and Democrats since the 2000 census. One notorious case took place in Texas. Texas lawmakers were unable to agree on new congressional districts because the Republicans controlled the state senate and the Democrats controlled the state house of representatives. A compromise plan was forced on the parties by a panel of federal judges, essentially leaving the current partisan balance in place. However, after Republicans took control of the state house in 2002, they sought to reopen the redistricting question, breaking an unwritten rule that remapping was to be a matter dealt with once every ten years to avoid incessant wrangling on

the subject. To resist, Democrats in both the state house and senate fled to Oklahoma and New Mexico to prevent the creation of a quorum (the minimum number of representatives present to conduct business) and thwart the ability of the Republicans to push through their redistricting plan.

In the end, the Democrats gave in and the congressional districts were redrawn, with the potential that the Republicans would pick up seven seats in the 2004 elections. Staff lawyers in the U.S. Department of Justice approved the plan, even though lawyers for the department had concluded that the redistricting plan undercut minority voting rights. In fact, Republicans won twenty-one of Texas's thirty-two seats in the house of representatives in 2004, up from fifteen. The U.S. Supreme Court announced on December 12, 2005, that it would consider the constitutionality of the redistricted congressional map. On June 28, 2006, the Court ruled that the redistricting violated the rights of some Hispanics, but did not violate the rights of African-American voters in the state. Furthermore, it ruled that nothing in the U.S. Constitution barred states from redrawing political lines at any time, and it established no timetable for reviewing the redistricting that had violated the rights of Hispanics.

A redistricting effort in Pennsylvania also drew a great deal of attention. After losing two seats in Congress due to a drop in population, Pennsylvania redrew its districts, a process that the Republican majority in the General Assembly openly sought to benefit their party through the latest techniques in gerrymandering. Some of the unusually shaped districts that resulted were called the "supine seahorse" and the "upside-down Chinese dragon." Even though a Democrat won the governor's race in Pennsylvania in 2002, Republicans took twelve of the nineteen U.S. House of Representatives seats.

Vieth v. Jubelirer (541 U.S. 267, 2004) contended that Republicans went too far in their efforts to favor their own party in redrawing congressional lines. However, in May 2004 the Supreme Court upheld the Pennsylvania map in a 5–4 decision. Justice Antonin Scalia (1936–) and others of the majority opinion maintained that it was the responsibility of Congress and not the Court to define fair districting practices. Justice John Paul Stevens (1920–), a minority opinion holder, characterized the decision as "a failure of judicial will to condemn even the most blatant violations of a state legislature's fundamental duty to govern impartially."

IMPORTANT NAMES
AND ADDRESSES

Center for Women's Business Research
1411 K St. NW, Ste. 1350
Washington, DC 20005
(202) 638-3060
FAX: (202) 638-3064
E-mail: info@womensbusinessresearch.org
URL: http://www.cfwbr.org/

Children's Defense Fund
25 E St. NW
Washington, DC 20001
(202) 628-8787
1-800-233-1200
E-mail: cdfinfo@childrensdefense.org
URL: http://www.childrensdefense.org/

Civil Rights Project
8370 Math Sciences, Box 951521
Los Angeles, CA 90095-1521
(310) 267-5562
FAX: (310) 206-6293
URL: http://
www.civilrightsproject.ucla.edu/

Congressional Black Caucus Foundation
1720 Massachusetts Ave. NW
Washington, DC 20036
(202) 263-2800
FAX: (202) 775-0773
E-mail: info@cbcfinc.org
URL: http://www.cbcfinc.org/

Congressional Hispanic Caucus Institute
911 Second St. NE
Washington, DC 20002
(202) 543-1771
1-800-EXCEL-DC
FAX: (202) 546-2143
URL: http://www.chci.org/

Lawyers' Committee for Civil Rights under Law
1401 New York Ave. NW, Ste. 400
Washington, DC 20005
(202) 662-8600
FAX: (202) 783-0857
URL: http://www.lawyerscommittee.org/
2005website/home/home.html

League of United Latin American Citizens
2000 L St. NW, Ste. 610
Washington, DC 20036
(202) 833-6130
FAX: (202) 833-6135
URL: http://www.lulac.org/

National Association for the Advancement of Colored People
4805 Mount Hope Dr.
Baltimore, MD 21215
(410) 580-5777
1-877-NAACP-98
URL: http://www.naacp.org/

National Association of Latino Elected and Appointed Officials Educational Fund
1122 W. Washington Blvd., Third Fl.
Los Angeles, CA 90015
(213) 747-7606
FAX: (213) 747-7664
URL: http://www.naleo.org/

National Black Child Development Institute
1313 L St. NW, Ste. 110
Washington, DC 20005-4110
(202) 883-2220
FAX: (202) 833-8222
URL: http://www.nbcdi.org/

National Caucus and Center on Black Aged
1220 L St. NW, Ste. 800
Washington, DC 20005
(202) 637-8400
FAX: (202) 347-0895
E-mail: info@ncba-aged.org
URL: http://www.ncba-aged.org/

National Hispanic Council on Aging
734 Fifteenth St. NW, Ste. 1050
Washington, DC 20005
(202) 347-9733
FAX: (202) 347-9735
URL: http://www.nhcoa.org/

National Urban League
120 Wall St., Eighth Fl.
New York, NY 10005

(212) 558-5300
E-mail: info@nul.org
URL: http://www.nul.org/

Organization of Chinese Americans
1322 Eighteenth St. NW
Washington, DC 20036-1803
(202) 223-5500
FAX: (202) 296-0540
E-mail: oca@ocanational.org
URL: http://www.ocanational.org/

Pew Hispanic Center
1615 L St. NW, Ste. 700
Washington, DC 20036-5610
(202) 419-3600
FAX: (202) 419-3608
E-mail: info@pewhispanic.org
URL: http://pewhispanic.org/

Poverty and Race Research Action Council
1015 Fifteenth St. NW, Ste. 400
Washington, DC 20005
(202) 906-8023
FAX: (202) 842-2885
E-mail: info@prrac.org
URL: http://www.prrac.org/

Sentencing Project
514 Tenth St. NW, Ste. 1000
Washington, DC 20004
(202) 628-0871
FAX: (202) 628-1091
E-mail: staff@sentencingproject.org
URL: http://www.sentencingproject.org/

Southern Poverty Law Center
400 Washington Ave.
Montgomery, AL 36104
(334) 956-8200
URL: http://www.splcenter.org/

U.S. Equal Employment Opportunity Commission
1801 L St. NW
Washington, DC 20507
(202) 663-4900
URL: http://www.eeoc.gov/

RESOURCES

The U.S. Census Bureau collects and distributes the nation's statistics. Demographic data from the bureau include *Profiles of General Demographic Characteristics* and *Population Projections Program* (projections released periodically). The Census Bureau also produces studies on racial and ethnic groups, including *The Asian Alone Population in the United States: March 2004* (March 2006), *The American Community—Blacks: 2004* (February 2007), *The American Community—Hispanics: 2004* (February 2007), and *U.S. Hispanic Population: 2006* (October 2007).

The Census Bureau releases the *Statistical Abstract* each year; the latest edition is *Statistical Abstract of the United States: 2008* (December 2007). It releases financial and family statistics in *America's Families and Living Arrangements: 2006* (March 2007) and *Income, Poverty, and Health Insurance Coverage in the United States: 2006* (Carmen DeNavas-Walt, Bernadette D. Proctor, and Jessica Smith, August 2007). It also compiles statistics on homeownership rates, business data, state and metropolitan population data, and voting data. Publications include *Housing Vacancies and Homeownership Annual Statistics: 2006* (February 2007), *Characteristics of Businesses: 2002* (September 2006), *State and Metropolitan Area Data Book: 2006* (July 2006), and *Voting and Registration in the Election of November 2004* (March 2006). The Census Bureau periodically publishes the *Survey of Minority-Owned Business Enterprises.*

The U.S. Bureau of Labor Statistics (BLS) provides labor force data. The BLS publishes *Employment and Earnings, Household Data Annual Averages*, and the monthly *Employment Situation Summary*. The *Monthly Labor Review* provides detailed analysis of labor force statistics on a periodic basis. Other job-related sources published by the U.S. Equal Employment Opportunity Commission are *Job Patterns for Minorities and Women in Private Industry* (January 2007) and *Enforcement Statistics and Litigation* (January 2007). The Center for

Women's Business Statistics provided information on businesses owned by minority women in *Businesses Owned by Women of Color in the United States, 2006: A Fact Sheet* (2007).

A variety of government resources on minority health proved invaluable. The National Center for Health Statistics produces *Health, United States, 2007* (2007) and the monthly *National Vital Statistics Reports*, which provide birth and mortality statistics. The Centers for Disease Control and Prevention publishes the annual *HIV/AIDS Surveillance Report*. Another helpful source, *America's Children: Key National Indicators of Well-Being, 2007* (July 2007), is published by the Federal Interagency Forum on Child and Family Statistics. The *SEER Cancer Statistics Review, 1975–2004* (L. A. G. Ries et al., 2007), published by the National Cancer Institute, provides invaluable data on cancer.

A number of U.S. Department of Health and Human Services publications were used in this book. The *2006 National Healthcare Disparities Report* (December 2006) is helpful in examining differences in health-care access and utilization among minority populations. *Indicators of Welfare Dependence, Annual Report to Congress, 2007* (2007) examines rates of utilization of a variety of social programs. *Results from the 2006 National Survey on Drug Use and Health: Detailed Tables* (September 2007) provides information on tobacco, alcohol, and illicit drug use.

The U.S. Department of Education's National Center for Education Statistics (NCES) publishes the annual report *The Condition of Education, 2007* (June 2007). Other NCES reports that proved helpful were *Status and Trends in the Education of American Indians and Alaska Natives* (Catherine Freeman and Mary Ann Fox, August 2005), *Status and Trends in the Education of Racial and Ethnic Minorities* (Angelina KewalRamani et al., September 2007), *American Indian and Alaska Native Children: Findings from the Base Year of the Early Childhood Longitudinal Study, Birth Cohort* (Kristin Denton Flanagan and Jen Park, August 2005), and *Indicators of School Crime and Safety: 2007* (Rachel Dinkes, Emily Forrest Cataldi, and Wendy Lin-Kelly, December 2007), which is jointly published with the U.S. Bureau of Justice Statistics (BJS). The College Board provides useful data in *College-Bound Seniors 2007* (2007). The Civil Rights Project published "Charter Schools and Race: A Lost Opportunity for Integrated Education" (Erica Frankenberg and Chungmei Lee, September 2003), a report on charter schools.

The BJS produces *Homicide Trends in the United States* (James Alan Fox and Marianne W. Zawitz, July 2007) as well as numerous other reports. Other BJS reports used in this publication include *Criminal Victimization 2006* (Michael Rand and Shannan M. Catalano, December 2007), *Prison and Jail Inmates at Midyear 2006* (William J. Sabol, Todd D. Minton, and Paige M. Harrison, June 2007), *Probation and Parole in the United States, 2006* (Lauren E. Glaze and Thomas P. Bonczar, December 2007), and *Capital Punishment, 2006* (Tracy L. Snell, December 2007). *Hate Crime Statistics, 2006* (November 2007) was published by the Federal Bureau of Investigation.

Finally, the Gallup Organization provides valuable polling information. Gallup publications used in this book include *Black Democrats Move into Obama's Column* (Lydia Saad, January 2008), *Blacks Convinced Discrimination Still Exists in College Admission Process* (Frank Newport, August 2007), *Black-White Educational Opportunities Widely Seen as Equal* (Lydia Saad, July 2007), *Whites, Blacks, Hispanics Assess Race Relations in the U.S.* (Joseph Carroll, August 2007), and *Whites, Minorities Differ in Views of Economic Opportunities in U.S.* (Joseph Carroll, July 2006).

INDEX

of Hispanics, 4, 6 (f1.3)

of Native Americans and Alaskan Natives, 12

of Puerto Ricans, 6

region of residence for Asians, non-Hispanic whites, 11f

See also Regions

Gerry, Elbridge, 131

Gerrymandering, 131–132

Gibson, Campbell, 10

Glasser, Ruth, 5

GlobalSecurity.org, 6

Gore, Albert, Jr., 128

Government. See Federal government

Government programs

free/reduced-price lunch, percentage of 4th-graders eligible for, 79t

income, percentage of total family income from various sources, 81t

means-tested assistance program recipients by race/ethnicity, 79, 81

means-tested assistance programs, total family income from, 80 (t5.7)

TANF, Food Stamps and/or SSI, population receiving, 80 (t5.8)

welfare reform, 78

Grade point average (GPA), 43–44

Graduation. See High school

Graffiti, hate-related, 115–116, 118f

Grandchildren, 23–24

Grandparents, 23–24

Great Depression, 52

Green card, 53

Grieco, Elizabeth M., 11

Grigg, Wendy, 38–39

Grutter v. Bollinger, 48–49

GSR (General Schedule and Related) grades, 66

Guatemalans, 3

Guest-worker program, 53

H

Handley, John, 26

Harrell, Erika, 122

Hate Crime Statistics Act of 1990, 114

Hate crimes

hate-bias incidents, 115t

against minorities, 114

at school, 115–116, 118f

Haves/have-nots, 76–78, 79f

Hawaiians. See Native Hawaiians and Pacific Islanders

Health

AIDS, 101, 103–106

AIDS, female adult/adolescent cases by exposure category, race/ethnicity, 105t

AIDS, male adult/adolescent cases by exposure category, race/ethnicity, 104t

AIDS cases in children less than 13 years of age, 103t

AIDS/HIV cases among persons aged 13 and older, 103f

alcohol use, binge/heavy in past month, 108t

of babies born to teenagers, 19

behaviors that threaten, 106–108

births, low-birthweight live births by race/ethnicity/smoking status of mother, 92t

births, total/percentage by race/ethnicity of mother, 91t

cancer, colon/rectum, incidence/death rates, 102 (f6.6)

cancer, female breast, incidence/death rates, 99f

cancer, lung/bronchus, incidence/death rates, 101f

cancer, prostate, incidence/death rates, 100f

cancer incidence rates/trends for top 15 cancer sites, 96t–97t

cancer mortality rates/trends for top 15 cancer sites, 98t–99t

death, leading causes of, 108–110

deaths by causes of death, race/ethnicity, sex, 110 (t6.18)

deaths of persons with AIDS, by year of death, race/ethnicity, 110 (t6.19)

diabetes, 102 (f6.7)

diseases, 91–101

drug use, illicit, by age, gender, race/ethnicity, 109t

health care, 83–87, 89

health care, access to, 85f

health care, quality of, 84f

health care visits to doctor offices, emergency departments, home visits, 88t

health insurance coverage, people without, 85t

health insurance coverage for persons 65 years and over, 87t

of Hispanics, 83

infant, neonatal, postneonatal mortality rates, by race/ethnicity of mother, 93t–95t

life expectancy, 108, 109f

median age by sex, race/ethnicity, 84t

Medicaid coverage among persons under 65 years of age, by race/ethnicity, 86t

pregnancy/birth, 89–91

prenatal care for live births by race/ethnicity of mother, 90t

tobacco product use, 107t

Health care

access to, 84–87, 85f, 89

health care visits to doctor offices, emergency departments, home visits, 88t

health insurance coverage for persons 65 years and over, 87t

health insurance coverage, people without, 85t

Medicaid coverage among persons under 65 years of age, by race/ethnicity, 86t

prenatal care for live births by race/ethnicity of mother, 90t

quality of care, 83–84, 84f

"Health Care Professionals: Data and Statistics" (CDC), 106

Health insurance

coverage for persons 65 years and over, 87t

Medicaid coverage among persons under 65 years of age, by race/ethnicity, 86t

minorities' access to, 84–86

people without, by race/Hispanic origin, 85t

Health, behaviors that threaten

alcohol use, binge/heavy in past month, 108t

cigarette smoking, 106

diet/nutrition, 106–107

drug abuse, 107–108

drug use, illicit, by age, gender, race/ethnicity, 109t

tobacco product use by age, gender, race/ethnicity, 107t

Health, United States, 2007 (NCHS)

on death, leading causes of, 108, 109–110

on deaths from heart disease, 97–98

on diabetes, 101

Healthy Eating Index, 106

Heart disease

deaths from, 97–98, 108

hypertension, 97

Heterosexual contact, 104–105

HHS. See U.S. Department of Health and Human Services

High blood pressure, 97

High school

college preparation in, 41–43

graduates, by highest level of foreign language course completed, race/ethnicity, 45 (t3.10)

graduates, by highest level of mathematics course completed, race/ethnicity, 44 (t3.8)

graduates, by highest level of science course completed and race/ethnicity, 44 (t3.7)

graduates, by type of English course taken, race/ethnicity, 45 (t3.9)

graduation by African-Americans, 33–34

graduation by Hispanics, 36

NAEP mathematics achievement levels, 36f

NAEP reading achievement levels, 33f

High School Coursetaking: Findings from the Condition of Education 2007 (NCES), 43

High school dropouts

Native Americans, 36

by nativity/race/ethnicity, 37t, 38f

rates by race/ethnicity, 31–32

Higher education
    Advanced Placement exams, students taking, by race/ethnicity, 46t
    affirmative action in, 47–48
    African-Americans in, 34
    bachelor's degree, earning, 46–47
    bachelor's degree or higher, percentage of adults ages 25 and over with, by race/ethnicity, 41f
    bachelor's degree or higher, persons ages 25 to 29 with, by race/ethnicity, 48t
    black colleges/universities, 50
    colleges/universities, 18- to 24-year-olds enrolled in, by race/ethnicity, 47f
    educational opportunities, views of, 49
    minority college attendance, 46
    preparation for, 41–44
    SAT/ACT scores, 44–46
    tribal colleges, 49–50
Hill, Paul T., 41
"Hispanic Health: Divergent and Changing" (Pew Hispanic Center), 91
Hispanic Population in the United States (U.S. Census Bureau), 73
The Hispanic Population in the United States: 2006 (U.S. Census Bureau), 71–72, 83
The Hispanic Population in the United States: March 2002 (U.S. Census Bureau), 4, 83
"Hispanic Prisoners in the United States" (Sentencing Project), 121
Hispanic, use of term, 3
Hispanics
    achievement scores of, 30–31
    affirmative action and, 48
    AIDS and, 103, 104, 105
    Alzheimer's disease and, 100
    bachelor's degree, earning, 46–47
    business ownership, 67
    cancer, breast, 94–95
    cancer, colon/rectum, 96–97
    cancer, prostate and lung, 95
    cancer incidence/morality rates, 91, 92
    college, preparation for, 41–42, 43
    college attendance, 46
    in criminal justice system, 121
    Cuban Americans, 6–7
    deaths, leading causes of, 108–109
    diabetes and, 101
    discriminatory employment practices, 59
    divorce rate of, 18
    drug abuse by, 107–108
    drugs at school and, 115
    education, preschool children's literacy, 28–29
    education preparation for children, 27–28
    educational attainment of, 35–36
    electoral districts and, 131–132

employed Hispanic workers by sex, occupation, class of workers, full- or part-time status, 65t
employment status of Hispanic population by sex, age, 56t
employment status of Mexican, Puerto Rican, Cuban population, by sex, age, 57t
in federal government workforce, 66
geographic distribution of, 4
GPA of students, 43–44
hate crimes against, 114
haves/have-nots, views of, 77–78
health care, access to, 84
health insurance for, 85, 86
heart disease and, 97, 98
high school dropouts, 31–32
homeownership, 25
income of, 71–73
in labor force, historical perspective, 52–53
labor force participation, unemployment, 55
labor force projections for 2016, 60, 62
life expectancy of, 108
living arrangements of children, 21, 22, 23
marital status of, 15
married-couple families, 20
Mexican-Americans, 4–5
nativity, citizenship status by detailed ethnic group, 5f
No Child Left Behind Act and, 39
occupations of, 62–64
official designation for, 1
origins of, 4, 6 (f1.2)
on parole/probation, 120–121
percent by region, 6 (f1.3)
political participation by, 130–131
population of, 3
poverty, children living in, 75–76
poverty rate for, 73, 75
pregnancy/birth, 89, 90
preprimary education, 29
in prisons/jails, 117
public opinion on equal job opportunities, 60, 60f
public opinion on race relations between non-Hispanic whites/Hispanics, 13f
public school enrollment, 27
Puerto Ricans, 5–6
SAT scores, 45–46
school "choice," 39
school segregation and, 35
sentencing, racial disparities in, 122
single-parent households, 21
teenage birth rates, 20
tobacco smoking by, 106
unemployment, 53
violent crimes, victims of, 111

voter registration, 125, 126
voter turnout, 126, 127, 128
welfare recipients, 79, 81
whites and, 12
widows, 19
Hispanics and the 2008 Election: A Swing Vote? (Pew Research Center), 131
Historic Reversals, Accelerating Resegregation, and the Need for New Integration Strategies (Orfield & Lee), 35
Historical Census Statistics on Population Totals by Race, 1790 to 1990, and by Hispanic Origin, 1970 to 1990, for the United States, Regions, Division, and States (U.S. Census Bureau), 10
Historical Voting and Registration Reports (U.S. Census Bureau), 127
Historically Black Colleges and Universities, 1976 to 2001 (Provasnik & Shafer), 50
HIV. *See* Human immunodeficiency virus
"HIV and Its Transmission" (CDC), 103
HIV/AIDS Surveillance Report 2005 (HHS & CDC), 103
Hobbs, Frank, 3
Hoefer, Michael, 3
Hoffman, Charlene M., 33–34
Holding NCLB Accountable: Achieving Accountability, Equity, and School Reform (Civil Rights Project at Harvard University & Sunderman), 38
Hollinger David A., 125
A Home of Your Own: Expanding Opportunities for All Americans (White House), 26
Homeownership
    growth of, 25–26
    rates by race/ethnicity, 24–25, 26t
Homicide
    deaths from, 109–110
    gang-related homicide, 122, 123
    homicide type by race, 113 (t7.4)
    homicide victimization rates per 100,000 population, 113 (t7.3)
    minorities as victims of, 111–112, 114
    offenders, 116
Homicide Trends in the United States (Fox & Zawitz), 114
Hondurans, 3
Hopes, Fears, and Reality: A Balanced Look at American Charter Schools (Lake & Hill), 41
Hopwood v. Texas, 48
House Committee on Ways and Means, 79
Household and Family Characteristics: March 1994 (U.S. Census Bureau), 20
Households
    children living in poverty, 76
    definition of, 20
    income differences by, 71
    income of African-Americans, 73
    living arrangements of children, 21–24